to Freedom

13 QUANTUM LEAPS FOR THE SOUL

Leslie Kenton

HarperCollins*Publishers*

HarperCollins*Publishers*
77–85 Fulham Palace Road,
Hammersmith, London W6 8JB

Published by HarperCollins 1998
10 9 8 7 6 5 4 3 2 1

A catalogue record for this book
is available from the British Library

ISBN 0 7225 3722 0

Printed and bound in Great Britain by
The Bath Press, Bath

CONTENTS

For my son Jesse
who has the mind of a scientist
and the heart of a poet

ACKNOWLEDGEMENTS

Writing this book has been my greatest challenge as well as my greatest joy. Researching it has brought me in touch with men and women whose qualities of mind and soul have been an honour to touch. It would be impossible to list them all. I hope those I have omitted to mention by name will forgive me. It would be equally impossible not to mention a few whose work and teachings have been central in shaping my own: Michael Harner, Sandra Ingerman, Christina Stack, Ervin Laszlo, Stanislav and Christina Grof, Joseph Campbell, Brian Swimme, Rupert Sheldrake, Mathew Fox, Gary Zukav, David Bohm and Ken Carey.

I need also to give thanks for the passion of my editor Michelle Pilley who virtually insisted that I write this book although at first I resisted at every turn, and all those from designers to managing editors and publicists at HarperCollins who worked right along beside me to create such visual beauty and inspire my own labours. I have never worked with a more talented or enthusiastic group of people. Thanks go to all of them: Eileen Campbell, Paul Redhead, Nicky Vimpany, Jo Ridgeway, David Hearn, Megan Slyfield, Dominic Forbes. Thanks, too, to Doug Blanks for the cover photo.

It was Simon Buxton of the Sacred Trust who told me again and again why I had to write the book and stood by as I did it – even though we were at times separated by 12,000 miles. It was my best friend Graham Jones – the world's most caustic critic – whom I need to thank for his infinite patience and his editorial suggestions. And my daughter Susannah who read everything via email and made suggestions on how to make it more accessible.

It was the wisdom of Grandfather and the Circle of Thirteen who, together, cajoled me into overcoming my resistance and taking the plunge. I have them to thank for any wisdom which may appear in these pages. I need to thank Jaguar for his power and his love – the most beautiful animal I have ever seen, in every way. He, whose task it is to preserve the essence of shamanism throughout history has cared for me with the gentleness of a kitten despite his proud nature and his great power. I am enormously grateful to Michael for his wings and Lacemaker for her beauty.

Finally, and in many ways most important of all, I want to thank three woman who have given up days and nights week after week to work with me: Yvette Brown – better known as FOX has worked on every book I have in print, as friend, helpmate, editor and inspiration. I doubt that I could ever write a book without her. Lorraine Maytum has been indefatigable in her support, bringing wholeness to us every day, even when she had to lay aside her own life for a time to give it. Finally Joy John, the newcomer on the scene, has blessed us all with her light and her willingness to go far beyond what should be expected of anyone.

Thank you all for everything.

Leslie – Pembrokeshire, August 1998

AUTHOR'S NOTE

The contents of this book – the exercises, the journeys, the visions and the processes – have grown out of a marriage of nature, science and shamanism. Each of these elements have a long history of practice. They are designed to expand your awareness, deepen your understanding and enrich your experience of this magnificent universe in which we live. They are not, in any way meant to be therapeutic or to replace medical or psychiatric care where it is needed. They are tools and techniques designed to expand your experience of freedom, increase your connections with your own soul and help you bring the blessings that only you can bring to the world.

CHAPTER I

Born Free

This is a book about freedom – not as an idea but as a living experience. It centres around a thirteen-week integrated programme of practical tools and techniques designed to enrich the experience of freedom in your own life and then keep on expanding it. The process has been developed out of a marriage of the most ancient techniques known to man for expanding consciousness – shamanism – together with leading-edge physics, biology, systems theory and the rapidly developing science of consciousness itself.

> Man is born free, and everywhere he is in chains.
> *Jean Jacques Rousseau*

I will take you on a journey. It is an old and well-worn track, along the way you are likely to experience some surprising, some beautiful and some life-changing events. We will wind through the well-lit avenues of modern scientific research as well as down magical twisting paths which man walked long before he wrote things down. In the end you may discover that the fount of power and creativity, healing and joy, to which both routes lead is exactly the same.

MIDWIFE TO FREEDOM

Journey to Freedom has grown out of workshops and seminars I give throughout the English-speaking world. I love teaching this stuff more than anything else I do. Sometimes I ask myself why. I guess it's because the most inspiring thing I ever come face to face with is the magnificence of the individual human soul. I love playing the role of midwife – the woman who is present as witness to its blossoming in the people I work with. But there is something else I love about it too. The workshops I teach are filled with the

A certain naïveté is prerequisite to all learning. A certain optimism is prerequisite to all action.

George Leonard

most remarkable men and women. You find the president of a European bank sitting next to a woman bus driver. On her other side is a sculptor and next to him a doctor, next to her a man just returned from Alaska where he climbed Mount McKinley. This kind of work somehow attracts highly independent, intelligent people from an enormously diverse cross section of the population.

Freedom is an experience unique to each of us. Yet its essence is universal. All freedom comes from within. Live free and you feel fully alive. It is like taking a deep, spontaneous breath. It is like laughter. Freedom is also full of surprises. There is a boldness to it. You dare to say what you think and feel, yet are not afraid to listen to the words and hearts of others who think differently. Living free brings with it a sense that you can trust yourself as well as the universe even though you may 'understand' neither. It also means becoming liberated from having to conform to other people's rules, the slavery of imprisoning ideologies, as well as being able to transmute the life-draining powers of addiction and the crippling influences of ancient emotions that would strangle your creative power. The freer you get the more self-determining your life becomes and the more exciting. Even when huge challenges arise, instead of appearing as crushing forces they turn into worthy opponents. Wrestling with them helps you break through to an even wider experience of liberation.

TECHNOLOGY OF LIBERATION

If you are able to handle the uncertainty of being beyond ego, you are ready for inner creativity.

Amit Goswami

The quantum leap programme is in its essence a technology of liberation which takes its name from science. Please don't worry about the word *quantum*. This is not some kind of new-age hype. 'Quantum' has a very specific meaning both in the science of physics and in the way the journey to freedom process happens.

In physics the word *quantum* means a bundle of energy. *Quantum leap* is the term used to describe the movement of an electron from the orbit of one atom to another in a very special way: it moves from one place to the other by making a *discontinuous jump*. In other words, it leaves one place and arrives at the next without passing through the space in between. By doing this a quantum leap transcends the rules of time and space which for so long scientists believed to be an inescapable restriction in reality. The quantum leap programme works in a similar, inexplicable, way. It also brings about changes which are discontinuous – changes which cannot be described or measured by the laws of mechanistic science or psychology. For these are changes of the soul.

Journey to Freedom

Journey

Freedom knows no age-barriers. Neither is it the province of an elite few while the rest of us just get by and hope that a few crumbs will fall our way if only we are patient enough, virtuous enough, or spend enough money buying the right product. Freedom belongs to all people – indeed it is encoded within our genetic makeup – part of our very DNA. Perhaps this is why we so long for it.

POWERS OF CREATION

The old skin has to be shed before the new one can come.
Joseph Campbell

Sometimes when I look around me at the world that we humans have created, I am dazzled by what I see. It is full of magnificent technological achievements. Silver birds fly in the sky and men walk upon the moon. The entire globe is capable of being connected up electronically so that when I am in the wilderness in New Zealand I can instantaneously send a message to New York or receive one from Tokyo through the ether over my mobile phone. Yet often I shudder at the way in which many of the things which we have created seem not to serve life but to deplete it – the herbicides and pesticides that are seriously disrupting the reproductive lives of men and women and our animal friends, the continuing build up of arms throughout the world and the excessive worship of profit at any cost to life. I believe these life-destroying practices have come about because our vision has not yet widened enough. We have been perceiving power as something external to us rather than recognising that authentic power, like authentic freedom comes from within. Once we reclaim authentic power and freedom and make them a part of our day-to-day existence, and once our vision of reality has widened enough, then we can choose to work together to recreate a world which honours life instead of undermines it.

NEW BEGINNINGS

We stand poised at the edge of a millennium – a time of healing and new beginnings. It is a time during which we can experience freedom together for the first time among millions of people of all different races, creeds and colours if only each of us can gain deeper access to our wisdom and creativity, our vision and our compassion both for ourselves and for the world we see around us. We can also learn to work together with respect for other living things around us to create a world of great beauty and balance and joy. To bring such a world into being in a way that honours

The techniques you will be using in your journey to freedom make use of the thoughts and findings of some of the world's most forward-thinking scientists and philosophers – from David Bohm and Karl Pibram to Rupert Sheldrake and Ervin Laszlo. These visionary men are each, in their own fields, wrestling with the, as yet undescribed, *fifth entity* – a subtle field of energy with universal effects. This increasingly appears to be the ground of being which lies beneath the quantum realms you will be accessing in your own journey to freedom. We will be looking at their work in more detail in later chapters, I think you will find it truly fascinating.

Journey to Freedom is not an intellectual programme. It is a process which involves the whole of your being. It requires active participation daily for thirteen weeks during which you will be making one quantum leap after another:

✦ You will learn to move in and out of *quantum consciousness* at will – these vast transpersonal realms of freedom, awareness, creativity, healing and bliss which lie beyond time and space and are accessible only through your *quantum mind*.

✦ You will make friends with compassionate non-physical energies – 'spirits' if you like – in the quantum realms. You will learn to work in collaboration with their power, and make good use of their wisdom, inspiration, and strength to create what you want in your life.

✦ You will learn to bring back the wealth you find there to enrich the day-to-day world of your life, the lives of others and the life of the earth as a whole.

✦ You will come more and more to live as the multi-sensory being which you naturally are – someone not limited to the perceptions of the five senses alone.

✦ Gradually, progressively, you will find a natural alignment of your personality with your soul taking place. So that the inside of you and the outside sing the same song. As this happens you will come in touch with your own authentic power and experience freedom of the highest order.

✦ As a natural outcome of this alignment between soul and personality you will move towards an experience of even greater co-operation with others in both the mundane world and in the quantum realms.

✦ When this occurs freedom and responsibility become natural partners fused together by joy in the service of life.

the highest potentials in ourselves, the animals and plants, rocks and sea, sun and sky – who are our brothers and sisters – we need access to authentic power and authentic freedom. We need to experience clarity of mind and compassion. And we need to learn to use our freedom wisely. Such gifts will never be found in religions or political systems, in philosophies or psychological ideas. The very best of their teachings may inspire us to open up our thinking in a way that sparks our own creative ideas and urges us to look deeper and dream vaster dreams for our future. The real wisdom which leads us to create our own future lies not outside us in the words of politicians or bankers, scientists, doctors or philosophers, but rather within each individual soul.

THE THIRTEEN STEPS

The programme is made up of thirteen quantum leaps which are designed to be taken over thirteen consecutive weeks. To work with it at this speed will ask an hour a day of your time, no more. If your busy life does not permit a time commitment at this level, the course can be stretched over twenty-six weeks, thirteen months, or even thirteen years for that matter, provided that you do this systematically and continuously so that you do a little work on the journey to freedom process every day.

Chapters 2 through to 6 will guide you through some of the revolutionary global shifts taking place in consensus reality. They will show you how these things are affecting your life and tell you how you can make use of them to empower your own journey towards authentic power and freedom. These shifts are the result of a growing alignment between leading edge science and the mysticism of the great religious traditions. Mystics are people who have been able to access quantum consciousness and have returned to tell the tale. If you are impatient to begin your journey to freedom immediately, you can skip these early chapters for the moment and go on to Chapter 7 The Basic Tools – where the quantum leap process is introduced. Then you can come back and read them at your leisure. But do read them. For, in addition to the very practical journey work that you will be doing, it is also important to become aware in a conscious way of the things contained in these early chapters. They set the scene in which your quantum leaps can most easily be taken. However, all the way through the thirteen quantum leap chapters which follow, we will be exploring in even greater depth phenomenal changes taking place in biology, consciousness research, cosmology, medicine,

If a man is at any time to have a chance of escape, then he must first of all realize that he is in prison. So long as he fails to realize this, so long as he thinks he is free, he has no chance whatsoever.
Jean Danielou

Ultimately; it is in the experience of the journey that we heal ourselves, not in its analysis.
Carl A. Hammerschlag

physics and ecology which are in one way or another directly related to the journey to freedom you will be taking.

There is a far-reaching magic to this journey. Its reverberations can echo way beyond the confines of your own life. For the freer you become – the more your outer life becomes an authentic expression of your soul – the easier it gets for each of the rest of us to embrace and live our own freedom. That is an idea, I believe, whose time has come. They say that each of us teaches what we most need to learn ourselves and creates what we most love. This is certainly the case with me and freedom. And so I offer you a journey towards freedom, a process you can go through for accessing freedom and authentic power from within, drawing them forth, and living them out. May it serve you well.

CHAPTER 2

The Scent of Freedom

Freedom has always fascinated me. I love the smell of the word. I like its sense of possibility. I taste freedom when I listen to the music of Aaron Copland – music that could only have been written in a country which once had vast prairies and seemingly infinite wilderness. I feel it in my body when I run along cliffs in the rain. I rejoice in the sense of it that comes when, after hours of shifting dead words and sentences, something suddenly comes alive and beauty spills out all over the page.

In an outer way, to be free means to enjoy liberty of action under a government which is not despotic and does not encroach on individual human rights. In an inner way to be free means becoming liberated from the relentless forces of doubt, self-criticism and fear which we all inherit growing up in emotional and educational environments which split our mind from our body and teach us not to trust ourselves. They teach us to put our faith in 'experts'. They fail to teach us to honour the splendour of the individual human soul, and they fail to tell us that the universe is filled with compassion on which we can draw whenever we need support and power and which we can direct to create whatever we want.

What we need is more people who specialize in the impossible.
Theodore Roethke

PACKAGED FREEDOM

It makes me laugh to see the way our commercial world tries to sell the experience of freedom: freedom? It means wearing a pair of Levi 501s doesn't it? Sipping white rum on a tropical beach with a sexy lover. Taking a 100 miles an hour ride on a Harley across the desert at sunset. Or surfing that seventh wave. On film these things carry the *freedom*

One must make room in
oneself for the immensities
of the universe.
Brian Swimme

buzz. For a little while they let us imagine the real thing, even though they are only a pale facsimile of it. These days we get offered freedom in all sorts of 'packages'. They range from TV ads offering telephone sex, to weekend seminars promising instant enlightenment.

Some people, in their search for freedom, end up sniffing cocaine. Others dance all weekend at a rave. A few turn to philosophy or look for freedom in ancient religious practices. They head off to India or to California to sit at the foot of the guru and hope that somehow he will hand it to them. All of these things – from rum and cocaine to raves and yoga – offer a taste of freedom. Some – like drugs and alcohol – are more transitory than others. When they wear off, so does the sense of liberation they once promised, to be replaced by a *post-freedom hangover*. Others, like transpersonal psychology, or Mahayana Buddhism run deeper. The freedom they offer is slower in the making but it lasts longer. Every experience of freedom brings with it a sense of being released from imprisonment – of being able, even for a short time, to respond to life spontaneously with the whole of your being.

I go anywhere
I don't feel a thing
Everyplace opens to me
Spirit Spirit Shaman Songs;
David Cloutier

Look up the verb *to free* in the dictionary. It will tell you it means to release from bondage or constraint, to deliver, to disentangle from obstruction or encumbrance. And quite right. When we talk of freedom we often speak of it as freedom *from*. Money worries for instance, or responsibility. Sometimes we tell ourselves, 'If only I had this or didn't have that, then I'd be free'. Other times we indulge in dreams of freedom – sailing across great expanses of sea with the wind in our hair, or crossing the Sahara on a camel, or building a wooden hut in the woods and living there, or partying until dawn every night. Yet how many times have we gone on vacation to be 'free of worries' only to find we packed them in the suitcase under the new underpants?

HOW DEEP IS THE SEA?

If you realize what the problem is – losing yourself, giving yourself to some higher end, or to another – you realize that this itself is the ultimate trial. When we quit thinking primarily about ourselves and our own self-preservation, we undergo a truly heroic transformation of consciousness.
Joseph Campbell

Like the proverbial iceberg, most of us live with the lion's share of our potential for freedom, joy, creativity and power submerged beneath a sea of unknowing. We go about our day-to-day duties and pleasures conscious only of what comes to us through our five senses. How does it taste and feel? What does it sound like? What do we see in front of our eyes? Meanwhile beneath the vast ocean of consciousness that constitutes what it is to be fully human our greater selves hibernate waiting to be awakened.

Sometimes, when we fall in love perhaps, or when we are faced with an event of life-shattering proportions like a critical illness or the death of a close friend, the submerged area of our being erupts in magic or horror, in surges of passion, energy and beauty. Then for a time the mundane quality of our everyday life is replaced with a sense of expanded being. We not only *feel* more alive, we wake up to find that familiar things – the tree that stands outside a bedroom window, a cat that greets us when we come home each day, the simple shell we picked up and slipped into our pocket while walking on the beach, have taken on a luminosity that we can't explain. Other times without warning, while listening to music or walking down a city street we are suddenly hit with a feeling that the world is far greater than we ever imagined it to be, or a sense that all we see around us somehow *is* us – we are all part of the same stuff. While the experience lasts everything seems right in the world. Then, like the sun at the point of setting, it all fades beneath the mundane horizon leaving only the faintest wisp of colour to remind us that we once stood in its glory, felt the rays of the sun upon our bodies and *knew* that sense of being at one with the universe which makes every struggle seem to have a meaning.

The distance between you and your understanding of the creation of matter from energy is equal to the distance that exists between the awareness of your personality and the energy of your soul.
Gary Zukav

ROAD TO FREEDOM

Gary Zukav, author of *Authentic Power*, believes that we are no longer five-sensory beings evolving through our exploration of the physical world. We are, he insists, evolving into a multi-sensory species, men and women no longer limited to five-sensory perception. In the process we are beginning to turn away from our fascination with *external* power, to replace it with the kind of *authentic* creative power that comes from building a bridge between the individual soul and the outer personality. It is this evolution which lies at the core of journey to freedom.

To be human is to live in a limited world. It has to be limited to allow us to move about, act upon our environment and bring our visions into being. If we experienced a sense of continual connection with multi-dimensional quantum consciousness, we probably would not have the drive to go about our daily lives. In fact some people whom I have met who make this kind of connection easily seem to have little desire to go on living in a physical body. Instead they want to escape from life and space out. This is not the road to freedom, it is a road taken in fear which disempowers you. So does the cynical materialist route that denies the importance of everything you cannot see for gold. Without a sense of connection to the majesty of transcendent realms our

To fully understand, one has to sit down and wait for the universe to enter.
Brian Swimme

lives become narrow to such a degree that we can feel ourselves incarcerated in a prison of our own making. We don't experience the love we long for. We seem unable to create the wealth we want. We feel ourselves to be not good enough so that we 'need' an expensive car, a new suit, a special eye shadow to feel OK. When we get them we think they are great for a time. Then they too lose their lustre and we our fascination. So we go on wanting something else, caught up in the belief that 'if only … ' then everything would be all right in our lives.

AUTHENTIC POWER

We have a genius for overlooking openings to extraordinary life.
Michael Murphy

I have learned, both from wrestling with my own sense of dissatisfaction and longings and from working with people in the realms of personal growth and healing for some twenty-five years, that authentic freedom and power are never gained by acquiring things from outside. Far too many people have climbed to the top of the ladder only to find to their dismay that it is leaning against the wrong wall. In the process they have lost touch with their soul. Don't get me wrong. I love beautiful stuff. I love living in a wonderful eighteenth-century house. I love white linen sheets, fine paintings and delicious food. I love travelling to see the things that fascinate me. However, the greatest freedom I have ever felt has little to do with these things. It comes in times when the part of that iceberg of my own being which lies submerged beneath the sea of mundane consciousness rises up to greet me with a vision of what is possible and the energy for me to bring it into being.

SEEDS OF THE SOUL

You have the power in the present moment to change limiting beliefs and consciously plant the seeds for the future of your choosing. As you change your mind you change your experience.
Serge Kahili King

Each human being is utterly unique. Like the seed of a plant which has encoded within its genetic material the potential for everything it can become as a full blown flower, each of us comes into this world carrying a package of as yet unrealized potential for energy, health, creativity and joy. It is physical, psychological and spiritual potential that creates our uniqueness. The fullest expression of it leads to the fullest experience of authentic freedom. It is rather like the brushstroke a zen painter uses to represent a single leaf on a shaft of bamboo. The leaf he paints is totally singular – like no other leaf that has ever existed. Yet within its uniqueness is encompassed universal beauty and life energy of the highest order. So it is with each of us.

Within the individual genetic package which is you is nestled your very own brand of seedpower – an essential soul energy that encompasses far greater physical, creative and spiritual potential than you could ever hope to realize in one life time. The more fully this seedpower is allowed to unfold the richer your experience of authentic power and freedom will be. So focused is the energy of spirit within a tiny seed that it opens and reaches towards the light, regardless of what is in its way. Once I pulled up a weed growing in my garden to discover within its roots a marble that had been crushed out of all recognition by the life-force of the growing plant.

The wonderful thing about any little seed is that it doesn't take much for it to develop into the plant it is designed to be: some good rich organic soil, a little rain and a dose of sunlight. For the power and the intelligence that makes growth possible lies not outside of it but within the seed itself. People – you and me, and the woman you saw when you got on the bus this morning – are just like plants. All we need is a good healthy environment which allows our unfolding to take place.

> To believe your own thought, to believe that what is true for you in your private heart is true for all men – that is genius.
> *Ralph Waldo Emerson*

PAINFUL DISTORTIONS

The problem is that few of us get it. For as we are unfolding – as we are passing through the superbly orchestrated phases of our physical and spiritual development – more often than not our environment does not provide the rich soil, clean water and sunlight we need for full unfolding. More often than not it truncates our development. Then, like a little plant trying to push through depleted soil with too little water and not enough sunlight our growth becomes stunted or twisted. Or like a seedling trying to push through earth with a stone on top of it we develop 'distortions'.

All sorts of things can cause distortions: accidents, illnesses, emotional or physical abuse. Even being raised in a wonderful family if you happen to be a 'fish' and the rest of your family are 'ducks'. Distortions can be physical in nature – a sunken chest or an excess of fat which our bodies create as a cushion against a harsh world around us. They can also be emotional, leaving us with a sense that there is something *wrong* with us, that we cannot rely on our judgement, that we are unworthy, or incompetent or guilty even though we may have no idea why or how. And they can be spiritual. When we grow up in an environment which lacks an awareness of the interconnectedness of all life, when we feel ourselves to be isolated and living in a boxed-in world of the five senses, then we can end up with a nihilistic sense of life. We feel we have nowhere to go, nothing to do and no purpose in remaining alive.

> Our own life is the instrument with which we experiment with Truth.
> *Thich Nhat Hanh*

> You already have the precious mixture that will make you well. Use it.
> *Rumi*

POWERFUL VALUES

Losing your mind can
be a peak experience.
Jane Wagner

That's the bad news. The good news is that, because of the enormous capacity of a living organism to heal itself, most of these distortions can be cleared through such practices as detoxifying the body, through meditation, through shamanic work that brings you closer and closer to your soul. Of course, some distortions can't be cleared. I recently did some shamanic healing for a young man who had spent the first six years of his life trying to stay alive while all around him the Khmer Rouge threw people into open graves and shot them. I am not sure if the distortions that come from such an experience are ever cleared. They may be like genetic defects which remain with us throughout our lives. Or they may not. For I have witnessed many so-called miracles and learned that the universe moves in wonderful and mysterious ways. But what's exciting about distortions that can't be corrected is that, once we come face to face with them, they often bring us a deep sense of compassion and help us define the values by which we choose to live our lives. The young man I worked with has become highly skilled in working with abused children in war zones. I myself would never have been concerned with issues of health and freedom had I not had to struggle in my early life with chronic illness, depression, and straitjackets.

THE REAL McCOY

As we recognize that the fragmentation to which we are subject is due to a disconnection from the source of our life, the immortal self, it follows that our path to wholeness must involve a 're-membering' of that self.
Ralph Metzner

Authentic freedom brings a sense of ease in being who you are – distortions and all. It is feeling OK about yourself and being able to make use of your creative power to bring your unique visions into form. It is feeling good about what you have created too. Tap into freedom and you release energy. You feel like you are connected to life with your whole being. You are no longer trapped within what Alan Watts used to call 'a skin-encapsulated ego'. Freedom gives you easier access to some of the submerged iceberg of your being where creative power and joy live. Most of the time you feel unencumbered by your past, no longer constrained by other people's ideas or pressures from your education or your religious and family origins. You experience life from moment to moment and life is something you feel safe enough to risk living to the full.

Such freedom – the real McCoy – bears little resemblance to what the freedom salesmen would have us believe can only come to us by having the latest fast car, Ph.D., a new lover – or three. It carries no post-freedom hangover in its wake. True freedom is as wild and trusting as we are at our core. It is living with your feet firmly planted on the earth as you stretch your arms towards heaven. Feeling free makes laughter rise up and spill over. But freedom is not just a sense of open-ended possibility. It is also an ease when you find yourself confronted by delays or restrictions. You feel pretty sure that you have the strength and support of the universe to do what you are trying to do and you know that all will unfold in the best possible way.

FREEDOM THIEVES

So, born as we are with a passion for freedom and an enormous capacity for realizing it, what keeps us from living it out? There are many things. The most important fall into three categories:

> We did not come over on the same ship, but we are all in the same boat.
> *Bernard Baruch*

- ✦ Our parental training.
- ✦ Our religious training.
- ✦ Our restricted worldview.

As kids we grow up learning to conform to our parents' expectations. We have to. We need their love and care. We learn that we have to earn love by being 'good'. Usually being 'good' has little to do with being who you are. It is about being quiet when someone is talking. It is about using the right fork, or not sucking your thumb, or not telling the truth lest what you say offends the neighbours. All of these imperatives become encoded within our psyche as though they were major rules by which we should live our lives. Each is bound to the fear that if we cannot do this we will not get the love and care we need. There are other things from childhood too. Like our parents' beliefs and the comments they make about us all the time which we take to be gospel truth.

> You can't sing praises until you confront your own rages, because bullshit steals your heart's song and that's where the spirit lives.
> *Carl A. Hammerschlag*

I was raised during the early part of my life by my maternal grandmother – an incredibly powerful woman who had lost her mother at the age of six and spent the next eight years raised in a convent in Canada where little girls were locked in a cupboard for three days if they wet the bed. My grandmother held certain truths to be self-evident: that no child should be fed when it is hungry but rather on a regular schedule so you did not 'spoil' it; that every baby should be fully toilet trained by five months – long before an infant physiologically has control of its functions. Any baby who did not comply was a 'bad, bad child'. Later, her undeniable 'truths' took on new forms.

They came to include: you should never show anger; and whenever you are sick, unhappy or troubled about anything you should: 1. Eat. 2. Go to bed with an eider-down. 3. Never complain.

To this day I live with echoes of her words in my head. I grew up sure that I was a 'bad girl'. In my teenage years that turned into an 'evil woman'. I spent a lot of years afterwards trying to do everything right so I could redeem myself. Of course I never succeeded because the very notion that I needed redemption was nonsense. My grandmother – an amazing woman for whom I have much love and admiration – is long dead; yet the imprisonment of her words and actions, which came from her trying to do her best for me, is part of what has forged the bars of my own prison.

We get all sorts of imperatives thrown at us as children: 'Keep clean!' 'Try harder!' 'Stop being selfish!' It is because of all this that the search for freedom for many people becomes a desperate attempt to escape from authority or to rebel against it. What few parents realize is that, no matter how they treat their children, children love them and want nothing more than to be whatever is asked of them. Yet many of the things that are asked of you as a child are profoundly imprisoning simply because they have nothing to do with what you came to the earth to do – namely to live out the truth of your soul and bring its unique brand of seedpower fully into being.

RELIGIOUS STRAITJACKETS

Organized religion does its share of imprisoning too. Although the mystical teachings from all the world's great religions can be a wonderful source of inspiration to remind us of what is real and true when we get tied up in the day-to-day struggles of our materialistic world, the political structure of organized religion is a different story. It tends to be highly orientated towards the control of the people it claims to be freeing. Some religions have endless lists of 'dos' and 'don'ts'. Others traffic in fear, based on the notion that our god is the only god. If you do not believe in him you are doomed forever to damnation. This kind of religious indoctrination dwarfs your sense of self and tries to turn you into an automaton who follows rules slavishly. For some, the controlling and exploitative nature of organized religion revolts them so completely that they come to hate even the words associated with spiritual experience like 'transcendent', 'numinous' and 'sacred'.

Life is not a problem to be solved, but a mystery to be lived.
Thomas Merton

Ideologies are toxic. They poison perception and happiness. They block access to the intelligence that is designed to guide people's lives.
Ken Carey

GOD? WHICH GOD?

I remember an incident that happened many years ago which brought me face to face with the kind of fear and aggressive energy religion instils in its worshippers. One Saturday afternoon when my children were five, seven and ten the doorbell rang. I opened it with the three of them grouped around. There stood a small man with huge hands and a stooped body. He told me that the world was ending, that the sheep were going to be separated from the goats and unless we were among the sheep we would be damned in hell forever. My children listened with huge eyes thinking that this was a wonderful tale in which the hero would surely leap up at any moment to save the world from hellfire. The little man then went on to say that his church were holding a service this evening at 6 o'clock and we were invited.

Having dealt with this kind of Bible-basher before, I had learned that if you stand and talk to them they go on and on. So I had developed a strategy which always seemed to work. I would say, 'Well, that is very kind of you, but actually we are Buddhists.' This wasn't strictly true, although I had spent a lot of my childhood steeped in Buddhist mythology in a Japanese family where the father was a Buddhist priest. I had found that doorstep missionaries would usually shrug their shoulders at this and leave.

Not so this gentleman. He rubbed his huge hands together with glee, 'There is only one god,' he said. Moved by the breadth of his understanding – something I had not encountered in a fundamentalist proselytizer before – I was about to tell him that I could not agree with him more. I was just going to say how wonderful it was to meet someone of his faith who acknowledged that the divine is the divine in whatever form it comes cloaked, when he spoke again, 'I am only sorry you chose the wrong one!' My jaw fell open. My three children burst out laughing, in part at my naïveté, in part, because even they could see the absurdity of his assertion. Yet such is the power for imprisonment which religions hold.

EXIT MEANS THE WAY OUT

The quantum leap journey is designed to help you transcend the distortions that may have been restricting your freedom, clear out the false ideas and help you move gracefully towards the full expression of your unique self. The programme is a practical guide to the expansion of consciousness and the release of power. From beginning to end, all

> The most beautiful experience we can have is the mysterious … He to whom this emotion is a stranger, who can no longer pause to wonder and stand rapt in awe, is as good as dead.
> *Albert Einstein*

> I obey only my own instincts and intuition. I know nothing in advance. Often I put down things which I do not understand myself, secure in the knowledge that later they will become clear and meaningful to me. I have faith in the man who is writing, who is myself, the writer.
> *Henry Miller*

of the exercises it uses remain entirely within your own control. *Journey to Freedom* does not ask you to buy into any belief system, any psychological framework or any external authority. It consists of a collection of simple techniques for accessing energy, power, vision, healing and creativity by expanding consciousness. They will give you rich and direct access to both the world of form – the world of ordinary reality in which we live most of our lives – and to the world of consciousness (or non-ordinary reality) which encompasses a world of mythological images and energies of practical use to your unfolding.

It is important to remember that freedom doesn't depend on the external circumstances in which you find yourself. One of the most moving accounts of freedom I have ever read came from a political dissident imprisoned in a concentration camp in the early forties. It told of how he came to experience the true nature of freedom while living in the most inhumane conditions of physical incarceration imaginable. He reclaimed his freedom in the only way any of us ever can or will – by coming to live from ever deeper levels of himself so that eventually his soul and his outer personality became authentic echoes of each other. This is what your journey to freedom is all about.

Mother, show me how to love
Beyond my human fear
Teach me all the joys of life
Beyond the veil of tears
Jamie Sams

CHAPTER 3

Breaking Out

We can get trapped in another kind of prison too. It is a prison of our own making and we don't even realize it. The bars have been forged out of the worldview we have grown up with. A worldview is never something that you sit down and figure out. It is a collection of ideas inherited from your culture, your educational background and what is known as consensus reality – notions about what is real on which most people tend to agree. A package of beliefs learned in childhood that make the world seem coherent. These notions become so deeply ingrained in our thinking that we are usually not even aware of them, yet they define the breadth of our lives. They limit our ability to see whatever exists around us that is not consistent with what we 'allow' ourselves to believe. A worldview remains unconscious in a culture yet it governs the judgements we all make as part of that culture.

> **Do not sacrifice upon the altar of your mind the sacred wisdom that rises with each beat of your heart.**
> *Ken Carey*

WHAT DO YOU BELIEVE?

Here are just a few of the basic assumptions on which the worldview we have inherited rests. Every statement has now been scientifically disproved yet we all go on living as if they were true. And we remain imprisoned by them.

- ✦ There is a clear distinction between the objective world around us and our own subjective experience.
- ✦ Mind is a function of the physical brain. It has no existence apart from the body.
- ✦ Our consciousness cannot affect the material world.

The Electric Monk was a
labour-saving device ...
Electric Monks believed things
for you thus saving you what
was becoming an increasingly
onerous task, that of believing
all the things the world
expected you to believe.
Douglas Adams

◆ Fundamentally the only way we can gain knowledge is through our five senses.
◆ Psychic gifts such as ESP, out-of-body experiences and near-death experiences are figments of imagination. They don't stand up to scientific scrutiny.
◆ The universe can be reduced to nothing but a collection of material particles.

Whether or not you are a scientist, whether or not you have read the philosophy or understand the mathematics out of which today's materialistic worldview has evolved, it nonetheless affects you. It limits your reality to what you experience through five senses alone. And it blinds you completely to what else may be present. As a result it blocks freedom, entraps creativity and limits joy.

THE SCIENCE OF REALITY

Throughout history we humans have constructed hundreds of different methods for describing what is real. These include a wide variety of political systems, moral philosophies and religions. They have shaped our worldviews and our history. In the last three centuries, however, we have relied for our information about what is real not on religion, or philosophy, or cosmology, as we once did but rather on the system we call 'science'. Since the seventeenth century, science has pushed aside political and philosophical thinking, religions and mythology to take centre stage as the global authority in shaping our worldview.

Without connection there is
something dangerous and
wrong about the world.
David Nichols

Since we give such authority to science it becomes absolutely essential that the science which we are relying on to define consensus reality be up to the task. For basing the functioning of a culture on a system of knowledge which is either incomplete or which contains some fundamental flaw in its assumptions means the society based on it will not function properly. Yet this is exactly what we have been doing. As a result we find ourselves rushing headlong towards a massive dissolution of the political, moral and social structures on which we once relied to orientate our lives and give meaning to our activities. We also find ourselves faced with both disintegration of the biosphere and degradation of life. And both are happening so dramatically that the ecological destruction around us may soon become irreversible.

WEEDING OUT THE FLAWS

There are two basic flaws in the science out of which the twentieth-century worldview has developed. They form the cross bars of the prison we have unwittingly constructed to limit our freedom by shaping a consensus reality that is too small to serve us. The first is the assumption that we live in a mechanical universe made up of bits and pieces – atoms, protons, neutrons, what-have-you – which can be taken apart, studied and manipulated to our own advantage, then used to build whatever we want without concern for the effect that what we make might have on the rest. Our science, until relatively recently almost entirely concerned with the parts, has neglected the whole. It has remained blind to the complex interactions and feedback loops on living systems and the planet as a whole. This is why it is called *mechanistic*, *reductionist* or *atomistic* science.

The more you examine the major problems of our time the more obvious it becomes that they will never be solved at this level. They are far too interrelated in complex ways for any of them ever to be understood in isolation. World population growth, for example, will never be stabilized until poverty is reduced. The devastation of the rainforest as well as the destruction of thousands of species of plants and animals will continue just as long as developing countries in the Southern Hemisphere are being crushed under massive debts. At the same time a dearth of natural resources plus the degradation of living environments in a world of expanding population is destroying cohesion in local communities and creating ethnic cleansing and tribal wars. For such problems to be addressed we need to move beyond the mechanistic, reductionist worldview and to expand the science out of which it has developed by a more *holistic, organic,* or *ecological* perspective – one which takes into account these complex interactions. And this is exactly what is happening.

> Newtonian physics still is applicable to the large-scale world, but it does not work in the subatomic realm. Quantum mechanics resulted from the study of the subatomic realm, that invisible universe underlying, embedded in, and forming the fabric of, everything around us.
> *Gary Zukav*

MARRIAGE OF SCIENCE AND MYSTICISM

A worldview for freedom looks at living systems as integrated wholes and takes into account the interconnectedness of all things in the universe. Such an expanded sense of reality has long been held by mystics from every religious tradition in history. They have always insisted that the universe is one and that all things in it affect each other. Traditional mystic teachings are being reinforced by recent scientific findings in quantum mechanics, systems thinking in biology and leading-edge consciousness research.

> For the deepest passion of the Western mind has been to reunite with the ground of its own being.
> *Richard Tarnas*

But all this has by no means filtered down to consensus reality yet. So our worldview still imprisons us.

This expanded worldview is known as the holistic, holographic or *systemic* paradigm after the work of scientists who have demonstrated that living organisms are integrated energetic systems within an integrated universe. These things simply cannot be reduced to their parts if you are to understand and work with them. The tension between mechanism, which has developed out of a sense of separation between spirit and matter, form and substance, and holism in twentieth-century science is important to resolve if you are to break out of any self-imposed prison that may be limiting your life. You need to be willing for a time to let go of all your preconceived notions about what is real in order for you to explore the further reaches of the wider universe and discover what you have been missing. This is part of taking your first quantum leap towards freedom.

THE POWER OF CONSCIOUSNESS

The second flaw in the science out of which our current worldview has come is equally huge. Mechanistic science has completely ignored – left out altogether – one critical factor in its description of reality: the power of consciousness. By consciousness I mean both our everyday sense of awareness as well as the vast uncharted realms of the quantum mind which psychologists call the unconscious. In quantum realms you find the seat of our creative powers, our intuition, our dreams, our spiritual experiences, and our sense of ultimate meaning and values.

Although consciousness is not something you can hold in your hand or draw a picture of, it has enormous power to affect material reality. This is not just an empty statement. Literally hundreds of researchers throughout the world have carried out well-designed multidisciplinary, multicultural research as part of what might be called the Human Consciousness Project. Their intention is to map the whole spectrum of the various states of human awareness, including those generally categorized as unconscious. In many ways their work parallels the research of the Human Genome Project where scientists are now intensively studying the whole sequence of human DNA in the endeavour to map all our gene sequences. The efforts of scientists and doctors involved in consciousness research have converged to form a surprisingly coherent picture of the various states of consciousness available to men and women and the remarkably

Our own generation is simply the one to emerge at the time when human consciousness has become subtle enough and complex enough to awaken to what the universe has been telling us from the beginning.
Brian Swimme

Whoever has parted from his source
Longs to return to that state of union
Rumi

different experiences that can come out of each one. They are also discovering that the quantum realms – source of creativity, mythology and spiritual experience – can be mapped just as we have mapped ordinary reality. This is some of the mind-blowing stuff you will be looking at and working with during your journey to freedom.

BREAKING THE MOULD

Yet despite all this most of us continue to follow the values of our society: we keep learning in school, buying the things we are told to buy and trying to make sense of a world while somewhere deep inside we feel that we are imprisoned. We experience very little sense of freedom. When things get really bad it can even seem we are living in a wasteland, a mechanical world without meaning or purpose. In short we have become separated from our own authentic power. Sometimes we get so far from it we come to doubt its very existence. And as far as the experience of freedom is concerned, it is in such times that we become easy prey to the purveyors of facsimile. We keep buying the goods they tell us to buy, we keep playing the games they tell us to play only to discover they lead nowhere.

DO IT YOURSELF

Our longing for freedom asks that we reconnect with our instincts, for instinct is the voice of the multi-sensory quantum realms. In short, it asks that we come home to ourselves. You can do this without drugs, without gurus, without becoming a disciple or having to belong to any privileged group. You can do it regardless of your age, your physical condition or your religious beliefs. Freedom becomes part of your day-to-day experience as soon as you are ready to:

> The mind of the beginner is empty, free of the habits of the expert, ready to accept, to doubt, and open to all the possibilities.
> *Shunryu Suzuki*

+ Become an explorer of the multi-dimensional universe in which you live.
+ Learn to recognize, honour and respect the beauty of the individual soul and give it authentic expression in your life.
+ Allow your worldview to expand until it gets large enough to encompass the whole of reality.
+ Let go of the restrictions imposed on you from childhood, religion and education.
+ Seek out your individual place within the order of the universe.

✦ Develop a deep and abiding friendship with the inhabitants of the multi-dimensional universe in which we make our homes – from the moles and the stars, the grass and the trees, the rocks and the quasars, to the helping spirits who guide, bless and inform us, the muses who inspire us, the angels who shine for us and the maggots who eat away decaying matter so that new life may come forth from old.

✦ Learn to build powerful bridges between the rich inner world of consciousness and your day-to-day existence.

✦ Commit yourself to bringing your own unique creations into being.

In its essence *Journey to Freedom* is a spiritual course for freedom designed to bring you home to that sense of bliss and wholeness which we all know should be in our lives but which we often experience only fleetingly. It is a process that depends on simple-to-use skills giving direct access to the wisdom that lies within *you* by awakening your *consciousness matrix* and putting it into practice in your life.

ACTIVATING THE MATRIX

The consciousness matrix is what I call the facility which we all have that gives us access to the quantum realms of multi-dimensional reality. It is like an interface encoded within your physical body, probably within your DNA or in your energy field. Using this matrix Einstein was able to see himself riding on a beam of light, and this led to the formulation of his theory of relativity. This matrix made it possible for Blake to write his poetry and etch his pictures, and for Copernicus, Galileo, Kepler and Newton to transform our world by introducing us to their expanded perceptions of reality.

Throughout human history the consciousness matrix has provided those who knew how to make use of it with direct experience of wisdom, vision, creativity and sometimes also a luminous sense of freedom. Until recently, however, such experience has been accessible only to a few – mystics, prophets, religious leaders, shamans, artists and great scientists who one way or another were able to activate it and by doing so to move into the multi-dimensional universe, and access the wisdom, insight and power which resides there.

The world is rapidly changing. At the turn of the millennium we are living in the midst of a revolution in knowledge and vision so vast that nothing like it has ever been experienced by mankind. As science approaches new thresholds of meaning the scientific view of reality moves ever closer to the mystics' cosmology. It is a cosmology often referred to as the *perennial philosophy*, and it crosses all cultural barriers.

YOU HAVE WHAT YOU NEED

On a practical level, well-tested methods for shifting consciousness are widely available to anyone who wants to use them to dive into the ocean of the vast universe and immerse himself in its richness. At this point in history ancient and modern are coming together on a wide scale to present us with the knowledge and skills we need to access authentic power and freedom. Each of us seems to be asked just what we can make from them. The philosophy on which *Journey to Freedom* is built is aligned with the latest scientific discoveries about how the mind can move beyond space and time to heal, to create, to know, to expand, and to make changes in the material world. This may sound very new to your ears. Rest assured. For the techniques the programme uses to help you make the freedom passage are rooted in the most ancient practices for consciousness expansion known to human history. They are derived from what has come to be known as *shamanism*.

CHAPTER 4

The Art of Consciousness

Say the word shamanism. Does it bring images of Native American medicine men dressed in feathers dancing around campfires? Or huddled naked in 'sweat lodges'? Some get pictures of Zulu witchdoctors throwing bones or casting spells. For a few – especially those steeped in fundamentalist religion – the word strikes fear into the heart. 'Shamans? Oh God. Aren't they those people who consort with spooky spirits? That's dangerous. I will pray for you.' Such fears come out of ignorance. Shamanism does not involve trucking with dangerous spirits and, far from being associated with any particular ethnic group, it has near-universal origins which can be traced back to the dawn of recorded history.

DIRECT LINE TO QUANTUM REALITY

Shamanism is a direct method for expanding consciousness. It consists of a collection of simple techniques for accessing energy, power, vision, healing and creativity. It is neither a religion nor a philosophy. Pre-religious, pre-political and pre-philosophical in nature, shamanism is a highly democratic methodology which gives you direct access to revelations and spiritual experiences unmediated by restricting worldviews or organized religion. It requires no guru, no priest, no religious hierarchy to intervene on your behalf. I think this is one of the reasons some people are afraid of it. For since shamanic methods connect you directly to spiritual power and healing they create an experience of autonomy and independence in the person using them. Shamanic methods put authority back in the hands of the individual. As such they undermine

Pursuing their shamanic practices, they have come to realize that what most people describe as 'reality' only barely touches the grandeur, power, and mystery of the universe. The new shamans often cry tears of ecstasy when undergoing and recounting their experiences. They talk with mutual understanding to persons who have had near-death experiences, and see hope where others may see hopelessness.

Michael Harner

whatever structures of church or state imprison us because neither is wide enough to embrace the power of the human spirit. Now this is dangerous stuff. Nothing short of revolutionary.

So old are shamanic practices that the knowledge of these methods seems to be encoded within our genes. I am no longer surprised when teaching these techniques to find my students report 'but it is like remembering something I have always known – like being a child again – like coming home.'

Shamanism is very down to earth. Practising shamanic techniques brings you not an intellectual understanding of the spiritual, but an *experience* of it. Shamanic practices developed long before spiritual experiences became beaurocratized and formalized into religious dogma. Long before established political systems and religions, shamanism grew not out of ideology, but out of practice. It is highly pragmatic. Its techniques have been used for at least 30,000 to 50,000 years by people all over the world. Why? Because they work.

Tribal groups relied on the shaman who journeyed into quantum realms on their behalf. He went for healing, for guidance and wisdom when challenges and crises arose, for vision about where best to hunt, or how best to plan for the winter. Shamanism pre-dates the world's great religions. In fact shamanic practices form the seedbed out of which civilization's religions and philosophies have been developed by pioneers who – either consciously or unconsciously – knew how to make use of their consciousness matrix to experience quantum awareness and then returned to codify what they had found there in words or paintings, dance or sculpture, mathematical formulae, music, or religious teachings. However, it is important to realize that it is never the experience in quantum realms that imprisons us: it is rather the way that it is turned into a codified system and passed on to us. It becomes something that is imposed on us from the outside, restricting the way we live our lives. This is why I feel it is essential that each of us develops the skills to draw on the power of the quantum realms for ourselves.

> Imagination connects us with the web of power and the spirit in all things.
> *Jose Stevens & Lena Stevens*

THE WORLD IS ALIVE

Like the child before its perceptions have been restricted by schooling, a shaman perceives the world around him as pure energy – a universe in which all things and thoughts, all dreams and visions, are alive with power. This sense of all-encompassing vitality brings with it a related ability to view even the most ordinary things in life –

from the pen that lays on the desk before you to the mysterious morning fog billowing in from the sea – as alive and therefore sacred.

The word shaman is of Tungus origins. It means 'see-er' – one who sees simultaneously both the material aspect of form and the invisible aspect of consciousness. But a shaman's skills go way beyond seeing. He also has the ability to change material reality through a combination of compassion and intention.

The techniques of shamanism, out of which the quantum leap programme has developed, are common practices in tribal cultures throughout history. Throughout history, too, shamanism has demonstrated a remarkable ability to shape-shift and mould itself to fit the needs of changing times, cultures and local values. This is happening once again. Here you will find that ancient and modern methods for activating the consciousness matrix have been adapted for a mainstream audience at the turn of the millennium.

> The two worlds, the divine and the human … are actually one. The realm of the gods is a forgotten dimension of the world we know.
> *Joseph Campbell*

SCIENTIST AS EXPLORER

Journey to Freedom has certain things in common with the journey that science has taken in its exploration of the cosmos. The data which scientists use to construct theories of the cosmos has been carried to them by particles of light, or *photons*. And photons have been in existence since the birth of the universe some 15 billion light-years ago. Yet it has taken scientists a long time – about 4 million years – to be able to view them. Light from a photon is so dim that it cannot be picked up by an unassisted human eye. Scientists have had to do three things to be able to see them:

> It is the imagination that gives shape to the universe.
> *Barry Lopez*

✦ Develop the sensitivities necessary to expand their vision so that they stop behaving like blinkered horses.
✦ Create specific tools and techniques – from mathematics, infrared detectors, x-ray defraction, spectroscopic devices and optical telescopes – to assist them in the seeing process.
✦ Let go of a lot of sacred cows.

They needed to expand vision, use new tools and leave behind assumptions they had made about the nature of the reality they were trying to study. One of the most exciting things about living right now is that our scientists are the first generation to develop the sensitivity and subtlety to be able to see with scientific eyes and hear with scientific ears what the universe has been whispering to our mystics all along.

TECHNOLOGIES OF THE SACRED

As explorers in the realms of consciousness, we need to go through a similar process.

✦ We need to develop our sensitivities and expand our vision to embrace the sacred nature of reality as well as its material face.

✦ We need to use tools and techniques that will assist us in experiencing the nature of quantum reality and in expanding our ability to perceive it. These include practices that shift awareness to carry us forward, exercises for enhancing vision, and allies to help point the way.

✦ We need to examine our assumptions about reality and to find which of these are useful companions to assist us as we move forward and which, like dead-wood, are no longer appropriate and need to be cut away to make our exploration and passage as light as possible.

This is what *Journey to Freedom* is all about. It works by accessing your consciousness matrix and putting it into gear.

Man, in his search for freedom, has developed hundreds of ways of activating the consciousness matrix throughout the ages. The matrix has been used by artists, scientists, mystics, prophets and saints as well as healers, poets, myth-makers and visionaries to make the silent passage into luminous realms. These methods range from physical means such as yoga, fasting, intense physical exertion and breathing techniques to mental practices like meditation, prayer and active imagination. Some activate the matrix by the use of consciousness-altering substances from LSD to ayahuasca – the plants used by natives of the Upper Amazon. Others make use of ritual, alchemy, or magic. Yet, go back far enough and you will find that every one of these methods has one way or another developed out of shamanism.

TECHNICIANS OF ECSTASY

Shamanism is not a religion, nor is it the exclusive province of Native Americans with their feathers and their sweat lodges, Siberian dancers with their bells and drums, or Australian Aboriginals with their walkabouts and dreamtime. It is a highly practical and easily learned technology for empowerment which belongs to everyone regardless of race, colour, creed or origin. Shamanic practices awaken our natural ability to enter quantum reality. When you begin to use them you are likely to get the feeling not of 'learning' something new but, of 'remembering' what you already know. Shamanic practices are the most disciplined way to access quantum realms – those zones of consciousness that are variously called the 'transcendent', 'the mystical', 'non-ordinary reality', the 'sacred', the 'numinous', the 'mystery', the 'otherworld', or the 'inner world' – at will while remaining in control.

There is something wonderfully ecstatic about moving beyond space and time, body relaxed and awareness heightened as you enter the altered state of consciousness characteristic of shamanic work. Once there you can connect with the spirits of the land and of the air, with gods and goddesses, angels, archetypes and power animals and then return to ordinary reality with healing energy, new understanding, or simply a sense of wonder at the magnificence of the universe we live in.

A shaman is a visionary. In his classic work, *Shamanism – Archaic Techniques of Ecstasy* Mircea Eliade describes him as a 'technician of ecstasy'. 'Shamans,' he says, 'are of the "elect". As such they have access to a region of the sacred inaccessible to other members of the community.' Shamanism is not only ancient, it is universal. You find it in North and South America, Asia, Africa, Europe, Polynesia and Micronesia. In all of these areas shamanic practices have been preserved to this very day by a small number of people. The service they have unwittingly provided to the rest of us is immense. If they had not maintained a shamanic tradition all of these simple yet powerful practices would have been lost to us forever. In the modern materialistic world we need a pathway back to the sacred: shamanism provides it.

To see a World in a Grain
  of Sand
And a heaven in a
  Wild Flower
Hold infinity in the palm
  of your hand
And eternity in an hour.
William Blake

The shaman is simply a guide, who conducts the initiate to the spirits. The initiate picks up the information revealed by the spirits and does what he or she wants with it.
Jeremy Narby

We must be willing to get rid of the life we've planned, so as to have the life that is waiting for us.
Joseph Campbell

INDIANA JONES FOR REAL

One man, almost single handed, has brought the ancient practice of shamanism into modern times: Michael Harner is a brilliant anthropologist who has at various times been visiting professor at Columbia, Yale and University of California at Berkeley as well as Professor and Chair at the Graduate Faculty Anthropology Department at the New School for Social Research in New York. Harner, who looks like a latter day Indiana Jones, carries a profound respect for the spirit world in which he works, as well as a deep compassion for all life. Like the shamans from whom he learned his skills, he is also the most ordinary of men – a man whose feet are planted firmly on the ground while his head touches the stars. And he has a sense of humour that puts W.C. Fields to shame.

It is a sacrality that unveils the deepest structures of the world.
Mircea Eliade

As a young man in the fifties and sixties, Harner carried out anthropological field work in South America, travelling first to the Jivare in the Ecuadorian Amazon and then to the Ucayali River in the Peruvian Amazon to study the culture of the Conibo Indians. He got on well with the Indians. It was not long before the highly intellectual sense of detachment which his education had instilled in him gave way to a sense of wonder and respect for the people he was working with and the shamanic practices he saw around him. Harner found himself wanting more than just an outsider's understanding of what he was witnessing. He wanted to know for himself what these Indian shamans experienced when they journeyed with the spirits and then returned to the tribe to enrich it with spiritual wisdom, healing, and practical advice. He asked his new friends to show him what they knew. They told him they were willing to introduce him to their magical reality but that he would have to drink their sacred drink *ayahuasca* – a potion based on the tree-climbing Banisteriopsis forest vine – to be able to 'see'. This vine contains the consciousness-altering harmala alkaloids, harmaline and harmine, which trigger visions, telepathy, and out-of-body experiences. Harner took the sacred mixture in the presence of a village elder and found himself plunged into another world. His experiences are recorded in a wonderful book that has now become a classic, *The Way of The Shaman*.

VISIONS OF THE OTHER WORLD

His mind began to work on many levels at once. He had visions of great spirits and was given knowledge about the birth and evolution of life and consciousness from them. At one point a giant crocodile appeared with waters gushing from its open mouth to create a sea on which a dragon-headed boat propelled by hundreds of oars glided towards him. Harner heard the music of other worlds: '… the most beautiful singing I have ever heard in my life, ' he says, 'high pitched and ethereal, emanating from myriad voices on board the galley. As I looked more closely at the deck, I could make out large numbers of people with the heads of blue jays and the bodies of humans, not unlike the bird-headed gods of ancient Egyptian tomb paintings. At the same time, some energy-essence began to float from my chest up into the boat.' What was even more astounding, once the journey had completed itself he discovered, while discussing his experiences with those who had initiated him, that far from being mere projections of his individual mind, these visions were very much the same visions they too experience on shamanic journeys. In some way which Harner at that point could barely fathom he was experiencing something which was *external* to himself. He realized that in a very real sense the realms accessed when the consciousness matrix has been activated have some kind of objective reality. They are accessible only through altered states, yet they are verifiable by the experience of others.

I felt a great, inexplicable joy so powerful that I could not restrain it but had to break into song, a mighty song with room for only one word: joy, joy! … and then in the midst of such a fit of mysterious and overwhelming delight I became a shaman, not knowing myself how it came about. I have gained my enlightenment, the shaman's light of brain and body.
Eskimo shaman

MAGNIFICENT OBSESSION

Thus began Michael Harner's lifelong fascination with shamans and shamanism – a passion which led him not only to read virtually everything that has been written on the subject but also to travel the world working with indigenous cultures from both the Old and New Worlds, then to pass on what he has learned to tens of thousands of people. He was amazed to discover that each of the cultures in which some vestiges of shamanism remain have a number of universal or near-universal practices and principles despite their distance from each other and the fact that there has been no contact between them. These practices he dubbed *core shamanism*. The journey to freedom process has largely developed out of the principles and techniques that Harner calls core practices. Here are some of them.

Try to suspend any critical prejudgements as you first practise shamanic methods. Simply enjoy the adventures of the shamanic approach; absorb and practise what you read, and then see where your explorations take you.
Michael Harner

- Using song, rattling and rituals the shamanic practitioner sanctifies space, rendering sacred the setting in which he will carry out his work.
- He places value on ritual objects including masks and costumes as well as on natural settings which facilitate shamanic practices.
- He communicates with plants, animals and all of nature in ways that to our culture can seem very strange.
- With the help of the spirit energies he performs healing rituals such as soul retrievals, extractions, de-possessions and power restorations. He also accesses information in the form of divination or prophecy.
- Fuelled by compassion and with a clear desire to help those in need, he focuses his intention.
- He uses the energy of a drum or rattle or song to journey into *non-ordinary reality* to seek help and healing for others.
- His body coupled with heightened mental and emotional awareness produces a *shamanic state of consciousness* (Harner's words).
- In this state he becomes acquainted with benevolent spirits including power animals, spirits of the land and trees, rocks and place, sacred beings known to the mythology of the world's great religions, ancestors and others, and forms long-lasting bonds of friendship with many of them.
- Finally – and in many ways most important of all – the shaman is an ordinary member of a community with a job just like everybody else, yet with the extra gift of being able to do work for the good of all.

Michael Harner's first training in shamanism took place using plant mixtures to induce the shamanic state as this is the practice of the native people in the upper Amazon who were his first teachers. His work with other indigenous cultures soon led to the discovery that this is not the most widespread method for altering consciousness. The most common tools for activating the consciousness matrix are the drum and the rattle. Harner insists that drumming and rattling commonly have significant advantages over the use of psychoactive plants. They give far greater control to the shamanic practitioner. As he says, 'I found out that the sound of the drum alone is capable of transporting a person to the same place as a psychedelic yet in a safer and more integrated way.'

SPIRITUAL ACTIVIST

The issue of control is central to working shamanically. Shamanism differs greatly from channelling and spirit possession where a person gives over his or her control to some spiritual agency, allowing it to speak or act through him, often not even recollecting what has happened afterwards. While a medium is a passive instrument of the energies that possess him, the shaman is highly active. It is more a case of the shaman possessing his spirits than them possessing him.

Harner often refers to the shaman as a spiritual activist. It is an excellent way of describing the self-directing, aware power that shamanism brings. The quantum leap programme is based on this power. The skilled shamanic practitioner has a high degree of dexterity which enables him to move at will from ordinary to non-ordinary reality and back again bringing full recollection of what has happened during his journey. He lives as successfully in ordinary life as in quantum realms.

The old indians say that if you give away something that's important to you, your life is renewed. It means that *you* have the things: the things don't have you. If you can't give away your possessions, they will destroy you.
Carl A. Hammerschlag

COMPASSIONATE SERVICE

Shamans do all sorts of service for the community. A shaman may help the dead find peace in the realms beyond life as well as bring healing to the living. There are two powerful forces behind all shamanic healing. The first is *compassion* for the ailing person. Second is the shaman's *intention* – his willingness to go into non-ordinary reality on that person's behalf to seek help for them. The stronger the compassion and the clearer the intention, the more powerful are the shaman's results. A shaman is also very different from the ordinary healer versed, say, in plant lore. The information he brings back from quantum realms about what plants or foods or healing practices to use for a particular person will come almost entirely from his helping spirits. It is not passed on from one generation to another in his culture. Shamanic healing is also very pragmatic. It makes plenty of room for support from both conventional and alternative medicine. And shamanic healing is spiritual healing. It concentrates on one of two things – either eliminating from the body of the person being treated some kind of energy which does not belong there or replacing power that has been lost.

A shaman is neither a priest nor a magician. The magician or sorcerer simply uses power, whether for good or evil. The shaman's work is always infused with humility and compassion. He knows that the power he works with is not his. It is a gift of his helping

For the caged bird
Sings of freedom
Maya Angelou

spirit and as such is meant to be used for the benefit of all life. Where a priest carries out his rituals in ordinary reality, the shaman's rituals are practised in the shamanic state of consciousness – while connected with the vastness of the universe. Go to a priest for advice when you have a pressing problem in your life and he is likely to refer you to a holy book as an authority on how to handle things. Go to a shaman and he is likely to suggest you trot down the road and consult a tree.

FEAR OF FREEDOM

It is perhaps the strangeness of such suggestions coupled with the fear that has been instilled in us by organized religions that has created a wariness of shamanism in the average person who has little knowledge of its real nature. After all, who but a madman would talk to trees? Indeed, from the vantage point of most Western psychology people who talk to trees and rocks and animals are thought to be at best deluded, at worst psychotic. Such practices tend to be viewed with fear in our society and 'treated' with powerful mind-suppressing drugs. These drugs immobilize some of the most creative people, stigmatizing them, sometimes even institutionalizing them, for we have been taught to fear those who don't fit in.

The galaxies exist in you, not printed as mere images within your skull, but in your every cell, your every atom.
George Leonard

The shaman, like the creative artist, is one who lives in freedom. Both ride the waves of freedom which the rest of us too often only dip our toes into. For we have been taught that real freedom is not allowed in our lives. We have been taught to fear the realms of expanded consciousness. We have been told either that they don't exist or that they are dangerous – filled with demons that belong to the mentally ill – places that are fundamentally dangerous to explore lest you get sucked into them and can't get out.

Michael Harner considers the Western world generally to be cognocentric. In other words, it takes into consideration and takes seriously only what one experiences in an ordinary state of consciousness while it virtually ignores and doesn't want to deal with anything that comes out of altered states of awareness. In our society this whole area is relegated to the realm of pathology; something we want nothing to do with as part of normal life. So we have pathologized the experience of every saint, prophet and shaman throughout history. They have all been treated as psychotics who, sadly, did not have the benefits of modern psychiatric treatment to sort them out. Meanwhile, we long to ride the waves ourselves but have forgotten how.

CHAPTER 5

The Science of Consciousness

Superstitious nonsense about quantum reality is on the wane. But we still have a long way to go. Well-conducted scientific research into expanded states of consciousness carried out by leading-edge psychiatrists such as Stanislav Grof are already mapping the transpersonal realms. Psychologists like Ralph Metzner, Jack Kornfield and Jeanne Achterberg – an expert in the use of shamanism for healing – have done fascinating clinical work in these areas and have written in depth about them. Meanwhile, the development of holographic models of the universe from physicists such as the late David Bohm as well as holographic models of the brain from many other scientists are making it more and more difficult to dismiss the importance of non-ordinary realms to our survival as a species.

Even the most materialistically-minded institutions in society – from multi-national pharmaceutical companies to government offices in search of new methods of gathering strategic military information – are making use of information gathered in quantum realms by people who already make good use of the consciousness matrix to shift realities. I am much amused by stories of left-brained chemists sent off by their companies to indigenous rainforest cultures in search of efficacious plants from which active ingredients may be extracted to develop new drug patents. 'How do you *know* that this plant cures back pain?' one chemist asks the village elder sitting in his longhouse in the midst of the Borneo jungle. 'How do we know?' comes the incredulous reply, 'Why the plants tell us of course.'

Tribal people who still live in close proximity to the living earth often retain an awareness of the sacredness of all life. They have an ability to communicate with the

Much madness is
divinest sense.
Much sense the
starkest madness.
Emily Dickinson

A universe comes to birth
from its centre; it spreads
out from a central point
that is, as it were, its navel.
Mircea Eliade

The body feels the things
of our spirits that the mind
never thought of.
Carl A. Hammerschlag

mythic, imaginal realms which we, in our alienation from nature and from ourselves, seem to have lost. The quantum leap programme can help you regain them.

KEY TO SURVIVAL

I believe our doing this on a wide scale is central to our very survival as a species as well as to the survival of many plants and animals – perhaps the living earth itself. For when we are disconnected from quantum consciousness and largely unaware of the multi-dimensional universe of which we are a part, the decisions we make can never be made in true wisdom. Neither can we live in authentic power or find creative solutions to the spiritual and ecological challenges which face us. I have heard Michael Harner comment, 'Many in our culture think it strange when they find out that shamans carry on conversations with animals, plants, rocks and trees – in fact all of nature. Yet deranged? I don't think so. For 3 million years our ancestors survived well doing this. Now, in the so-called civilized world where people no longer communicate with the planet and those who share it with us, we find ourselves in the midst of ecological catastrophes. That in itself should be enough to make us wonder which cultural assumptions are the most sane.'

Although shamanic practices predate all the world's great religions by tens of thousands of years, shamanism itself is no religion. It is rather a means of exploring the nature of reality and skilfully making use of energy for the benefit of all beings – both seen and unseen – who people the universe. Unlike the devout Buddhist or mystic Christian or Muslim, the shamanic practitioner is seldom focused on achieving self-enlightenment. He is instead intent upon connecting with the everyday world and the numinous powers of the universe for the benefit of both. His work enhances the quality of life itself. Death too for that matter since shamans also work a great deal with the dead to help them make the passage from this world to the next as gracefully as possible. The shaman looks on the universe itself as the ultimate reality and celebrates the *mysterium tremendum* that informs it.

QUANTUM ANIMISM

Behind the cosmology of shamanism lies a rich *animism* which grows out of the shaman's experience of working with and communicating with 'spirits' of whose existence he has practical experience (more about these spirits in a moment). Animism is a view of the world which attributes living spirit to all things, even inanimate objects. Once animism was considered a quaint primitive notion. Since the advent of quantum physics it is taken far more seriously. It can be considered a logical extension of the discovery that consciousness affects the quantum wave. The entire world may well turn out to be constructed from nothing but consciousness. Consciousness – insist a growing number of leading-edge scientists – appears to be primary. The forms of material objects are secondary. Consciousness is the stuff out of which material reality emerges.

From the vantage point of physics there are four fundamental and mathematically verifiable quantum properties which dovetail beautifully with the animism of traditional shamanism. Each of them is paradoxical and blasts wide open our worldview of a dead universe.

> That which blossomed forth as cosmic egg fifteen billion years ago now blossoms forth as yourself, as one's family, as one's community of living beings, as our blue planet, as our ocean of galaxy clusters. The same fecund source – then and now; the same numinous energy – then and now. To enter the omnicentric unfolding universe is to taste the joy of radical relational mutuality.
> *Brian Swimme*

- ✦ *The wave property:* Physicists have verified that a quantum object such as an electron can be at more than one place at the same time.
- ✦ *The quantum leap:* An object can simultaneously come into existence in one place and cease to exist at another without passing through the space in-between.
- ✦ *Wave collapses:* An object cannot be considered to exist within space and time until it is observed as a particle.
- ✦ *Action at a distance:* One quantum object, which comes into existence as a result of our observation of it, simultaneously influences the twin object associated with it no matter how far apart they happen to be.

Explain this to a practising shaman and he is likely to agree with each statement. For although it is expressed in a different language, it coincides with his own experience working in non-ordinary realms.

> May God us keep
> From single vision and
> Newton's sleep.
> *William Blake*

SPIRITS? WHAT SPIRITS?

Shamans say they work with spirits. What are these spirits? Projections of the mind? Hallucinations? Mental constructs? Or do they have a life of their own, separate from the person experiencing them? To the traditional shaman they are very real indeed – and a far cry even from figures conjured up through active imagination techniques employed by new age psychologists. They also bear no resemblance to what classical psychoanalysts view as fragmented elements of a psyche in need of reintegration.

Meanwhile, science of consciousness researchers have much to say themselves in answer to such questions. Stanislav Grof's work stands at the forefront of twentieth-century psychology. A scholar in residence at Esalen Institute in California for many years, Grof is a medical doctor who has carried out research into altered states of consciousness for almost half a century – first in his native Czechoslovakia and then in the United States. Some of the most important early work with LSD was done by him in the fifties. Later on, with his wife Christina, he developed non-drug methods for accessing non-ordinary reality. Working with these, together they have conducted some 30,000 sessions where participants access the consciousness matrix to explore non-ordinary realms. This has enabled Grof to witness the exploration of transpersonal realms in depth. His findings are recorded in numerous books, some of which are mind boggling in their implications. In fact his work is transforming the whole way we view reality. His latest book, *The Cosmic Game*, is a veritable bible of consciousness.

SHATTERING ASSUMPTIONS

'Transpersonal experiences,' writes Grof, 'have many strange characteristics that shatter the most fundamental assumptions of materialistic science and of the mechanistic world view, pointing to a paradigm closer to that which characterizes shamanic belief systems and the various branches of mystical or "perennial" philosophy.' Any unbiased study of the experiences of people journeying within transpersonal realms, says Grof, is forced to conclude that such journeying gives access to sources of information which are simply not accessible to an individual any other way. In these realms many people make connections with ancestors – and then return from quantum reality with information that can be verified by historical records. Others find themselves tapping into past and future events. Such things can only be experienced when accessing non-ordinary reality beyond

Everyone may educate and regulate his imagination so as to come thereby into contact with spirits, and be taught by them.
Paracelsus

In transpersonal states, we have the potential to experience ourselves as anything that is part of creation, as well as the creative principle itself. The same is true for other people who can experience themselves as anything and anybody else, including ourselves. In this sense, each human being is not only a small constituent part of the universe, but also the entire field of creation.
Stanislav Grof

time and space. Grof calls these realms *holotropic*. It is a word made out of the Greek *holos* meaning whole and *trepein* meaning moving towards or in the direction of.

According to Grof, in holotropic states a person can move across space and time, reliving past events such as birth. The journeyer is also given access to a panoply of gods and goddesses, the blissful and wrathful beings of Christian, Hindu and Buddhist cosmology, animal helpers, legendary heroes, superhuman entities and spirit guides – in short, the spirits which traditional shamans have always worked with. 'Deep personal experiences of this realm help us realize that the images of the cosmos found in pre-industrial societies are not based on superstition or primitive "magical thinking" but on direct experiences of alternate realities,' says Grof. 'A particularly convincing proof of the authenticity of these experiences is the fact that, like other transpersonal phenomena, they can bring us new and accurate information about various archetypal beings and realms. The nature, scope and quality of this information often far surpasses our previous intellectual knowledge concerning the respective mythologies.'

> I welcome all creatures
> of the world with grace.
> *Hildegard of Bingen*

TRANSPARENT TO TRANSCENDENT

Grof seems to treat the spirits of non-ordinary reality as personified universal energies, principles, and archetypes – mysterious figures – ultimately creations of or manifestations of a higher spiritual principal or energy which transcends them. Mythologist Joseph Campbell always insisted that deities need to be viewed – in the words of his mentor Karlfried Graf Dürkheim – as beings who are 'transparent to the transcendent' – in other words energies acting as bridges to the divine source.

> We are not human beings
> having a spiritual experience.
> We are spiritual beings
> having a human experience.
> *Teilhard de Chardin*

From the point of view of the shaman who interacts with these beings, they are spirits who inform his world with wisdom and healing, creativity and vision. As such they become his closest companions, teachers and 'friends' in non-ordinary reality. It is with them he works for the benefit of all in ordinary reality. The shaman too speaks of some higher energy which informs the spirits. He might call it the Creation, Great Mystery, or Divine Power. The shaman's relationship to his helping spirits is very much that of a partnership – spirit to spirit. Out of such partnerships miracles happen, great art is created and visionary scientific work done. A spirit to the shaman is as muse to the artist or daemon to the visionary scientist.

> Everything that is
> Is alive.
> *Spirit Spirit Shaman Songs;*
> *David Cloutier*

FRIENDS

One of the reasons our
society has become such a
mess is that we're isolated
from each other.
Maggie Kuhn

For me it is very much an experience of friendship which characterizes all shamanic work. Activating the consciousness matrix reveals to us connections with the whole cosmos on a highly personal level – connections which are by no means yet fully comprehensible. These relationships not only bring us endless wisdom on every level – from what kind of food is most health-giving for us or others to maximize health and energy to how to go about planning and executing a creative project: a book, a painting or the building of a community centre. They also help us forge deep connections with our own inner being and its purposes. They help make it possible to build bridges of authentic power between who we are at a soul level and how we express our identity in the outside world.

I died a mineral, and became
a plant.
I died a plant, and rose
an animal.
I died an animal and I was
a man.
Why should I fear?
When was I less by dying?
Yet once more I shall die
as a man.
Rumi

The friendship of the helping and tutelary spirits also creates for us a wonderful 'cocoon' within which deep inner change in our lives can take place safely and gracefully surrounded by their love and wisdom. In a world in which few of us have grown up in real security this can be quite a gift. Another observation I have made in the years I have been doing shamanic work is that practising shamanism transforms your life. I had the privilege of taking part in one of Michael Harner's advanced shamanic training programmes. It was carried out over a three-year period during which the same fifty participants met for one week twice a year to explore what Grof calls holotropic realms, and to work with traditional shamanic healing, ritual, and divination. I watched in wonder as the highly individual members of the circle (shamanic practitioners tend to be very much individualists) grew in wisdom, compassion, tolerance and authenticity. I saw this happen without any of the loss of autonomy you sometimes see in other kinds of groups. A shamanic circle provides the opportunity to explore a common interest while at the same time strengthening each participant individually and intensifying his trust in his own perceptions. In effect it leaves each of its members free to live out the nature of his individual soul. For me the shamanic circle has become an interesting model for future communities which, instead of exploiting an individual's spiritual power by trafficking in facsimiles of freedom, can encourage each member's ability to expand freedom. Such freedom, I believe, not only benefits the individual but the community, and even the earth as a whole.

CHAPTER 6

Myth and Magic

The goals and values of psychotherapy are quite different from those of shamanism. Psychotherapy comes out of a vision of reality in which there is a split between body, mind and spirit. It does not generally concern itself with spiritual or ethical values nor does it aim to bring about physical healing. It chooses to focus instead on resolving inner conflicts, and fostering psycho-social adjustment. Psychotherapy is primarily directed towards reductive analysis and interpretation according to a system of belief that is *external* to the person being treated. This may or may not be useful depending on the breadth of understanding on which the particular psychological method is based and on how appropriate it is to the patient. But no matter how broad a system the therapist is working with, it is still a system imposed on someone from *outside*. No manmade system no matter how wide in its visions (some are much wider than others), can come anywhere near the breadth of the human spirit. This is why in my experience all psychotherapeutic methods remain useful – sometimes very useful – yet limited in their effectiveness. No psychological system can lead to an experience of the very deepest levels of freedom. I find that shamanic work can.

If you have to be someplace other than where you are, you'll never see the here and now.
Carl A. Hammerschlag

THE PSYCHOLOGIST AND THE SHAMAN

Psychologists refer to quantum realms as 'the unconscious' or even the 'collective unconscious'. Yet what they mean by this is far too limiting to encompass the vast worlds of beauty, wisdom and healing in which the shaman travels. For psychologists take the unconscious to mean something found only *within* an individual or group, while shamanic practices lead to the exploration not only of the hidden aspects of our inner psyche but also of the entire universe – both seen and unseen.

Despite the positive effects it can have on individual growth, shamanism is not dedicated to psychological problem solving. It has developed out of a worldview in which body, mind and spirit are one energy within a sea of energy which is all life. It is concerned with exploring sacred realms, for spiritual guidance, physical and psychological healing, and caring for the needs of the family and community group. Where psychotherapy focuses primarily on helping the client overcome some debilitating problem, shamanism concerns itself with energy transformation so that you experience the sacredness all around you from moment to moment, restore order where it has been lost and find your natural place within that order. The fact that physical and/or psychological healing often takes place as a natural consequence of the practice is really part of the process not the end goal. All of these goals, which are part of creating harmony in the universe, can be simultaneously pursued through your shamanic practice. For example, a shamanic prayer or invocation can at the same time bring healing to a person, restore energetic order to the environment, and express reverence for life.

ONE WORLD

Shamanism recognizes none of the 'splits' common to our worldview: between body, mind and spirit, for instance, or between the visible, material world of matter and the world of angels, helping spirits, power animals, devas, gods, goddesses and archetypes. From a shamanic perspective spirits are just as real as the rocks in our garden and the teaspoons in our kitchen drawer. Indeed these things too have spirit. Traditionally the shaman, having been through a process of development and training by which the consciousness matrix had become fully activated, was able to undertake quests of the soul into sacred places, both on the earth and in imaginal realms, in order to bring back healing wisdom and guidance on matters of cosmic importance – as well as information of practical use, such as where to find food, which plant to use to cure an illness or how to find a lost possession. The traditional shaman is the intermediary between the numinous realms of sprits and gods and the everyday domestic world. He is at the same time a healer, a teacher, a storyteller and a sorcerer capable of harnessing unseen energies for the benefit of all. Like alchemy, which developed out of shamanic practices, shamanism ventures out into unknown spaces to find methods for transforming reality which reach

The psychological rule says that when an inner situation is not made conscious, it happens outside, as fate. That is to say, when the individual remains undivided and does not become conscious of his inner contradictions, the world must perforce act out the conflict and be torn into opposite halves.
Carl Jung

Man has not body distinct from his soul: for that called Body is a portion of Soul discerned by the five senses, the chief inlets of Soul in this age.
William Blake

way beyond the goals of depth psychology. They are always founded on compassion and a profound respect for Nature. To the shaman the entire world around us is alive – the trees and rocks, air and fire and sea. And his relation to each of these things is a highly personal one.

PASSING THROUGH

I am reminded of a charming story I heard once about someone who was questioning a shaman about the aliveness of trees and plants. 'That sounds like a pretty weird idea,' he said to the shaman, 'OK so if rocks and trees are alive then tell me what do the rocks think of the trees?' The shaman paused and looked out across the cliffs at the sea for a few moments, letting the question sink in. Then he turned back and began to speak. 'To tell you the truth, I don't think they worry much about them. After all the rock people know that the tree people are just passing through.'

The history of shamanism is the history of man's earliest spiritual awareness, beliefs and practices. It is written on the walls of prehistoric caves in Central Asia and in Africa. And in the graves of the Orient. In Uzbekistan archaeologists have uncovered a Neanderthal grave where, in sacred rituals, shamans have surrounded the body of a dead child with ibex horns. In the primordial darkness of les Trois-Frères caves at Montesquieu-Aventes in the Pyrenees of France, drawings reveal Palaeolithic rites probably carried out to the beat of a drum used to transport shamans to sacred realms. There they learned the where and how of the kill needed to feed the tribe and carried out rituals to bless the animal that would feed them so he could return to his source and be born anew. There too a 15,000 year old figure 2½ feet high and 15 inches across known as the Sorcerer of Trois Frères stares at us from a craggy apse. He is the animal master – the great shaman who presides over all the animals. With the round eyes of an owl, the chest and dancing legs of a man, the paws of a lion, the tail of a wolf or a wild horse and the powerful sex organs of a stallion, he has forged deep psychic bonds with his prey, made friends with their essence and learned to dance with their power. In South Africa all the way south from the Zambezi river to the Cape and stretching from Mozambique to Damaraland, Stone Age rock paintings and engravings created by primitive hunters and gatherers attest to shamanic practices carried out over thousands of years of communing with gods and goddesses, animals and elements.

A plant may not talk, but there is a spirit in it that is conscious, that sees everything, which is the soul of the plant, its essence, what makes it alive.
Pablo Amaringo

WEAVERS OF MYTH

It's all a question of story. We are in trouble now because we do not have a good story. We are in between stories. The old story, the account of how we fit into it, is no longer effective. Yet we have not learned the new story.
Thomas Berry

It was the shamans who worked the magic, the shamans who journeyed into numinous realms and brought back descriptions of reality that others missed. It was the shamans who returned from their travels to weave a mythology that inspired the tribe, one that made it possible for its members to make sense of their lives and their dreams, their aspirations and their suffering. Later the 'shamans' became 'prophets', and 'seers' but the sacred technology used to work their magic remained the same. As Joseph Campbell says in volume I of his *Historical Atlas of World Mythologies*, 'It has always been the business of the great seer, known in India as "rishis", in biblical terms as "prophets", to primitive folk as "shamans", and in our own day as "poets" and "artists", to perform the work of the first and second functions of a mythology by recognizing through the veil of nature, as viewed in the science of their times, the radiance, terrible yet gentle, of the dark, unspeakable light beyond, and through their words and images to reveal the sense of the vast silence that is the ground of us all and of all beings.'

CORRUPTION

In our own time the word 'myth' has been corrupted. You read the word in tabloid newspapers or hear it on television used in a totally different way to its real meaning. We hear a spokesman from some government when asked if he can confirm the story that his country will soon be testing a nuclear device respond by insisting, 'Nonsense. That is nothing more than a myth perpetrated by our enemies.' The word myth in its true meaning does not mean something false. A myth is a story which has emerged out of encounters in numinous realms and which carries the unmistakable fragrance of what is true in the widest sense. It is a tale that resonates at the level of our soul, one which cannot be reduced to meaning by analytical probing, and one which, in the hearing, transports us to a place of knowing within ourselves that is undeniable. A culture's cohesiveness is constructed around its myths. Our myths form the very foundations of our world views, values and sense of meaning – or the lack of it. If a culture's mythology does not nourish its people, bring them joy and meaning, then it becomes destructive.

The truth dazzles gradually, or else the world would be blind.
Emily Dickinson

Campbell, who was the greatest mythologist of the twentieth century – probably of all time – described the first two functions of mythology. The first is to awaken and maintain in an individual a sense of wonder and participation in the great mystery –

mysterium tremendum et fascinans – which sits at the very ground of being, including our own. The second is to create a cosmology for a people replete with mystical import that is directly related to the environment within which a people live so that a people's lives have a sense of purpose and meaning. From the earliest of times the shaman has been the instrument by which mythologies, cosmologies and religions have been brought into being. This is because he knows how to travel beyond the limited realms of time and space and move at will between ordinary reality and quantum realms.

AWAKEN THE GIANT

The consciousness matrix embedded within us – the means by which such wisdom and healing and power has been accessed since the beginnings of human history – remains intact. A gift once given to humankind, it has never been revoked. In most of us it sleeps like a great giant beneath the earth just waiting to be called. In some it has already stirred as we explore the powers of healing and self-help through active imagination, meditation, yoga or prayer in our search for truth and beauty, joy and freedom.

Now of course we no longer live in tribal cultures. The borders between peoples, between countries and between ritual practices have become blurred and broken down. In some cases they have been obliterated altogether. Where our ancestors gathered around the fire of an evening to be dazzled by the mythic tales of the shaman and sink into the safety of a shared cosmology that brought meaning, television has become the 'hearth' around which we now sit. Our children are raised on the mythology of advertizers. They tell their tales with great skill and persuasion. Yet their stories, instead of nourishing us from numinous realms and empowering our lives, undermine our power and encourage us instead to place it in the hands of the commercial world that would have us believe that the only way we can be free is to consume what they are selling us.

Yes, we live in different times. Yes, we have different challenges. Our concerns are no longer those of locating an animal on the hunt or performing rituals that honour the gods and goddesses asking them to protect our people through winter. Today's challenges are far greater. How, for instance, do we move forward as a global community faced with progressive extinction of animals and plant species on a massive scale? How do we live in a world burdened by massive debts? How do we recover our own power and experience our own freedom when the very political and economic systems we have created are structured in a way that makes us feel powerless? And finally, how do we come face to face

Man cannot live without mystery. He has a great need of it.
Lame Deer

Our nature lies in movement; complete calm is death.
Blaise Pascal

Yes, creation is moving toward us; life is moving toward us all the time. We back away, but it keeps pushing towards us.
Joan Halifax

with the earthshaking discoveries and dramatic shifts in worldview that are taking place as a result of findings filtering down from physics, astronomy, biology and consciousness research? These discoveries are not only wiping out our trust in every religious, moral and political philosophy we once clung to, they are quite literally turning our sense of reality upside down while providing us with nothing new in which to trust.

LEAP TOWARDS AUTONOMY

The world is full of people that have stopped listening to themselves or have listened only to their neighbours to learn what they ought to do, how they ought to behave, and what the values are that they should be living for.

Joseph Campbell

For me the answer is simple. Yet it has only come from over 25 years spent searching, experimenting, learning, yearning, suffering and discovering. It is no longer appropriate for us to rely on outside 'experts' whether they be doctors, priests or politicians. We can listen to their words of course, but we can no longer follow them blindly as human beings have so often done in the past, fearful that if we did not behave like good children some misfortune might befall us. It is time we embraced our journey into individual maturity by learning to activate our own consciousness matrix. Doing so enables us to expand our limited three-dimensional, five-sensory minds into those of the multi-dimensional beings that we are meant to be. It is time we made the leap – each one of us – into our own power and our own freedom, to learn to build powerful bridges between the truth of our own soul and the expression of our personality. It is time we expanded our vision, helped to heal the wounds in ourselves, in others and our planet. Time each of us explored the simple yet profound practices once known only by the great artists, scientists and shamans and used them to become everything that each of us is destined to be. In the process, I believe we will recover our power, experience our freedom and gain access to healing wisdom and vision of the highest order. Then, and only then will we be prepared together to meet the challenges that face us and take part in the communal process of reshaping our global future.

Ancient shamanic skills are surfacing in new forms. They are no longer the province of a few gifted people. They belong to us all. So let us pay respects to tribal cultures from the Inuit of the Arctic and Tamang of Nepal to the Sumatran Kubu and Native Americans, giving thanks to them for having preserved living shamanic skills. Then let us then turn these skills – which belong not just to tribal groups but to all people – into power for life. We stand poised at a new millennium and it is high time we demystified the whole realm of shamanism and made its marvellous techniques available to all who want to use them to help us move forward into a new age.

Today, the planet is the only proper 'in group'.

Joseph Campbell

CHAPTER 7

Hit The Road

There are two central techniques which act as the locomotive for journey to freedom: *Quantum Break* and *Bridge building*. Moving towards authentic power and freedom requires the continual use of both. I'd like to introduce them right away and explain what they are about as well as to answer the most common questions that arise about the use of each. Please take time to read about them, how they work and what purpose they serve before you go any further. Then come back and read all this again whenever you have a chance until the daily practice of each becomes second nature.

> If the Angel deigns to come it will be because you have convinced her, not by tears but by your humble resolve to be always beginning: to be a beginner.
> *Rainer Maria Rilke*

QUANTUM BREAK

Journey to Freedom requires that you develop the ability at will to move from an ordinary state of five-sensory awareness into quantum realms of consciousness. This only comes with practice. During the Quantum Break you will use various methods to activate your consciousness matrix and move temporarily away from your day-to-day time and space delineated reality into a shamanic state of consciousness. Once there you will be exploring the sacred world – what you might call the space between the molecules – out of which all creativity, all spiritual insight and healing come. You will be taking a Quantum Break at least once a day. The best time to do this for most people is first thing in the morning, before you do anything else. Immediately after the Quantum Break you will be Bridge building – that is recording in some form the experience you have just had.

Relax into the awareness that lies in the genetic structure of your cells, the awareness that has long been waiting for admission into your thoughts. Open to the design pattern in which you are conceived, the original vision of your incarnate perfection, the archetypal vibratory envelope of eternal awareness that has individualized as you in this locality. Accept it, welcome it, awaken to awareness of your home.

Ken Carey

The goal of the hero's journey is yourself, finding yourself.

Joseph Campbell

You will be rediscovering and reconnecting with the powers of instinct within. As you do you will come more and more to trust yourself and your own perceptions. You will make friends in quantum realms with the energies of compassionate spirits and archetypes who are sources of great power and wisdom. They can work with you in practical, effective ways to bring you in touch with your own authentic power and align your outer personality with the seedpower of your soul. As this happens you will experience the release of a lot of dead wood in your life. It will quite simply and naturally rise to the surface of your psyche to be cleared away. (More about this in quantum leap II.) Emotions, memories, even physical symptoms may also surface temporarily in order to be lifted off. The way to deal with these experiences if they do happen is to create a very small space between your awareness of what you are experiencing and the experience itself which will allow you both to experience these things as fully as possible and at the same time simply to be aware of what is going on, from a distance. This is very much the same process that you go through whenever you carry out a physical detoxification where you find you temporarily have a headache, need extra rest, or feel a bit different while physical toxins that have been stored in your body are cleared away. Remind yourself that you are always much better off without them.

As the weeks go by, you will find it easier and easier to let go of restricting worldviews, restricting emotional and religious constrictions which may have kept you from living as creatively as you can. Week by week too, you will find the whole of your life enriched – not by the teachings of someone else – but by the expansion of your own consciousness as a result of your own experience of spiritual energy. Step by step your sense of power will shift. You will come more and more to see yourself not as someone prey to the false power of outside influences, but as a centre of creative energy and authentic power. You will come to feel, working in friendship with beings both in ordinary reality and quantum realms, that you have the ability to create what is most precious to you and to live out the very highest nature of your soul.

BRIDGE BUILDING

The second pivotal tool in your journey to freedom is Bridge building. It is exactly what it sounds like – building bridges between non-ordinary reality and the mundane world. This step in the process is every bit as important as the Quantum Break.

It is all very well to experience the wonderful freedom and excitement of moving in and out of transcendent realms. It can be great to visit non-ordinary reality for the purposes of relaxation or to renew mind and body. And these are perfectly good reasons for taking a Quantum Break. When you begin to learn shamanic techniques you will be amazed at how powerfully renewing a shamanic journey can be. It cuts through habitual thought patterns, shifts neurological functioning in your body and alters brainwaves so that you can experience deep states of psychological and physical relaxation – sometimes even deeper than self-hypnosis, autogenic training, or meditation. For some, just touching these states can bring spontaneous healing and relieve persistent stress.

But becoming familiar with the magnificent richness and vast terrain of non-ordinary reality can do far more than simply help you deal with stress and renew your energies. It can bring you support from the universe during times of profound change in your life and guidance as to what the next step is even when you feel you have no idea. It can expand your awareness of what is *real*. It teaches you compassion for yourself (the hardest kind of compassion to come by), for others and for the earth itself. It teaches you to trust your own perceptions and it enriches your life enormously – so enormously that addictions – to food, to drugs, to work, to alcohol, to cigarettes, to sex – which you may have struggled with for years gradually fall away to be replaced by the knowledge that you can move whenever you want into numinous realms. Once there, you experience the whole universe as being rich in its nourishment of you and all of a piece. This sense will carry over more and more into your daily life so you feel more and more of the time that all is right with the world. But this only happens with practice and provided you Bridge build regularly.

GIVE POWER TO DREAMS

So it is not enough just to take a Quantum Break and bask in the beauty and wonder of what you find there. You need to bring back some of the extraordinary energy you connect with and translate it into physical form. Doing so not only enriches your own life

> Our knowledge base is so primitive that merely tweaking assumptions here or there in computer models of climate change can alter predictions from an impending ice age to catastrophic heating. That is not an indictment of scientists but indicates that there are gaps in our knowledge large enough for the future of the planet to fall through.
> *David Suzuki*

but also brings blessings to everything around you. It is what the artist does, the poet, the great visionary, scientist or inventor. It is what makes it possible for them to draw on inspiration and insight and then bring some of the beauty and truth they have perceived into form. Bridge building is what we all need to do when, in a flash of inspiration, we see or feel something in a new way. We need to manifest this inspiration into the world of ordinary reality, for it is only when we do so that we bring real transformation to our lives by aligning the power of the personality with the richness of our soul. We need to bring our dreams and our vision into being.

I cannot tell you how important Bridge building is to your journey to freedom. The world is filled with dreamers who either have a natural ability to dip into numinous realms or who choose to make use of consciousness-altering drugs or alcohol to shift their consciousness in an attempt to escape the difficulties of ordinary life. When they do they feel temporarily wonderful. Sometimes they even feel they have come face to face with a real sense of what the universe is all about and where they belong in it. But the wonder of such experiences soon dissipates because these people have not developed the skills needed to walk between the worlds. They make no attempt to bring back to ordinary reality the insights and gifts they find in quantum realms. So they become 'turn on junkies' able to touch the beauty of the transcendent yet completely unable to manifest any of its spiritual power in their ordinary lives. Bridge building grounds spiritual energy. It brings creative power into material form. If you do not know how to build Bridges you will never move fully into your own authentic power nor live your freedom.

CREATING STRUCTURE

How do you build Bridges? You do it by creating something concrete in physical reality. You take up a pen and write. Or you sit down in front of a computer and pour words onto the screen without stopping – simply recording the experience you had while in the shamanic state of consciousness during your Quantum Break. Or you dance the feeling you have brought back with you or you sing it in simple words and then record them on tape or in your journal – or even without words in simple melodies. Or you pick up paper and draw images freely – letting them pour forth from your heart to express the experience you have just had in quantum realms. Or, wherever it seems appropriate, you create a ritual which you then carry out in ordinary reality to ground whatever healing, learning, energies you have touched to make them part of your ordinary world.

You will have specific exercises to carry out during each Quantum Break. It is important to work with each of them in turn, one after another. You will be moving quite quickly in the process of learning the tools and techniques that will make it simple to access quantum realms and return with their gifts. Each technique requires practice to make it part of your life. Reading about it is less than useless. There is nothing theoretical about your journey to freedom.

DO IT THEN GROUND IT

Each quantum leap needs to be made and then integrated into mind and body before you are ready to tackle the next. Each builds upon the previous one in your process of unfolding. Each week you will have two 'Free Break' days during which you can put the current technique or any previously learned technique into practice for whatever personal purposes you like. For instance, you may find yourself or a friend in need of healing. You may want to explore some aspect of non-ordinary reality and begin to map these quantum realms. You may want advice on what the next step for a project is or you may need an overall view on some personal or business scheme. You may need something simple yet practical – like help for a houseplant which is ailing. Your two 'Free Breaks' can be used for these purposes.

In a very real sense we are the authors of our own lives.
Mandy Aftel

Of course you do not have to limit yourself to one Quantum Break a day. Once you have done your quantum leaps and Bridge building for the day you are free to use the Quantum Break technique as many more times as you like so long as you Bridge build on your return. But journey to freedom is an intensive process. It moves fast and deep. Most people find an hour a day is ideal to keep moving ahead without overdoing it. Each week too you will be asked to spend at least one day working on a project – creating sacred space in your home for instance, or making a journey to 'see' in a new way. You will then be recording your experience of these things in your Travelogue at the end of each week.

Patience is the companion of wisdom.
St Augustine

HOW MUCH TIME WILL IT TAKE?

So count on spending one hour a day during your journey to freedom. This time will include the reading you will be doing as well as both Quantum Break and Bridge building. I know this sounds like a lot. You may say, 'How am I going to find an extra hour for this?' The answer is you will not *find* it, you will *make* it. The first two quantum leaps are a little longer than those that follow, just because they introduce the whole process of shifting consciousness, so they may need a little more reading time. The commitment you make to doing this is a commitment to your own authentic power and freedom. And, just in case you think this sounds selfish or self-indulgent, think again. The truth is, the more you honour your own seedpower and move towards your own authentic power and freedom, the richer becomes your compassion for others and the more you can give to them. In fact it is pretty much automatic. As you become more truly who you are you cannot help but honour all others, including the rocks and trees, animals and people – what Native Americans call 'all our relations'.

For most people journey to freedom works best when they get up an hour earlier to do their shamanic work in the morning before anybody else in the house stirs. There are many advantages to this. This way you know that you have completed your journey work and will be able to go on with your day without the worry and fuss of fitting it in later or during the evening. Also the morning, before you have picked up the psychic and physical pollution of the day, is a great time for shamanic work. Taking your Quantum Break and doing your Bridge building begins your day from a position of clarity, energy, strength and power. As you work with Quantum Break and Bridge building, as the days and weeks pass you will find that you are making better and more efficient use of your time. Journey work creates an energetic architecture that reduces stress and seems to make everything work better. It helps get rid of what I call 'hamster syndrome' where much of our energy is wasted on a treadmill.

If you cannot manage your journey work first thing in the morning, or if one day you have to miss your morning session, then structure your day to include an hour in the afternoon or evening when you can carry it out. Generally just before bed is not a good time, however, since shamanic work can be very energizing. Not the best thing to be doing before going to sleep.

FORGET THE GOLD STAR

Whenever you decide to do your work, the important thing is to *do* it each and every day. It is also important to remember that you have committed yourself to journey to freedom because you want to come fully into your own authentic power and to make the experience of freedom a central part of your life. This is major transformation stuff. The thirteen quantum leaps are cumulative in their effects. They keep you continually moving forward. The journey to freedom process gets easier and easier as you go on, with each leap building on the previous one.

The thirteen quantum leaps need to be taken in the order in which they appear in the book. If ever you miss a day, don't beat yourself up about it. Simply go back to your intention the next day and carry on as usual. You are not an automaton and you are not doing this programme to satisfy some external taskmaster or get a gold star. You are doing it to enhance your own life. Compassion and forgiveness towards yourself for not being able to fulfil your intention 24 hours a day seven days a week is as important as honouring your commitments.

A frontier is never a place; it is a time and a way of life.
Hal Borland

GATHER YOUR GEAR

There are certain things you will need to gather together during the first week of the quantum leap programme.

✦ An A4 size book with blank pages in it which will serve as your journal. This you will use to record quantum experiences in words as well as to make drawings of them for Bridge building. It is best that this book be either unlined or one which has both lined and unlined pages in it to accommodate your writing as well as your drawing. If you prefer to write on a computer and print up what you have written each day, then buy a loose leaf binder in which the pages can be stored in consecutive order. If you prefer to record your journeys by hand in a smaller notebook, that will work too. Then purchase an artists sketch pad in a big size. In lots of ways it works better for Bridge building if the drawings are large. I sometimes hang a drawing of a particularly useful or important Bridge I've built on the wall of the room I work in or sleep in so that I can continue to interact with and expand the effects of the sacred energy of the Quantum Break that lies behind it.

✦ Coloured pens and pencils or pastels or oil pastels – even paints if you like. Buy a packet or two of colours that inspire you. When you choose them, pretend you are a child again and that you have the freedom to buy whichever ones you want with nobody to stand over you and tell you what is allowed and what is not. As you work through the programme, you may want to expand your collection of art materials – especially when you begin to see just how powerful working with shapes and colours, textures and form can be for your Bridge building.

✦ A rattle. This can be as simple as a little yoghurt container washed out, dried and filled with rice or lentils. If you prefer a ready made rattle, you can pick one up from the percussion department of any shop that sells musical instruments or buy a gourd or Native American rattle from a street market or speciality shop.

✦ A drumming tape for shamanic journeying. Your tape needs to be one specifically made for this purpose. It will have a monotonous beat with a call back beat on it. Sometimes you can buy such a tape in a bookstore. Otherwise you can order it by post (see resources). You can also make a tape of your own if you have a drum of any kind. (You will find the instructions for doing this in quantum leap 2.)

✦ A walkman. This is not absolutely essential, but it is so useful that you will probably want to have one. It means that you can journey without the sound of drumming disturbing anyone who may be near by. It has other advantages too in that, if you happen to have a little dictation tape recorder as well, a walkman will enable you to journey to the sound of drumming while at the same time recording your journey in words. (This is something you can experiment with if you like later on in the journey to freedom process.)

✦ You won't actually make use of some of these things until the second week or later, but now is the time to gather them so they are at hand when the need arises.

GATEWAY TO FREEDOM

A step-by-step process, journey to freedom is a programme to be carried out over thirteen weeks. Thirteen is a very special number. Thirteen is the number of the full moons and the tide changes within a year. It is the number most closely associated with the rhythms of the universe – a number that carries the power of wiping away the old and allowing the new to come to birth organically from within. The exercises you will be working with are designed to help you reconnect with your own instinct and restore lost trust in your own individual path. So you can walk it with joy. That too is the nature of thirteen – the number of individuality and freedom. It may also be why the number thirteen has been so often a source of fear in the Western world. It puts power back where it belongs: at the seat of the individual soul.

The number twelve belongs to the man-made traditions and to many of the social and cultural structures we have inherited. It is the number by which man has divided space and time – being the product of the four points of the compass multiplied by the three mythological levels of the universe. It is the number of the man-made months of the year and the number of a completed cycle. There are twelve-point programmes for recovery from alcoholism and from other addictions. There are twelve houses in the zodiac. These are the structures man has built in his evolution. These are the things which we are all familiar with.

Yet any man-made structure or philosophy or system, no matter how wonderful will never be large enough to contain the human spirit. Twelve-point systems are to be used for what each has to offer and then transcended. Even the most wonderful and effective system for transformation or healing or growth can become yet another prison for the human spirit. The prison it puts us in may be a bigger prison than we were in before. It may be a more interesting prison or a more comfortable prison, but it is nonetheless a place that ultimately restricts our freedom and prevents us from living our truth from the soul. That is not the goal here. Twelve completes the circle and thirteen breaks the mould. It is the all important thirteenth step that leads out from the beauty of what others have created into living out your authentic power and experiencing your freedom. This, the thirteenth quantum leap, is the most important of them all.

This programme is like no other you may have tried. It does not ask you to buy into a belief system. It only presents you with the tools and techniques most useful for activating your consciousness matrix and exploring the universe and all its mysteries for

The privilege of a lifetime is being who you are.
Joseph Campbell

yourself. It also trains you in the use of them – for healing, for creativity, for divination, for calling forth your authentic power and living out your freedom. Once you have these tools, once you have been through the quantum leap process, made the connections and learned the skills then you are free to do what you want with them or to throw them all away.

If your life does not allow you to work at this speed, the course can be spread over 26 weeks or even thirteen months. The important thing is to do your journeywork regularly – preferably a little each day. The journey to freedom process is designed like a ladder you use to climb the tree of awareness. Once you get to the top, once you have been through the process, then it will be time to throw the ladder away. For it is the experience of working through the climb that is of value not the rungs of the ladder itself.

The great path has no gates,
Thousands of roads
enter into it,
When one passes through
this gateless gate,
He walks freely between
heaven and earth.
Arthur Young

FREEDOM CONTRACT

I, _____, choose to undertake an intensive step-by-step process of unfolding to access my authentic power and freedom. I commit myself to the thirteen-week duration of the journey. I understand that the programme I will be working with is both progressive and cumulative and therefore requires that I work with one quantum leap after another in order. I, _____, commit to weekly reading, and carrying out daily Quantum Breaks, Bridge building, and sacred projects.

I, _____, further understand that working through the journey to freedom can bring to the surface psychological deadwood accumulated from such things as parental training, religious training and restricted world-views which have been blocking my experience of authentic power and freedom, and that this is part of the process of clearing them away permanently.

I, _____, here make clear my intention of allowing whatever deadwood in my life no longer serves my highest good to be lifted away.

I, _____, will persistently move forward on my journey and, for the duration of the freedom process, look after myself consistently by getting enough sleep, eating well, exercising my body and treating myself, and the universe as a whole, with patience and compassion.

_____

(signature)

_____

(date)

If the doors of perception
were cleansed
Everything would appear to
man as it is – infinite.
William Blake

KEEP ON TRUCKIN'!

When I teach journey to freedom I ask that my students make a contractual agreement with themselves. This helps them focus their intention and compassion – two of the three forces which make the whole freedom process work for you. It also commits them to the third driving force – persistence – just keep on truckin'. These three make anything work anywhere. Can you honour the seedpower of your own soul by giving yourself the gift of these three powers? Say yes by carrying out a simple sacred ritual. Pick a flower and put it in a small vase, or light a candle. Read the contract, amend it in any way you like – for this is your contract with yourself and has to be written in a way that suits you. Then sign it and date it. Return to it whenever you feel the need to refocus your intention, your compassion and your persistence. Then these three powerhouses will serve you well from beginning to end.

The whole scattered world of lower things is gathered up to oneness when the soul climbs up to that life in which there are no opposites.
Meister Eckhart

No system, no programme, philosophy, psychology, science or religion has ever been or ever will be as vast as the human spirit. It is only in coming in touch with the great depth and beauty of your soul, getting to know and work with its compassion and power, gaining access to your own sources of wisdom and spiritual guidance from within and learning to trust the whispers of your own soul that authentic freedom comes into being. It is at this point that we forsake our *idea* of the divine for a living experience of it. As someone once so wisely said, 'You have to forsake god for God'.

TRANSFORMATION FROM WITHIN

Please remember that the quantum leap programme is here to serve you. You are not here to serve it. It is not like some diet regime you go on, trying to be a 'good girl' or a 'good boy'. Those kind of programmes we begin with enthusiasm one day only to quit a few days later (and often feel very guilty). We all quit whenever a programme is imposed on us from outside without honouring our own individual needs, pathways and truths. As you work through *Journey to Freedom* you will see that what comes out of it comes from your experience alone – experience far richer than anyone else's. *Journey to Freedom* helps you transcend whatever distortions may have been restricting your experience. It helps you move forward into a way of living that is ever closer to the full expression of your individual divine essence. It allows the nature of your soul to unfold in all its beauty.

The programme is a practical guide to the expansion of consciousness and the release of power. From beginning to end it rests within your own control. It does not ask you to buy into any belief system, any psychological framework or any external control. A collection of simple techniques for accessing energy, power, vision, healing and creativity, it provides you with tools and techniques that give you direct access to a richer and richer experience of both your world of form – the world of ordinary reality – and the realms of quantum consciousness. I can't wait to see what creative use you will make of all this in the end. And when you have finished the programme, I would love to know. Please write to me at the address you will find in the resources at the end of the book.

quantum leap 1

Enter the Sacred

Guardian of the centre, keeper of truth, I hide within each breath you take, in every heart beat, in every thought that wings its way through your mind. I am the great rock in the wilderness and the tiny pebbles beneath your feet. I am the gossamer a spider weaves. You will find me in the fresh air of a morning and in the cardboard shanties of families who live in the streets of the metropolis. Smell my spirit in honeysuckle, feel my spikiness in a handful of sand, taste my brightness in a crunchy apple. All around you I sit silently, waiting to be noticed. Open your eyes and see me, open your ears and hear me. I transform wastelands into rich forests. I turn decay into new life.

I am the Spirit of the Sacred

You may feel dizzy, excited, curious or sceptical as you take your first step out of mundane reality into the quantum realms. The words, games and exercises are designed to make the passage as smooth and blissful as possible. So take a deep breath and jump.

Your journey to freedom begins with making friends with the sacred. And the sacred is everywhere. You don't have to travel to Stonehenge or Machu Picchu to find it. Neither do you need to swallow a consciousness-altering drug. The sacred continually pours forth from the centre of the universe, which, according to religious traditions as well as leading-edge science is simultaneously right here and now and everywhere, at any time. More about this amazing fact in quantum leap 8. The problem is that most of us have become blinded by the mechanically-orientated worldview we have inherited. We have forgotten how to see it.

Rediscovering the sacred is the simplest thing in the world. It happens through a shift of consciousness – a break in time and space through which you can watch the sacred realm come into being. Sometimes this takes place spontaneously. It is given by grace. You can also create structures in your life that invite it to happen more often. You can organize the space you live and work in, for instance, to make a place in your life for rituals which honour the radiance of the world around you and within you. These processes can be a lot of fun too. Think of them as adventures, a game, a childlike exploration. We will be doing some of this in this week as part of the first quantum leap.

ADVENTURE IN THE SACRED

I remember my first experience of the sacred as a grownup. I was 18 years old, just finishing my second year at Stanford University. Five months earlier I had fallen in love for the first time with a man three years older than me. I found myself in the unenviable position of having to leave him to go to live in New York. I knew it would be a long time before we met again – maybe never. We had one day to spend together in San Francisco before my plane left. So we went for a walk in Golden Gate Park. I had been in the park many times before, visiting the Japanese garden or the museum. But I had paid little attention to what was around me except in the rather vague way we all 'appreciate' being amidst trees, grass and flowers.

That morning the world of the sacred cracked wide open for me. As he and I wandered across grass, through trees, knowing that in a few hours we would no longer be together, I could feel death sitting at my shoulder. I had no idea why. I loved this man with an intensity I had not before dreamed possible. I could hardly bear the fire that burned in my flesh when he touched me, let alone the surges of power that came when he held me in his arms or whispered in my ear. The love between us had arisen simultaneously a few months before. From the moment we met both of us had experienced the sense that it was a love that had always existed and always would.

CRACK IN THE COSMOS

That morning we crossed a road and stepped up on to the curb. In front of us a group of old men were bowling on the green. They were dressed in the shabby clothes the old sometimes wear – garments which, like old friends, you have lived with so long you don't want to be parted from them. None of the men paid the least attention to us, absorbed as they were in their game. All at once the scene before me shifted from that of a pleasant ordinary morning spent in nature – nice trees, green grass, a small knoll behind the old men rising to a copse above – to something at once joyous and terrifying. Space expanded in all directions. A million tiny holes appeared in reality – each emitting light – so that the air and grass, the pavement we had just crossed, the bodies of the men in their shabby clothes, the clouds above us, and the trees around us, trembled with radiance. Time burst wide open to break in great waves over the lawn. My heart seemed to grow to immense proportions. I did not understand what was happening. I knew that I had never experienced any of this before. In some way that seemed totally crazy, I was all at the same time being wiped out and brought into being in a brand new form.

When an experience of the sacred arises spontaneously – often at times of great emotional joy or loss – it is both blissful and awe-filled. In whatever guise it shows itself, the sacred is a far cry from any 'orchestrated' experience of pink-flowers-and-soft-music which false purveyors of freedom with their easy answers offer us. It is an experience full of beauty and terror, fascination and majesty. In the presence of an overwhelming power you find yourself standing before a mystery that is wholly other. I knew nothing about what was happening that morning in Golden Gate Park. Only that it was an epiphany in my life and that I wanted to live more and more from this level of being.

MYSTERIUM TREMENDUM

In 1917 Rudolf Otto published one of the most important books on spirituality ever written, *Das Heilige – The Sacred*. In it he describes the awe-inspiring mystery (*mysterium tremendum*) we feel in the presence of sacred energy. He characterizes it as a perfect

Are you willing to be sponged
out, erased, cancelled,
made nothing?
Are you willing to be
made nothing?
Dipped into oblivion?
If not, you will never
really change.
D.H. Lawrence

What the people of the city
do not realize is that the
roots of all living things
are tied together.
Chan K'in Viejo

fullness of being, a flowering which dissolves away our conditioned thinking and breaks down all the barriers to our being fully present in the moment. Every time we are touched by the sacred it urges us to live a little more from the deepest levels of our being. Experience of the sacred opens the door to freedom. Make room in your life for the sacred and you take the first quantum leap towards freedom.

Otto characterizes the qualities of the sacred as numinous (from the Latin *numen*, god), for they are brought about by the sudden revelation of some aspect of divine power within the paraphernalia of day-to-day living. Such is the nature of the sacred when it bursts forth into our life. One minute you are waiting for a bus, standing beneath a tree you have stood under a hundred times before. The next this tree has become suddenly something else as well. It has been transmuted in some mysterious way into a supernatural reality. Of course it is still a tree to you and to everybody else standing there. In fact nothing in particular may distinguish this tree from all the other trees on the street. Yet because it has, at that moment, chosen to reveal itself to you as sacred, your immediate experience of it is transmuted into something wild and free, great and wonderful. It seems as though the tree has opened to you its secret nature and become a repository of all that is awesome – so much so that sometimes experiencing the sacred can make it hard to catch your breath. It can even, for a time, make you wonder who you are and what on earth you are doing there.

Another great philosopher of the sacred is religious philosopher Mircea Eliade. Eliade calls the manifestation of the sacred – during which the numinous realms open to reveal themselves – an *hierophany*. It is a great word. For it does not imply any religious or philosophical bias that would indicate that you need to belong to some in-group to have a right to sacred experience. Hierophanies belong to all who have eyes to see and ears to hear. In early civilizations hierophanies were common occurrences. In tribal cultures they are to this day – wherever people live with an awareness of the sacred nature of even the most ordinary things. To them, rocks are sacred, as are the wind, the stars, the Earth, the trees, the animals, the changes of the seasons, the sun and the rain, the birth of a child, the death of an elder. Wherever you find an awareness of the sacred you also find rituals designed to celebrate as well as set the stage for hierophanies to happen more often.

FEAR OF THE SACRED

Our modern world feels profoundly uneasy before such experiences. We are the only age in history that lives in a desacralized culture. Limited worldviews imprison us, forcing us to live in an almost totally profane world. Today a tree is nothing but a tree. The wind is but the movement of air caused by nothing more than mechanical shifts in currents. As far as rocks are concerned, what could possibly be more mundane? We make fun of 'primitive' people and their 'quaint' superstitions. At the same time we often exploit their land and force the values of our materialistic world on them. What we forget is that cultures for whom the sacred appears through ordinary objects know very well that a rock is a rock. They don't venerate the rock itself, or the wind. They worship the hierophanies which appear through these things to reveal the spirit of each – something totally other and vast in its beauty. They know that whenever and wherever the sacred erupts into the mundane world, no matter what form it takes, a deeper, wider, richer dimension of reality is asking them to dance with its power and celebrate its beauty.

Become as little children.
Jesus

MAKE WAY FOR THE SACRED

Most of us have to relearn how. Once we do, we find ourselves continually renewed, energized, ecstatic. It is as though a wild blessing has been given – a blessing which nourishes us and heals. In *The Sacred and the Profane*, Eliade speaks of the basic need we as humans have 'to plunge periodically into this sacred and indestructible time … the eternal present.' It is a need so deeply ingrained in our very being that when we are unable to fulfil it from time to time we end up living in a nihilistic wasteland. Then our lives become narrow, no matter how many fast cars we buy, how many drugs we take, how many lovers we have. Eating, sex, and getting up in the morning become nothing more than physiological events in a mechanical existence. Reawakening an awareness of the sacred in your life and making room for it turns these events into much more than bodily functions. Each one can evolve into a 'sacrament' – the meaning of which is communion with the sacred. When it does, our experience of vitality, joy and creativity just goes on expanding.

There is a place that opens only to tears.
Danah Zohar

Welcoming the sacred into your life is the first step in awakening the shamanic matrix and opening the gateway to freedom. It is not hard to do. We all knew how when we were children. It is just that our educational system with its emphasis on the rational, the abstract and mass conformity has taught us to forget. It has taught us to be 'serious' to 'work hard', not to 'daydream' nor to 'be silly'. Luckily, like learning to ride a bicycle, you never really lose the skill. To recover your lost ability to bring hierophanies into your life, you need only remember what you may have temporarily forgotten and begin to play again.

THE WEEK AHEAD

During quantum leap 1 you will be working with three different Quantum Break exercises: Inner Reaches of Sacred Space, Cocoon Spinning and Tree Talk. It is important to do them in this order for each builds upon the other: practising Inner Reaches of Sacred Space – which you will do in the first two days of your week – builds the foundations for Cocoon Spinning – done for the next two days. They, in turn will have begun to activate your consciousness matrix for the next Quantum Break – Tree Talk, which you will do the following day. They all prepare the way for your two Free Breaks. In these you might like to explore further, connecting on a sacred level with plants by repeating Tree Talk, deepening your experience of your special inner sanctuary in nature through using the Inner Reaches Break, or using Cocoon Spinning again, especially if you find yourself at a place in your life where you need extra emotional, physical and spiritual support to make the changes you want to make. The choice of exercises on 'free' days is up to you. With each of the Quantum Breaks you must be sure to do your Bridge building. For it is in bringing back the gifts from quantum realms and recording them in some form that requires a physical act such as writing or drawing, movement or singing, that powerful connections between the soul and the personality are forged. This, in turn, brings more and more authentic power into your life and expands your freedom.

As you are preparing for each Quantum Break, I suggest you read and then reread (at least three times) each exercise before you do it. This will enable you to become familiar with it before you begin. I also suggest, at least in the beginning of your journey work, that you do each exercise with the book open in your lap so that if you find yourself at a place in the exercise where you need to remind yourself of what comes next you can gently open your eyes, go back to the description of it to refresh your memory and then return to the process itself. This is easier to do than you might think. Try it. On the other hand, remember that the steps in each exercise are not to be followed slavishly. They are here as guides for you. So you can easily get the gist of the whole thing before you begin and just rely on what you remember of it. After you have done an exercise once, remember to read through it again just before you do it again. In time, of course, you will find that it almost becomes a part of you. Once that happens you need never look at it again. On pages 81–2 at the end of the chapter you will find your checklist where the whole of each week's exercises are set out step by step, day by day for quick reference.

SACRED NATURE

Nature is a great carrier of sacred power for us. This is probably because the energies of nature, in which we have lived as human beings throughout 4 million years of our evolution, are *our* energies. Our bodies and our beings are in communication through our DNA with those of plants and animals. At a cellular level, we know the familiar taste of herbs and smells of the earth. This knowing is built right into our being. Throughout the thirteen quantum leap programme you will be interacting with nature, aligning yourself with her power, coming into harmony with the different directions and the energies she carries, and with the elements of air and fire, water and earth. You will be exploring the centring power of the circle – the most basic of all shapes which is the energetic blueprint for mandalas and medicine wheels, for the seasons, for the sun and the moon, even for life itself. And you will be creating an energetic architecture in your life that welcomes hierophanies. Quantum Break 1 asks you to begin reconnecting with nature in two ways:

… according to my hypotheses, DNA was, like the axis mundi, the source of shamanic knowledge and visions.
Jeremy Narby

◆ By coming into contact with your own personal, internal sacred place in imaginal realms and returning to it frequently.
◆ By making friends with nature in the world around you, whether this means going out into the fields, by the sea, into the hills and woods and mountains or, if you are a city dweller, learning to dialogue with any natural object in your environment – a rock, a flower, even the food you eat.

These two processes are equally important. They reinforce each other. Your first Quantum Break is to leap into inner space.

Quantum Break 1

INNER REACHES OF SACRED SPACE

This is an exercise which you will use again and again throughout the thirteen quantum leap programme. It starts your daily practice. I give it in my workshops as a means of beginning to connect up ordinary reality and the mythic realms. But it is also far more. In practising it you will discover your very own sacred place of silence and natural beauty – a sanctuary of absolute safety and a place to which you can return, no matter where you are or in what circumstances you find yourself. Use it for healing, for renewing your physical and mental energy, for cleansing your body or your psyche and for tapping into creativity whenever you wish.

Here's how:

Take the phone off the hook so you won't be disturbed for the next ten minutes.

+ Sit on a straight-backed chair, or on the floor if you prefer. Take three or four nice deep breaths through your nose letting the air escape gently through your mouth on the outbreath.
+ Close your eyes.
+ Put your imagination into gear. Let your mind go back to some place in nature which you have seen and which you especially like. This is a place in ordinary reality, not somewhere from a dream or a story. It may be a place familiar to you, say at the end of your garden. Or it can be somewhere you have visited only once.
+ When you have found the place you like, sit for a moment quietly remembering as much about it as you can.
+ Now see what happens when you activate your senses.
+ What do you smell?
+ How does the air feel against your skin?

- Sense the earth beneath your body. What is it like?
- What do you see?
- Are there any herbs or fruits or flowers around you?
- What do you hear?
- Is there any water there? If so, can you hear it?
- Touch it?
- Drink some of it if you like.
- What does it feel like? Taste like?
- Are there rocks nearby? If so, pick one up in your hand and feel the weight of it. Is it rough or smooth?
- What is the atmosphere like? Is the sun shining? Is there mist? Rain? Feel it on your body. Let it penetrate your clothes.
- Let yourself sink into the beauty that surrounds you. In a very real sense this beauty *is* you. All that you see in this special place is part of you and you are part of it.
- Are there any others there with you? Animals? People? Nature spirits? Angels?
- Forget for a few minutes any concerns you may have about your day-to-day life. (Don't worry, you can think about them again when you return from your sacred place if you want to.) For the moment, just let these things lift away from you. Allow the wind to carry them high into the sky and far away. Just get in your skin in your sacred place and breathe softly.
- This place is yours and yours alone. You can return to it whenever you need help with an answer to a question, whenever you need healing, or clarity, renewal or refreshment.
- Let yourself sense the energy of love that surrounds you. It is embedded within your very body by the beauty and the friendship that you take in.
- When you are ready, give thanks for the friendship and the beauty around you and say goodbye for the moment to your inner sanctuary, knowing that you can return to it whenever you like. The more often you return the richer the experience will become and the more valuable will be the gifts you will bring back for yourself and others.

Now, very gently, in your own time, open your eyes and come back into the room.

Man can learn nothing except by going from the known to the unknown.
Claude Bernard

The return is seeing radiance everywhere.
Joseph Campbell

No more words. Hear only the voice within.
Rumi

Bridge Building

Now it is time to build your Bridges. Take out your notebook and record what you have experienced. Describe it in words – where you went, what you saw, felt, tasted, sensed, who was there, what happened there. Just let the words flow. Don't read what you are writing while you write it. Allow your pen to move across the page. Keep writing, without stopping, until you have finished.

Remember this is not an essay for school. There is no right or wrong way of doing it. If you are lucky enough to still be able to see or hear, taste or smell the atmosphere while you are describing it, great. If not it is of no matter. Your sacred place will work for you beautifully even if you only 'sense' the place but see nothing. However you experience it, it is the little details that give this sacred place its vibrancy.

If you prefer you can draw what you have seen. This does not have to be literal drawing – that is of a tree, a flower, a rock. It can be simply colours swirled together to give the feeling of the place or – what I like best to do – use a combination of words and colours to record your experience. When you are using colour, the same guidelines apply as for the words – just let rip. You are not trying to be an artist and there is no judgement involved. Simply let whatever comes onto the page happen as you create a record in ordinary reality of what you have experienced in imaginal realms.

STRAND BY STRAND

Bridges between the sacred realms and ordinary reality, as well as the enegetic cocoons which make transformation a more graceful experience, are woven strand by strand. That is why all the way through the quantum leaps you will be recording the results of your journeys and experiences, divinations and insights. You will be expressing them in concrete form in ordinary reality. There is a very important reason for this. The key to using the consciousness matrix to expand freedom rests in your learning to bring the two realms of reality into harmony with each other and in being able at will to access whichever realm is most appropriate at any particular moment in time.

There are a number of spiritual practices which can bring all sorts of wonderful experiences – union with the angels, visions, a sense of being freed for a time from the cares of the world. But unless the transcendent energy you have touched can afterwards be brought back into your day-to-day existence and grounded in ordinary reality it will not yield an experience of progressively unfolding power, authenticity and freedom. In fact, spiritual experiences that are not grounded in action in the ordinary world can actually take you further and further away from freedom. They can become not a means of expanding consciousness, creativity and joy, but rather an escape from a world that seems too tough to handle. It is just as easy to become enchanted by a spiritual buzz as it is by a materialistic one. And just as imprisoning. Like the traditional shaman, each of us is meant to walk between the worlds of the sacred and the ordinary. Each of us needs to learn continually to infuse ordinary reality with energy by calling in the numinous power of the sacred. That is when authentic power and freedom become living experiences.

NO WRONG WAY

The important thing to remember as you are working with all of the techniques in the journey to freedom process – from quantum leap 1 onwards – is THERE IS NO WRONG WAY TO DO IT. I can't stress this enough. Because of our upbringing and education all of us have been taught to think that there is one 'right answer' to any question, only one 'right way' to do something, only one 'right result' from any practice. These beliefs, which have been so deeply ingrained in us, die hard. Yet it is important to let them die and then bury them once and for all.

Every person's experience of each quantum leap will be absolutely individual. More than that, each time you repeat the same exercise it will be different for you. That is in the nature not only of doing shamanic work but of life itself. What you will find, however, is that there may be 'themes' that run through your work for a time. These are qualities and myths, insights and energies that will be very important to you right now. In a week's time or a month's time they may well have completed whatever process they have been part of only to be replaced by others. This kind of work is very organic in its nature. One thing after another, one focus of awareness or one kind of energy will tend to surface into awareness for you to use to create in ordinary reality whatever is appropriate to you. Then once its cycle has completed itself it will gracefully and automatically be replaced by whatever comes next. The whole process of your journey to freedom unfolds in this way. It is not intellectual. It is unique to you. This is the hard-

Practice is a seedbed of miracles.
Michael Murphy

est thing for my students to get – but it is very important to understand right from the beginning – YOUR EXPERIENCE OF AN EXERCISE IS RIGHT FOR YOU.

Meaning seems to leap out
of matter, like a tiger out
of a dark cave.
Ramakrishna

There are some people for whom shamanic work is as easy as falling off a log right from the first day. They access the consciousness matrix with ease and shift from ordinary reality to non-ordinary reality quickly. When they begin to journey, they do this with similar alacrity. Their journeys are filled with symbols or visual images galore. You would think that they would be the ones who make the best shamanic practitioners in the end and whose journey to freedom would go forward most easily and successfully.

IT AIN'T NECESSARILY SO

The irony is that this is not the case at all. I have worked with people who when they begin the exercises feel frustrated because 'nothing seems to happen to me,' 'I can't do it,' 'I have never been able to do anything right,' 'I never could visualize anything,' 'I know I am a failure,' or any number of other self-deprecating comments. This kind of stuff comes from the wrong kind of education – education that is constantly trying to make you fit into a mould instead of encouraging you to find your own shape and explore your own way of doing things. *Don't buy into it.* Any trouble you have at the beginning of your journey work is brought about by one of two things:

✦ *Beginner's worries*: Everybody feels uncertain when they begin to learn something new. Part of the challenge is to let yourself feel any fear that surfaces then do it anyway. All those niggling anxieties will eventually float away as you continue day by day to do your Quantum Breaks and Bridge building. Gradually you will forget about all those worries as you become fascinated by the wonderful sacred energies you will be connecting with and the exciting new territories of reality which you will be exploring.

✦ *Trying too hard*: Journey work is never accomplished by trying. Yet we are all filled with the notion that if something doesn't come easy in the beginning what we should do is, 'Try harder next time.' The secret to making all of your quantum leaps rich and profitable comes in gradually letting go of the whole idea of trying harder altogether. Whatever comes to you during an exercise is exactly what the compassionate spirits who will be working with you know is most appropriate for you.

My experience from teaching is that it is often those who struggle the most with their tasks in the beginning who end up gaining the most from the journey to freedom. I don't know why this is. I have often wondered. Maybe it is because to make things work for them they continually restate their intention, they learn patience and compassion for themselves when things don't work as they think they 'should' and – maybe most important of all – they just keep on truckin'. Gentle persistence brings incredible power for transformation. As you will see for yourself within the first six weeks of your journey work. So persevere.

The Inner Reaches of Sacred Space is not only a useful exercise to use when you want to regenerate your energy, clear a muzzy head, calm unsettled feelings and gain objectivity over something that is troubling you, it is the first step in *cocoon-building*. What I mean is, it can help see you through many deep changes in your life when they arise – from the loss of a lover, physical illness or injury, changes in your work, to the challenge of creating something when you have not the faintest idea where to begin.

LESSONS FROM THE CATERPILLAR

In nature, when the humble caterpillar prepares to turn itself into a butterfly – something we as human beings are, metaphorically at least, called on to do over and over in our lives – it builds a cocoon. A cocoon is a sacred structure within which metamorphosis – transformation of the deepest order – can *safely* occur. It is sacred because, whether it be hard and crisp or soft and flexible, a cocoon simply 'holds the space' while the powers of transformation encoded within every organism work their magic. They dissolve the caterpillar into a soft jelly. Then, knowing exactly what needs to happen from moment to moment, they reshape this jelly into the butterfly. Finally, the newly-born butterfly destroys the cocoon, which has served its purpose for protection in the midst of change, to emerge in all its glory.

We all need cocoons to help us through transformations – whether they be life passages like puberty or menopause, traumas such as the death of a close friend, or a spiritual crisis that leads to rebirth. Many of the practices of shamanism – including Inner Reaches of Outer Space – help provide them.

Now is the time to begin working with cocoon building. There are many ways of doing this. We will be working with others later on in your freedom journey. Meanwhile, Quantum Break 2 builds the foundation of Cocoon Spinning which empowers more graceful transformation. Simple though it is, once you learn it, the healing and supportive

Ask now the beasts and they shall teach thee; and the fowls of the air, and they shall teach thee; or speak to the earth, and it shall teach thee; and the fishes of the sea shall declare unto thee.
Job 12:7-8

Today I do affirm that I am Divinely guided ... There is That within which knows what to do and how to do it, and It compels me to act on what It knows.
Ernest Holmes

energy it offers whenever you need it is phenomenal. It helps clear dead wood. It brings renewing energy. It cossets you in an environment of wholeness and safety. One of my students described this rather well. 'I have always wanted to be surrounded by the wings of a 30-foot angel,' she said. 'To have enough space that I could move about, dance my dance and do my things, yet know that the safety of his wings was always there around me, to bless me, renew me and make me conscious that, even when things get hard for me, I am loved.' Such is the experience of cocoon making once you get the hang of it.

Quantum Break 2

COCOON SPINNING

- ◆ Enter your Inner Reaches of Sacred Space.
- ◆ Activate your senses as in Quantum Break 1 until you feel yourself to be fully present in your special place in nature.
- ◆ Call to the spirits of the trees and grass, water and air, rocks and earth around you asking them to be present.
- ◆ Call to any other helping spirits – animals, people, teachers, angels – whom you have met in your special place before or who show up now.
- ◆ Ask all of these spirits to weave for you a cocoon of safety and support within which the changes your soul is bringing to your life – no matter how difficult these changes may seem in ordinary reality – can take place gracefully with no *unnecessary* stress.
- ◆ Feel what happens when you do this. How does your body feel? Enjoy the blessings and the love of these spirits whose greatest wish right now is to give you the support that you need.
- ◆ Sit in their presence and enjoy the feelings for a few minutes.
- ◆ Now thank each one for its gift.
- ◆ In your own time gently bring your consciousness back to ordinary reality and open your eyes.

Bridge Building

Now record what you have brought back from your cocoon exercise in your notebook, either in words that you just let flow onto the page, or drawings, or any other way you choose. You may find you have been given a sacred symbol that you will want to draw, or a simple poem to record, or a sound. These things are great gifts. Record them and keep interacting with them. They will continue to bring you the particular quality of supportive energy they carry as long as you need it and as long as you keep 'playing' with it by allowing your consciousness to interact with whatever form you have chosen for recording your experience. Eventually the energy will have become part of you. At this point simply give thanks to it and file it away with your other records of Bridge building. You never know, it might be appropriate in the future to reconnect with it.

THE NATURAL WORLD

Throughout the thirteen quantum leaps you will also be reconnecting with the natural world around you. Our bonds with forests and plants, water, light and earth are so much a part of our being that it is very hard for us to be separated from them and still thrive. When we are not aware of our connections with nature it can seem like we are being tossed out naked onto the top of a lonely mountain while the hurricane of life swirls round us. As you move deeper and deeper into communion and friendship with nature, you come to perceive that even a hurricane is nothing but life power. Align yourself with it and far from being a force used against you, its energy can become an ally for you to use for whatever creative purpose you want.

As human beings we are inextricably enmeshed in nature. It is the matrix out of which we were born, the medium in which we live the whole of our lives and the resting place to which we return at death. In a very real sense we are nature – one of the infinite strands of her beauty that, woven together, create the tapestry of the world. Yet almost everything in modern life would have us forget this fact. The more successfully we forget it, the more alienated we feel from ourselves. It is this very experience of alienation that has us reaching into addictions.

From the shamanic perspective, all of the natural world is alive – the rocks and trees, every valley, each flower and raindrop. 'Listen to them,' the shaman tells you, 'they will speak to you.' When you cut flowers, talk to them, tell them how much you love their beauty and where you intend to put them in your house. Ask permission to take some

> Life is not a problem to be solved, but a mystery to be lived.
> *Thomas Merton*

> Your future has nothing to do with getting somewhere you think you need to be. It has to do with the awareness that getting <u>there</u> means <u>being</u> here.
> *Carl A. Hammerschlag*

of them. Ask them what they like. This was the way I discovered that lilies – my favourite flowers – love sugar. When I add sugar to the water I place cut lilies in I am able to prolong their life. Often I can more than double it. Your consciousness matrix gives you a natural ability to communicate with nature around you. Working with the plant world is a wonderful way of awakening it.

SACRED MEDICINE

Earth with her thousand voices praises God.
Samuel Taylor Coleridge

Plants are made of the same photons we are – the same photons the sun is and the same photons that appeared out of the big bang at the beginning of the universe. They give us medicines, the air we breathe, building materials from which we make shelters. They bring us beauty for its own sake, wood for burning and for paper and food for us to eat. Rooted in the earth they grow upwards towards the heavens connecting lower, middle and upper worlds. The spirit of plant growth is a greening spirit. It is the 'greening' which Hildegard of Bingen so loved and expressed in her music, her prayers and her healing practices. When it is personified in myth it comes to us in the form of the Egyptian Isis, the Greek Demeter, the Native American White Buffalo Woman and the Celtic Brigit – all manifestations of the nurturing mother.

Plants not only communicate with each other they also speak with animals and with us. I remember my astonishment when years ago in the African bush I learned that acacia trees, on which giraffes feed, protect themselves from death by giving out signals to the giraffes when they have been fed on enough. They do this by producing a chemical which to the giraffe has an unpleasant smell and a bad taste. The chemical filtering through the acacia's leaves keeps the animals away until the tree has had a chance to regenerate itself. Then, after a week or so, the protective chemical disappears and the giraffes are free to return for another lunch.

Only when you truly inhabit your body can you begin the healing journey.
Gabrielle Roth

The second Quantum Break involves reconnecting with the world of nature directly by conversing with a plant. It can be a tree you see at the end of your street, a bush in your garden or a simple potted herb sitting on the windowsill of your kitchen.

Quantum Break 3

TREE TALK

- Choose a bush or herb, flower, plant or tree that attracts you.
- Whichever plant you choose, sit with it and begin to become aware of the gentle yet powerful energy that growing things carry.
- Take a few deep breaths to relax. Let your eyes go soft and all your consciousness shift gently. Don't force anything. This does not require effort, only a little time and repetition for it to happen by itself. So be patient. There is no right way of doing shamanic work.
- Sit or stand in front of the plant or tree and thank it for bringing its life into your circle of awareness.
- Now in your imagination honour the spirit of the plant and open your awareness to it.
- Close your eyes, imagine that you are this plant or tree. See what your body feels like.
- Now imagine your roots going deep into the ground and your stems and branches reaching to the light. Notice how supported you feel.
- Feel your roots plunging deep into the soil, drawing nutrients and water from it to sustain you.
- Pay attention to your experience of time. Has it changed? If so how? How does it feel to be a 'plant person'? Open your eyes and look at the plant or tree in front of you.
- If the plant in front of you were talking to you, what would it want to tell you?
- If you have chosen a tree, lean against it or sit under it and ask it a question about something you want to know about in your own life. Then wait patiently and see what it tells you. Plant people are slow speaking but enormously profound since their roots sink so deep into earth. In one of your Quantum Breaks, if you are lucky enough to have the time, curl up under the tree and go to sleep. See what dreams come to you.

> One day, it was suddenly revealed to me that everything is pure spirit.
> *Ramakrishna*

> Reverence is a perception of the soul. Only the personality can perceive Life without reverence. Reverence is a natural aspect of authentic empowerment because the soul reveres all of life.
> *Gary Zukav*

The rhythm of my heart
is the birth and death
of all that are alive.
Thich Nhat Hanh

- ✦ When interacting with plants, always ask their permission to pick a leaf or flower before you do and then listen for an answer.
- ✦ If you have chosen a herb or bush or a flowering plant, ask it if you may pick one or two of its leaves or a flower and then, holding them in your hand, touch them, smell them, taste them. If it is an edible plant, put a leaf into your mouth, close your eyes and see what comes to you.
- ✦ Now thank the plant for its time and let your consciousness shift back to ordinary state.

Bridge Building

Let the beauty we
love be what we do
Rumi

Record in your journal what you have experienced. You might like to draw it, or sculpt it using coloured paper or whatever bits and pieces you have at hand. If you choose to do this you might like to hang your drawing on the wall of your room or inside a closet door so that you see it whenever you open the door. Then you can continue to interact with sacred plant energy.

WHAT PLANTS CAN TELL US

It is looking at things
for a long time that ripens
you and gives you a
deeper understanding.
Vincent van Gogh

The first time I worked with an edible plant I chose sage since I like it very much and it grows profusely in the rockeries in front of my house. I asked it if I could pick a couple of its leaves which I then held in my hand. I asked it to reveal to me its nature. I asked it if there was any way in which I could use it to alleviate any of my own symptoms, or those that members of my family sometimes suffered from. If so, I asked it how should I prepare it. The results of my little meeting with sage surprised me.

THE GREAT SAGE

He told me – not out loud but telepathically – that he has the power to clear away whatever is murky or irrelevant or polluted because he is strong and dry and clear. Later on I communed with the spirit of sage (see quantum leap 28 for plant communion). I learned that the great sage spirit resides in a desert. He is huge and dome-shaped and proud by nature. In the sacred silence I connected with him – friend to friend. He told me I could make tea of him or put one of his leaves in my mouth in the morning and that it would remind me to take nothing into my body which is not essential. He told me I needed to learn this quality of essentiality and that interacting with him could teach it to me. 'It will make you as strong as I,' he said. 'I am clarity of purpose, I am your medicine plant. I am indomitable strength because I carry no excess baggage. That is something you need to learn. I can teach you to live a life of essentials,' he told me. Then he invited me to play on his leaves, which I did. He told me that he was 'well pleased' I had come. "I am your reminder of essence and truth. Burn me while you work. I will be with you. You may play on my leaves and branches. Your fatigue (which I had been feeling for some weeks around the time of the journey) will pass as soon as you remove all that is non-essential in your life.' He then proceeded to tell me a couple of dozen things that his leaves could be used for and tell me how to go about using them. His personality was a bit like one of those men who sit across from you at dinner and tell you one thing after another about how clever they are, all the amazing things they have done. I tend to be suspicious of so much self-praise so I really didn't take his words all that seriously.

This happened fairly early on in my shamanic work and I was more than a little stunned by what came of the communion with sage. Nevertheless, I wrote down everything I could remember afterwards in my journal. Then promptly forgot it. Two years later I came across this record by accident in my journey book. Curious about the validity of the information I had recorded, I went to the shelves where I keep my many books on herbs and plant medicine. I opened the three best ones I own. I was stunned to find that 80% of what I had learned during my plant communion corresponded with the indications for the medicinal use of sage. I suddenly knew what all those left-brained chemists must feel like when they are sent into the rainforest by pharmaceutical corporations in search of new plants suitable for making wonder drugs. No wonder native people find the question, 'How do you know what a plant does?' strange – all you have to do is ask it. I laughed at myself and my intellectual schooling that had taught me to trust only what came from 'experts' and books. This proud, self-centred great sage spirit had spoken the truth to me.

Enthusiasm literally means 'being filled with spirit.'
Stephen Larsen

Just remain in the centre, watching. And then forget that you are there.
Lao Tzu

I try to apply colours like words that shape poems. Like notes that shape music.
Jean Miro

Some people will never learn anything … because they understand everything too soon.
Alexander Pope

◆

FREE BREAKS

You are free to choose for yourself what you would like to do over the next two days. Perhaps you would like to practise connecting on a sacred level with plants, or deepen your experience of the Inner Reaches of Sacred Space. Taking a little time to get the hang of Cocoon Spinning is always useful – you never know when you might need it.

◆

SEARCH FOR THE SACRED
Week One Project

Your project this week is a simple one. Yet it can serve as the beginning of a whole new way of relating to the world around you. The secrets of its gifts will reveal themselves as we move further into your journey to freedom. For the moment please just take this on trust and do it without thinking too much about what you are doing. Here it is:

As you go through week one of your journey to freedom, keep your eyes open for things around you that you particularly like. You may see a brightly coloured ribbon that attracts you. There may be a small box sitting on your desk that you have a particular affection for. You may be walking along the street and notice a feather on the pavement in front of you that you find yourself wanting to pick up. Without analyzing why, whenever you have any experience of being drawn to something, pick it up (not in other people's houses). Spend a moment just being with it. Move it around in your hand. Get to know it. If, after doing this, you still feel good about it, then keep it. During the week you will be collecting one or two – maybe several – things which hold beauty or fun or a sense of wonder in them for you. Have fun making your choices. You may find there is a special post card with a photograph of an animal on it or a cartoon that makes you laugh. Whatever you are drawn to, explore what it is like to relate to it and keep those things you are instinctively drawn to. Put them in a safe place. In your next quantum leap you will be coming back to them.

So that is it. This is all there is to taking your first quantum leap. See if you can approach each of your Quantum Breaks in the spirit of play and adventure. Have fun with it. Children are so naturally good at this kind of thing for, provided they are young enough and provided they have not been too damaged by their early upbringing, their consciousness matrix remains alive and well and eager for adventure. It takes the rest of us a little time to recover their sense of joy and curiosity and to lay aside our need to 'do it right', but don't worry, that will come. Clear intention, compassion and persistence plus a little time are all you need to make it happen for you.

Normally we do not as much look at things as overlook them.
Alan Watts

CHECKLIST

Day One

+ Read through the chapter at least as far as Quantum Break 1.
+ Do Quantum Break 1 Inner Reaches of Sacred Space.
+ Bridge build.
+ Read the instructions for your project, Search for the Sacred on the opposite page and begin your week's work with it.

Nothing in all creation is so like God as stillness.
Meister Eckhart

Day Two

+ Read more of the chapter if you have time and have not already done so.
+ Repeat Inner Reaches of Sacred Space.
+ Bridge build. Notice and record how your experience of it may have changed since yesterday as well as any other Bridge building you will be doing.

Belief consists in accepting the affirmations of the soul; unbelief in denying them.
Ralph Waldo Emerson

Day Three

- ✦ Read more of the chapter if you have time and have not already done so.
- ✦ Do Quantum Break 2 Cocoon Spinning.
- ✦ Bridge build.
- ✦ Don't forget that all the way through the week you will be carrying out your project.

Day Four

- ✦ Repeat Cocoon Spinning.
- ✦ Bridge build.

Day Five

- ✦ Do Quantum Break 3 Tree Talk.
- ✦ Bridge build.
- ✦ How are you getting on with your sacred project?

Day Six

- ✦ Do a Free Break exercise.
- ✦ Bridge build.

Day Seven

- ✦ Do another Free Break exercise.
- ✦ Bridge build.
- ✦ Gather together what you have collected for the week in preparation for quantum leap 2.
- ✦ Spend 20 minutes doing your Travelogue.

Travelogue

Congratulations. You have got through the first week of journey to freedom. Now it is time to record your experience. This you will do in your Travelogue. Make a special place for it at the back of your journal. Or if you prefer, buy a big scrap book – the kind kids use to paste pictures in. You can use it not only to record your impressions and your progress in words and drawings, but also to stick into it pictures, momentos, and bits and pieces which have caught your eye during each particular week. These can be things which amuse you or make you feel good or delight you – a leaf maybe from the plant you have spoken with, a picture you came across in a magazine that reminds you of your sacred space, or some silk threads in wonderful colours which remind you of the Cocoon Spinning exercise and how safe it can make you feel. These objects may well be things you have chosen as part of your Week One Project in the first week.

Your Travelogue will become a record of your journey to freedom put together in any way you choose – writing your impressions along the way if you like to use words or using a combination of many ways of record keeping.

How was this week for you? What did you like and not like? What discoveries did you make about yourself? About ordinary reality? About the quantum realms?

You will do your Travelogue each week on day seven. So if you choose to begin your journey to freedom on a Saturday then the Travelogue for each week will be written on a Friday. If you choose to treat Sunday as day one of each quantum leap week then you will be recording these things on Saturday.

Your Travelogue is important. When I am teaching, I always get my students to report back their reactions – whatever they may be: excitement, discouragement, fun, anger and frustration, wonder. It makes no difference. The important thing is just to honour your own experience and voice it. Travelogue is the way you will do this. 'Inner Reaches was great. It mopped up that big ball of stress I came home with on Tuesday.' 'I just can't get the hang of Cocoon Spinning.' Remember that the journey you are taking is yours and yours alone. What you think and feel about it all from week to week matters. Write it down.

We are shaped and fashioned by what we love ...
Goethe

Not I, nor anyone else can travel that road for you.

You must travel it by yourself. It is not far; it is within reach.

Perhaps you have been on it since you were born, and did not know.

Perhaps it is everywhere – on water and on land.
Walt Whitman

quantum leap 2

Over the Threshold

Come explore the diamond universe with me — more wonderful than words can describe. Find your roots in a green and leafy valley and learn to bask in safety. Run across golden savannahs and reclaim the powers of instinct, wildness and creativity. Journey to gather healing for yourself, for others, for the Earth herself. Come to gaze far into the future or the past. Discover the nature of your own essence. The journey is free, the rewards endless. Come travel with me.

I am the Journeymaster

This week your journeys begin. You will be exploring quantum realms which you may only have dipped your toe into previously. The spiritual energy which you will be working with is your power source for freedom. The techniques you will be learning are your tools for accessing it. Once you practise a bit you are likely to find it as easy as child's play. And just as much fun.

A shaman is a walker between the worlds. With a clear sense of purpose, he or she activates the consciousness matrix then journeys to explore the heights, breadths and depths of the unseen universe and returns with its gifts. The most powerful of all shamanic techniques for expanding freedom is the shamanic journey. A shamanic journey is a journey of the soul. What makes journeying so different from every other encounter with the numinous realms is that the shamanic traveller enters these realms *deliberately* and with *clear intention*. Unlike the mystic or the channel who opens himself to non-ordinary reality and hopes for the best, the shaman maintains skilful control – going and coming between the realms in an orderly and skilful way. He knows exactly where he is leaving from in ordinary reality, where he is going to and for what purpose. He also knows how and when to return to the place from which he started.

CLEAR INTENTION

This is one of the most valuable and reassuring aspects of shamanic work. I have personally never bought into the notions that:

✦ We should at all times be *vulnerable* in order to be fulfilled spiritual beings.
✦ That in some way we need to 'let it all hang out' in order to break out of the psychological bonds that imprison us.

Real freedom comes from a combination of conscious control and intention. You move towards it progressively. It demands skill, clarity of purpose and a sense of being grounded in everyday reality, yet never restricted by it. Such is the promise of learning the skills of journeying and practising them daily. This is what your second quantum leap is all about.

Some people feel uneasy about learning to journey because they associate the mythological, imaginal realms of non-ordinary reality with mental illness. The imagery of mythology derives from the shaman's experience in non-ordinary reality. So does the imagery of the schizophrenic. But that is where the similarity ends. In mental illness the mythic world has erupted suddenly, precipitating spiritual emergency. The schizophrenic has broken off from the structure of his society and dissociated himself completely from consensus reality. He is cut off from his starting point and from the social order. He has no control over where his consciousness goes and no idea how to get

There are time-tested techniques whereby you can work on a problem – as you should – in ordinary reality, and then make a journey to your teacher in non-ordinary reality to get the answer to your question. In this way you will often get tremendous detail, so that you come back with knowledge for the week, the month, the year ... whatever you are seeking – perhaps even for a lifetime. There is no need to wait for accidental revelations.
Michael Harner

back. In short he is not capable of normal functioning. He can only live out of a chaotic imaginal world which overwhelms him. The shaman is very different. The shaman has not rejected the social order and its forms. He journeys into quantum realms to gather wisdom, vision and healing energy as well as the creative power that resides there, not for escape but in order to bring back these gifts and *enrich* the culture in which he lives. Both the shaman and the psychotic dive into the waters of expanded consciousness. But while the psychotic *drowns* in them, the shaman, skilled in the art of journeying and working with the compassionate energies he finds there, *swims* in ecstasy and then returns to shore refreshed, renewed and rewarded.

ALL YOU NEED

There are two secret ingredients that make every kind of shamanic technique work superbly. They are so simple that although I mention them a hundred times in every workshop I teach seldom do my students take me seriously. (That is until they find out for themselves.) Let me give you the secret right now. All you need is:

INTENTION and COMPASSION.

That is virtually all there is to journeying, divination, healing, and tapping into creativity. If you only remember one thing let it be this; for it will not only make your journeys rich and fulfilling. It works equally well to enrich your life as a whole. The formula looks like this:

INTENTION + COMPASSION = FREEDOM

You could also make other equally valid equations such as these:

INTENTION + COMPASSION = HEALING
INTENTION + COMPASSION = VISION
INTENTION + COMPASSION = ECSTASY
INTENTION + COMPASSION = CREATIVITY
INTENTION + COMPASSION = BLESSINGS

Shamanism is people directly helping others. It is a kind of spiritual activism in which one works with the powers that connect human beings to the incredible power of the universe – a work that involves journeying and shifting back and forth between realities.
Michael Harner

You see, shamanism is colourful, it is earthy, it is sacred, it is fun. That is why it has been called a form of ecstasy. It is the place where the imminent and the transcendent meet.
Leslie Gray

Any way you measure it, intention and compassion adds up to something pretty wonderful.

JOURNEY WITH YOUR HEART

Always journey with your heart open – full of compassion not only for the spirit energies and all beings in ordinary reality but also for yourself. For most people compassion for themselves is the biggest challenge. Leave your starting place with a clear intention about where you are going to go and what you are going to do. Then a little practice is all you need to make consciousness bridging a joyous and rewarding art.

A journey is just that – it is a passage from the three-dimensional space-and-time bound reality, via some kind of 'bridge' that activates your consciousness matrix and takes you into the imaginal realms of expanded awareness. It is a little like shifting gear. You move out of your fragmented daytime world of things, ideas and thought patterns, into the unified and creative quantum realms. Once there, the boundaries of what you know as reality expand exponentially. In time, through journeying, they may even dissolve away for a while so you experience yourself as an organic part of all creation. Once you learn to journey to quantum realms and can move about in them with ease, you gain easy access to healing, wisdom and spiritual guidance of the highest order. Then spirituality becomes an actual experience from within – not an intellectual idea or set of rules imposed upon you from outside.

As you journey again and again you will get to know the ins and outs of moving from one zone to another in non-ordinary reality. In time you will be able to make your own maps of these realms. Journeying in quantum realms is very much like making a journey over land in ordinary reality or through the streets of a city. The more times you traverse the same route the more familiar you are with the way and the easier it becomes. Once you get to know the 'lay of the land' what is likely to amaze you – it never ceases to surprise the people I teach – is how closely the maps you draw of non-ordinary reality parallel maps drawn by fellow journeyers. This is one of the advantages of learning to journey in a group. It can be reassuring when others perceive what you do. For non-ordinary reality is just as real as ordinary reality – but in a different way.

COSMOLOGY OF CONSCIOUSNESS

Don't worry if you believe nothing of what I've said so far. That's normal. In fact I think that's important. Each of us begins to journey full of scepticism. This is exactly how it should be. You only find out what you *know* when you *experience* it. The wonderful thing about working with shamanic techniques is that gradually, week after week, month after month, you learn *to trust* your own experience so there is much less need to look outside yourself for truth and power. Both are to be found in infinite abundance within. That, after all, is where real *knowing* comes from: experience.

It is helpful when you begin to journey to know something about the general cosmology of non-ordinary reality as reported by shamans and recorded in world mythologies – all of which are based on their explorations. This helps you get a sketchy lay of the land and makes it easier to get started developing your journeying skills. It is a cosmology which, with minor exceptions, is pretty universal in the way it describes the imaginal realms, even though most of the various cultures it comes from have had no physical connections with each other. Mircea Eliade spent much of his life researching the cosmologies of shamanic cultures. Almost all of them describe the universe as being divided into three cosmic zones which are connected via a central axis known as the world pillar or *axis mundi*. You will be working with this central axis in a later quantum leap. For the moment what is important are these three cosmic regions – sky realms, earth realms, and lower realms. In shamanic language these are called the upperworld, middleworld and lowerworld. The shaman travels back and forth between these zones by passing through openings in the imaginal world that give entrance to quantum reality at large – or what the Celts call the Otherworld. Make use of this traditional cosmology for now. Later on you will come to know the nature of these realms through your own experience.

PLUMB THE DEPTHS

You access the lowerworld by walking, tumbling or sailing downwards through the earth until you cross the threshold between ordinary reality and non-ordinary reality and enter the imaginal world. From a psychological point of view lowerworld journeys take you beneath the lumen of your conscious mind. They allow you to plumb the depths of dreams and power, memories and instinct. Psychologically, lowerworld journeys are

From your centre in Eternal Being, energy intent swirls outward to become beings, individualized forms of your expression: angels, pattern beings, generations of light.
Ken Carey

… many different sorts of people can be visionaries – artists, mystics, psychologists, hospital victims, founders of religion. These are the people who in various ways and often in quite different circumstances have achieved a major experiential breakthrough: a radical shift in consciousness which has provided access to more profound domains of inner spiritual knowledge. Sometimes this visionary perception has revealed states of ecstasy and transcendence, sometimes it has summoned the devils and demons from the darker recesses of the mind. But in all instances the borders of normal consciousness have been crossed and in many instances the boundaries between subject and object have dissolved altogether.
Nevill Drury

often self-confrontational passages epitomized in the archetypal hero's journey which Joseph Campbell has written of so elegantly. Each of us is asked to make a hero's journey several times in our lives. We leave the structures of what we know to be true, shift our centre of gravity and move into numinous realms. Once there we encounter helping spirits, wrestle with our challenges, and transform what appear to be our enemies into allies. Emotionally, on lowerworld journeys, we descend into the deepest regions of the psyche and eventually enter the inner sanctum of the soul where we are asked to confront our own individual greatest challenge of all and then transmute it into power and creativity. Such an experience in turn transforms our life by enlarging the very frame of reference by which we measure ourselves. It also gives us access to the archetypal treasures – healing and creative powers. They in turn become our offerings to our family community when, at the end of each hero's journey, we return with them to our ordinary everyday life.

In movies, fairy tales and sagas you will find hundreds of lowerworld hero's journeys: Alice tumbles down the rabbit hole to experience a complete reversal of all she knows to be true and then returns an older and wiser young lady. Demeter the great goddess of nourishment and blessings loses her beautiful daughter Persephone who has been abducted into the Greek underworld by Hades, lord of death. Persephone later returns having matured from an adolescent to a woman in full flower. Psychologically underworld journeys are transformative journeys out of which you become more authentically on the outside what you are on the inside. By making them you gain access to creative energies that have until then been sequestered away by fears or social conditioning.

RECOVERING INSTINCT

From a shamanic point of view, lowerworld journeys lead you into the depths of non-ordinary reality which you access by journeying through a cave maybe, or a tunnel, a crack in the earth, or a well. They take you beneath the surface of the earth and beyond into the realm of earth-related compassionate spirit energies. The lowerworld is the home territory of *power animals*. These are the most important spirits shamans work with in traditional cultures. (We will be doing a lot of work and play with power animals during quantum leap 3.) The lowerworld is a place you might choose to go to learn about how to work with plant energies or elementals. It is a realm you might visit for healing, advice about practical things in life, or information about the weather. Lowerworld journeys can also take you deep into your body for you to discover the slumbering soul energies waiting to be set free, or to re-order life energies which have temporarily lost their harmony.

By contrast, the upperworld is the realm of magical flights. Journeying there – which you do by leaping, flying, or floating upwards through openings in the sky into the mythic realms – has something in common with the experience of flying in your dreams. It can elevate your spirits. The quality of an upperworld journey is akin to the phenomenon of 'remote viewing' used for crime detection where a clairvoyant is asked to send his awareness beyond space and time to discover and describe the place where a crime was committed or to discover the meaning of a clue. It is also akin to out-of-body experiences which have been so widely investigated in the last two decades.

We may well be entering a new phase in history which will see the gradual diminution of formal religious structures and their replacement not by empty nihilism or reductionist materialism but by frameworks of belief based on experiential consciousness research.
Nevill Drury

EXHILARATION AND CLARITY

From a psychological point of view, the upperworld is a place of spiritual clarity and exhilaration. It is a realm from which the inspiration for a work of art might come. In the fourth century, Christian theologian Gregory of Nyssa described the nature of an upperworld journey when he wrote, 'The human soul has but one vehicle by which to journey heavenward, that is to make itself into the flying dove.' More than 1,500 years later Native American prophet Black Elk spoke of a similar experience, '... birds leave the earth with their wings, and we humans may also leave this world, not with wings but in the spirit.' To the shaman the upperworld is the zone of gods and goddesses, angels and archetypes. It is the place of divine inspiration and cosmic wisdom to which one may choose to journey for spiritual instruction. It is a finer, somehow more etheric zone than the lowerworld. And, because of this, clearly focusing your intention while you are travelling in the upperworld becomes especially important.

The shaman travels lightly. His (her) most powerful tool is the condition of willingness practised with discernment.
Karen Berggren

These are only very sketchy descriptions of what you will encounter as you journey into these realms. What is important to remember is that upper and lowerworld are elaborately interlinked as are the energies or spirits that inhabit them. So you can be accompanied on a journey to the upperworld by a power animal, for instance. Or you might make a lowerworld journey only to be met at the side of a lake by a dancing angel waiting to show you something or take you somewhere. In shamanic work there are never any hard and fast rules. You discover for yourself what is there in quantum realms by exploration. In the process of journeying over and over again gradually you learn to

The plunge within is the way of the shaman.
Stephen Larsen

trust what you find there and you come to *know* it. Knowledge, gleaned from shamanic work, is never theoretical. It is the knowing that comes from experiencing – the only kind that is of real value.

MEET THE MIDDLEWORLD

The *middleworld* is ordinary reality – the place in which we live on the earth – the planet itself and all the stars above and beyond us as well as the earth beneath our feet. But there is also a non-ordinary aspect to the middleworld. The traditional tribal shaman journeyed to this non-ordinary zone of the middleworld whenever his tribe needed to find a herd of animals for the hunt or to search out a child who had wandered too far from the village and got lost. Today's shaman might do a middleworld journey if asked for help from the family of someone in a coma. In this case he would go to the patient in non-ordinary reality to find out from his soul whether he is trying to return to life and take up his place in the world again or to let go of his body and be released from the world. You will be exploring the wonders of middleworld journeys in a later quantum leap. They are journeys to be taken only after you have become proficient in journeying in the upper and lowerworlds and after you have made strong connections with your power animal and other helping spirits.

We must assume our existence as broadly as we in any way can; Everything, even the unheard of, must be possible in it. This is at bottom the only courage that is demanded of us: To have courage for the most strange, the most inexplicable.
Rainer Maria Rilke

SECURE IN THE KNOWLEDGE

One of the most common questions I am asked by people learning to journey is, 'Is it safe?' Quite simply, the answer is 'Yes it is.' You need only learn the skills and follow the guidelines of core shamanism. When I first started to do shamanic work this was a question I myself asked Michael Harner – the most knowledgeable man in the world about *core shamanism* (in fact it is he who coined the phrase). His answer was simple. 'While you are journeying in either the upper or lowerworld you are completely safe. When working in non-ordinary reality in the middleworld you must always make sure you are filled with power – in other words in close connection with your power animal. It is only in the middleworld that you might come across troubled spirits like ghosts (who are themselves suffering and confused) who may try to be disruptive.' As long as you are filled with power from your power animal you have nothing to worry about.

By now I have made thousands of journeys to the upper and lowerworlds. I have never encountered any difficulties. This does not mean that occasionally while journeying in the upperworld or the lowerworld you won't encounter surprising spirits or undergo amazing – sometimes unsettling – experiences. But the experiences invariably carry with them deep healing and gifts of grace. For instance, I once did a journey to the upperworld to find myself quite literally blown apart. It was more than a little surprising I can tell you. Yet I had journeyed a lot and I knew I was safe there. So, more curious than worried, I simply stayed present and watched what was to unfold with an open heart. It was completely amazing. After having been completely wiped out – blown into a million fragments of light – I found myself spontaneously at one with the cosmos in all its beauty. It was as though I had somehow become it, and it me. I then experienced the wondrous cycles of death and rebirth in nature. When I returned from the journey to my starting place in ordinary reality, I felt as though I had been blessed with a kind of renewal and given a new insight into our interconnectedness with all things. While on this journey I was also given a simple song by the spirits which I brought back and wrote down.

Ecstasy and sacrifice are shamanic experiences needed in the midst of the modern global breakdown of traditions … so that regenerative powers within us can be summoned.
Rowena Pattee

I am the stardust
I am the sea
I am the hedgehog
I am the tree

I am the storm and the wind and the soil
I am the leaves and the fleas and the toil

I am the fire
I am the one
I am the moose and the goose and the sun

*Our task is to cross
the thresholds
Into unknown lands
Where our teachers
May provoke our initiation
And our demons summon
our illumination.
May the Great Spirit smile
within us
Making our spirits strong
And our souls light.*

Such a song is typical of power songs that you may find are given to you from time to time as you do your own journeying. Listen for them. They are usually as simple and childlike as this one. They are a gift from the quantum realms which you can use over and over again to shift your consciousness and call your spirit helpers. Some have words, some only have sounds. When such a song comes to you, give thanks. It is a great blessing. (More about power songs in Quantum Break 26, page 194.)

*And what we learn, may
we carry it back
Whole or in part
And share it with our village.*
Nadu

STAGE FRIGHT

I think it is natural to be slightly worried about learning a new set of skills whether they be for white water rafting, giving lectures, or anything else. When the skills you are taking on are those that give you access to vast realms of consciousness into which until now you may have only inadvertently dipped your toe, it is little wonder if you are a little hesitant. My answer to the people whom I teach in workshops is simple: we are going to be working with methods that have been time tested over thousands and thousands of years. To make the best use of them you will be following specific protocols and structures, making good strong connections with your helping spirits, your tutelary spirits, and your power animals. You will be getting the skills you need under your belt step by step. Before long they become second nature. That is what the first twelve quantum leaps are all about. By the time you come to the thirteenth leap you will not only have become familiar with the terrain, you will feel completely at home in quantum realms and be able to move easily from one level to another. You will also know how to make good use of the two secrets on which all shamanic work depends: compassion and intention.

The real teachers of shamanism are the spirits themselves. The tools and techniques you are learning here are only the ladder by which you climb the steps of consciousness to make good connections with them. Once you have gained the skills and come to know your spirits, then you can throw the ladder away. Such is the thirteenth quantum leap – the final leap to freedom.

Rhythm touches deep chords of resonance in our ancestral memories; whenever we connect with other human beings through rhythmic music, dance, or drumming, the memory of humankind as one family arises.
Reinhard Flatischler

TECHNOLOGY OF ENTRAINMENT

Rhythm is the language of creation.
Charles Johnston

At first glance it may seem that the Japanese monk sitting in meditation practising zazen is doing something quite different than the Native American drumming or the teenager at a rave. In truth all three of these people are instigating the psychophysical process for activating the consciousness matrix known as *entrainment*. Entrainment, which is a word derived quite literally from the idea of getting on a train and travelling, induces altered states. It provides the passage from one realm to another. There are many tools that can be used to carry you from here to quantum consciousness: meditation, music, drumming and dancing, for instance, strobe lights, special breathing exercises, singing, rattling, whirling as the dervishes do, psychoactive plants, sensory isolation, running – even sleep deprivation. Even silence can do it. In time, simply moving into stillness and directing your attention towards the journey will make it happen. This is the way the Polynesian *kalakupua* – master shamans – do it.

Most of the methods for entrainment depend on focusing your attention on a regularly repeating pattern of stimuli such as a mantra repeated over and over or drumming or rubbing your hands together in a steady monotonous rhythm. Scientists investigating the neurobiology of entrainment rituals suggest that the repetitive 'driving' stimuli of, say, a drum may create sensory overload. This blocks, they believe, the sequential processing functions of our left brain (the part of the brain largely responsible for rational, linear thought processes) enabling activity in this part of the brain to remain constant. In effect it helps us stop the world for a time. This is what Buddhists call stilling the mind – silencing the constant chatter that goes on in our head all the time and switching off external impressions that continually bombard our senses. Once your attention gets absorbed in a monotonous drumming sound or other entrainment tool, this brings about physiological changes leading to heightened concentration. With practice it can bring easy access not only to deep states of relaxation in which healing energies act spontaneously but also to journeying.

Whatever entrainment tool you use, what you are doing is setting up a Pavlov's dog situation. Ringing a bell at the same time as offering the dog food created a conditioned response in the dog. It smelled the food, heard the bell and salivated. In time Pavlov found the dog would salivate when the bell rang, even when there was no food offered. So it is with entrainment tools. Listening to the beat of a drum over and over in a relaxed state with the intention of shifting consciousness from ordinary reality to nonordinary reality soon makes the experience of altering consciousness almost instantaneous. In time just hearing the sound of the same drumbeat quickly focuses your mind and body on the task at hand and enables you to shift consciousness instantaneously. A drumbeat of 205–220 beats a minute is particularly useful as a tool for entrainment. It seems to activate the four to seven cycles per second brain waves measured by electroencephalograph equipment. Known as the theta state, these frequencies are associated with hypnosis and very deep states of meditation, creative thought, trance and lucid dreaming.

The human mind, heart, and spirit are lying dormant, waiting for the ancient sound of the drum and for certain basic types of training in order to come alive.
Michael Harner

The tree birthed the drum so that we and spirit could speak with common tongue.
E. Bonnie Devlin

THE SHAMANIC TRANCE

The shamanic 'trance' is a very special state in which your body is relaxed. Perhaps, 10–20% of your awareness remains with the body and the rest is involved in the journeying process. A shamanic trance bears little resemblance to what most people think of as trance – being knocked out and unaware of what is going on or taken over by something outside yourself. It is a relaxed yet controlled state in which you are to one degree or another aware of both ordinary and non-ordinary reality. It is rather like standing comfortably with a foot in both worlds. Harner believes that the monotonous drumbeat used to induce the shamanic state also simulates the beat of the human heart – the most primal and reassuring of all sounds to a human being. So effective a tool is drumming that, in one project designed to explore the effects of it, researchers discovered that in ten minutes a shaman listening to it can achieve a scientifically measurable state only duplicated by Japanese Zen masters after six hours of meditation.

The drumming on a tape or a CD made specifically for journeying will be a steady beat. You will find on your tape journey sessions lasting 15, 20, or 30 minutes so you can choose the length of journey you want to do. (I generally suggest a journey of 20 minutes for the first few times. Then it is up to you.) Some people journey much faster than others. This is no indication of competence – just of style. Generally, as you continue to journey to the lowerworld you will find it takes you less time to get there and get back so your journeys can become shorter. At the end of the journey session – which is marked by a steady monotonous drumming – you will hear the *call back*. This consists of four bursts of drumming faster than the beat you have been journeying to. Usually each burst has seven beats to it and the four bursts will be interspersed with a short pause. Then will come a faster steady beat that will last between 30 seconds and a minute. You will use this beat to retrace your steps. (On any journey when the call-back beat comes, you need to stop what you are doing immediately, thank any spirits you have been working with, tell them they can go now, turn around and immediately leave the imaginal realms, go back through the tunnel and come out in the same place you began your journey – the place you have chosen from your memory in ordinary reality.) Finally, you will hear another four bursts. This tells you that you should be back now where you started from. You can gently open your eyes and come back into the room.

GO FOR DRUMMING

I favour a drumbeat as a means of entrainment for many reasons. First because it is so comforting, probably because it mimics the earliest sound any of us ever hear – that of our mother's heartbeat in the womb. Second, it is the most widely used tool for entrainment among cultures with a shamanic tradition. Thirdly, the drumbeat soon becomes like a horse or vehicle you can ride into and throughout the journey. Listening to it, you quickly come to feel totally supported, secure and focused while you journey. Finally, of all of the methods that I have tried, I find the drumbeat the simplest to use when you are beginning.

Since it is unlikely that you will have your own private drummer to drum for you as you journey, you have three alternatives:

- ◆ You can make a tape of steady monotonous drumming for yourself – with call back as described above which you play on a walkman or other tape player.
- ◆ You can use a rattle instead of a drum which you shake yourself as you are journeying.
- ◆ You can buy a tape designed for shamanic work and use that.

I rose above the limits of the world ... my feet were walking on the far side of heaven.
A Chuckchee Shaman

SECOND NATURE

There are a number of tapes of shamanic drumming which you can buy (see Resources page 348) and listen to on a walkman so that there is no worry about disturbing anyone with the sound while you are journeying. Using a walkman has two other advantages. First the containment of the sound through earphones acts as a reinforcement to switching realities and powerfully focuses your consciousness on journeying since it provides an inner world within which you are working. Secondly, when you are listening to a drumming tape you also have the option of quietly recording your journey onto one of those little dictation tape machines without having your voice drowned out by the drumbeat. (Walkmans these days can be bought very cheaply, too.)

So, while it may seem a nuisance at the beginning to have to rely on the paraphernalia of earphones and tapes, by the end of the thirteen-week programme you will be glad you have. They will have served you well at least until the whole experience of journeying becomes second nature. By that time you probably will have become so at

A shaman is a man or woman who enters into an altered state of consciousness – at will – to contact and utilize an ordinarily hidden reality in order to acquire knowledge, power, and to help other persons.
Michael Harner

ease with the inner landscape and be so familiar with the process of getting there that you will be able to use other methods as well. I myself often journey simply by moving into what I call the *sacred silence*. I do this when I am in public and want to connect with the energies of the land or place I am visiting. It goes unnoticed by anyone who happens to be nearby. However, I still make most of my journeys to a drumbeat. Why? I guess because I have grown to love the sound and because, whenever I am tired, the drum beat makes it far easier for me to journey effectively by providing me with a clear structure to keep my heart and mind focused on my all-important intention.

Rattling with the same 205–220 beats per minute rhythm is another easy way to journey. The advantage of a rattle is that you can easily pick up a small rattle at a music shop (some are no larger than the size of an egg) or even make one with a small yoghurt carton filled with rice or corn kernels. You can also buy tapes with rattling on them. I love journeying to the sound of a rattle sometimes. It is gentler than a drum. I find I can cover my eyes and rattle throughout the whole journey without this interfering with the journey itself whereas drumming for yourself is highly demanding physically. (It also creates a lot of noise and can make enemies of your neighbours.)

Once you have got your entrainment tool sorted out it is time to decide where you are going to journey from.

During the second week of journey work – all the work you will be doing in the next thirteen weeks of your journey to freedom – you will be making your first journeys. Journey protocols have been set out in Ticket to Ride. You can use them for each of your journeys, wherever you are journeying to. It is worth familiarizing yourself with them right from the start.

Here are your guidelines. You need to be familiar with them before embarking on any journey work. Get to know them well and they will be valuable friends. They are also here for you to refer back to if during future quantum leaps you need to refresh your memory about the journey process.

Rhythmic stimulation, not only from sound but from other factors, influences consciousness.
Holger Kalweit

Living nature is not a mechanism but a poem.
Thomas Huxley

Ticket to Ride – Journey Protocols

BEFORE THE DRUMMING BEGINS

STATE YOUR INTENTION

Actually write it down so you are really clear about it. Remember the secret to doing powerful shamanic work has two parts to it: **intention** and **compassion**. Together they make everything work. Without both, journeying can be a bit like getting into a rudder-less boat on a big lake – turning the engine on and just letting it career around without control. You don't want to end up hitting a bank. So, as you prepare to journey keep your heart open as much as you can with a feeling of friendship for all things and keep repeating your intention. Be sure too that your intention has meaning for you. For the world of expanded consciousness responds far better to what comes from our heart than from our head.

CHOOSE YOUR STARTING POINT

Decide what place you are going to journey from to the lowerworld. Go to this place, in your mind, and activate your senses. What do you see, hear, touch, taste, smell? You will leave and return from here. Take a moment to look around you and engage your senses so you are really present before you begin your journey.

LET GO

Lie down or sit down if your prefer; but lying is usually easier – especially in the beginning. Take a few gentle but deep breaths, stating your intention a few more times. Let go if you can of thoughts about what you have to do later or what you did yesterday and be present as much as you can in the moment.

Until one is committed there is hesitancy, the chance to draw back, always ineffectiveness, concerning all acts of initiation (and creation) ... the moment one definitely commits, the Providence comes too. All sorts of things occur to help one that would never otherwise have occurred ... Whatever you can do or dream you can begin it. Boldness has genius, power and magic in it. Begin now.
Goethe

BE HERE NOW

Now move deeply into your body. Feel the floor beneath it. Listen to the sound of your breath and feel the air going in and out of your body. Be aware of any tensions anywhere. In fact let them get stronger, then, taking another deep breath, let go of them and sink deeper into the surface on which you are lying. Bring all of your senses into play. What do you touch, smell, taste, see, hear? And what about your inner sensing?

GET EXCITED

This is the real teaching of all the greatest teachers – not to disengage yourself from natural law, but, at the same time, not to become bound to the world of sensory fact.
Joseph Campbell

Remember when you were a child at Christmas and you couldn't wait to find out what was inside all those bright, ribboned packages sitting beneath the tree? See if you can let that kind of anticipation and curiosity rise up in you now. Journeying is like adventuring. You never know what you are going to meet, learn, experience. When we grow up we often become jaded and lose our sense of fascination and curiosity. See if you can let yours arise.

AS THE BEAT BEGINS

SEND OUT A HERALD

Go back once again to your intention. This time send it out from your heart. It will go before you as a herald to announce to the world of non-ordinary reality that you are coming and what you are coming for. You need to do this only *once* the way a trumpet sounds to announce an event. Let your heart sound echo before you and you are ready to journey.

SHIFT YOUR BREATH

Notice if your breath changes. I find as I begin to journey, my breath grows deeper and slower. Others find the opposite is true for them. Stan Grof, who has done more than anyone in the world to systematically explore altered states of consciousness, uses accelerated breathing together with evocative music in what he calls holotropic therapy (holos means whole and trepin means moving in the direction of something) as a method for bridging ordinary and non-ordinary consciousness. Be aware of your breathing as you begin your journey: it may want to become faster, it may slow down. In any case, it is likely to change.

IMAGINE YOUR WAY

'I don't want to imagine things, I want to experience what is real.' Quite right. Except, believe it or not, at the beginning of a journey allowing your imagination to flow within the context of your intention gets things going easily – especially when you first begin to journey. I always smile when someone in a workshop complains to Michael Harner, 'but I might be imagining it.' Harner replies with just the hint of a smile, 'OK. But then you might want to ask yourself, "Why am I imagining *this* instead of something else?"'

ALL SYSTEMS GO

Move with your heart along the passage you have chosen to your destination – either the upper or lowerworld. The heart is important here. Journeying is not a question of forcing anything with your will but rather of *allowing* it to happen by simply being aware in your heart of your intention. Then trust what happens. The drumbeat is your entrainment – your method of movement – but remember it is your intention that is riding the train to your chosen destination. As in any journey – even in ordinary reality – what you see in the scenery along the way is not decided by you. It is just what you get.

COME ALIVE

Let your senses run wild on the journey. Be aware of what you see, feel, taste, smell and hear in non-ordinary reality. But don't try to force anything. Your senses come alive by themselves when they are ready. By the way, everybody is

If we had a keen vision and feeling of all ordinary human life, it would be like hearing the grass grow and the squirrel's heart beat, and we should die of the roar which lies on the other side of silence. As it is, the quickest of us walk about well wadded with stupidity.
George Eliot

different. Some of us 'see' more than we 'feel', others 'hear' more than we 'see'. Some people actually journey with 'words' rather than seeing or feeling much. Just be aware that if you are, say, a visual artist in ordinary reality, in non-ordinary reality you may not 'see' at all. You may find another sense dominant.

STAY COOL

While you are journeying, try to remain neutral to what you see and to whatever happens. This is not the place to call in your self-criticism or decide that you like this but don't like that. There will be plenty of time for that when you return. If you lose your concentration, just take yourself back to the place on the journey where it faded, restate your intention and wait there with an open heart. Your journey will resume in its own time.

TRUST YOUR EXPERIENCE

Trust whatever happens on your journey. After hundreds of journeys I finally realized that we *always* get the teachings that we need from a journey – even when at the time it may not seem so. When flashes of insight come, pay attention but don't analyze anything – save that for later. You may feel, as most people do in the beginning, that you don't trust yourself. You may even be inclined to criticize yourself. Don't. Just be present there, heart open to what 'speaks to you', be truthful, and remain neutral about what you receive on the journey. It will all work just as it is meant to.

THE RETURN

When the call back – four short bursts of drumming – comes, or when you yourself decide you are ready to return to ordinary reality, thank all of your helping spirits and let them know they can go. Then follow the same path you took into non-ordinary reality to come home. This is a much quicker process as you are simply retracing your steps. It usually takes no more than 30 seconds to 1 minute. Give yourself a moment to reorientate yourself and then open your eyes.

And is it mere coincidence that different and widely separated cultures, as well as various branches of art and science, come up with striking parallelisms and 'synchronicities' from time to time?
Ervin Laszlo

BRIDGE BUILDING

Bridge building is one of the most important parts of your work. It does just what it says it does: it builds a bridge between non-ordinary reality and ordinary reality. After each journey you will make notes about it in your journal. Record what you saw, what you felt, what you were told. Record any symbols or metaphors that have come up even if you don't immediately understand them. Often the 'meaning' of a journey will continue to unfold long after the journey has finished. You may well find in time that you are getting so much information, healing, guidance from your journeys that it is vital to write it all down in order to be able to make use of it. I have a tendency when journeying to feel that really nothing is happening to me. Often I come back and record my journey only to find when I read it back that it has been immensely rich and helpful.

Certainly some shamans will say you can learn from exposure to an older and wiser person, one who has lived and done the work longer. But they could also tell you that the best teacher is a tree.
Leslie Gray

THE WEEK AHEAD

You will be making five journeys to the lowerworld in this week: to have a look around, to meet an animal, to work with water, to work with growing things, and to see how it feels to do something physical in this realm.

Your two Free Breaks this week are for you to use for whatever purposes you like, calling on the skills you have learned during quantum leap one or two. You might like to talk to a houseplant that is ailing to find out what is wrong with it for instance. Or perhaps practise your Cocoon Spinning. It's a good idea to do this when you don't really need a cocoon so that when you find yourself needing its protection you can access it instantly. As the weeks go by with your practice try to be aware of the threads that strengthen your cocoon in your life. You could perhaps go to your inner sacred space, or journey, to find out if there are any changes you can make in your environment that will continue to shape the power and the beauty of your cocoon. Or journey to ask who in your life strengthens your cocoon.

INTO THE LOWERWORLD

The first journey you will be undertaking is to the lowerworld. To get to the lowerworld you need to choose a place in ordinary reality from which you will leave and to which you will return afterwards. This place needs to have some kind of an opening into the earth that will carry you deeper and deeper into the earth and then beyond into the imaginal realms that are the lowerworld. The place you choose can be a place that you have only seen once in ordinary reality or one that is very familiar to you such as a pond at the bottom of your garden or a staircase down into the basement if you live in a big apartment building. Choose a place you like. It could be your sacred place in nature that you have been working with in quantum leap one, provided this gives you some access downwards.

The place you choose might have a crack in the ground through which your awareness can travel downwards. Or you could travel down through a spring, the roots of a tree, or a tunnel into the earth. I have even had people in my groups that got to the lowerworld by lying down on the grass and 'dissolving' into the ground, although I think it is probably better to look for an opening of some kind. I most often journey to the lowerworld by diving off the rocks into the sea near where I live. I then swim down in my awareness beneath the waves and continue to travel through cracks in the rocks until gradually they turn to the right and open out into a kind of rabbit hole at the end of which I see light and tumble into the lowerworld.

Quantum Break 4

JOURNEY TO THE LOWERWORLD

Your intention:
TO GO TO THE LOWERWORLD TO LOOK AT THE LANDSCAPE
Explore the area of the lowerworld you are in and then return to record your journey.

♦ Review the guidelines for journeying on page 99. Read the following
   instructions over three times and you are ready to begin.
♦ Be clear about the place you have chosen to start from. It has to be a place
   which gives you access to movement downwards. Go there in your imagination and look around. Activate your senses.
♦ Turn on your drumming tape and begin your journey.

- Enter into whatever passageway you have chosen to take you down and give you access to the lowerworld. Notice what the tunnel is like going down. What do you smell? Feel? See? Hear?

- Just keep going downwards. Remember you are not looking for moles and worms and wood lice (unless of course one of these friends can be of help to you in getting down), you are using this tunnel into the earth to give you access to the imaginal realms beyond it.

- Just keep moving down. If you happen to see any tunnels coming back up again just ignore them and go downwards. (These are used for different purposes – not as a passage to the lowerworld.)

- Keep looking for the light at the end of the tunnel that will indicate you are coming out into the lowerworld. If you don't see it after a few minutes, create it for yourself. This is a good way of focusing your intention.

- When you get to the end of the tunnel it will open out into some kind of a landscape. What is the light like? Is it much like the light in ordinary reality or is it different? If so, notice how. You will record all these things in your Bridge building when you return.

- Now come out into the lowerworld. What do you see? There are often one or two things you see or sense that will always be there each time you reach the lowerworld. For one person it might be white pebbles, for another a particular quality of light, or a tree, or a pond. As you do your first full journeys notice if there is some particular 'marker' like this for you that will always tell you when you have arrived in the lowerworld.

- What do you feel? Smell? Hear? Sense? What is the landscape like? Are you in a glen? Are you on a beach? Are there mountains? Trees? Are you in a cave? Pay attention to what is around you. Also notice what feelings you have when you enter the tunnel and then afterwards when you come out into the lowerworld space.

- Is there anyone there? An animal? A person? If so then say hello to them.

- When the call-back comes on the drumming tape, thank any helping spirits, animals or guides that have helped you go down or met you there and retrace your steps right back to the place from which you began your journey in ordinary reality.

The natural world is the larger sacred community to which we belong. To be alienated from this community is to become destitute in all that makes us human. To damage this community is to diminish our own existence.
Thomas Berry

Bridge Building

When you return to do your Bridge building, record everything that happened or didn't happen including any negative feelings. If they come, honour them. Ask yourself, how big a part your Carping Critic is playing in all this. We all have one. Mine used to be giant–sized. He criticized everything I did. As you keep journeying, focus on your intention and do what you do with compassion for yourself and others, and these feelings will clear away so Mr C Critic will in time forsake you. He will just get bored and wander off. Good riddance!

BE PATIENT

Giving voice to Earth's voice has been a specific human task since the beginning, according to the stories we tell ourselves, the songs we sing, our rituals and our poetry. Repetition, rhythm, rhyme, patterns of gesture, movements and language: these are the ways we speak out and give coherence to experience, assert our connection with everything else.
David Suzuki

Journeying with grace and ease is a question of learning to step out of the way and just let it happen. This is something each of us has to learn in our own way. This is the way to make it all work for you. Shamanic work is about bringing yourself back to your intention, connecting with your compassion (for yourself as well as anything else) and persisting. I promise you that when you are working with these three things it will all come beautifully in time. And it doesn't matter how long this takes. Remember the power of the consciousness matrix which you are learning to activate and which you access each time you do shamanic work. It is the product of a million years of human evolution. It will not let you down provided you just keep making skilful use of it.

Every time you journey to the lowerworld you will use the same place in ordinary reality for coming and going and you will travel down the same tunnel. The reason for this is that it makes the whole process much more efficient since you become familiar with the route and can travel down and up it more and more easily. Getting down and back are only the means by which you reach the lowerworld to do whatever you have set out to do there. There is no point in reinventing the wheel.

If you do not get fully down the tunnel on your first journey, or if you get through the tunnel and emerge in the lowerworld but then don't see anything around you on your first few journeys, that's fine. Don't worry. It will come. Just be aware of any thoughts or feelings that show up while journeying so that you can record them during your Bridge building afterwards.

PUT OUT A CALL

While you are journeying remember to call for whatever you need. This is non-ordinary reality which means you can create whatever you need to make your journey run more smoothly. If you find yourself on the way down coming up against a stone wall, then call on a mole or a helper with a sledge hammer to break through a rock and speed you on your way. Remember you are not journeying with your body here, but with your spirit. Your spirit can become any size or shape it needs to get the job done. This is where your imagination comes in. Don't be afraid of it. It is a powerful tool for focusing a journey and a good way to gather your intention when you begin.

Animals and spirit helpers communicate in all sorts of ways. It can be through words or through gesture or symbol or metaphor. Metaphor is the most powerful language of the quantum realms. Or an animal may simply put you on their back and sail off to explore the territory.

You will notice with each journey you do that more impressions come and there is likely to be more information to bring back. When you go down the tunnel call out for the animal spirit you want to consult. If there is no spirit then simply call out once you get to the lowerworld. Sometimes you have to ask several times before you get any of the spirits to pay attention to you. I think this is often because the spirits want to test out the power of our intention and compassion when we journey.

If ever any spirit in non-ordinary reality gives you anything, treat it like the rich blessing that it is. Thank them, clasp it to your heart and bring it back with you to ordinary reality. The energies given in this way can bring healing, wisdom and power. Such gifts are a sign of friendship from the spirit world. These friendships will continue to deepen the more you journey.

The shaman returns to earth-consciousness with the same sorts of 'spiritual revelations' as those gained in transcendental NDE's and in traditional shamanic societies such revelations become part of that culture's accumulated 'wisdom teaching'.
Nevill Drury

TROUBLESHOOTING

If you find on your first journey, or second or third journey that you have trouble getting down to the lowerworld or become confused once you arrive there, simply keep bringing your awareness back to your intention for the journey and restate it to yourself, i.e. 'My intention is to go to the lowerworld and meet an animal.' It is exactly like meditation. It is quite normal to have a lot of 'junk' thoughts enter your head while you are meditating – stuff like, 'I must remember to buy tomatoes,' or 'Oh god, I can't do this

The task is to go as deeply as possible into the darkness ... and to emerge on the other side with permission to name one's own point of view.
Anthea Francine

Myth is the bubbling
lifespring of our consciousness
... of our highest creativity as
well as our worst delusions,
and the secret is all in how it
is tended ... the shaman is
man's basic creative response
to the presence of the
mythic dimension.
Stephen Larsen

right, I am hopeless at everything.' The same thing can happen while you are journeying. That's OK. Don't worry about it. These thoughts are not important. When they come just very gently direct your awareness back to your intention and repeat it again to yourself. Intention is the power that directs every journey – keep coming back to it and you will be amazed at how effective this is. Remember too to call for whatever you need to fulfil that intention. If it is dark going down the tunnel and you want some light, call on a lot of fireflies to give it to you, or manufacture a torch and use it to light your way. If you need help getting down, then call on a guide – maybe a bird or a mole or an angel or helping spirit in some form. Let them take you. This is non-ordinary reality. Here you can create whatever you need to fulfil whatever your intention for a journey is.

It is important to remember that learning to journey is like learning anything else – it comes with practice. Some of the most successful shamanic healers began their career with early journeys which they felt were pretty lean. When I began to journey I would get down to the entrance to the lowerworld and there would be cardboard cut out animals sitting there. I would speak to them and they would do nothing. I usually had to ask them for what I wanted at least three times before they would respond at all. Having had these experiences, and thinking myself such a failure at first, I now realize they were enormously helpful to me in learning to journey. It taught me the power of intention, compassion and *persistence*. It taught me to lay aside the psychological junk I had carried around with me all of my life that told me I was 'never any good at anything,' that I was just 'imagining things,' that I 'could never get the hang of journeying.'

TAKE WHAT YOU GET

One last thing that is important to remember about any shamanic journey: accept and record whatever advice, healing, or experience you are offered *faithfully*. In time you will come to know that it is exactly what you need at this particular moment in time. The compassionate spirits have enormous wisdom. They communicate exactly what you need to know and give you what you need (not always what you *think* you need and want). If you find yourself struggling with your journeys and criticizing yourself for 'not doing it well enough' then this is what you need to hear right now. Record it during your Bridge building. Then reflect on just what message the spirits are giving you with this. It could be that what they are trying to teach you is to stop trying so hard and relax. Just persevere with your journeys to the lowerworld outlined below, one for each of the next four days. It will all come in time.

Quantum Break 5

MEET AN ANIMAL

Your intention:

TO GO TO THE LOWERWORLD AND MEET AN ANIMAL

- ✦ Re-read Ticket to Ride – Journey Protocols if you need to refresh your memory.
- ✦ Journey to the lowerworld as you did in Quantum Break 4.
- ✦ Is there an animal waiting for you?
- ✦ If not, wait a while and see who shows up.
- ✦ If there is, greet them and get to know them.
- ✦ Ask them to reveal to you something about their nature.
- ✦ Ask them to show you what they do best.
- ✦ When the call-back comes, thank them for their help, let them know they can go now, and come back.

For if our body is the matter upon which our consciousness applies itself, it is coextensive with our consciousness. It includes everything that we perceive; it extends unto the stars.

Henri Bergson

Bridge Building

It is a good idea to draw the animal or animals you met, but if you really feel you are so bad at drawing you are more likely to offend your new friend than capture their personality, then jot down your experience in words. Drawing, however, is an excellent way to Bridge build, whatever you may think of your attempts. This is not an attempt to make art but to record in some simple form your connection with quantum energies so they are more available to you when you need them in your day-to-day world.

If we stick to a plan without trying any of the byways, the end of the journey is just a place of preconception, not experience.

Carl A. Hammerschlag

Quantum Break 6

DIVE INTO THE LOWERWORLD

No man, however civilised, can listen for very long to African drumming, or Indian chanting, or Welsh hymn singing, and retain intact his critical and self-conscious personality.

Aldous Huxley

Your intention:

TO GO TO THE LOWERWORLD AND FIND A BODY OF WATER

✦ Journey to the lowerworld and see if any of your animal spirits are waiting for you.

✦ If there is an animal friend there, ask him or her to take you to water.

✦ Go with them, or on your own if you wish, to find a body of water – a lake, a well, a pool, an ocean.

✦ Dive into the water and activate your senses. What do you see around you? What do you feel?

✦ As you leave the water, cup your hands and take a cupful of water. Pour it or sprinkle it on the ground.

✦ Thank any friends or helpers you may have had, and come back.

To be the One and simultaneously the many – this is your calling, your purpose, the ultimate destiny of your kind.

Ken Carey

Bridge Building

Note down, or draw, the body of water you visited and what surrounded it. Record how it felt to dive into it. Were you shocked by any of the sensations? Were they very different from what you expected? Make a note, too, of where you sprinkled your water.

Quantum Break 7

JOURNEY TO GROWTH

Your intention:
TO GO TO THE LOWERWORLD AND SEE WHAT HAS GROWN

+ Journey to the lowerworld.
+ Go back to the place where you sprinkled your water.
+ Notice if anything has grown there. Is it a plant? What does it look like? Smell like?
+ Is your animal friend there?
+ If so, ask it to help you find one thing which will be of value to you back in ordinary reality.
+ When you find it, hold it to your heart, thank your friend and come back.

Sea Spirit
Sea Spirit
Calm the waves
For me
I'm tired
Yo ho lo
Calm the sea
For me
Shaman Song

Bridge Building

Write down as much as you can about anything that grew in the water. Did your animal friend meet you? What did he give you? Does it relate in any way to whatever grew in the water? Write down any meaning you attach now to what you were given and why it should be of value now. You may want to come back to this later and see if this changes.

Beyond words, in the silencing of thought, we are already there.
Alan Watts

Quantum Break 8

LOWERWORLD WORKOUT

Shamanic experience is present in the lives of those of us in the modern world who are searching for the whole, the eternal, the ecstatically true embrace of reality amid the fragmented, chaotic, and false remnants of lost traditions.

Rowena Pattee

Your intention:
TO GO TO THE LOWERWORLD AND MOVE ABOUT

✦ Journey to the lowerworld.
✦ Take a look around you and choose to do something physical – climb a mountain, run across a landscape, leap great distances, fly.
✦ Notice how your body feels.
✦ Notice the experience of doing something physical in the lowerworld.
✦ While you are exploring, see if there is some special place that is particularly nourishing to you.
✦ Ask any animal friend to guide you to new areas of the lowerworld and to show you the places they like best and what they like most to do.
✦ Thank your friend for their help with your exploration, and come back.

Bridge Building

If you chose something to do that you do regularly in ordinary reality – go for a run, perhaps – note down in what ways it felt different to do this activity in the lowerworld. If you chose to do something radically different – like flying – simply describe how that felt. Did you find somewhere that was especially nourishing for you? Did your animal friend take you there? What was it like? How did it nourish you? Do you feel able to deal with some situation in ordinary reality more easily now that you have been there?

MAKE A SANCTUARY
Week Two Project

Your project for the week is to create a sacred place in your home which will serve as a small sanctuary. This week you are beginning to work with the architecture of energy and exploring how it changes the quality of material reality. Your intention will be focused on defining energetic structures that separate out this small part of your living space from the rest and welcome the sacredness of anything you choose to put in this area to manifest its own sacred spirit. It is hard to explain this process for, like all things sacred, it can only be moved towards intuitively with a sense of play and wonder. This can be a lot of fun to do.

It is time to gather together the various things you collected together last week and arrange them within the space you have chosen. You will be creating a place where you can carry out your journeys, do your Bridge building or even just be reminded of quantum reality every time you look at or interact with the objects you have chosen to place in this special area. Now it is ready to be consecrated.

To consecrate means to dedicate a place or object or collection of objects to something or some purpose. Although the table or desktop or windowsill you have chosen may also serve a mundane purpose, it will now be used primarily for transpersonal reasons. Your sanctuary will be created by you, maintained by you, used by you and altered by you in whatever way is appropriate during the weeks ahead while you are doing your journey work. It will be dedicated, consecrated, and created as an offering to whatever, at a soul level, you love most. Is it beauty? Freedom? Creativity? What? If you are not sure what this is then you might like to use one of your Free Breaks to go to your sacred place within and ask the question 'what do I most love and value?' You may find the answer comes from within. You may find it is given to you by some spirit energy that is present.

The sanctuary or altar which you create does not have to be large or in any way showy. In fact the simpler it is the better. It could be on a shelf in the corner of a room, on a small table – even on a portion of your desk or a bedside table will

The only thing of value in a man is the soul. That is why it is the soul that is given everlasting life, either in the Land of the Sky or in the Underworld. The soul is man's greatest power, it is the soul that makes us human, but how it does so we do not know. Our flesh and blood, our body, is nothing but an envelope about our vital power.
Ikinilik

I arise today
Through the strength
    of heaven
Light of sun,
Radiance of moon,
Splendour of fire
Speed of lightning
Swiftness of wind.
Depth of sea
Stability of earth,
Firmness of rock.
St Patrick

do. You might like to place a candle on it, which you can light once a day while you are doing your journey work, and a small glass or vase in which you can place fresh flowers. Place there too any other objects that have attracted you or have special meaning for you – the photo of a child you love perhaps or an animal whom you have met and worked with in non-ordinary reality. It is also the place to keep your Travelogue. Make a play of it and see what comes. Let the sacred spirit of it shine forth. Be aware of this spirit every time you come in contact with it then watch how creating a space in which the energetic intention is clear can enrich your days. Objects too have spirit. They can become extraordinary friends. Record in your journal what you perceive.

FREE BREAKS

The lack of awareness of spirit in everything comes out of years of indoctrination. We are often shamed as a child when we come into the house or the school room to report that 'the corn told me it is ready to be cut' or that 'the pussy cat said it doesn't want any more milk'. We are taught not to believe anything unless it comes out of a book or some 'expert' tells it to us. A valuable journey you might like to do during one of your Free Breaks this week is to go to the lower world and ask whatever animal or spirit you meet to help you discover the moment or moments in your life at which the world taught you to disbelieve.

Call on the skills you have learned during quantum leaps one and two. It may be particularly useful to practise Cocoon Spinning so that you are really proficient at it when you need to call on it. Or simply go to the lowerworld and do some more exploring.

CHECKLIST

Day One

+ Read through the chapter at least as far as Journey to the Lowerworld.
+ Do Quantum Break 4 Journey to the Lowerworld *to go to the lowerworld to look at the landscape.*
+ Bridge build.
+ Read the instructions for Make a Sanctuary on page 113 and begin to plan what you are going to do.

Day Two

+ Take a look at Troubleshooting on page 107 if you have not already done so.
+ Do Quantum Break 5 Meet an animal *to go to the lowerworld and meet an animal.*
+ Bridge build.
+ Are you beginning to find yourself looking at the world around you any differently?

Day Three

+ Do Quantum Break 6 Dive into The Lowerworld *to go to the lowerworld and find a body of water.*
+ Bridge build.
+ Don't forget that all the way through the week you will be carrying out your sacred project.

Day Four

+ Do Quantum Break 7 Journey for Growth *to go to the lowerworld and see what has grown.*
+ Bridge build.
+ Find a way of building this experience into your project.

... the greatest insight into truth and causality may be gained by entering the 'supernatural' world. In modern western society we may no longer regard the world of the paranormal as 'supernatural' – indeed, the NDE and OBE are increasingly commonplace and simply represent a fascinating dimension of normal human experience. However, the principle is clear enough. It seems to me that the shamans of pre-literate hunter-gatherer societies have been attuned to the universe in ways we are only now beginning to understand.

Nevill Drury

Day Five

✦ Do Quantum Break 8 Lowerworld Workout *to go to the lowerworld and move about.*

✦ Bridge build.

✦ How are you getting on with your project?

Day Six

✦ Do a Free Break exercise of your choice.

✦ Bridge build.

Day Seven

✦ Do a Free Break exercise of your choice.

✦ Bridge build.

✦ Spend 20 minutes writing your Travelogue.

✦ Complete anything still to do on this week's project.

Travelogue

✦ How many days this week did you take your Quantum Break? (Seven I hope!) How was beginning to journey in non-ordinary reality for you? How did you choose to Bridge build? Did you use words? Song? Colours? Sculpture? If you have only used one or two of these ways so far why not try a different method next week.

✦ How was your experience of creating sacred space in your home? Did you do it all in one go or bit by bit over the week?

✦ Have you been aware of any significant issues for you that have arisen this week? If so what are they?

✦ Has your experience of journeying changed significantly since the first day you did it? If so describe how in your Travelogue.

Quantum leap 3

Enter the Allies

I am the glue of the universe. I forge the links connecting all things. I tie an artist to his muse, a tree to the earth, an electron to its atom. I bind your hopes and dreams to the energies that help you bring them into being. Whatever you do, call my name and it will be done with grace. Wherever you go I am present. Touch me, taste me, reach out your hand and open your heart. You will learn that you are never alone.

I am the Spirit of Friendship

This week the play begins. You will meet and begin to work with your power animal. This is the most intimate relationship you will have in quantum realms. Power animals are great people, witty, wise and reliable. They carry your power – for health, for creativity, for joy. Each is unique and each a joy. Have fun.

We do not see things as
they are but as we are.
Jewish Proverb

Some say the most powerful force in the universe is love. I would call it friendship. Like the air we breathe and the thoughts we think, friendship is everywhere. It is carried on the spirit of the morning breeze, you find it gazing at a pebble you pick up on the beach, you breathe it in the scent of a lily. Yet often as not we do not see the spirit of a thing, or feel it. Nor do we allow ourselves to relax into the warm embrace of the friendship that connects our spirit to the spirit of another thing.

Shamans work with spirits which they have come to know and to trust. These spirit energies include devas who care for the plants on the earth, ancestral spirits, power animals, angels, gods and goddesses, elementals and spirits of specific objects in their environment. Throughout history there has been an awareness that everything in the world has both a physical nature and a spiritual one – a tree, a fox, the wind, a house, a knife, a boat. Early peoples were deeply attuned to communion with their environment. When Neolithic man sang the rising of the moon, the moon returned to him its grace. When he poured his care into the fashioning of a weapon, the spirit of the weapon grew strong for the hunt. When he called to his power animal for help and protection in crossing a prairie swarming with predators, he experienced greater strength in his limbs and his senses became heightened. Our culture has largely lost its ability to connect with spirits, whether it is the spirit of a tree or rock, a house or sunset, let alone the spirits of animal powers and angels in non-ordinary realms. This week's quantum leap is about learning to look with new eyes at what is around you and to hear with new ears. It is about rediscovering the power of friendship by reconnecting with spirit. And what better place to begin than in the realm of the animal powers.

… the eagle is not just a
'symbol' of the Great Spirit.
The eagle is the Great Spirit.
It's not as if the earth is holy,
the earth is holy. It is not
some 'special dirt' but this
dirt, right here under our feet,
that is holy. The 'holy land' is
not way off somewhere in the
Middle East or Jerusalem or
Bethlehem, but right here
where we stand.
Leslie Gray

ANIMAL FRIENDS

When I was six years old my best friend was a huge golden collie. His name was Tuffy. I had called him that because my greatest ambition was to be tough and I was about as far away from being tough as anybody could get. Tuffy let me bury my face in his glorious ruff, protected me, and listened to me when I needed to pour my heart out. His patience was infinite. His love gave me strength. It made it possible for me to go on living in a world with which I felt I had nothing in common. That was the first inkling I had of the deep connections we humans have with animals and the power of their friendship. Perhaps this is because we *are* animals. Yet so often we find ourselves in conflict with our own animal nature.

Later on, when I was ten, I went to see Jean Cocteau's magical film *La Belle et La Bête*. It was then that I fell in love with the Beast. Really in love – the way young girls fall for teen idols. The Beast was a magnificent creature – so deep, so full of passion and of pathos. Later in the film when he turned into the prince dressed in brocades and gold, I cried. The Beast himself was infinitely more interesting to me than this rather contrived blond-haired, bow-legged prince in all his jewels. Throughout the film the Beast, played by French actor Jean Marais, suffered terribly as a result of the conflict between the instincts of his heavy animal body and the longing to express his spiritual love for Beauty. I remember at one point Beast was walking with Beauty along the ramparts of his castle. His eyes had softened with love for her. All at once a young roe deer darted by in the woods to his left. Instantly love was ripped away to be replaced by blood lust and longing for a kill. Then, just as suddenly, the eyes of the Beast flooded with tears.

Such is our human experience. We find ourselves caught between our earth-bound animal nature and our longing to soar in the realms of spirit. In our culture the two have become split, leaving us uneasy about the animal part of our being, disconnecting us from instinct and, too often, rendering us powerless. Rediscover the spirit of the animal and it will help you reconnect with your fundamental power.

In religious traditions only the inspired are truly considered transmitters of the truth.
Rowena Pattee

SPIRIT OF THE WILD

Wisdom teachings from ancient times tell us that at a soul level we are deeply tied to animals. Even the English word *animal* comes from *anima* in Latin which means 'soul'. Ancient stories tell of animals and humans sharing strength and characteristics. The Oriental system of astrology categorizes people according to animals. It speaks of those born in the year of the snake, the ox, the boar, the rat, and compares their characteristics with the animal used to describe their nature. World mythology tells of a time when many of our greatest teachers came from the animal world. How 'before the fall' we could converse with animals and they with us. Yet, like Cocteau's wonderful Beast, most of us have inherited a worldview in which mind is split from body and spirit from instinct, and mind is the more valued. So we feel uneasy about the animal part of us. It is the carrier of all those irrational impulses which our religious upbringing has taught us to fear. It is the home of our instincts, which the left-brained educational system that we have been put through has done its best to burn out of us. The animal spirit in us is

Our next breaths, yours and mine, will sample the snorts, sighs, bellows, shrieks, cheers and spoken prayers of the prehistoric and historic past.
Harlow Shapley

a wild spirit – an instinctual spirit that lives close to nature and moves spontaneously. It is a spirit which acts without the self-doubt, guilt and inhibition that so often plague our lives. And the animal spirit in us is – more than any other part of us – a *free* spirit. It responds to life from moment to moment wholeheartedly whether we are confronted with food, pain or affection.

When we are in touch with our own animal spirit, we are in touch with personal power, strength and wisdom which are virtually impossible to access in any other way. We are also in touch with the earth so that quite naturally we act responsibly towards the land, the sea and the air. We are less likely to pollute them – not out of some external code of morality which tells us we shouldn't – but because we feel more deeply our dependence on them and our connections with other forms of animal life. The friendship between us and other kinds of spirits can be equally important.

THE COMPANY OF SPIRITS

Spirit energies manifest in very specific forms. You will meet them as power animals, teachers, guides, gods and goddesses, ancestral spirits of the place, spirits of nature, spirits of the elements and of the sky, the earth and sea. Just as Bridge building forges powerful connections between your soul and personality – making the experience of authentic power and freedom a living experience – the friendship of compassionate spirits brings a high degree of power for healing, for creativity, for creating harmony in the universe, as well as for fun and simple joy. Spirits are a shaman's friends in non-ordinary reality. His relationship with each of them is highly personal like your relationship to a brother or a lover, a best friend, or someone you admire.

Each spirit, like each human being, is unique. Some are solemn. Others make you laugh. Friendships with your helping spirits will draw you into great adventures. It is they who bring you power. It is your compassion and intention which gather and direct it. From such partnerships miracles can be made. But it is important to know that shamanic work is always based on first-hand experience. It does not depend on any belief system. It is not what you *believe* that matters, it is what you *experience*.

In a British television interview in the 1950s Jung was asked by the interviewer, 'Do you *believe* in God?' Jung paused, looked down and then looked up again with an enormous smile on his face. 'I don't *believe*,' he said. 'I *know*.' Michael Harner has a similar response when somebody asks him if you have to believe in spirits to practise shamanism. 'Shamans don't *believe* in spirits,' he replies, 'Shamans talk with them, interact with them. But they no more "believe" there are spirits than they "believe" they have a house to live in or have a family.' This is a very important issue because shamanism is not a system of faith. It is a system of knowledge based on first-hand experience.

GUARDIAN SPIRITS

There is no better way to acquire first-hand experience of the friendship of spirits than working and playing with power animals. Power animals are guardian spirits in animal form known to tribal cultures throughout the world – from the Coast Salish of California to the Lapps in the northern reaches of Scandinavia. A power animal can appear in almost any form – a deer, a wolf, an elephant, a lynx, a bird, an aardvark or even a mouse.

Power animals help protect you from illness and misfortune. They bring knowledge, wisdom and, above all, both physical and spiritual power. Power animals are different in character from angels yet they all have certain things in common with the guardian angels of Christian and Muslim traditions. For, like guardian angels, they are said to help us through the birth process and then to remain with us as protectors throughout our lives. According to tribal cultures when we are born each one of us comes into the world with a specific power animal as a guardian. He or she is a compassionate spirit who having once lived on the earth, knows the difficulties we face and wants to help us in what we do and to care for us by keeping us in a good state of health and spiritual power throughout our lives. When we are not aware of our power animals and we do not respect and honour the gifts they bring us, power animals can sometimes leave. If they do, we experience a loss of power that makes us susceptible to repeated or chronic illness, spates of bad luck or low physical, mental and emotional vitality.

Only human beings have come to a point where they no longer know why they exist. They ... have forgotten the secret knowledge of their bodies, their senses, their dreams.
Lame Deer

UP CLOSE AND PERSONAL

Your relationship with your power animal is likely to be the most personal of all your spirit friendships. Probably the most fun too. Your power animal, say it's a bear, not only carries the power from the whole bear species, he or she also has a highly individual nature and a totally unique personality. You may have the same animal as someone else as your guardian spirit, yet the personality of their power animal may be as differ-

A shaman is a man who has immediate, concrete experiences with gods and spirits; he sees them face to face, he talks with them, prays to them, implores them – but he does not 'control' more than a limited number of them.
Mircea Eliade

ent from yours as night and day. You can have more than one power animal, too. If so, each will be different. I have worked with some power animals who never speak, conveying all of their information and energy through symbolic gestures. I have worked with others who never stop talking. Some are almost stand-offish. They convey their power and their wisdom from a distance. Others seem to metaphorically roll up their sleeves and take a real hands-on approach to everything. A power animal's behaviour can change from time to time, too. One power animal, who came to me in a dream and of whom I am inordinately fond, used to work with me all the time in healing. But for the past year he has simply not participated. During one of my trips to the lowerworld I approached him with tears in my eyes saying, 'Why do you no longer work with me? I miss you a lot.' He told me he would no longer be doing healing work with me but that he had no intention of leaving me. He said that from now on he would be acting only as my personal guardian and that is what all his power would be going into.

Your power animal is likely to show itself to you in a physical form that is most appropriate to you. My main power animal is a very beautiful bird. I love her beauty and delight in it each time I see her. A man I recently taught has an amusing snake as a power animal, with a head that looks like Scooby Doo. He adored Scooby Doo as a child and delights now in travelling in non-ordinary reality by holding onto his snake's tail and being towed along – often at breakneck speed.

HERE COME THE ANIMALS

A power animal can come to you in many different ways. You can journey in search of one. You may find in ordinary reality that a particular animal is 'calling to you'. You may sense an animal or keep thinking of it, see pictures of it, be given an ornament of this animal, or receive a postcard of it. This kind of thing can make it seem as though the animal is trying to signal to you that he is here waiting for you to discover him. This happened to me once. I had done some shamanic healing for someone and found myself working with a new animal. I made the assumption that the animal was somehow connected with the person I was doing the healing for. Then the next time I gave some healing the same animal showed up. Still the penny didn't drop. Around the same time, a favourite cousin of mine gave me a lovely tray with a drawing of this animal on it. I thanked her and thought no more of it. I put it on my dressing table under my perfume bottles. Over the next three months no less than four people separately gave me a gift of this animal – ornaments, pictures, you name it. I finally got the message.

Since then I have worked almost exclusively with this power animal in my healing and creative work. Each time I journey, she is always waiting for me at the entrance to the lower world. It is this power animal, who took so long to get through to me, who has taught me just how wide-ranging is the help and healing power animals can bring. When I need information or guidance on any particular project I will simply go to her and say, 'Please take me to whatever spirit in the universe is most appropriate to help me with …' And off we go.

By the way, if you're wondering why I don't just tell you straight out what this animal is, it's not because she's weird or shy – quite the opposite. It's just that often power animals don't much like to be talked about. They prefer to be asked before you go around telling people about them.

THE WEEK AHEAD

This week you will identify and begin working with your own power animal or animals. You may already have met an animal or two during your lowerworld journeys last week. Perhaps one persisted in reappearing a number of times in the same journey or repeatedly each time you went to the lowerworld. If so, this may be a power animal for you. You will be journeying specifically to find out. You will also be exploring methods for meeting your power animal such as moving into your inner sacred space and calling one, as well as becoming more aware in ordinary reality to see if one is calling to you. During your two Free Breaks this week you can experiment with ways to deepen your friendship with your power animal. The week's project will deepen your connections with your animal's energy.

Once upon a time – but this is neither a fairy tale nor a bedtime story – we knew less about the natural world than we do today. Much less. But we understood that world better, much better, for we lived ever so much closer to its rhythms.
Most of us have wandered far from our earlier understanding, from our long-ago intimacy. We take for granted what our ancestors could not, dared to, take for granted; we have set ourselves apart from the world of the seasons, the world of floods and rainbows and new moons. Nor, acknowledging our loss, can we simply reverse course, pretend to innocence in order to rediscover intimacy. Too much has intervened.
Daniel Swartz

$\mathcal{Q}$uantum $\mathcal{B}$reak 9

TRACKING YOUR POWER ANIMAL

Your intention:
TO GO TO THE LOWERWORLD AND FIND YOUR POWER ANIMAL

You are going to visit the lowerworld to find your power animal. You will be following the same journey practice you used last week. You might like to refresh your memory by going back over Ticket to Ride on page 99 before you begin.

✦ As always you will leave from and return to the same place, call on whatever you need to help you on your way and use your drumming tape for travel.

✦ Be sure you are clear about your intention and keep reminding yourself of it as you journey. Remember it is *compassion and intention* that gets the job done.

✦ When you get to the lowerworld you may find that an animal is waiting for you. Or you may be greeted by an animal who has been present on your previous journeys. In either case, ask the question 'Are you my power animal?'

✦ If it is it will give you some clear sign like a call or a movement. It may start to play hide and seek with you, for instance.

✦ If there is no animal waiting then look around and call out for one. (Often the spirits test our sincerity and perseverance before they show up.)

✦ If you see several animals ask them to indicate to you which is your power animal by some distinct sign.

✦ If a power animal doesn't show up, don't worry. This isn't a sign that you are 'doing it wrong'. The spirits know what they are doing. It may be that your power animal needs to make itself known to you in one of the other ways we will be working with, or that it is not yet time for you to come to know it. In this case explore the lowerworld further until the call back comes and then describe what you have experienced in your Bridge building.

- ✦ Once you identify your power animal have fun. Ask it to show you the place in non-ordinary reality it likes best. Ask it to show you which games it likes best to play. Ask it if it has anything to tell you.
- ✦ Then watch what it does. Sometimes power animals speak to you telepathically in words. Often they convey their meaning in actions – by some gesture or by indicating something with a wing or a paw.
- ✦ Spend the rest of your journey time (15–20 minutes) until the call back comes exploring the lowerworld with your new ally. It is a wonderful friend who is likely to stay with you just as long as you honour it and give thanks for the power that it brings.
- ✦ When the call back comes thank your power animal, let it know that it can go now, and return.

> Since individuation is an archetypal process, it seems clear we must recognize the archetype of the wild creature in the human psyche as a transpersonal complex on a par with the shadow, the animus, and the anima.
>
> *Marie-Louise von Franz*

Bridge Building

Whether or not you met a power animal, record what happened during your journey in your journal using words or drawings. Remember that whatever experience you get on your journey is right for you. Whatever happened or did not happen is part of the messages that the spirits are bringing to you. What are those messages?

LOVE DREAMS

You can dream a power animal. The dreams in which they come are vivid, sometimes *lucid* dreams – where you know you are dreaming. I have dreamed two animals. One dream happened in what I would have said to be the most unlikely environment in the world for it to occur. I was in a motel room near San Francisco airport waiting to catch a plane the next morning. It was one of those dreadful artificial environments where not only the air was artificial but even the 'cream' you are invited to dump in your coffee seemed to be made of plastic. I went to sleep hoping morning would come quickly and I could get out of the place. I dreamed of a coyote – the most beautiful animal I had ever seen. I could make out every hair on its body. So splendid was this animal that

> We're in trouble because we don't recognize that the god's energies are our own energies. We don't understand that the energies personified in the god are the very energies of our own lives. We don't realize that the gods are not out there somewhere. They live in us all. They are the energies of life itself.
>
> *Joseph Campbell*

even in the dream I could hardly bear his beauty. When I awakened I knew, despite the absurdity of it all, that I had fallen in love. I laughed out loud. How on earth could I ever tell somebody that I had fallen in love with a coyote? My blessed coyote remained with me for a very long time. When I was carrying out extraction work (where you remove from someone's body energies which would be more appropriately placed in other parts of the universe) he was amazing. He had the ability to ferret out whatever needed clearing, no matter how hidden.

Power animals can sometimes shape-shift and take on other forms – even human forms. One of mine takes human form occasionally. A power animal can also merge its spiritual essence with you for a time – to give healing to someone or to bring you extra strength when you need it. In this case it also acts as an alter ego, bringing you power and connecting you with your own instinctual or animal nature. Athletes often work with power animals, sometimes without even realizing what they are doing. A runner might call on the power of an eagle during a marathon. A high jumper will visualize himself as a jaguar leaping into a tree. Each is accessing instinctual animal power and directing it to the ends they seek.

Quantum Break 10

CONNECTING WITH POWER

You cannot travel into yourself without exploring the infinite reaches of eternal consciousness.
Ken Carey

Your intention:
TO ACCESS THE POWER OF YOUR ANIMAL GUARDIAN

Another method for connecting with your power animal is to rattle or drum for it. You can use this equally to identify a new power animal or to forge a deeper bond with one you already know about. It is best to darken the room or use an eye mask so that you are not distracted by light.

◆ Give yourself a few minutes to breathe gently and deeply, letting your body become relaxed and allowing your heart to be open.

- Begin to rattle gently. It need not make much noise. If you are concerned about disturbing anyone else in the house rattle softly with the rattle right next to your ear. (The little plastic egg-shaped rattles you can buy in shops that sell percussion instruments are ideal for this.)
- Allow images or sounds or a sense of animals to pass through your mind and body.
- After ten minutes or so you may find that one animal is persistent in appearing in some form. Or it may seem that a particular animal energy is in the room.
- Telepathically, ask if this is your power animal. If it is, it will give you some clear sign. You will sense a movement, a call or a feeling in your body or some affirmation in your heart.
- If you already know your power animal then while you are doing this exercise simply call it to you and ask it to be present. See what it feels like in your body while it is there. Are your own senses heightened? Do you find yourself more connected with your own powers of instinct?
- Animal spirits are not only protectors and providers of power, they also have much to teach us about how to reclaim the power of our own animal instincts. What can yours teach you?
- Thank the animal for its presence and let it know that it can go now.
- Return to ordinary reality.
- Stop rattling.

Bridge Building

Now record your experience, whatever it has been. You might like to use colour and drawing for this. I find when working with animal energies that words can be inadequate to describe them.

You do not have to face the truth if you hire a belief system to do it in your place.
Ken Carey

Ecstasy and sacrifice are shamanic experiences needed in the midst of the modern global breakdown of traditions and its resulting disorientation, so that regenerative powers within us can be summoned.
Rowena Pattee

Quantum Break 11

INNER REACHES ANIMAL TRACKING

Your intention:
TO CONNECT WITH YOUR POWER ANIMAL IN INNER SPACE

You may also find a power animal or connect with one you already know in that special place in nature you first entered during the first week of your journey work. Go back and read The Inner Reaches of Sacred Space exercise (see page 68).

✦ Once your senses are heightened and you feel really comfortable in your special place ask that your power animal show up.
✦ Look around you. What do you see? What do you smell? What do you sense?
✦ Now reach out and touch your animal. Ask it to touch you. If it is a cat, it might push its head against you. A bird might brush you with its wings.
✦ Spend ten minutes exploring the inner reaches with your animal. Ask it to show you things you may have missed before in the environment.
✦ Now thank it for its friendship and gently return to the room.

... all too often those who seek alternative spirituality are unconscious of the basically Calvinist ethic that permeates their world view. This then leads them to focus on the rigorous and most stringent practices of, rather than the earthiness and sensuality of, Eastern forms of spirituality. Shamanism is so completely a down-to-earth spirituality that I suspect it will be nearly impossible to use it as a cloak for Anglo-European dualism. But, of course anything is possible.
Leslie Gray

Bridge Building

Record whatever has happened during your inner animal tracking in any way you choose. You might even ask the animal before you say goodbye to it how it would like to be recorded and see what it tells you.

TROUBLESHOOTING

The biggest problem most of my students face when learning to journey is lack of confidence. They find it difficult to believe that the stuff they get on their journeys is relevant or coming from anywhere other than their imagination. My daughter Susannah had this problem a lot in the beginning of her shamanic work. And she does phenomenal healing. 'Sometimes I got such fleeting, wispy images that it was hard for me to believe them', she says. 'I only know that journeying and feedback from others about the value of the wisdom or the healing which you bring back from the spirits was what helped me gain confidence. I once did some healing – a soul retrieval – for a woman who had tried to commit suicide at the age of 19. The soul part that came back told me three times to remind her of the skirt made of leaves. It sounded so absurd. But of course I dutifully passed on the message. When I did the woman's eyes flooded with tears. She told me of a beautiful skirt she had once made by sewing cocoa leaves together. She explained that she had denied her femaleness for many years and had dressed in a very butch way. As a result of the message she went out and bought herself three new skirts to wear.'

One power animal, two power animals, power animals that are so real you feel you could stroke them with your ordinary reality hand, power animals that are so vague you can only sense them. There are as many ways to experience a power animal as there are people. We all have a tendency to feel that our experience is a wrong one. Well, lay that belief aside. In the beginning you may only see the simplest suggestion of an animal – the eye of an eagle, a sketchy shape of a swan. You may not even 'see', You may only sense the presence of an animal spirit. You may also not be sure if an animal is your power animal. Give it time. If he is, he will show up again and again … and again. As far as how many power animals you have, this is entirely a personal matter – personal to the power animals themselves. For they choose you, you do not choose them. I used to work with seven or eight. I don't know why. Now I have two – one who is only my protector and the other who does most of the work for me in non-ordinary reality. I have not noticed in my own work that it was any better when I had more. Sometimes less can be more. Just be patient and allow your relationship with this very important spirit to begin and to unfold in whatever way it will.

Quantum Break 12

POWER GATHERING

The urge toward individuation is a true instinct, probably the strongest of all. Therefore, it first appears as an animal, a spontaneous instinctual force in the unconscious.

Marie-Louise von Franz

Your intention:
TO GET HEALING FROM YOUR POWER ANIMAL
Or
TO GET GOOD ADVICE FROM YOUR POWER ANIMAL

Power animals not only bring protection and energy they can also offer a lot of wisdom and good advice as well as bring you healing. Now that you have begun to forge a friendship with your animal spirit, it is time to begin calling on it for help. (This is the only way you ever get to know how rich a power animal's help can be.)

✦ Choose one of the three different means you have been exploring for connecting with your power animal – Quantum Break 9, 10, or 11.

✦ Follow the method and, when your power animal shows up, either:

✦ Ask it for healing if there is something you would like healed in you: or ask for healing in someone else – an animal, a plant or even a person (provided of course that you have the person's permission to do so). Or:

✦ Ask it for advice about something in your life you want insight into.

✦ Watch carefully what your animal does. Often the meaning of things that happen on a journey will not be immediately apparent. It can unfold later – even days or weeks afterwards.

✦ If you have asked for healing you may find that the animal gives it to you there and then. Or he may tell you something that you need to do later in ordinary reality to further your own healing – cut out coffee for instance, take a certain herb, perform a ritual for cleansing or detoxifying yourself, or sleep in a different room.

- If you have asked for advice on some issue he may tell you something specific which you will discern telepathically in words or he may take you somewhere and show you something that you need to embrace or explore to find your guidance.
- Ask your power animal how he feels about your speaking to others about him. Many power animals don't like you to reveal their identity except perhaps to others who are working shamanically as you are. But each power animal is different. Yours may want you to make him known – expecially to certain people in your life. Ask yours what he wants you to do about this.
- When you are ready, thank your power animal and return to ordinary reality.

> The individual goes right to the very bottom of his being to find who or what is doing the seeing and he ultimately finds – instead of a transpersonal self – nothing other than what is seen, which Blyth called 'the experience by the universe of the universe'.
> *Ken Wilber*

Bridge Building

Now record the results of your journey work. You can also make notes of any further insights that come to you afterwards in your Travelogue at the end of the week.

FREE BREAKS

Use any of the Quantum Breaks you have used so far this week to get to know your power animal better. Or just go to the lowerworld and hang out with them, explore and play. The idea is to deepen your friendship with them, so simply ask them how best you might do that.

> Never doubt that a small group of thoughtful, committed people can change the world. Indeed, it is the only thing that ever can.
> *Margaret Mead*

Week Three Project

Your power animal is the guardian spirit who will accompany you on all your journeys. He will do divining, healing, and guide you in the work you do for others. He will bring you information. He will be your scout in various areas of non-ordinary reality. He is a kind of psychic pal, tour guide, spiritual advisor and playmate all wrapped up in one package. As you spend time together and work together you will get to know his likes and dislikes and his idiosyncrasies. Chances are he already knows yours or he would not have chosen to be with you in the first place.

Power animals love certain things:

✦ Say a silent good morning to your power animal when you get up each day.

✦ Keep a small picture or a postcard of your power animal somewhere where you see it regularly and are reminded of him.

✦ Be aware of the *fragrance* of your animal's power, even when you are not specifically working with him. The fragrance of his power remains always with you to strengthen you and bring you wisdom and protect you as you go about your day-to-day life in ordinary reality.

✦ Call on his power specifically when you are challenged by anything in ordinary reality – say when you are tired or facing an exam or having to put together a creative project.

✦ Wear a piece of jewellery that reminds you of him and lets him know you are thinking of him.

✦ Ask him to join you when you are doing something physical – actually call him into your body. Power animals love this and the strength they bring your body is remarkable.

✦ The next time you journey ask your power animal how *he* would like you to honour him. See what he says.

✦ Draw your power animal or sculpt it in wax, or clay, or soap.

✦ Become aware of how your power animal speaks to you in daily life.

Old Man said to the people: 'Now, if you are overcome you may go to sleep and get power. Something will come to you in your dream that will help you. Whatever these animals tell you to do, you must obey them, as they appear to you in your sleep. Be guided by them.'
Blackfoot Lodge Tales

Which would have the greater effect in your life: my compassion for you or your compassion for yourself?
Running Wolf

- Dance your power animal. Put on music or a drumming tape or simply pick up your rattle and dance your power animal. Call him into your body and let him move within you. The movements may be elaborate but it is more likely that they will be very simple. The important thing is the inner experience of connecting with your power animal as you move.

Your project this week will be to choose four of the suggestions above and carry them out this week. Record the experience of doing this in your Travelogue. You might choose to place a photo of your animal in your sanctuary and honour him by recognizing your new friendship each time you see it, for instance. Or you might even like to dance your power animal and then write about the experience. You might like to find some physical reminder of him that you wear or carry about with you each day to connect you with the new friend you have made and give thanks for the blessings such friendship brings. It's up to you.

Each new gain in comprehension brings a corresponding reduction of complexity. You become simpler as you become wiser, until the day arrives when once again your understanding is your own, no longer polluted with what you have been told or what you have heard, but fresh as new perception, pure as a mountain spring, clear as the guileless eyes of a conscious child.
Ken Carey

CHECKLIST

Day One

- Read through the chapter as far as Quantum Break 9.
- Do Quantum Break 9 Tracking Your Power Animal *to go to the lowerworld and find your power animal.*
- Bridge build.

Day Two

- Do Quantum Break 10 Connecting With Power *to access the power of your animal guardian.*
- Bridge build. Notice and record how the meeting you had today with your power animal differs from the Tracking Your Power Animal exercise where you are journeying. Which was the richest for you?

In the house of long life,
there I wander,
In the house of happiness,
there I wander.
Beauty before me, with it
I wander.
Beauty behind me, with it
I wander.
Beauty below me, with it
I wander.
Beauty all around me, with it
I wander.
In old age travelling, with it
I wander.
I am on the beautiful trail,
with it I wander.

Navaho refrain

The world is a mirror of
Infinite Beauty, yet no man
sees it. It is a Temple of
Majesty, yet no man regards it.

Thomas Traherne

◆ Read the instructions for Week Three Project on pages 132–3 and decide which four methods you are going to use this week to deepen your friendship. Begin to play with them.

Day Three

◆ Do Quantum Break 11 Inner Reaches Animal Tracking *to connect with your power animal in inner space.*

◆ Bridge build.

Day Four

◆ Do Quantum Break 12 Power Gathering *to get healing from your power animal or to get good advice from your power animal.*

◆ Bridge build.

Day Five

◆ Repeat Quantum Break 12. If you asked for healing yesterday, ask for advice today, advice yesterday, healing today.

◆ Bridge build.

◆ How is your work with your week's project coming?

Day Six

◆ Do a Free Break exercise. Journey or simply shift consciousness and connect with your power animal for healing or advice or just to hang out with your new friend and play together.

◆ Bridge build.

Day Seven

◆ Do another Free Break exercise. Journey silently or shift consciousness and connect with your power animal for healing, advice or just to hang out with your new friend and play.

◆ Bridge build.

◆ Spend 20 minutes doing your Travelogue.

◆ Remind yourself of the commitments you have made for Week Three Project.

Travelogue

+ How many days this week did you do your Quantum Breaks? If you skipped a day or even two, why did you skip it? Record this in your Travelogue.

+ How was your experience of your power animal? What have you learned about his nature? What does he like and dislike?

+ Were there any 'struggle' issues that came up this week? If so, how did you handle them? If you ever felt you were not 'doing it right' see if you can figure out what message the spirits are sending you and how you need to deal with this. Are there any preconceived notions that you need to lay aside? If so what are they? Are you willing to let them go and play?

+ Which experience of connecting with your power animal did you like best? Describe it.

Painting is just another way of keeping a diary.

Pablo Picasso

quantum leap 4

Soar to the Heavens

I sweep aside concern with trivia. I have the vision of the eagle and hold the power of the angels. I am a winged being who soars above the mundane. I can introduce you to clarity, to lightness and to joy. I can tell you tales of past and future. I can bless you with the healing of golden light. My mind is cool but my love is great. Climb a rainbow, take flight and meet me in realms so fine you have no need of a body. I am the keeper of secrets of long ago and I have eyes to the future. My realms are fine as gossamer – made of pure light. Come float in the wonder of such crystalline beauty. Leap to the heavens. I will be there.

I am the Master of the Upper Realms

This week your journeying really takes off. You take your maiden voyage to the upperworld to meet the Wise One. Here in the domain of angels and archetypes you can seek healing or ask for answers to questions that concern you. You can transcend the everyday world for a time and be renewed by the radiance of these realms. You can even bring the fragrance of its beauty back with you on your return. Get ready to soar.

We live our lives inscrutably
included within the steaming
mutual life of the universe.
Martin Buber

It always seems a little strange to me that some people have so much trouble with the notion that everything in the universe is alive. I remember as a child knowing this very clearly. For instance I knew that the roses at the front of our house smiled on misty mornings when at last the sun reached their petals. I heard pleasant groans from the empty house next door when one morning a big furniture van pulled up in front of it and men with huge arms and hands loaded sofas and boxes and tables and mirrors into it. It licked its paws the way a dog does after finishing off a leg of lamb stolen from the kitchen counter.

TALKING TO MACHINES

That the world was full of spirits was of course something nobody had ever said to me. I somehow just took it for granted because I sensed them everywhere. And because I did, occasionally, I would talk to things. Like washing machines for instance. Washing machines? I know. It sounds pretty weird. What could be more absurd than talking to a washing machine? Well of course I didn't just stand there and pass the day conversing with our washer. But when something would go wrong with it, my mother – who was not the most patient of women – would throw up her hands and shout to me, 'For god's sake Leslie, see if you can't do something with this thing.' Then she would waft through the kitchen doors to leave me alone with the offending appliance.

I knew absolutely nothing about washing machines. Neither had I any particular interest in them. But since my mother had put me on the spot I did the only thing I could think of doing: I stood in front of the washing machine and asked it what was wrong. Usually I would do this silently – telepathically I suppose. To my surprise, often I found I got some kind of answer. It didn't come in words, of course. I would get a sense that I should unscrew this bolt or move that thing from here to there, or pull something out from inside the drum. As I carried out these rather vague instructions, I would find myself muttering simple, childish things out loud like, 'But what is it you *need* me to do?' or 'Come on now, let's put you *right*.' Or 'Oh you *poor* thing.' More often than not, after fiddling with something here and twisting something there, the offending machine would start to work again. Then for a short time in our house I was a 'hero'. 'So clever,' my mother said, 'with mechanical things.' Only I knew the real truth. I was not clever at all – machines just told me what to do for them and I did it.

No pessimist ever discovered
the secrets of the stars,
or sailed to an uncharted
land, or opened a new
heaven to the human spirit.
Helen Keller

ANACONDAS AND OUTBOARD MOTORS

I think it takes a bit of time to become aware of the spirit in everything especially when, in our culture, the very notion that anything exists which is not totally material in nature is so drummed into us in school. When Michael Harner was first introduced to shamanism and began to practise it – some 37 years ago – in the upper Amazon, he had trouble with this 'spirit thing' too. He would hear the tribal people who were his teachers speak of 'the spirit of the anaconda' or the 'spirit of the tree'. At first he balked at their words. They sounded strange to his Western ear, trained as it was in left-brained thinking. But after experiencing for himself these powerful spirits on journeys in non-ordinary reality, he came to accept their reality. 'It was when they started talking about "the spirit of the outboard motor" that they really lost me,' says Harner. 'Then I began to think about it. I realized that if you are a native of the Amazon living deep in the forest and somebody breaks their neck, being able to connect with the spirit of the outboard motor can be life-saving. After all it is the only thing that can get you to a Western hospital where you can get it set.'

When it comes to spirits in human form, history is full of people who have encountered them. They usually appear only after someone has experienced great loneliness, is exhausted, has been carrying out monotonous tasks or finds himself in the midst of life-threatening circumstances. Such experiences activate the consciousness matrix by reducing our usual cognitive functions and triggering awareness shifts thereby creating openings into quantum realms. They can also bring about a temporary disintegration of our personality and ego structures, forcing us to lay aside our cultural conditioning, reducing the stream of habitual thoughts and behavioural patterns and opening the way to transpersonal dimensions of experience in which we are more aware of spirit energies.

It's only when we truly know and understand that we have a limited time on earth – and that we have no way of knowing when our time is up – that we will begin to love each day to the fullest, as if it was the only one we had.
Elisabeth Kübler Ross

Where there is great love there are always miracles.
Willa Cather

THE GREATER THE NEED

From the point of view of traditional shamanism, compassionate spirits are said to show up wherever there is great human need for healing, comfort, wisdom or advice. The greater the need, the more their compassion is aroused, and the more likely they are to come to our aid. Mountaineer Reinhold Messner in 1978 found himself accompanied by helping spirits in life-threatening conditions during his solo ascent of Nanga Parbat. Scientist Thelma Moss at UCLA, known for her research in Kirlian

… I speak of 'spirits', it is because that is the way shamans talk within the system. To practice shamanism, it is unnecessary and even distracting to be preoccupied with achieving a scientific understanding of what 'spirits' may really represent and why shamanism works.

Michael Harner

photography, was contacted repeatedly by a spirit who called himself 'Benjamin Franklin'. She preferred to think of him as the 'Old Wise Man archetype'. At one point when she had come to a total impasse in her work, he arrived to give her the name of a book which she then went to and found the information she needed to continue her research.

Some spirit stories make great adventure reading. Like that of Captain Joshua Slocum who sailed round the world at the turn of the century. A life-threatening storm overtook him mid-Atlantic while he was seriously ill and too weak to handle the boat. At that point a spirit appeared looking completely lifelike. He told Slocum that in his lifetime he had been the helmsman of Christopher Columbus' ship the *Pinta*. He said that he liked to come to the rescue of sailors in trouble. He took the wheel from Slocum and looked after the boat until the storm had passed. In the history of shamanism such occurrences are commonplace. A shaman is often given his guardian spirit after a vision quest where he goes out into the wilderness to fast and pray for power and direction in his life.

PROJECTION OR REALITY

I don't believe; I know.

Carl Jung

Twentieth-century psychologists once dismissed spirits completely, insisting that people who saw them are naïve, only anthropomorphizing – 'projecting' their human feelings onto inanimate or imaginary objects. In more recent years most psychologists have tended to explain them as 'psychic forces' within an individual's subconscious that are in need of integrating. But with the advent of so much evidence from consciousness research, coupled with the more holistic and ecological worldviews now being used in physics and biology to describe reality, this is changing rapidly.

They tend to undergo transformation as they discover the incredible safety and love of the normally hidden universe. The cosmic love they repeatedly encounter in their journeys is increasingly expressed in their daily lives.

Michael Harner

Mathematician and cosmologist Brian Swimme, author of *The Hidden Heart of the Cosmos,* believes that we have somehow lost our ability to commune with the spirit of things around us. 'Early humanity,' he says, 'was profoundly attuned to communion, community and mutuality. They were deeply embedded in communion and literally identified with all the environment in which they found themselves. For early humans the rivers literally sang and the sun had feelings.' His work – a mixture of well-founded science and heart-felt poetry epitomizes the changing views on spirit and its relationship to consciousness.

SPIRITS OF THE HEIGHTS

Meanwhile, the meticulous research of Stanislav Grof into altered states of consciousness shows that when his subjects shift into quantum states – which Grof refers to as *holotropic* states – they consistently encounter spirit guides, teachers, animals and other guardians. In his book *The Adventure of Self-Discovery* Grof says, 'The subjects perceive these beings as suprahuman entities existing on higher planes of consciousness and higher energy levels. Sometimes they appear quite spontaneously at a certain stage of the spiritual development of the individual; other times they suddenly emerge during an inner crisis, responding to an urgent call for help … Sometimes the spirit guides have a human form with a distinctly numinous quality. Other times they appear as a source of radiant light or a powerful energy field. Many subjects explain that they do not actually have any sensory perceptions of their guides; they simply sense their presence.' He then goes on to describe in some detail the elaborate guidance, healing and useful practical information which can be given to subjects by these spirit friends encountered in non-ordinary reality.

SNAKES AND LADDERS

In most shamanic traditions and in the world myths that have developed out of them there are three levels of non-ordinary reality. You have learned to journey to the lowerworld. In quantum leap 7 you will be travelling in the middle realms. Now it is time to sail upwards to the heavens.

Just as the lowerworld is to be found by going downwards into the earth and then beyond into mythic domains, so the upperworld is a mythological realm that is found at the end of a path leading through a hole in the sky. In some cultures this opening can be a star such as the Pole Star which you go into, through and out the other side into the quantum realms of the Otherworld. Yakut shamans think of the stars as holes in the great tent of the sky which give access to the upperworld. Carib shamans in Guyana dance on ropes and swing in the air until a spirit invites them to come up, then they climb a spiral ladder. In Australia aboriginal shamans climb a rope too. Other cultures access the upperworld by entering into a sunrise or a sunset, by climbing the world tree, or going up twisted serpents which look a lot like the DNA molecule, or riding up a rainbow.

> We are not human beings having a spiritual experience. We are spiritual beings having a human experience.
> *Teilhard de Chardin*

The upperworld is quite a different place to the lowerworld – lighter, more ethereal somehow. Because of this, travel in the upper realms requires greater focus of intention than in the lowerworld. The practice you have had in the last two quantum leaps will have stood you in good stead for your upperworld explorations. Just keep coming back to your intention as you go and repeat it. That way you will find it quite a simple matter to focus as you move through these marvellous domains.

PLAN YOUR TRIP

You will begin your journey to the upperworld very much as you have your journey to the lowerworld – from a place in ordinary reality which you particularly like and which gives you access to some kind of movement upwards. It can even be the same place from which you journey to the lowerworld if, for instance, there is a tree which you can climb and then leap off upwards into the mythological realms. Or you can choose another place where you can go up a pole, a mountain, or the spire of a cathedral. You can go up on smoke if you like, like shamans in the Middle Ages did. The practice that women shamans had of going up the chimney to carry out upperworld journeys was demonized by the church. The women, who did much of the healing in the communities in which they lived, were ostracized, called witches, and punished for their ability to access spiritual power and healing directly without the intercession of a priest. When someone has direct access to spiritual power, established religion – and the medieval church had more power than anyone or anything – often sees this as a threat to its authority. As a result an estimated 7 million women were killed in Europe during the Middle Ages.

This was not a one-off occurrence, it has been true throughout history. In the twentieth century in the Soviet Union the state put to death every shaman they could find, almost wiping out the rich shamanic traditions there. Now, with the advent of religious tolerance and the work of the Foundation for Shamanic Studies which upon invitation sends teachers into areas that have largely lost their local shamanic practices, this is changing. One of the amazing things about teaching core shamanic practices to communities who have had most of their own local traditions destroyed is that they not only quickly learn the near-universal techniques such as those you have been working with in the past few weeks, but the learning of them brings them access to local practices that have been lost. It is as though such knowledge is embedded in our genetic material to be recovered with ease once you learn to access the consciousness matrix.

Here are some of the ways you can travel to the upperworld:

+ From a skyscraper.
+ From the top of a pyramid.
+ Up a stairway of the sun's rays.
+ From a cathedral spire.
+ From the top of a tree.
+ From the top of a tower.
+ From the top of a mountain.
+ Up a rainbow.
+ On a tornado or whirlwind.
+ Up the smoke from a fire.
+ Up a ladder.

MAKE YOUR CHOICE

Stop reading. Put the book down. Close your eyes and revisit in your imagination some place in ordinary reality you particularly like that provides access upwards into the sky and beyond to the mythological realms of the upperworld. It can be a place you are very familiar with or somewhere you have only seen once. Now go to that place and look around. Activate your senses so that it becomes very real for you. Decide where you are going to begin and end your upperworld journeys. Now write a description of your special place in your journal.

Like the lowerworld entrance, which was not into actual soil but rather through the earth and beyond, your upperworld entrance is not into outer space. Outer space with all the stars and galaxies is still ordinary reality. You will be going beyond the sky through an opening in time and space. You may find that you will gently drift through, or push through or even pop through some kind of a membrane. You may see it as a cloud or even a sheet of paper. If you need help then call on your power animal. Sometimes there is a white bird there to help you through. The upperworld has a number of levels to it – each one separated by a similar fine sheath which you will pass through as you go from one level to the next.

How is it that as many as a quarter of all people – and not just sensitives – have the ability to 'read' some aspect of the mind of the person with whom they interact?
Ervin Laszlo

But a symbol, a mythic symbol, does not refer to something which is known or knowable in that rational way. It refers to a spiritual power that is operative in life and is known only through its effects.
Joseph Campbell

THE WEEK AHEAD

Wherever shamanism is still
encountered today, whether in
Asia, Australia, Africa, or
North and South America, the
shaman functions fundamentally in much the same way
and with similar techniques –
as guardian of the psychic and
ecological equilibrium of his
group and its members, as
intermediary between the seen
and unseen worlds, as master
of spirits, as supernatural
curer, etc. The shaman is able
'to transcend the human
condition and pass freely back
and forth through the different
cosmological planes …'

Peter T. Furst

This week all the journey work you will be doing will be to the upperworld. You will be going to check out the lay of the land there, to meet a Wise One, to ask a question, to ask for healing, and to explore the various levels of the upperworld.

During your Free Breaks you can use the time either to further explore these realms, or to go back and use any of the previous techniques that we have done in any of the earlier Quantum Breaks for healing, for information, relieving stress, or any other purpose to which you want to put them. This week's project will be to represent in physical reality the qualities that you have perceived in the lowerworld and the upperworld.

READY, STEADY, GO

You are about to take your first journey to the upperworld. Please go back to page 99 and review Ticket to Ride – Journey Protocols before you begin if you need to. You will be using the sound of the drum to carry you there and back again – leaving from the place you have chosen and returning there afterwards. The upperworld is the hangout in non-ordinary reality of archetypal energies: gods and goddesses, wise old men and women, teachers, guides – even angels and other beings most of which you will probably experience in human form. From a shamanic point of view, the superhuman beings which Grof refers to are the spiritual connections you are going to begin making this week. You will be journeying to find the Wise One who will in the future act as your teacher and guide. You can take your power animal with you as you journey. Either call him to you as the drumming begins so he can help you on your path upwards or ask that he meet you there as soon as you pass into the upperworld. He can accompany you on your travels in the upperworld and return with you afterwards.

Quantum Break 13

MEET THE WISE ONE

Your intention:
TO GO THE UPPERWORLD AND FIND THE WISE ONE

✦ Be clear about where you are journeying from to the upperworld and where you will be returning to. Give yourself a moment to experience this place.

✦ Make arrangements with your power animal as to how and where you will meet up. Ask him for what you will need from him on this journey.

✦ Repeat to yourself your intention for the journey: TO GO TO THE UPPER-WORLD AND FIND THE WISE ONE. Remember that travel in the upper-world demands that you are very clear about your intention. Keep repeating it and you will have a focused journey and get to where you are going.

✦ As the drumming begins start your passage upwards moving to the top of what is going to carry you to the upperworld and then beyond.

✦ Look for the membrane. What is it like? Call for any help if you feel you need it to pass through.

✦ Now you will be at the first level of the upperworld. Look around you. You are looking for your Wise One – the one who will now and in the future act as your guide, spirit helper, and a major fount of healing, knowledge and wisdom for you.

✦ Is there anyone there? If so, ask them if they are your Wise One. If they don't indicate that they are, simply go up another level.

✦ Repeat the same procedure with the next spirit you encounter in human form and so on until you find a spirit who indicates in some way that it is your Wise One.

✦ Once you find your Wise One stop travelling.

✦ Now ask him or her to tell you about themselves and their origins. Do they have a name? Where do they come from? Have they ever lived upon the earth and if so when? If not where do they come from and from what time?

The Earth family has been not just all humans of diverse societies, but all beings. The mountains and rivers are beings too. In Hindi, the words Vasudhaiva Kutumbam mean 'Earth Family' the democracy of all life, all the little beings and the big ones with no hierarchy because you have no idea ecologically how things fit in the web of life.
Vandana Shiva

The shaman, however, has a social rather than a personal reason for opening the psyche as he or she is concerned with the community and its well-being; sacred action, then, is directed towards the creation of order out of chaos.
Joan Halifax

To the heavens, to the well at
the end of the world, to the
depth of the Underworld, to
the bottoms of spirit-filled
lakes and seas, around the
earth, to the moon and sun, to
distant stars and back again
does the shaman-bird travel.
All the cosmos is accessible
when the art of transformation
has been mastered.

Joan Halifax

♦ Ask your Wise One if there is anything in the upperworld that he or she wants to show you or tell you about.

♦ When the call back comes, thank your Wise One and any of your helpers or spirits and return quickly by retracing your steps to the place from which you began your journey.

Bridge Building

Make a record of your journey in your journal, whether or not you met your Wise One, what the upperworld is like, what was shown to you. If you did not meet your Wise One, don't worry, it will come next time. Did you remember to restate your intention whenever you lost focus? Did you remember to ask for whatever help you needed in finding the Wise One and moving upward? Don't forget you are travelling in quantum realms. Here you can call for and get whatever you need to help you fulfil any intention.

TROUBLESHOOTING

In my life's chain of events
nothing was accidental.
Everything happened
according to an inner need.

Hannah Senesh

There are two questions which I am frequently asked when I am teaching. The first is, 'What if I get disturbed while I am journeying? What should I do?' First of all, before you begin a journey you should make every effort you can to make it unlikely that you will be disturbed. Take the phone off the hook. Let others in the house know you will need to be undisturbed for half an hour. If despite all this you are interrupted while journeying, say someone comes into the room or the phone rings, simply deal with this intrusion from ordinary reality and then as soon as you can, using your drumming tape, journey back to the place in non-ordinary reality at which you were disturbed and return back again to your usual starting place. This is important since one of the basic principles of shamanic work is that you know very clearly where you are at any particular moment and that you always return to your starting place after a journey. In this way there is never any 'confusion' about anything.

The other question people ask is, 'Will I ever get "stuck" in non-ordinary reality?' The answer is no. You will not. You are working in very precise ways as you learn these practices. Precision is important too. It imparts skill and clarity to your travelling between realms of consciousness. Every shift in consciousness and every journey involves a commitment to carry it through to the end, at which time you emerge in the same place and state of consciousness from which you began. This makes all travel absolutely safe and means that consciousness shifting remains always under your control.

Quantum Break 14

QUESTIONING THE WISE ONE

Your intention:
TO MEET YOUR WISE ONE AND ASK A QUESTION

This time you will again journey to the upperworld and go to your Wise One. Once you get to him or her you will ask a question. It should be a question that you *care* about the answer to. It is rather useless to ask something like 'What colour is most appropriate for me to wear tomorrow' unless this particular issue happens to be of monumental concern you.

When asking a question of a wise spirit make sure that it is a *rich* question, one that does not just demand a 'yes' or 'no' answer. It could start with 'who', 'what,' 'why', 'how'. Generally speaking it is not best to use the words 'will' or 'should' because the answer you get will not be anywhere near so rich. It is also important not to have any words like 'or' or 'and' in your question simply because you will not know whether the answer you get relates to one part of the question or the other.

Before you begin your journey, write down the question you are seeking an answer to.

If you have to be sure about what you're experiencing in the moment you'll always subordinate the reality of the present to the certainties of the past.
Carl A. Hammerschlag

So the lively force of his mind
Has broken down all barriers,
And he has passed far beyond,
The fiery walls of the world,
And in mind and spirit
Has traversed the
boundless universe.
Lucretius

Living is a form of not
being sure, not knowing
what comes next or how …
The artist never entirely
knows. We guess. We may
be wrong, but we take leap
after leap in the dark.

Agnes de Mille

✦ Journey to the upperworld, and if you have not yet met your Wise One seek to meet him or her on this journey.

✦ If you have met your Wise One you will be returning to the place where you last met, following exactly the same pathway with your power animal and any other helpers that helped you on your first journey to the heavens.

✦ Once you meet the Wise One pay close attention to the first thing he or she does – do they show you something? Do they take you somewhere? Do they reach out to you or give you something? In the upperworld the Wise One tends to orchestrate everything that happens so from the moment you ask your question, be conscious of everything you see and everything that happens.

✦ You may get an answer to your question in words. More likely you will get symbols and experiences that you will then bring back and record.

✦ When the call back comes, thank the Wise One for the help that they have given, and retrace your steps as usual.

Bridge Building

Record everything that you remember from your journey. When doing an upperworld journey in search of an answer to a question, very often the full richness of the answer does not develop until after you are back in ordinary reality. So be aware over the next few days of anything else that comes to you in relation to the answer to this question which would be worthwhile adding to your journal.

Quantum Break 15

JOURNEY FOR HEALING

Your intention:
TO JOURNEY TO THE UPPERWORLD AND ASK FOR HEALING

✦ Journey to the upperworld and seek out your Wise One.

✦ Ask for healing.

✦ You may find that it is given immediately in the form of light or warmth being poured into you, you may find that you are given specific advice on diet or herbs or medical care that would be worthwhile seeking for your condition.

✦ You may find that your Wise One takes you someplace or shows you something that is directly related to the healing that you are asking for.

✦ Ask the Wise One if it is important that you return again to the upperworld for more healing.

✦ Thank your Wise One and any helpers for what is given and retrace your steps to where you started from.

Bridge Building

Come back and record what has occurred on your journey. Make sure you take note of any advice that your Wise One has given you in relation to things you can do in ordinary reality to encourage further healing. If you are given the names of specific foods, herbs, or health practices that may be useful to you, be sure to check them out by reading about them or speaking to people who know about them before you follow any advice of this kind.

Here in the West we have exorcized the spirits and cut ourselves loose from the living web of the world. Instead of seeing ourselves as physically and spiritually connected to family, clan and land, we now live chiefly by the mind, as separate individuals acting on and relating to other separate individuals and on a lifeless, dumb world beyond the body.
David Suzuki

Now we are no longer primitive; now the whole world seems not-holy. We have drained the light from the boughs in the sacred grove and snuffed it in the high places and along the banks of the sacred streams. We as a people have moved from pantheism to pan-atheism.
Annie Dillard

Hawaiians traditionally have viewed the entire world as being alive in the same way that humans are alive. They have thought of all of nature as conscious – able to know and act – and able to interrelate with humans … Hawaiians also viewed the land, the sky, the sea, and all the other species of nature preceding them as family – as conscious ancestral beings who had evolved earlier on the evolutionary ladder, who cared for and protected humans, and who deserved similar treatment (aloha'aina [love for the land]) in return.

Michael Koni Dudley

Quantum Break 16

CHARTING THE UPPER REALMS

Your intention:
TO GO TO THE UPPERWORLD AND EXPLORE

✦ Journey to the upperworld and go directly to your Wise One.
✦ Ask them to guide you in exploring the various levels of reality in the upperworld and teach you about the nature of each and what is to be found there.
✦ On the call back, thank them for what is given, for their time and attention, and for what they have shown or told you. Now retrace your steps to where you started from.

Bridge Building

This Bridge building begins the process of mapping the upperworld for you. You might like to write about your exploration, you might also like to begin to draw a preliminary map of the upperworld and what is found there. You will find that this 'map' will develop and become more and more rich as you journey there in the future.

FREE BREAKS

This week you can use your Free Breaks to go back and repeat any of the journeys you have done in the past weeks, or practise any of the techniques you have learned so far for any purpose you wish. I highly recommend, however, using at least one of these Free Breaks to return to capture the spirits of the upper and lower realms to continue your mapping of it.

HONOURING THE REALMS

Week Four Project

This week's project is to make something or find something that represents the quality and the energy that you experience on an upperworld journey. It could be a drawing you make or a piece of sculpture made with coloured paper or plastic. You will be making something or finding an object or objects you can bring together to represent the quality of the upperworld. Then you will be adding what you have made to your sanctuary. This week you will also be looking for an object that represents for you the quality of energy in the lowerworld. This might be the figure of an animal, perhaps your power animal, it could be a rock or some sort of drawing that you make. Make this a part of your sanctuary too. This kind of Bridge building helps bring the spiritual essence of both lowerworld and upperworld into your day-to-day existence. It also further enhances your ability to become a person who lives at ease with a foot in both worlds.

Tell me the story of the river and the valley and the streams and woodlands and wetlands, of shellfish and finfish. A story of where we are and how we got here and the characters and roles that we play. Tell me a story, a story that will be my story as well as the story of everyone and everything about me, the story that brings us together in a valley community, a story that brings together the human community with every living being in the valley, a story that brings us together under the arc of the great blue sky in the day and the starry heavens at night …
Thomas Berry

Bless a thing and it will bless you. Curse it and it will curse you … If you bless a situation, it has no power to hurt you, and even if it is troublesome for a time, it will gradually fade out, if you sincerely bless it.
Emmet Fox

CHECKLIST

Day One

✦ Read through the chapter and refamiliarize yourself with Ticket to Ride – Journey Protocols on page 99.

✦ Do Quantum Break 13 Meet the Wise One *go to the upperworld and find the Wise One.*

✦ Bridge build.

Day Two

✦ Prepare a question you would like to ask.

✦ Do Quantum Break 14 Questioning the Wise One *go to meet your Wise One and ask a question.*

✦ Bridge build.

✦ Read the instructions for Week Four Project on page 151 and decide how you are going to go about creating something to reflect the quality of the upperworld.

Day Three

✦ Do Quantum Break 15 Journey to Ask for Healing *to journey to the upperworld and ask your Wise One for healing.*

✦ Bridge build. Did you notice anything today that came in answer to the question you asked yesterday?

✦ Check out any herbs, medical practices, foods or any other advice that you were given when you are back in ordinary reality.

Day Four

✦ Do Quantum Break 16 Charting the Upper Realms *to go to the upperworld and explore with your Wise One.*

✦ Bridge build.

In shamanism, the maintenance of one's personal power is fundamental to well-being.
Michael Harner

Perhaps the coming together of our insights about the world around us and the world inside us is a satisfying feature of the recent evolution in science …
Ilya Prigogine and Isabelle Stengers

Use the light that dwells within you to regain your natural clarity of sight.
Lao Tzu

Most of us don't become what we can be because we can't see it's what we already are.
Carl A. Hammerschlag

Day Five

+ Repeat Quantum Break 16 or 15 *to explore the upperworld or to ask for healing.*
+ Bridge build.
+ How is your work with your week's project coming? Have you made or found things to represent the lowerworld or upperworld?

Day Six

+ Do a Free Break exercise. Use any of the Quantum Break exercises in any of the quantum leaps for whatever purpose you would like.
+ Bridge build.

Day Seven

+ Do a Free Break exercise. Use any of the Quantum Break exercises in any of the quantum leaps for whatever purpose you would like.
+ Bridge build.
+ Spend 20 minutes doing your Travelogue.
+ Finish off your project.

Travelogue

+ How many days this week did you do your Quantum Breaks? Are they starting to be more fun or are they still something you are doing because you are 'supposed to'? Record this in your Travelogue.
+ What was your experience of the upperworld like? Do you have a preference for either upperworld or lowerworld journeys?
+ How is your project coming? Do you find yourself relating to your sanctuary or is it something you have just created as part of your journey to freedom process?
+ How did your power animal behave in the upperworld?
+ Are there any issues that are still concerning you about your shamanic work? If so, what are they?

Shamans, medicine people, seers, and visionaries still practise the arts of healing and trance in various parts of the world. Many, in their different ways, are endeavouring to pass on the wisdom of the Ancient Ones to the people of today. They know that the traditions of the past are threatened by modern technology. But, as one shaman said to this author 'Many non-traditional people of the West seem not only to appreciate the "road" of the shaman, but also appear to have an affinity for the "Medicine Way".'

Joan Halifax

Quantum leap 5

Back to the Future

I ride through past and future weaving beginnings into ends. I spin yesterdays and tomorrows into endless spirals of being. I will lead you back beyond conception. I will show you the energetic architecture of your soul. I will introduce you to your seedpower. Through me you will discover your roots – lines of blood and energy which carry your power, blessings and challenges. Through my eyes you can look towards your future. Enter the timeless void with me and let your soul song be sung. Prepare yourself for the most difficult challenge you will ever face – to bear the splendour of seeing your own beauty.

I am the Timeless One

In Newton's static universe time travel was pure science fiction. Then Einstein came along with his space-time continuum, matter began to dissolve and quantum-relativistic physics made possible what shamans had been doing for 40,000 years. This week we are going to be working in and out of linear time, exploring the mysteries of enfolded reality through the past and the future. Right here is your ticket to ride.

Time, they tell us, is of the essence. I have never quite figured out what that means. The essence of what? I know that for most of us, time rules our lives and impedes our freedom. I have learned that it doesn't need to. Linear time is not the rigid structure we perceive. You can expand time in ordinary reality when you need more of it. You can access the past and the future – sometimes with pretty amazing results. That is what you will be doing this week.

Consciousness researchers, the greatest of which is Stanislav Grof, divide quantum or transpersonal experiences into three categories:

✦ Those which transcend space.
✦ Those which take you into the domains of mythology.
✦ Those which transcend time.

You have already begun to experience the first two. We will be looking even more closely at them in the next few quantum leaps. But for now, let's look at time.

TIME TRAVEL

Normally we experience ourselves as only being here and now. In our daily consciousness we are simply not aware of anything except what is happening in the moment. In fact we are only aware of what is coming to us through our senses. Right now we can't experience what happened last night, for instance. Of course we have a memory of last night, but memory is a very different kind of experience than actually being there. When it comes to experiencing the future, this is where we really feel helpless. The future hasn't happened to us yet so how can we possibly experience it? Well, we could fantasize about it, or we might make a computer model of it, or we could anticipate it, but none of these things are the same as experiencing the future.

Yet when you enter quantum realities, you *can* experience the past. Activate your consciousness matrix, direct your intention with clarity and you can find yourself in Concord, Massachusetts during the American revolution lying wounded on the earth. You can hear the sounds of the soldier's breathing next to you. You can taste the blood. You see the horses and the flags. You feel the coldness of the frost. You can even bring back new information about what it was like in Concord during the revolution. Extraordinary as this may seem, Grof, like British psychiatrist Arthur Guirdham, and many others, has recorded numerous cases by now where this has happened to people in holotropic states. And the information they acquire by moving back in time has later been validated through historical records. I have even had this experience myself. It happened long before I ever got involved with shamanic work. In certain cases you get a similar experience of the future. Reliable research records many instances of people experiencing an event or seeing it long before it actually occurs. Techniques for time travel form the crux of the work you will be doing in quantum leap 5. But to get a grip on such an extraordinary idea as being able to transcend time we need to go back and look at how the concepts of time and space which are part of the accepted worldview came into being and how they are changing as a result of twentieth-century scientific discoveries about the nature of the universe, many of which have not yet worked their way through to consensus reality. What follows may seem like a bit of a digression, but bear with me for the ground we will be covering is really important in breaking through the bars of imprisonment erected out of the limitations of conscious reality. It is inportant for freedom that we come to realize how transparent they really are.

To return to the root is to find the meaning,
But to pursue appearances is to miss the source.
Sengtsan

MAN WATCHED OVER BY GOD

Until the sixteenth century the Western worldview was based on Aristotelian philosophy and Christian theology. Aristotle was the first biologist. He distinguished between *matter* – that is substance, structure and quantity – and *form* – that is pattern, order or quality. Aristotle believed that form had no existence separate from matter, nor could matter exist without form. For him matter held the essential nature of all things as potentiality. And thanks to a process he called *entelchy*, which means 'self-completion', this essential nature became real – it actualized itself – through form. Aristotle created a highly structured logic based on these principles. It became the backbone of Western scientific and philosophical thought for 2,000 years. And together with the teachings of the Christian church, it created the worldview of a living, organic, spiritual universe created by God in which man, watched over by God, stood on the earth at the centre of the universe.

In the sixteenth and seventeenth centuries, this worldview was turned upside down. This was when the Scientific Revolution, associated with the work of Galileo, Kepler, and Copernicus, Descartes, Newton and Bacon took place. Each of them in his own way contributed to the destruction of the medieval worldview. Nicholas Copernicus

There is no domain of human interest that shamanism does not touch, for its world view is of an interconnected whole.
Rowena Pattee

blew the whole Western world apart when he announced that the earth was no longer the centre of the universe around which the sun and stars turned. The earth revolves around the sun, he insists. Galileo Galilei wiped out every trace of Aristotle's *form* from science and turned science into a discipline which eliminated all references to pattern, order or quality and became only a study of *matter* – that which can be objectively measured and quantified. Rene Descartes turned philosophy into a cold, analytical mind game. He announced *cogito ergo sum* – I *think* therefore I *am* – and separated the whole of reality into mind and matter. He formulated a method of analytic thinking based on breaking up complex ideas as well as things in the objective world into small pieces. Study the pieces, he said, and you will understand the behaviour of the whole. Within 50 years the whole of the living universe became nothing but a machine to be analyzed, manipulated and ordered. Even animals had no soul. As for gaining information about reality in any other way than analysis and observation, that was a complete impossibility.

THE UNIVERSE AS MACHINE

Once Galileo and Descartes built the conceptual foundations for reality as a perfect machine governed by mathematical laws, Isaac Newton came along and synthesized their work into Newtonian mechanics. In 1687, having established the law of gravity and universal laws of motion, Isaac Newton published – at his own expense – his *Philosophia Naturalis Principia Mathematica* and ushered in the modern age and the worldview which went with it. The world had become a fully deterministic mechanical machine. This was an enormously successful paradigm. It quickly became the model for all scientific disciplines. So much so that the very definition of being 'scientific' became synonymous with thinking in mechanistic ways. However, the role of consciousness and the energy of spirit were completely ignored. A kind of philosophical materialism took their place. For Newton, God created the universe as a system governed by mechanical laws – a universe which, once established, could be studied and completely understood.

Until the advent of quantum physics, post-Newtonian scientists held to Newton's image of the universe as a deterministic super machine. However, they dismissed Newton's idea of an intelligent creative divine power behind it, choosing to treat God as well as any awareness of spirit as embarrassing residues of irrational dark ages. Data gained through the senses during the course of objective analysis of the material world became the only criteria for doing science. Cartesian–Newtonian dualism – the total separation of mind and matter – came to dominate thinking in medicine, psychology, psychiatry and the natural sciences, and to create the materialistic, reductionist worldview.

EATING THE MENU

The consequences of this worldview have been enormous. On the up side it has enabled us to study in depth the things in objective reality from animals and rocks to disease organisms and structural characteristics of metals. It has enabled us to develop a technology far greater than ever before in human history – a technology that has created computers which store and relay information worldwide, and send rockets to the moon. On the down side, our Newtonian–Cartesian inheritance has separated the divine from material form so that we no longer look at a flower or a deer and see spirit. It has also disconnected us from our spiritual roots, suppressing knowledge of how to activate and make use of the consciousness matrix embedded within our DNA to access other levels of reality. It has even blinded us to its existence and deprived us of direct access to the spiritual powers of creation, wisdom, and healing.

It is not that the data about man's ability to do these things has been lacking – far from it. An enormous amount of brilliant scientific work has been done into the nature and power of consciousness. But run-of-the-mill science, burdened by a worldview that is too restricting, has almost completely ignored its existence. It has had to reject data that is incompatible with its theoretical framework inherited from Newton and Descartes. Gregory Bateson, a brilliant scientist and thinker who has examined this situation in depth described it all rather well once when he made the remark that when our scientists continue to make errors and omissions of this kind, they might one day go into a restaurant for a meal and end up eating the menu instead of the food. Grof describes the kind of blinkered thinking that has resulted from trying to get square blocks into round holes:

> 'If the universe is essentially a material system and physics is a scientific discipline that studies matter, physicists are the ultimate experts concerning the nature of all things and the findings in other areas should not be allowed to be in conflict with the basic theories of physics. Determined application of this type of logic resulted in systematic suppression or misinterpretation of findings in many fields that could not be brought into consonance with the materialistic worldview.'

By the end of the third decade of the twentieth century, virtually every major postulate of the earlier scientific conception had been controverted: the atom as solid, indestructible, and separate building block of nature, space and time as independent absolutes, the strict mechanistic causality of all phenomena, the possibility of objective observation of nature. Such a fundamental transformation in the scientific world picture was staggering, and for no one was this more true than the physicists themselves.
Richard Tarnas

A SEA OF ENIGMAS

Then when quantum physics arrived, bringing with it an avalanche of new experimental evidence and observations, the 300-year-old worldview on which all our science and technology had been based began to crumble. Since Newton physicists had subscribed to the belief that all physical phenomena can be reduced to the properties of hard solid material particles. Suddenly these so-called particles were dissolving right and left in the shifting enigmas of quantum-relativistic physics. Matter as 'solid stuff' vanished altogether. With it went the beautifully defined dimensions of absolute time and space. They quickly became subsumed beneath Einstein's space-time continuum. Scientists discovered – often to their horror – that a particle becomes a wave and a wave a particle depending on the consciousness of the observer looking at it. Suddenly consciousness was back into the picture. The intention and viewpoint of an observer had to be recognized as playing a central part in creating external reality which, since Newton, had seemed to be purely objective and impersonal. In his *Passion of the Western Mind* Richard Tarnas gives a lucid and precise description of these profound changes:

> 'The solid Newtonian atoms were now discovered to be largely empty. Hard matter no longer constituted the fundamental substance of nature. Matter and energy were interchangeable. Three-dimensional space and uni-dimensional time had become relative aspects of a four dimensional space-time continuum. Time flowed at different rates for observers moving at different speeds. Time slowed down near heavy objects, and under certain circumstances could stop altogether.'

EMERGING PARADIGMS

One of the fascinating parallels between shifting scientific paradigms and consciousness studies is the discovery by researchers that people in whom the consciousness matrix has been activated to become familiar with experiences in non-ordinary reality report perceptions of the flexibility of time and space that parallel the findings of physicists. In *Beyond the Brain* Grof describes the way transpersonal experiences undermine the conventional belief in time and space based reality:

There is now a growing body of evidence that the interconnecting holofield is a specific manifestation of the cosmic quantum vacuum. But, just what is the quantum vacuum? The term seems mysterious, yet it refers to one of the most important, and as yet least understood, aspects of the physical universe. A deeper look at it is eminently worth our while.

Ervin Laszlo

'Matter tends to disintegrate not only into playful energy patterns but into cosmic vacuum. Form and emptiness become relative and ultimately interchangeable concepts. After the individual has been confronted with a considerable sample of transpersonal experiences, the Newtonian–Cartesian world view becomes untenable as a serious philosophical concept and is seen as a pragmatically useful, but simplistic, superficial, and arbitrary system of organizing one's every day experience.'

The whole scattered world of lower things is gathered up to oneness when the soul climbs up to that life in which there are no opposites.
Meister Eckhart

Other fascinating scientific breakthroughs are slowly transforming our worldview and creating what has come to be known as the *emerging paradigm* out of which a new worldview is emerging: Rupert Sheldrake created a storm of controversy with his book *A New Science of Life: The Hypothesis of Formative Causation.* He put forward the concept of *morphogenetic fields* – non-physical form-generating fields which he suggests are causal agents in the development and maintenance of biological forms. Later in his *The Presence of the Past* he suggested that all natural systems from crystals to hamsters to human beings inherit a collective memory of their kind which has been shaped by morphic fields that carry a collective or pooled memory. This inherent memory is a *process*. It involves action at a distance and transcends conventional laws of both time and space. We will be looking at the implications of his findings working with the consciousness matrix, particularly in relation to the power of ritual, in the next quantum leap.

THE MAGIC OF HOLOGRAMS

Physicists David Bohm and Karl Pribram's *holonomic* thinking looks at the universe as a hologram in which all parts receive information about the whole. A hologram is a three–dimensional photograph of something. It comes out of a wave-interference pattern created by two intersecting beams of light stored on film. One beam arrives at the film directly while the other is scattered off the object being photographed. These two beams interact. Their interactions produce an interference pattern which encodes its characteristics on the surface. As this pattern spreads over the whole film, all parts of it get information about the light-reflective surface of the object. It creates an unusual full 3-D image which can be retrieved anywhere, including in space, simply by rebuilding the wave-interference patterns stored on any part of the film. In effect any part of the film contains an image of the whole although the smaller the portion of the film you are looking at, the less clear the image will be. When two or

Many psychedelic experiences appear to have a general quality similar to those in everyday life, with the sequences occurring in three-dimensional space and unfolding along a linear time continuum. However, quite typically, additional dimensions and experiential alternatives are readily available. The psychedelic state has a multilevel and multidimensional quality and the Newtonian–Cartesian sequences, if they occur, appear to be arbitrarily teased out of a complex continuum of infinite possibilities.
Stanislav Grof

Modern physics offers some fascinating possibilities based on its broader understanding of the nature of time. Einstein's theory of relativity, which replaced three-dimensional space and linear time with the concept of a four-dimensional continuum of space-time, offers an interesting theoretical framework for understanding certain transpersonal experiences that involve other historical periods. The special theory of relativity allows for a reversed flow of time under certain circumstances. Modern physicists have grown used to treating time as a two-directional entity that can move forward or backward. Thus, for example, in the interpretation of the space-time diagrams of high-energy physics (Feynman diagrams), the movements of particles forward in time are equivalent to the movements of corresponding antiparticles backward in time.

Stanislav Grof

more parts of the film are looked at at the same time, each part will surrender the same information.

Holograms make it possible to store an amazing amount of information. A small part of a holographic plate can conserve a vast range of wave-interference patterns. It is estimated that the entire contents of the US Library of Congress could be stored on a multi-superposed hologram the size of a marble. What scientists such as Bohm and Pribram suggest is that these properties of holographic information storage are likely to be the way that temporal connections are stored in nature. Nature appears to have a holographic memory based on some kind of information-holding and transmitting field – a holofield – which transmits holographic interfering wave patterns. This could be what Sheldrake is talking about with his morphic resonance. The brain, suggests Pribram, may be a hologram. So may the whole universe. It may well be that, when you enter quantum realms via the consciousness matrix, you tap into this holofield and gain access to information that transcends time and space – information which you have no need of your five senses to access.

MYSTERIES OF ENFOLDED REALITY

English-born physicist David Bohm was the most important pioneer of trans-disciplinary science since Einstein. Although a physicist of high repute (a protégé of Einstein, he wrote the textbook on quantum mechanics which was used in every English-speaking university in the world), Bohm was a generalist. He was also a student of the spiritual teacher Krishnamurti. Bohm's concepts are elegantly simple and enormously profound. He says that there are two dimensions or realms of reality. There is one which shows itself at the surface in physical and biological form as the material world. This he calls the *explicate order*. There is also a deeper level of reality which is unseen and which we therefore can only know indirectly. This he calls the *implicate order*. Implicate means 'folding inward'. He says that everything that occurs in time and space – the whole material world of the explicate order – is enfolded within the implicate order. Think of a vortex – a form which is pretty regular and stable but which has no real existence apart from the movement of the fluid in which we see it. The vortex may seem to be independent, yet its 'existence' comes entirely out of the movement of the flowing water. This, says Bohm, is how particles in physics show up as independent entities although they are really derived from the underlying enfolded implicate order. For Bohm there are no accidents in the universe. All things we observe around us derive from the implicate order and are an expression of the order in that realm. His work may have a great deal to contribute to our understanding of how accessing the energy of transcendent realms – his implicate order – makes it possible to use that energy to create, heal and bring about other changes in ordinary reality.

There are many other scientists too that have contributed greatly to the emerging paradigm that continues to erode the mechanistic worldview still held by most people. Founder and Director of the General Evolution Research Group and president of the Club of Budapest, Ervin Laszlo has written over 50 books. He has the remarkable ability to maintain the clarity of a child's vision although he carries the intellect of a giant. In addition to his revolutionary theory of *unified interactive dynamics,* Laszlo has provided a rich overview of the evolution of consciousness as it seeks to understand the universe. His book *The Whispering Pond, A Personal Guide to the Emerging Vision of Science* (my favourite) is both a brilliant synthesis of the emerging paradigm and a magnificent vision full of wisdom and hope. Another scientist who's work is help laying to rest the mechanistic worldview is Belgian Nobel laureate thermodynamicist Ilya Prigogine. Prigogine's theory of *dissipative structures* is being used to investigate the dynamics that make it possible for the physical world to evolve sequentially towards phenomena that are no longer purely physical.

THE ROAD AHEAD

It is very exciting stuff. The work of forward-thinking scientists and other visionaries such as Michael Murphy, Ken Wilber, Charles Tart, Robert McDermott, Brother David Stundl-Rast, Gregory Batson, Mathew Fox, Gary Zukav and Brian Swimme, is helping us move us towards a new understanding of how the physical universe produces life and mind as part of its ongoing process of self-creation and self-organization. It suggests that both the brain itself and nature as a whole is in some way a continuous medium that carries information in the form of wave patterns of information-conceiving and transmitting field. It brings centre stage the role that consciousness plays not only in the creation of so-called objective reality but also in enabling us to expand our awareness that there are more ways of gathering information and exploring reality than merely through the five senses. It is helping to propel us towards taking our place as multi-dimensional beings living in a multi-dimensional universe. And it takes us full circle

Meaning seems to leap out of matter, like a tiger out of a dark cave.
Ramakrishna

Matter, as we have seen, is best viewed as a product of space – more exactly, of the vaccum's universal zero-point field that fills space. The seemingly solid objects that populate our world, and the flesh and bones that make up our body, are not constructed out of irreducible building blocks we could properly call 'matter'. The things we know as matter – and that scientists know as mass, with its associated properties of inertia and gravitation – are the results of subtle interactions in the depth of this space-pervading field. In the new vision there is no 'absolute matter', only an absolute matter-generating energy field.
Ervin Laszlo

Ecstasy is a union of time and eternity through love.
Rowena Pattee

back to the discoveries of psychiatrists like Grof and Guirdham. People in altered states of consciousness not only have access to verifiable information from other times, but even the belief in the mandatory nature of linear time is questioned. As Grof says:

'... the linearity of temporal sequences is transcended in unusual states of consciousness. Scenes from different historical contexts can occur simultaneously and appear to be meaningfully connected by their experiential characteristics. Thus a traumatic experience from childhood, a painful sequence of biological birth, and what seems to be the memory of a tragic event from a previous incarnation can all appear simultaneously as parts of one complex experiential pattern. And again, the individual has the choice of focusing selectively on any one of these scenes, experiencing them all simultaneously, or perceiving them in an alternating fashion, while discovering meaningful connections between them. The linear temporal distance that dominates everyday experience is disregarded, and events from different historical contexts appear in clusters when they share the same strong emotion or an intense physical sensation of a similar kind.'

> The quieter you become,
> the more you can hear.
> *Baba Ram Dass*

BACK TO WORK

Thank you for bearing with me through this rather lengthy examination of shifting scientific paradigms and crumbling worldviews. I believe it is important as you work through the consciousness matrix in exploring non-ordinary reality to be aware that you are likely to find that many of your discoveries in the inner realms have remarkable echoes in the emerging paradigms of science, cosmology and creation spirituality. It seems to me that explorations in the inner world and the outer world are converging at this moment in history to make the experience of authentic power and freedom for each one of us more easily accessible.

Until now in *Journey to Freedom* you have been gathering the skills you need to explore non-ordinary realms and access their power. You have formed a strong personal relationship with your power animal. You have met your Wise One in the upperworld and practised your journeying techniques so you can move at will when you hear the sound of the drum into either the upper or lowerworld. You have been perfecting your skills in creating sacred space in ordinary reality through your weekly projects and you hopefully have also begun to create the structures in your life that allow hierophanies – those spontaneous appearances of sacred energy – to become more and more a part of it.

> In our former lives, we were rocks, clouds, and trees. We may have been an oak tree ourselves. This is not just Buddhist; it is scientific. We humans are a very young species. We appeared on earth only recently. We were plants, we were trees, and now we have become humans. We have to remember our past existences and be humble. We can learn the Dharma from an oak tree.
> *Thich Nhat Hanh*

Now is a good time to stop for a moment and pat yourself on the back for all of the work you have done. You have actually covered an enormous amount of ground both intellectually and experientially in very little time. A lot of the stuff you have been working with would be mind-blowing to someone who had not yet been through the journey work process. These are things which you cannot explain to anyone, you can only *experience* them.

THE WEEK AHEAD

Now it is time to travel beyond linear time. This week we will be moving back and forward in time to access power and information about the nature of your seedpower – the unique energetic architecture of soul which you brought into this world when you were born. We will be seeking the answers to the questions: 'Who am I?' 'What do I want?' 'What do I *think* is stopping me?' We will be moving towards the intergration of soul and outer personality that creates authentic power. You will be doing five different journeys this week, each of which transcends time. As your week's project you will be experimenting with shifting time in ordinary reality by expanding and contracting it. It should not only be a lot of fun but also hold some wonderful surprises.

TROUBLESHOOTING

The area you are most likely to have trouble with this week is a big one. It is difficult for most people when they do the first journey to explore the nature of their seedpower not to feel overwhelmed by the beauty of what they are confronted with. Just as we need to continually expand our worldview and become aware of shifting discoveries in science to keep us from becoming blinkered in our vision, so too do we have to keep breaking through and moving beyond the limitations placed on us by false ideas and descriptions about ourselves which we have grown up with and which we still carry around. When, as a child, we are told that we are stupid, or worthless, or hopeless, or ugly, or incapable, these notions become mummified concepts. We swallow them like stones. They weigh down our movement and keep us from experiencing our real nature. Commit yourself to laying aside all of these notions at least for the week – just letting go of them altogether and coming to what you are doing with a fresh and open mind. Try not to feel daunted by the beauty of what you see. It is likely to be pretty dazzling.

Once every people in the world believed that trees were divine, and could take a human or grotesque shape and dance among the shadows; and that deer, and ravens and foxes, and wolves and bears, and clouds and pools, almost all things under the sun and moon, and the sun and moon, were not less divine and changeable. They saw in the rainbow the still bent bow of a god thrown down in his negligence; they heard in the thunder the sound of his beated water-jar, or the tumult of his chariot wheels; and when a sudden flight of wild ducks, or of crows, passed over their heads, they thought they were gazing at the dead hastening to their rest; while they dreamed of so great a mystery in little things that they believed the waving of a hand, or of a sacred bough, enough to trouble far-off hearts, or hood the moon with darkness.
W.B. Yeats

EXPANDING TIME
Week Five Project

The active imagination thus induced will not produce some arbitrary, even lyrical, construction standing between us and 'reality', but will, on the contrary, function directly as a faculty and organ of knowledge just as real as – if not more real than – the sense organs.

Rowena Pattee

This week you will be experimenting with the shifting nature of time. This sounds like a very surprising thing to do. Indeed it can be. The first time I learned it could be done I was not only amazed but also tremendously grateful. I was writing a book – *Passage to Power* – which turned out to be much larger and longer in the making than I had anticipated. One day I realized that there was no way I could get the book finished in time for the deadline.

I did not know what to do. At this point I did a journey to a helping spirit and asked if I could expand time so I would have more time to get the book written. I was told that this is a simple matter.

This week your project will be to work with your power animal or your Wise One in ordinary reality to do just that. Call to them from ordinary reality and ask them to teach you to either expand time when you need more time for a particular task, or to contract time should you be kept waiting for something. See what happens and record this in your journal. Learning to expand and contract time depends almost entirely on practice. The more you do it the easier it gets. Should you, after a few days, find that it's not working for you, then as part of your Free Break this week, journey to your Wise One and ask if he or she can give you advice or take you to someone who will show you how to expand time.

Quantum Break 17

STEP INTO SEEDPOWER

Your intention:
TO FIND THE ANSWER TO THE QUESTION 'WHO AM I?'

Today you will be exploring the unique nature of your seedpower and examining the energetic architecture of your soul.

+ Check back to Ticket to Ride – Journey Protocols on page 99 if you need to refresh your memory about journeying.
+ Go to the place in nature from which you journey to the lowerworld and prepare yourself by activating your senses.
+ Repeat your intention for the journey so it is clear in your mind.
+ When the drumming begins, journey to the lowerworld. Ask your power animal to take you way back in time to when your soul decided it would take on a material body – way back before birth, even before conception itself.
+ Look around you. Ask the questions 'Who am I?' 'What is my deepest nature?'
+ Explore the quality of the energy that is your soul.
+ Ask your soul to show you how it has structured the unique energetic architecture of your seedpower – that embryo which enables the soul's unique nature to take on form. What is your seedpower like?
+ Ask your soul why it has chosen this particular kind of seedpower for you to bring into the world. See what it has to show you or to tell you.
+ Now call on your power animals and helping spirits to gather as much information as you can about your own unique nature. They may speak to you in words, they may take you and show you something in metaphor or symbols.
+ Don't be surprised if what you are shown is far more beautiful than anything you have ever seen before.

To orient your life around a structure of some other human being's understanding is to worship a false god. It is to lock yourself into a framework of someone else's prejudice, however well intentioned. It is to prefer the past-oriented knowledge of another to your own present-moment perception. It is to doubt both yourself and the Creator who would, if you permit it, awaken within you.

Ken Carey

◆ For a few moments, let yourself bask in the wonder of what you experience.
◆ When the call back comes, thank whatever helping spirits have been present, let them know that they can go now, then return to ordinary reality.

Bridge Building

In the cosmology of the new
millennium the Sun's
extravagant bestowal of energy
can be regarded as a
spectacular manifestation of
an underlying impulse
pervading the universe. In
the star this impulse reveals
itself in the ongoing giveaway
of energy. In the human heart
it is felt as the urge to devote
one's life to the well-being of
the larger community.
Brian Swimme

Bridge building after this journey is enormously important. I find that generally it works better if you find some visual way of expressing what you have found – for instance drawing it using colour or sculpting it. You may even find that you can go out in nature and find various objects to put together to create a sculpture that epitomizes the quality of your soul energy. You can, of course, also make notes in your journal or add words to your drawing or sculpture.

One of the important things about Bridge building in this way when doing a seedpower journey, is that any images you get from the journey can be great to work with later in ordinary reality. Put them in the room you work in or hang them on the wall in the room you sleep in or spend a great deal of time in. Then just let yourself hang out with them. You will find as you do that the bonds between your seedpower and the outer expression of your personality become stronger and stronger and you experience more and more of your authentic power.

SACRED ENERGETIC ARCHITECTURE

It was Meister Eckhart who taught that the soul is generative in nature. It has, he insisted, the power to create form out of the intention which is encoded within its very substance. Being clear about smaller intentions is central to every journey you take and everything you choose to do in your life. Yet it is even more important to become conscious of your *master intention* which the very energetic architecture of your soul has been designed to carry out. To discover your master intention, you will need to penetrate deep into your own seedpower where this information is encoded. For in bringing to fruition what Eckhart calls our 'soul's generative power' each of us needs to uncover our unique master intention and align ourselves with the sacred architecture of our own soul. That is what your next journey is all about.

Quantum Break 18

DECODING THE SEED OF INTENTION

Your intention:
TO FIND OUT THE ANSWER TO THE QUESTION 'WHAT DO I WANT?'

◆ Follow the same protocols as in Quantum Break 17.

◆ Again you will be journeying beyond time and space.

◆ Ask your power animal, Wise One or other helping spirits to take you on a journey deep into the genetic encoding of your seedpower to discover what your master intention was in entering this life.

◆ Let yourself go right into the seed, deeper and deeper. What do your see? What is it like inside?

◆ Once you have journeyed deep into the soul-seed that is you, ask the question 'What is my master intention in coming into this life?' What is it your seedpower has been perfectly designed to grow into? What is it you most want to do or to be?

◆ Now allow yourself to connect as fully as possible with your master intention. Let the power of it enter every cell of your body, every sinew, every space between every molecule. How does it feel to do this?

◆ When the call back comes, thank your spirit helpers and return.

The body feels the things of our spirits that our minds never thought of.
Carl A. Hammerschlag

The only devils in the world are those running in our own hearts. That is where the battle should be fought.
Mahatma Gandhi

Bridge Building

Record the information that you have brought back about what your master intention was when you chose to take a human body. This will bring you the deepest answer to the question, 'What do I want?'. Note down in words what you discovered.

Quantum Break 19

GRACELAND

Only through being yourself
can you give to the others in
your world your greatest gifts.
To do any less betrays both
them and yourself.

Ken Carey

Your intention:
TO UNCOVER THE GIFTS OF GRACE THAT HELP YOU FULFIL
YOUR INTENTION

Like the tiny seed which knows exactly how to grow into the unique flower it is
designed to become, your own unique seedpower not only carries a clear master
intention. Within its encoding you will also find special gifts of grace which
empower the unfolding of that intention. You may be the kind of person who
has a wonderful ability to create harmony among those you live and work with.
Your grace-bestowed strengths may be things like determination or a natural
sense of beauty, a keen intellect, an ability to make just about anything with
your hands. Each of us have many strengths for living out our master intention.
The more aware we are of them the more graceful this process becomes.

I live near the abyss,
I hope to stay
Until my eyes look at
a brighter sun
As the thick shade of the
long night comes on.

Theodore Roethke

◆ Once again you will journey back in time to that time long before birth, before
conception, when the nature of your seedpower was being formed.
◆ Ask your power animal, Wise One or other helping spirits to make known to
you the special strengths and powers which have been woven into your seedpower as a gift of grace to enable you to carry out your master intention.
◆ Let yourself connect fully with your gifts of grace. What are they? Feel them
in every part of your being, enjoy and give thanks for them.
◆ When the call back comes thank your helpers and return.

Bridge Building

You might like to represent your gifts of grace either in visual form or through words, or both.

BLESS YOUR ENEMIES

I love the idea of worthy opponents. Life is just like that. Not only do we come into being with a master intention and gifts to help us carry it out, we also carry a collection of challenges which can strengthen our master intention and hone the clarity and beauty of its expression in our life. They are the fire that tempers steel – worthy opponents that help make the expression of who we really are more true, clear and powerful.

Quantum Break 20
WORTHY OPPONENT JOURNEY

Your intention:
TO DISCOVER WHAT CHALLENGES EMPOWER YOUR MASTER INTENTION

✦ Follow the protocols for Quantum Break 20 journeying deep into the past with the help of your power animal, Wise one and other helping spirits.
✦ Ask to be shown the worthy opponent challenges that your soul chose to weave into its seedpower. What are they? How have they been designed to express themselves in your life?
✦ Find out how best you can work with each to express your master intention in your life. Sometimes worthy opponent challenges carry the greatest power of all to help us become what we have chosen to be in this life.
✦ When the call back comes, thank your spirits and return.

Without suffering, happiness cannot be understood. The ideal passes through suffering like gold through fire.
Fyodor Dostoevsky

Bridge Building

What do your worthy opponents look like? Can you draw them? Try writing down your challenges and whatever insights you have about what they are asking from you and how they can empower you. We will have a chance to work with them in a future quantum leap.

Coming to know your master intention and working with it can be an enormously unifying experience. As you become more and more familiar with it – not in an intellectual way but by actually letting yourself sense its presence in every cell of your body – the more unified you begin to feel. The debris and confusion we all have from taking on other people's ideas of who we are and what we should do gradually dissolve away.

Quantum Break 21

LEAP FORWARD IN TIME

Your intention:
TO EXPLORE HOW YOUR MASTER INTENTION CAN UNFOLD IN THE FUTURE

✦ This time you will journey not into the past but into the future.
✦ Ask your power animal, Wise One or other helping spirits to take you five years ahead from today and show you what the graceful unfolding of your seedpower in service of your master intention can look like.
✦ Once more, pay close attention to what they do or show you. See where they take you. Notice how you feel as that alignment between your soul and your personality grows stronger. How does it feel to be more and more truly who you really are?
✦ What you find five years ahead may surprise you with its richness.
✦ Let yourself explore it and enjoy it.
✦ When the call back comes, thank your spirits and return.

Bridge Building

Record your findings in any way you feel is approproate.

FREE BREAKS

Use your two Free Breaks this week to explore any of the journeys you have already done this week in greater depth, or to go back and use any techniques in any previous leaps to fulfil any purpose to which you want to put them.

CHECKLIST

Day One

+ Read through the chapter as far as the first Quantum Break if you can.
+ Do Quantum Break 17 Step into Seedpower *to find the answer to the question 'Who am I?'*.
+ Bridge build.
+ Read the instructions for Week Five Project on page 166 and begin to work on it.

Day Two

+ Do Quantum Break 18 Decoding the Seed of Intention *to find out the answer to the question 'What do I want?'*.
+ Bridge build.
+ Notice if your worldview has shifted.

Day Three

+ Finish reading the chapter if you have not already done so.
+ Do Quantum Break 19 Graceland *to discover what you have been given by grace to carry out your master intention*.
+ Bridge build.
+ Don't forget to work on your project.

The real voyage of discovery consists not in seeking new landscapes, but in having new eyes.

Marcel Proust

A man might die a thousand deaths in one day and find a joyful life corresponding to each of them.

Johannes Tauler

Day Four

✦ Do Quantum Break 20 Worthy Opponent Journey *to discover what challenges empower your master intention.*
✦ Bridge build.

Day Five

✦ Do Quantum Break 21 Leap Forward in Time *to explore how your master intention can unfold in the future.*
✦ Bridge build.
✦ How are you getting on with your project?

Day Six

✦ Do a Free Break exercise of your choice.
✦ Bridge build.

Day Seven

✦ Do a Free Break exercise of your choice.
✦ Bridge build.
✦ Spend 20 minutes doing your Travelogue.
✦ Complete any work still left to do on your week's project.

Travelogue

✦ Be sure to write your Travelogue for the week. How many days did you do your Quantum Breaks this week? Are you beginning to enjoy them – at all?
✦ What was the experience of going back in time like for you? Was coming face to face with your own unique nature surprising?
✦ How did you find the expanding and contracting time experiences? Did they work for you? Did you do an extra journey to your Wise One for advice?
✦ Were there any issues that arose for you out of the difference between your ordinary perception of yourself in day-to-day life and meeting your seedpower?

quantum leap 6

Rites of Passage

I spin the threads of your intention. I weave patterns of energy into material form. I will teach you the power of ritual gleaned from your soul. Actions carried out to honour your truth and nurture its unfolding bless the world around you. I can show you how negative habits restrict your freedom and teach you to dissolve them away. For they are nothing more than ancient baggage, empty of meaning except to remind you that all is resonance. A gesture here, a word there, imbued with compassion and clear intent when repeated again and again marries the sacred with the mundane. Make the craft of ritual a part of your life and you learn the art of wholeness.

I am the Master of Ritual

Rituals are a powerful force in your life. They can either bind or free you depending on whether they are consciously chosen or unconsciously lived out as constricting habits. This week you will be looking at how to deal with rituals that don't serve your soul's purpose. We will also be exploring the immense power of sacred rituals – those that carry the fragrance of quantum reality practised with clear intention – life changing stuff.

The ability to ride the waves of life, letting even the hard times empower rather than diminish you depends on learning to live comfortably with a foot in both worlds. One of the most effective tools you can use to come to do this is ritual. The daily and weekly practice of life-affirming rituals gradually leads to an ongoing experience of the sacredness of the world around you. It is also another powerful method for Cocoon Building, so when challenging transformations arrive, going through them becomes a more graceful process. Practising simple rituals can help you experience a blessed connection to everything around you – from the plant on your desk, the food that you eat and the work that you do, to the drug-burdened homeless kids with stud-riddled bodies whose souls cry out for an experience of transcendence.

But there are rituals and rituals. Those that we enter into with full awareness, clear intention and compassion for all life (there's that old familiar duo, intention and compassion again) can change the whole quality of our existence. They anchor us in spiritual truth and they celebrate milestones on our journey by making us aware of the sacredness of our own pathway. The other kind of rituals, those which we take part in unconsciously – by this I mean the repeated acting out of destructive habits and the ceaseless repetition of negative thought patterns – imprison us. Each of us walks around with our own unconscious negative habits. Usually we have carried them around for so long that we come to think they are part of us. They restrict our freedom and impede our experience of authentic power. This week you can take a good hard look at negative unconscious rituals and see how they tend quite naturally to fade as you make stronger and stronger connections between your soul and your personality. You will also be working with powerful self-directed and consciously chosen rituals that bring more sacred energy into your life, enriching your relationship to yourself and to the world around you.

RITES OF PASSAGE

The lives of people from tribal cultures are full of positive rituals. They are used to mark the coming of a child, the death of an elder, the puberty of a boy, the first menses of a girl. A ritual is a form of worship, celebration or affirmation carried out through words, gestures or acts. It creates sacred time and space in ordinary reality through which we can come face to face with the important issues in our lives and give them the focus they are calling for. Rituals make it possible for you to find new ways of seeing, to open yourself to new growth and to transform crises into opportunities. The words, gestures and acts involved in a ritual have no power in themselves and no meaning either unless they have been imbued with sacred intention. A few years ago I attended a beautiful wedding. Everything was perfect – the setting, the costumes, the order of events, yet the experience was draining not only for me but for the other guests present because the rituals of the ceremony, instead of being made pregnant by an awareness of the sacredness of the act of joining man to woman and woman to man, had been replaced by concern for making a social impression. Everybody seemed obsessed with how it would all look to the camera. When it comes to ritual *intention* is everything.

The bad habit rituals we are prey to – addictive eating, self-blame, emotional dramas with people, self-criticism and abuse – are not fuelled by free choice and a sense of connection with the sacred soul. They are habitually learned responses which you absorb from childhood and the world around you. Yet both bad habits and positive rituals operate in very much the same way. To understand how this is so, the most useful model I have ever found is not psychological, but one that is developing out of the emerging paradigms of leading-edge science.

Many thinkers trace the origins of our particular and violent fall from grace, our exile from the garden, back to Plato and Aristotle, who began a powerful process of separating the world-as-abstract-principle from the world as experience – dividing the mind, that is, from body, and human beings from the world they inhabit. In the process they laid the groundwork for experimental science.
David Suzuki with Amanda McConnell

VACUUM-BASED HOLOFIELDS

It all goes back to theories that describe information-holding and transmitting fields – to the work of David Bohm and Karl Pribram, Rupert Sheldrake and other visionary scientists. They attempt to define and describe subtle yet all-pervasive connections in space and time which, by all the laws of mechanistic Newtonian–Cartesian science are impossible, yet which good experimental evidence now confirms most certainly exist. Quite apart from discoveries in physics, even the world's leading biologists from N.K. Kolciov in the former Soviet Union, Ervin Bauer in Hungary and Paul Weiss in Austria and the late Yale biologist Harold Saxon Burr all in one way or another have affirmed interconnections between all things in the universe that go far beyond the known laws of conventional science.

Until now science has recognized only four kinds of universal fields in nature: gravitational, electromagnetic, and strong and weak nuclear fields. What emerging paradigm scientists are suggesting is the existence of a fifth field which appears to behave like a holofield. Even as far back as 1967 the highly conservative Harvard astrophysicist Harlow Shapley asked if there is not 'an additional entity, a fifth one' in the universe.

Could it be that several people meditating together enjoy some kind of collective consciousness – and that the focused collective consciousness of a group of people affects the bodily condition of other people?
Ervin Laszlo

If this fifth entity exists many scientists believe it probably has to do with the creation and evolution of life.

THE FIFTH ENTITY

Until 1948 the universe was believed to have existed as a static object throughout all eternity. Then the Big Bang theory arrived which is now believed to have brought the universe into being. This 'new' universe is not something static ruled as Newton and his followers believed by a series of immutable laws. It is an evolving process which appears to be being continuously shaped and reshaped in the manner of its unfolding. And according to most scientists working within the emerging scientific paradigms, we humans can play a significant role in its evolution now and in the future.

Since the advent of quantum physics, scientists have been wrestling with how two photons which are separated in certain conditions – no matter how far apart they are, can change each other. Meanwhile parapsychologists have been trying to figure out how two people can connect with each other through telepathy and how prayer and visualization and shamanic practices can bring about measurable changes to ordinary reality. All the scientific explorations in these areas point to the existence of a fifth entity – perhaps a vacuum-based holofield – which cannot as yet be measured but which is affected by human consciousness and which most certainly acts upon our own lives and all things in the universe. Meanwhile, the evidence that mind affects machine – usually the hardest to accept from the Newtonian–Cartesian worldview – is growing rapidly.

At Princeton University researchers from the School of Engineering found that the output of random event generators is significantly altered when these machines are put in the presence of groups of people whose attention is focused on a particular goal, as well as when the members of the group share an emotional experience. The statistical probability of such things happening is more than 5,000 to 1 and yet it consistently happens. Such effects add fuel to the concept of a consciousness 'field' as an agency for creation order even in random physical processes.

Focusing your intention and carrying out simple rituals is a powerful means of creating order and harmony both in your own life and your environment as a whole. The scientist who has done more than any other to make known his own particular definition and approach to fifth entity research is Rupert Sheldrake. And his work is directly relevant to the power of ritual in our lives.

FIELDS OF INFLUENCE

A field is an area of influence. For Sheldrake the interconnected fifth entity is a field of morphic resonance. Like the well-accepted fields of influence – the electromagnetic, gravitational and weak and strong nuclear fields – it cannot be seen yet it is known by its effects. Everything in the physical world, says Sheldrake – from an atom to an elephant – has its own unique morphic field. These fields contain 'memories' of its past experience as well as potential information for its future development and behaviour. The caterpillar, for instance, holds the morphic field for the butterfly, the acorn for the oak tree. Morphic resonance works together with an organism's genetic inheritance to carry the memory of a species. It gives form to an individual organism's body and helps direct its growth.

In the realm of human behaviour our morphic resonance not only carries information of our ancestral memories but of our cultural conditioning, our belief systems, our mythology, our intentions, our emotional patterns and our thought patterns. And this is true of inanimate objects as well. The regularities of nature are more an outcome of habit registered as information in morphic fields than so-called natural law.

Salt, according to Sheldrake, crystallizes the way it does because it has crystallized in that particular way so many times before. The more salt crystallizes, regardless of when or where this happens, the memory of the process is carried on morphic fields to other saline solutions which then find it easier to crystallize the same way again simply because it has been done so often in this form before. The same is true of new ideas. This may well explain why so often in history the invention of a particular instrument or process has taken place simultaneously in different areas of the world by different people. Or why the principles of core shamanism have been practised throughout history by tribal people in various areas of the globe who have had no physical or cultural contact. Thanks to universal morphic resonance, new ideas and attitudes can spread much more quickly than they would otherwise – quite beyond the effect of the media and the Internet. The implications of the existence of such a fifth entity force in the universe is enormous. When enough people dream visionary dreams of the future, or experience expanded states of consciousness whether or not they are connected by culture, they may be able to raise the consciousness of the world and change the course of history thanks to the interconnectedness of everything in the universe.

I think this is a rich concept, morphic resonance. Its implications for ritual makers at the end of the twentieth century are profound.
Matthew Fox

We were born out of the Earth Community and its infinite creativity and delight and adventure. Our natural state is intimacy within the encompassing community. Our natural genetic inheritance presents us with the possibility of forming deeply bonded relationships throughout all the million species of life as well as the nonliving components of the universe. Any ultimate separation from this large and enveloping community is impossible, and any ideology that proposes that the universe is nothing but a collection of pre-consumer items is going to be maintained only at a terrible price.
Brian Swimme

THE BLUETIT ENIGMA

In the realm of evolution there are many examples to indicate that this really is what is going on. In England at the beginning of the twentieth century a system of milk delivery was started where bottles of milk were delivered to people's doorsteps. After 20 years or so, bluetits in Southampton started piercing the tops of milk bottles and drinking the cream from the top. This turned out to be a very successful habit. It spread like wildfire through the city. Of course there were a few tragic cases when bluetits were drowned when they got their heads stuck in milk bottles, but most of the birds ended up with a free meal each day.

Before long the same behaviour pattern showed up among bluetits in other cities. The rate at which this occurred was carefully monitored by curious observers throughout Britain. Now bluetits are home-loving birds. They almost never stray very far from their small territory. So, at the time, biologists concluded that all these enthusiastic bluetits must have been making independent discoveries about milk bottles in all these different cities at around the same time. Before long zoologists found that the habit was spreading and speeding up. Professor of Zoology at Oxford, Sir Alistair Hardy, found the phenomenon so remarkable that he went so far as to suggest it might have been the result of telepathy – a comment which probably did his scientific credibility little good. But from the point of view of the emerging paradigm this is exactly the kind of effect you would expect from the evolutionary nature of morphic resonance.

CATCH THE HABIT

The next chapter of the bluetit saga comes from Holland. Dutch birds began doing it. Soon the behaviour pattern spread so that by the time of the Second World War bluetits all over Holland were stealing milk. Then the Germans invaded and milk deliveries ceased. It was not until 1948 that they began again. Bluetits don't live more than three or four years. This means that there were no bluetits around in 1948 that could have remembered what Sheldrake calls 'the golden age of free cream.' Nonetheless the habit established itself once again all over Holland and Britain within two or three years. This is a beautifully documented case which illustrates very well what Sheldrake is talking about.

Another area where Sheldrake's fifth entity hypothesis has many implications is in the realm of memory. Morphic resonance depends on similarity. The more similar something is to something else the stronger the resonance between them will be. This is why organisms are most like themselves in terms of what they were like in the past. For instance, I, Leslie, am more like how I used to be than I am like you. So as a general principle the most powerful morphic resonance acting on a person is his own past experiences. This enables organisms to maintain their form through a stabilization of their morphic fields even though the chemicals and the cells of their body are constantly changing. In other words, the cells of your liver and your skin, your heart and your bones are constantly dying and new ones coming into being, yet you still retain the basic form of your body thanks to memory information carried in your morphic field. In the realm of behaviour, it enables all organisms to tune into their own past patterns of activity. If you learn to ride a bike when you are a child but don't look at a bike again until you are 30, you will still know what to do if you get back on one. There is a kind of habit memory that is transmitted through morphic resonance, and this is where habit patterns come in.

FIELD OF MEMORY

We are continually tuning into ourselves in the past. Morphic resonance is the transmitter of the past. It moves through time. Tuning into it involves a resonance through time with ourselves in the past. We have all been taught that memories are stored inside our brains as memory traces. Such an idea developed out of the mechanistic view of the mind as nothing more than a physical epiphenomenon of the brain. Consequently hundreds of scientists have been searching for physical evidence of it. Yet no scientist has ever found any trace of memory in the physical brain. The brain which was believed to store information in rather the same way it is kept on a computer disk or video tape, now appears to be more like a TV set – merely the 'hardware' which transmits memory to awareness rather than storing it. Consciousness, which may at least in part be carried by morphic resonance, is *not* physical nor is it local to the body alone. Consciousness is interpenetrating, throughout the universe. It now appears not only to be a controlling force in creating and sustaining material reality but a guiding force in the evolution of both man and the universe as a whole. This is probably why scientists have never found any trace of evidence that memory is stored in the brain (although millions of laboratory animals have been sacrificed to the search). After all, if you ripped out the wires in your TV set and looked at them you would still not be able to tell what programmes it

A holographically-functioning superweak field could exist in nature: physicists as well as biologists have found significant evidence of it. It now remains to 'discover' it as a bona fide element of the universe. This revolutionary development marks the next milestone along the way of our continued explorations.
Ervin Laszlo

Land then, is not merely soil; it is a fountain of energy flowing through a circuit of soils, plant and animals ... An ethic to supplement and guide the economic relation to land presupposes the existence of some mental image of land as a biotic mechanism. We can be ethical only in relation to something we can see, feel, understand, love, or otherwise have faith in.
Aldo Leopold

had been transmitting last night. Yes of course when there is damage to the brain you experience memory damage but that now appears to be damage to the 'receiver' not the memory 'storage system'.

Sheldrake suggests that we can not only tune into our own morphic resonance we can also tune into that of others. From a scientific viewpoint this could turn out to be what we are doing when we work with spirits in non-ordinary reality. It could also explain Jung's idea of archetypes and the collective unconscious, and Grof's discovery that, like shamans, people in holotropic states contact universal energies of gods, goddesses and mythic heroes which are recorded in world religion and mythology even when they have no previous knowledge of their existence.

TRACING THE ARCHETYPES

Where Jung only wrote about the collective unconscious in the human realm, Sheldrake suggests that this is part of a much wider field-based resonance phenomenon found in all nature. Jung's archetypes do not make any sense to scientists who are still working out of mechanistic Newtonian–Cartesian paradigms. Yet they play a central part in transpersonal psychology and in an understanding of the human mind. This collective memory is an important ingredient in understanding what we are. For all of these archetypes, like other compassionate spirits we work with in shamanic journeying, may each have their own morphic field. Repeated contact with them influences our own. I have come to suspect that this is a major reason why exploring quantum realms under the guidance of power animals and compassionate spirits changes people's lives so much for the better. It seems to bring everyone more wisdom, power, peace, security, compassion and creativity.

I suppose it is not so different from the kind of thing that happens when you spend a lot of time with people who are filled with negativity and despair. You can find yourself feeling as they do without any real idea of why, simply because your morphic field is continually influenced by theirs. It may also be why we love to hang out with the kind of people who are creative and positive. The more we are in their presence the better we feel. The exchange of energy that is taking place through morphic resonance enriches our own experience of life. The Buddha said that it is easy for a good man to be good and hard for him to do evil while it is easy for a bad man to be evil and difficult for him to do good. Our repeated thought and behaviour patterns become part of

The need for community and its rituals is an ancient need. It has been built into the human psyche over thousands of generations and hundreds of thousands of years. If it is frustrated, we feel 'alienated' and fall prey to psychiatric and psychosomatic ills.
Anthony Stevens

our morphic resonance as do our interactions with the morphic resonance of others, of objects, of animals, of a house, or a place in nature.

RITUAL HABITS

'Negative rituals' or bad habits are part of the morphic resonance phenomenon too. And the longer they go on the more they reinforce our tendency to fall into them and the harder they are to break. We develop ways of thinking about ourselves as 'not good enough', or 'always a bridesmaid, never a bride', or 'incompetent', or a 'bad person' from hearing these things said time and again. They form patterns that reinforce each other and we act on them until, gradually, we come to believe these things are true. Similarly we can get into the habit of taking a few glasses of wine when we get home from work every night just to wind down. Before long this behaviour pattern, recorded in our morphic field, becomes so powerful that this negative ritual begins to steal our power and rule our life. Bad habits are hard to break. Partly this is because they tend to be unconscious. We don't even know that we have them until a crisis raises its head and forces us to change by breaking down the structures in our lives that no longer serve us, and allows us to open up to new creative possibilities. And that is seldom a comfortable process.

SHAPING THE SACRED

Just as bad habits ingrain themselves in our memory fields and reinforce our self-defeating tendencies, positive rituals can be used to transform the way we relate to ourselves and to the world around us to an extent that is hard to imagine. That is until you experience their effect.

Ritual is a way of connecting us with sacred energy and then shaping and directing it to a particular end. Like morphic fields which, although we can not see them, affect the material world, the shape-shifting energy that is carried by our intention as we go through sacred rituals connects up clear lines of power between the quantum realms and ordinary reality. Through this connection vital energy can flow forth to transform day-to-day reality. And this happens energetically; not in a way that anybody can explain logically. Through ritual we experience either a presence of the past or a presence of the sacred or both.

The soul should always stand ajar, ready to welcome the ecstatic experience.
Emily Dickenson

RITUALS OLD AND NEW

Sheldrake speaks about how cultures and tribes are governed by morphic fields. All cultures have patterns of activity which are repeated again and again in order to recall or relate to a previous event or to affirm a particular important revelation or experience. Passover, for instance, is a recreation of the Passover dinner which Jews have celebrated since the first Passover dinner. In these kinds of past-linked rituals people do things as closely as possible to the way they have been done before. They use the same words and language, they make the same gestures, they eat the same foods. Through such rituals these people are consciously reinforcing a pattern of activity in order to connect with their ancestors who have done the same thing for centuries. I have watched in admiration as Tibetan monks carried out lengthy rituals to create a sacred space within which teachings and initiations into the archetypal energies with which their lineage is connected can be given.

The sacred becomes present as you participate in the ritual – there is a kind of collapse in space and time. In the Holy Communion it is believed that there is a presence of the original Last Supper and of Christ as well as all of those who have participated in the same ritual ever since – the communion of saints. Such practices are found all round the world in all societies. From a rational point of view what participants in such rituals are doing looks like meaningless mumbo jumbo and foolish superstition. From the point of view of morphic resonance the practising of ritual creates a perfect medium for connecting sacred energy and material gestures and in doing so brings its influence into your life.

New rituals – those you will be working with this week – all have connections to the past as well as to experiences of soul in quantum realms. They too consist of actions repeated again and again in ordinary reality using the same words or song or gestures. They are always carried out with clear, sacred intent. That is what links them to the transpersonal sources of power which make transformation in material reality possible. You can create powerful, positive, new patterns of morphic resonance in your life by creating and working with your own rituals which honour what you value most. Repeat them again and again. Each time you do this the energies that the ritual connects you with become more influential in your life.

The enduring gift from native Americans to us is the importance of ritual. Rituals and their symbols are the residue of culture. They invest the events in our lives with meaning. They illuminate and ultimately define our realities because they mark the milestone by which we define ourselves as individuals and as participants in a community. Without them, the potential richness of our lives loses its full depth and significance.
Carl A. Hammerschlag

THE WEEK AHEAD

This week we will be exploring symbols and rituals. They are designed to connect your experiences in transpersonal realms to your day-to-day life in a way that will enable positive changes to take place. Some days you will be journeying, some you will be working with objects in ordinary reality, others making use of your Inner Reaches of Sacred Space. All through the week you will be working with symbols and rituals derived directly from *your* connection with quantum realities. When you journey, you will as always be working with your power animal or animals and your Wise One but, if you have not already done so, you might like to begin making connections with other helpful spirits as well. For instance, you will be doing a journey to discover a symbol that you will use in one of your rituals. Why not ask your power animal or Wise One if there is a particular helping spirit that he or she can introduce you to who can guide you to finding that symbol, or give you advice on how to work with it. This is something I do all the time. When I am in need of some help or guidance, insight or healing, I will journey to my power animal and tell her what I need then say, 'Please take me to whatever compassionate spirit in the universe is most appropriate to help me with this.' Then she takes me on her back to whatever realm of non-ordinary reality this spirit inhabits and stays with me while I am learning what I am there to learn or being given the healing I have asked for. The quantum realms are vast as is the richness of the spiritual beings who inhabit them. Don't hesitate to expand your friendships there.

Later in the week you will be entering sacred space to find your own personal power song. Power songs are mentioned in many books on shamanism and are cited as being of great importance to its tradition and practice. Jose and Lena Stevens include a journey to find a power song in their book, *Secrets of Shamanism, Tapping the Spirit Power Within You*. They explain the function and importance of such songs as follows:

'These power songs remind shamans that they are protected from harm by their guardian spirit. In singing them they honour their allies and call forth their power to protect and help them. The songs are also a constant reminder that they are not lost in the "dream" of ordinary reality. Singing a power song fills them with power and a sense of certainty.'

Always be a first-rate version of yourself, instead of a second-rate version of somebody else. *Judy Garland*

THE LANGUAGE OF BUILDING

Just as a master builder takes a drawing of, say, a cathedral, and translates it into physical form using the language of columns and portcullises, vaults and buttresses, so we can work with the language of symbols to manifest our soul's unique energetic architecture in living form. Symbols are powerful tools for your soul to use in building its material form on the earth and in helping to express its master intention. They can be used to build powerful Bridges between your soul and your personality, bringing more and more freedom and authentic power into your life. In this Quantum Break we begin by discovering symbols in the inner world and then ask for rituals we can use to work with in shaping the evolution of our own morphic fields and becoming more fully who we really are. In the following Quantum Break we will be linking symbols from quantum realms with physical objects in the world around us to begin our ritual work and creative practices in ordinary reality.

Quantum Break 22

BLUEPRINTS INTO FORM

Your intention:
TO DISCOVER A PHYSICAL SYMBOL OF YOUR SOUL'S ENERGETIC ARCHITECTURE

✦ On this journey you will once again connect up with your seedpower – that particular soul energy which you brought into being in this life.
✦ Check back to Quantum Break 19 – Graceland if you need to refresh your memory about journeys beyond space and time.
✦ You will start at the place from which you always begin your journeys.
✦ You can choose to go to the upperworld or the lowerworld, whichever you feel is more appropriate for you to reconnect most easily with your soul's energetic architecture. Ask your power animal to take you directly to the right place in non-ordinary reality.

The shaman then is a master of play, dancing, and chanting in the field of human suffering. And through these acts, the people are awakened from the nightmare of sickness to the dream of Paradise. Playfulness and absurdity sharply rouse the slumbering ones. The beauty of poetry and the ferocity of keen wisdom remind the forgetful ones. Compassion and poise heal the diseased ones.
Joan Halifax

- ✦ Move right inside your soul's architecture. Ask it to give you a symbol which represents the essential nature of your seedpower. This could be a visual symbol such as a sun or a mountain, a flower or a sword, or it could be a sound or a word, even a sense of quality which represents its fundamental nature.
- ✦ Once you have been given this symbol, hold it to your heart. Let its beauty penetrate your senses.
- ✦ When you are ready, still poised within the energetic architecture of your soul, ask to be given a simple ritual using your symbol that you can carry out each day in ordinary reality to honour the beauty of your soul's architecture and help it to manifest itself more fully in your life.
- ✦ Watch carefully to see what the spirits give you. They may speak to you in words or show you something. They may act out a ritual for you, showing you what is appropriate for you to do each day in ordinary reality. They may use some other way of communicating with you.
- ✦ The ritual you are given may be as simple as to light a candle in your sanctuary to honour your soul's master intention each morning, or pouring water on the land each day as a gesture of offering from your soul to the earth.
- ✦ You might like to grasp the symbol and the ritual that goes with it to your heart both in non-ordinary reality and in ordinary reality by making a physical movement with your hand before returning through the tunnel to your starting place.
- ✦ Give thanks to your power animal and helping spirit, and, holding the symbol of your soul's architecture as well as your ritual within your heart, return to ordinary reality.

I implore you ... to submit to your own myths. Any postponement in doing so is a lie.
William Carlos Williams

Bridge Building

Make a drawing of the symbol you have received and write down in detail the ritual that will be carried out daily.

MODEL MAKING

Work with symbols and rituals is made more and more powerful when you ground its purposes by working with material forms that represent your symbols. It is like the architect who builds the building. First he familiarises himself with its energetic architecture, then he draws it on paper and finally he begins to make a physical model of it. The making of this model informs the nature of the building's morphic resonance and makes the building work itself a simple matter when the time comes. In this next Quantum Break you will be exploring the stage of model making by seeking a physical object that can represent the symbol you discovered in your last journey.

Quantum Break 23

TREASURE HUNT

Your intention:
TO FIND A PHYSICAL OBJECT TO CARRY YOUR SYMBOL

✦ Spend five minutes in the Inner Reaches of Sacred Space (see page 68) to calm and centre yourself. Now go out into nature or look around your immediate environment to locate an object that seems to represent the symbol you received in your last journey which represents the essential nature of your seedpower.

✦ Bring the object back to the place of sanctuary you have made in your home. Just sit with it for a few minutes. See whether the things you already have there need rearranging. Has anything outlived its purpose? If so, thank it and put it back in nature or somewhere else in the house. Do you need to bring anything else into your place of sanctuary now? If so what?

Many years ago I was given a small, round, silver box as a Christmas present by my daughter. It was so light I could hardly hold it in my hand. When I opened it I was surprised to find a very beautiful, ultra-light-weight powder puff. She told me that she had given it to me to remind me of the nature of my own soul. At that time the last thing I ever would have associated with myself was something so light you could hardly feel it was in your hand when you were holding it. I told Susannah this. She replied that I had very little awareness of the nature of my own soul and suggested that I go through the ritual of taking this ultra-light-weight ball out of the silver box daily and holding it in my hand in order to begin to be aware of what my soul nature was really like. When I carried out this ritual I found that it broke through a great many of the negative thought patterns about myself that kept me from accepting and liking who I was. You will be working in a similar way with your objects.

WORKING WITH OBJECTS

Week Six Project

Spend 10 minutes each day in a quiet state with the object which carries the nature of your seedpower. Touch it, look at it, hold it, move it in your hands. When you feel that you are in communion with the quality of your essence, represented by the object, it is time to carry out the particular daily ritual you were given in non-ordinary reality to honour that seedpower. After this week is finished you may like to continue this ritual either every day as you have been doing or whenever you feel you have lost touch with who you really are.

Everything as it moves, now and then here and there, makes stops. The bird as it flies stops in one place to make its nest, and in another to rest in its flight. A man when he goes forth stops when he wills. So the god has stopped. The sun, which is so bright and beautiful, is one place where he has stopped. The moon, the stars, the winds, he has been with. The trees, the animals, are all where he has stopped, and the Indian thinks of these places and sends his prayers there to reach the place where the god has stopped and win help and a blessing.

Ohiyesa, Santee Dakota physician and author

The eyes of my eyes
are opened.
e. e. cummings

Everything in life that
we really accept undergoes
a change.
Katherine Mansfield

China tea, the scent of
hyacinths, wood fires and
bowls of violets – that is my
mental picture of an agreeable
February afternoon.
Constance Spry

Sometime in your life you
will go on a journey. It will
be the longest journey you
have ever taken. It is the
journey to find yourself.
Katherine Sharp

Quantum Break 24

SEARCH FOR RESTRICTION

Your intention:
TO DISCOVER A SYMBOL FOR WHAT IS HINDERING THE FULL
EXPRESSION OF YOUR UNIQUE SEEDPOWER IN YOUR LIFE

+ Go to your Inner Reaches of Sacred Space (see page 68) and activate your senses.
+ Look around this inner place in nature and ask for a symbol of those things you feel are hindering you which are not worthy opponents but represent the 'junk' you have accumulated such as false ideas and negative habits.
+ You may have to look under a rock or up in a tree or beneath water to find your symbol of hindrance but it will be there. Ask your power animal and spirit friends to help you in your search.
+ It could be almost anything – barbed wire, a heavy rock, a box made of steel – anything.
+ Once you have found it, don't judge it, just hold it to your heart as you did the symbol for your seedpower and, thanking your helping spirits bring it back to ordinary reality.

Bridge Building

Immediately after your journey you will be Bridge building by going to find something or put something together that will represent the restrictions in your life. You can go out into the garden or a park if you like and collect dead pieces of wood to weave together with other things you find there. Always be sure to ask permission whenever you want to take something from nature – say a flower or a rock or leaves – and wait for an intuitive reply that you have permission for your sacred reason. It is almost always given. If ever it is not given or you get a no, then look for something else. If you do not have access to the outdoors then look among the things you have in your house, or draw a picture of the symbol you have been given to embody the restrictions in your life – those negative thought patterns and habits, many of them unconscious, that restrict your freedom and impede your ability to see the true beauty of your own soul.

Once you have gathered together whatever expresses these hindrances to experiencing your freedom and living your authentic power, tie them together in a bundle and put them in your sacred space. Ask that all of the negative unconscious rituals in your life become embodied in this bundle. Sit for a few minutes in your sacred place holding the bundle. Close your eyes and, focusing your attention, pour all the power of your negative thought patterns and unhelpful habits, both conscious and unconscious, into the physical bundle before you. When you sense that this has been accomplished, wrap the bundle in a cloth – it could be just a piece of cotton or a scarf – and, placing it in your sacred place, ask that it ripen. This is very much the same process of nature that produces compost for the garden when you gather together vegetable parings and place them in a bucket for them to ripen and become compost to support new life. You will be coming back to your bundle tomorrow.

'Hope' is the thing with feathers –
that perches in the soul …
Emily Dickenson

Quantum Break 25

RITUAL OF SACRIFICE

Your intention:
TO SACRIFICE YOUR HINDRANCES AND GIVE THANKS FOR THEIR TEACHINGS

I learned this ritual ten years ago from a wonderful shaman and healer who lives in Devon in England. Some people think of sacrifice as something that you do which wastes yourself, like giving over your life to something that does not really feed your soul, that you think you 'should' be doing. Others think of sacrifice as having to give up something that is precious to you – like a ring, for instance, or a relationship that means a lot to you. In truth sacrifice is a giving over or a

The opening of vision for the shaman unfolds in a transpersonal realization resulting from a crisis of death and rebirth, a transformation of the profane individual into one who is sacred. For many neophytes, this realization awakens in the dream-web when animal-tutors and spirits of the Other World appear. They come as emissaries of mythical beings, of gods and ancestors. And the candidate is doomed if he or she does not accept the instructions received in the dream from these presences of the Other World.
Joan Halifax

giving up on something that you have been holding to yourself which no longer serves your deepest purpose. And the hardest thing for everyone to give up is not a diamond ring or a lover or a broken dream but actually our negativity. This is what you will be doing in this Quantum Break.

The word 'sacrifice' means quite literally 'to make sacred'. When you sacrifice something you let go of it and in doing so you call in the sacred power embodied in it. Then, using your intention, you direct it to whatever place in the universe it is most appropriate for it to be. You will be using this powerful and transformative process to advantage again and again in the future, whenever the need arises.

To carry out this Quantum Break you will need a source either of fire, or earth, or water, or wind. You will need to decide before beginning which element is most easily accessible to you or, if you have the choice, which you prefer to act as the transformative element in the sacrifice. If you have a fireplace you might choose fire. If you have a river or the sea or a lake or a pond near you, you might choose water. If your ritual is taking place in windy weather and you have access to the outdoors it might be wind. If you prefer earth then you will need a little trowel or spade. For what you will be doing is offering the ripened negativity back to the universe as compost for new life wherever it is needed and most useful. Here is how to do it:

✦ Sitting in front of your sacred place where you have placed your bundle, which now also holds the symbol for the essence of your soul energy, close your eyes and go to your Inner Reaches of Sacred Space. Give thanks to this inner place and to the spirits that you find there for the symbol of your negative thought patterns and habits.
✦ Then ask that your power animal and your Wise One join you in ordinary reality to carry out the ritual of sacrifice which will help remove these patterns from your morphic fields.

On the steep bank of a river, there exists life. A voice is there, and speaks aloud. I saw the 'master' of the voice and spoke with him. He subjugated himself to me and sacrificed to me. He came yesterday and answered my questions. The small grey bird with the blue breast comes to me and sings shaman songs in the hollow of the bough, calls her spirits, and practises shamanism. The woodpecker strikes his drum in the tree with his drumming nose. Under the axe, the tree trembles and wails as a drum under the baton. All these come at my call.
W. Bogoras

- ✦ When you are peaceful and feel supported return to ordinary reality.
- ✦ Pick up your bundle wrapped in cloth and slowly unwrap it.
- ✦ Hold it in your hands, turn it over several times slowly. Feel the weight of it and the density.
- ✦ Letting yourself see with your inner eyes and hear with your heart, connect with compassion to the bundle of negative energy which has been ripening since yesterday.
- ✦ Let yourself ponder how the negative thought patterns and habits which it now holds may have served you in the past and give thanks, for our negativity has a role to play in our unfolding.
- ✦ Silently ask that the transformative power of your spirit helpers join you now in the sacrifice which you are going to carry out in ordinary reality.
- ✦ Go to whatever source you have chosen – fire, water, earth or air – carrying your bundle with you.
- ✦ With compassion you will now make an offering of the bundle and the ripened negativity with which it has been imbued to the universe.
- ✦ As you do, say a simple prayer stating your intention such as:
  I make this offering of my bundle of hindrances in the presence of my helping spirits. I give thanks for what it has taught me and how it has served me and now confirm that I am willing to release it. I ask that the ripening negativity which it embodies be made sacred through the transformation through _____ (earth, air, fire or water). I ask then that it be taken to whatever place in the universe is most appropriate for it . As it is consumed may it bring new life where it is needed in the universe.
- ✦ Now throw your bundle into the wind, or place it in the water or in the fire, or dig a hole and bury it in the earth. Be aware of how the experience of doing this makes you feel. You will already be experiencing a shift in your morphic resonance.
- ✦ Give thanks to your power animal and helping spirits and let them know that they may go now.

Consequently: he who wants
  to have
Right without wrong,
Order without disorder,
Does not understand the
  principles
Of heaven and earth.
He does not know how
Things hang together.
Chuang Tzu

Bridge Building

…that when we confront the
dark side of existence in a
focused and condensed form
in deliberately planned
sessions, we can significantly
reduce its various manifestations in our everyday life.
Stanislav Grof

The best way out is
always through.
Robert Frost

Record the experience of carrying out this ritual in your journal – how it felt from step to step. You might like to write down the prayer stating your intention. You can then use it (with minor alter-ations perhaps) the next time there is something that needs to be sacrificed – made sacred – in your life. Carrying out this ritual is unlikely to clear your life immediately of every negative habit or thought pattern you have ever collected since they are so deeply imbedded in us – although any-thing is possible. (To my amazement a not so very different ritual which I carried out to rid myself of jealousy which has always plagued me really did clear 90% of it – not immediately but within the next six weeks.) It is likely to cause a big shift in negative patterns that have been plaguing you and create a window for freedom and authentic power. But when you have access to a tool like this and choose to use it again and again whenever you have some kind of grief or negativity or confusion that needs to be made sacred, thanks to morphic resonance, or however you want to describe that fifth field of the emerging scientific paradigm, the freeing effects of this ritual become more and more powerful and the hold that negative thoughts and habits and painful upheavals have become weaker and weaker.

Who so knoweth himself
knoweth his Lord
Mohammed

Quantum Break 26

SEARCH FOR A POWER SONG IN SACRED SPACE

Your intention:
TO FIND A PERSONAL POWER SONG THAT YOU WILL USE IN
YOUR QUANTUM WORK

One of the most effective ways of being able to shift consciousness from ordi-nary reality into the quantum realms is by using a power song. You may have already come upon one or been given one in the journeying that you have done so far. It can be simply a melody or it can be simple words in a very sim-ple tune. It may even be words with no apparent meaning. Usually power songs are childlike in their simplicity, yet enormously powerful in that they carry the sacredness of the quantum realms in them. Before you begin any kind of a ritual, a journey, or shift in consciousness, all you will need to do is sing your power song and ask that all of the spirits that will be useful to you in carrying out your intention be present. You can use your song to call on the helpful spirits of your ancestors, to call on the spirit of a plant or a flower, to call on your power animal, or to call on the gods and goddesses – the archetypes that tend to inhabit the upperworld. A power song is a way of helping the everyday you – your personality – to move aside and connect with the sacred power of your soul and of the transpersonal realms.

- ✦ Enter Your Inner Reaches of Sacred Space.
- ✦ Activate your senses until you feel yourself to be fully present in your special place in nature.
- ✦ Call to your helping spirits, your power animals, your Wise One, and ask them to introduce you to your own power song or to take you to someone who can give it to you.
- ✦ Once you have sung your song, thank your helping spirits and come back immediately. Be sure to do your Bridge building right away.
- ✦ If you do not find a song, do not be concerned, it may not at this point be appropriate to have one. However, you might like to use your two Free Breaks to visit your Inner Reaches of Sacred Space to search for a power song again.

Bridge Building

Record the song that you have brought back in any way that you can. If you brought back words write them down, if you brought back a melody perhaps you would like to record it on a cassette, or simply sing it over and over to yourself until it becomes part of you. If on this sojourn into sacred space you don't find a power song be sure to keep your ears open on further sojourns and on journeys because they often come to us spontaneously. Power songs given this way should only be used when you are working with the consciousness matrix. Sing something else in the shower.

FREE BREAKS

Use your Free Breaks this week to explore any other ways in which ritual might be useful in your life. The important thing to remember is that whatever ritual you are doing the intention is what is most valuable. You might like to use ritual, for instance, in everyday activities. I know when I prepare a salad for my family I always focus my intention while chopping the vegetables and ask that all the love that's possible be put into the salad that I prepare. Having raised four children over a very long period of time and made many meals in my life I have often felt I don't ever need to make another meal for anyone. And yet when my youngest child comes home from school I find myself always preparing meals for him. It is not that he is not perfectly capable of preparing meals for himself, it is that I know that most food served is devoid of love. When he is at home with me I want him to have food that is as infused with love as possible.

In your Free Breaks this week see how you can bring ritual into the ordinary activities that you carry out each day. Remember, in making ritual work, the important thing is that old duo compassion and intention. They are absolutely unbeatable in transforming reality.

◆

CHECKLIST

Day One

✦ Read through the chapter as far as Quantum Break 22.
✦ Do Quantum Break 22 Blueprints into Form *to discover a physical symbol of your soul's energetic architecture.*
✦ Bridge build.

Day Two

✦ Do Quantum Break 23 Treasure Hunt *to find a physical object to carry your symbol.*
✦ Did you find it strange not to do a journey today?
✦ Read Week Six Project (page 185) and start work on it.

Day Three

✦ Do Quantum Break 24 Search for Restriction *to discover a symbol of what is hindering the full expression of your unique seedpower in your life.*
✦ Bridge build.
✦ Don't forget to do your ritual.

Day Four

✦ Do Quantum Break 25 Ritual of Sacrifice *to sacrifice your hindrances and give thanks for their teachings.*
✦ Bridge build.
✦ Are you aware of anything having lifted? Expanded?

Day Five

✦ Do Quantum Break 26 Search for a Power Song in Sacred Space *to find a personal power song that you will use in your quantum work.*
✦ Bridge build.

The solid Newtonian atoms were now discovered to be largely empty. Hard matter no longer constituted the fundamental substance of nature. Matter and energy were interchangeable. Three-dimensional space and unidimensional time had become relative aspects of a four-dimensional space-time continuum. Time flowed at different rates for observers moving a different speeds. Time slowed down near heavy objects, and under certain circumstances could stop altogether.

Richard Tarnas

> ### Day Six
>
> ✦ Do a Free Break exercise.
> ✦ Bridge build.
> ✦ Don't forget to do your daily ritual even if you have found new ones.
>
> ### Day Seven
>
> ✦ Do a Free Break exercise.
> ✦ Bridge build.
> ✦ Spend 20 minutes on your Travelogue.

Travelogue

✦ How many days this week did you do your Quantum Break?

✦ Have you allowed yourself to explore what ritual feels like in your life?

✦ Does it still make you feel uncomfortable to carry out ritual? (Our culture has for so long been riddled with empty rituals, activities that are carried out without real intention, that for many the idea of ritual seems like nothing but dumb show.)

✦ Have you noticed any difference in the way you think or feel about yourself since you have been working with the symbol of your seedpower?

✦ Were there any other significant issues for you in this week? If so describe them.

quantum leap 7

Walk on the Wild Side

Discover your wildness in every leaf, in every rock in every breeze. The death of autumn is your death. It gives way to winter and winter to spring and spring to summer. Do not attach yourself to one season only. That would be like trying to play but one melody of a great symphony. Wildness shines in the spirit of the sun and moon. It ripples in the tides. You can hear it in the voice of a bird's song. It flares forth from your core calling you home to your primordial roots in the soil. The earth is whispering to you and you to it. Let the reconciliation begin.

I am the Voice of Nature

You turn outwards this week to reconnect with the wildness of the living world, explore sacred sites in nature, learn from plants and to rattle in the spirits. It is time to explore the mysterious interconnecting energy fields which emerging paradigm scientists say carry messages from the past and promises for the future. Find out how they resonate with your own consciousness and you with theirs.

For 15 billion years the universe has been unfolding out of its inherent wildness. It has been generating new levels of organization, and new energetic architecture which in turn creates new physical structures and new beings. Consciousness, believe emerging paradigm scientists, predates life. It goes back to the birth of elementary particles – the primordial explosion – what Swimme calls the 'Primordial Flaring Forth' of potentiality from nothing. As human beings we bring a very special element to the evolving cosmos: our conscious self-awareness. Because of it we have an ability to explore the universe in ever more subtle ways. And, when we do explore, it not only engages our mind, it feeds our soul. It is little wonder that primordial wildness is the seat of all creative power – the earth's, the universe's, our own.

TAPPING THE SPIRIT OF THE WILD

When most people think of wild they think of chaos and they fear it. The truth is, within the wildness of the universe is to be found tremendous order. It is an order of a very special kind. We cannot understand it through the intellect but once we align ourselves with it, and come to trust it we can consciously work with it to create our visions, further our freedom and live out our authentic power. We come from wildness and we must return to it if we are to use our self-conscious awareness to help the world evolve.

Our animal bodies are made of light – the same protons that emerged from the big bang to form the galaxies and the sun. This light comes to us through the plants who photosynthesize oxygen, transmuting the sun's power into material form on which we feed to stay alive. Each of us carries a brand of wildness in our soul. When we connect with the spirits of nature their own wildness resonates with ours, awakening us to their beauty and their power, nourishing us with a sense of endless possibility. At its core wildness is the food of freedom.

Early man was naturally attuned to communion with the world around him. The dawn showered blessings upon him. The moon had feelings. Lightning brought a message from the gods. The earth, the universe, the whole shebang, was wild and free. He knew that he was wild in the same way the bear is wild and the salmon which he caught and ate. The universe is fecund with wildness. It is the same wildness that flared forth at that first instance and which continues to flare forth out of Bohm's implicate order – what physicists call the quantum vacuum – from which elementary particles and waves continue to emerge every moment of our lives.

THE WEEK AHEAD

This week we will be exploring ways of reconnecting with the wildness of the natural world around you and rediscovering your own wildness from within. And, for the first time during your journey to freedom, you will be working mostly in the middleworld. You will be exploring the non-ordinary domain of everyday reality with the help of your power animal. You will take a walk on the wild side – a simple vision quest to deepen your connections with the sacred nature of the living world around you. You will be making friends with the natural elements and exploring your relationship to sun or rain, mist or wind. You may find some new friends among the trees and the rocks as well. They have great wisdom to share if we choose to listen. You will also be learning to call in your helping spirits using your rattle. Finally, you will be journeying in a brand new way – without the use of drum or rattle, simply by entering the *sacred silence* and focusing your intention.

Shamans are typically very well grounded in this ordinary reality – so grounded that they can in fact move over into that other dimension with discipline and focus, which is the only way to be effective in helping others.
Michael Harner

RATTLE IN THE SPIRITS

Like power songs, which you worked with last week, rattling is a very powerful tool for calling in the spirits and shifting consciousness. Many cultures believe rattles hold the seeds that call our own seedpower into being. You can rattle rhythmically, in the same way that you would drum, and ask the rattle to tell you anything, such as whether it is appropriate to do a particular kind of healing at a particular time, or which path to take on a walk in nature.

The shaking of the rattle stimulates higher frequency pathways in the brain than does the drum beat. It can also intensify the experience of the drum beat when used with it. A shaman uses a rattle to call in his spirits before performing any sort of healing. He may also use a rattle together with his power song. He may rattle and whistle, or he may use a rattle on its own. One of the nice things about rattling is that it is of a sufficiently low amplitude that it doesn't cause pain in the ear receptors. There are many people who are very sensitive, particularly at the beginning of learning shamanic techniques, to the drum beat. For them rattling is ideal. Next week we will be looking at the medicine wheel and how you can use your rattle to call in the spirits of the six directions. For now you will be using your rattle to focus your intention and prepare for consciousness shifts. Start at a slow tempo then increase it as you feel the need to help shift

Where the spirit does not work with the hand there is no art.
Leonardo da Vinci

consciousness from ordinary reality into the quantum realms. You can also use rattling this way while you are walking in order to connect with the spirits of nature, listen to the spirit of a plant, or simply to prepare yourself to interact with your sanctuary at home.

The purpose of rattling before beginning shamanic work is both to call in the spirits and also to shift your consciousness from an ordinary state of mind to one in which you become like a *hollow bone*. This is the way that shamans often describe the state in which they work most effectively with the spirits. In practical terms what it means is allowing your personality to step aside so that you become filled with spiritual energy at the level of your soul.

You will be using your rattle a lot this week. You are likely to want to use it a great deal in the future as well. I have several rattles, each of which has a distinctive size and sound. There's one that I am particularly fond of which I travel with. It is a very simple little plastic egg with sand inside it. The sound is clear yet gentle. I can slip it into a pocket and carry it with me on a walk in nature. This is what you will doing during your first Quantum Break.

> Myth connects and relates us
> to our surrounding world.
> *Carolyn Bereznak Kenny*

Quantum Break 27

WALK ON THE WILD SIDE

Your intention:
TO TAKE AN HOUR'S WALK AND CONNECT WITH THE SPIRITS OF THE PLACE

A walk in nature acts like a mirror. It will reflect to you the signs and symbols of your own inward journey. You will seek to form relationships with the spirits of the place wherever you have chosen to walk. They have much to teach.

◆ Pick an area to walk in that you do not know well. Perhaps one that you have only been to once or twice but very much like the feel of.

> The indescribable innocence
> and beneficence of Nature – of
> sun and wind and rain, of
> summer and winter – such
> health, such cheer, they afford
> forever!….Shall I not have
> intelligence with the Earth?
> Am I not partly leaves and
> vegetable mould myself?
> *Henry David Thoreau*

- Although it is not absolutely necessary to do your walk on the wild side alone, it is important to remember that your intention is to interact with the presence of the place and the spirits that preside there. This can be difficult if there are other people with you, especially if they don't understand what you are attempting to do.
- Be sure to take your rattle with you.
- Spend three or four minutes gently rattling and directing your attention towards calling in the spirits of the place, your power animal, and any other helping spirits who you wish to have present during the next hour.
- Continue to rattle if you like or stop rattling once you sense yourself in the presence of spiritual power.
- Now become aware of the messages that you are picking up around you. What are the qualities of spirits that you sense are present? What do you hear?
- A walk on the wild side needs to be done quite slowly and always in silence, with gentle, diffused attention. This is very much like the kind of vision you have when you are gazing at a landscape without seeing any one thing in particular.
- As you wander, become aware of nature's awareness of you. Look for signs and symbols that may give you a key to your own life's purpose, to your inherent gifts, to your fears and your challenges.
- The spirits of nature are very wise and have much to share with us. As you walk be aware of any messages that you are receiving. Be aware of the quality of the leaves and the way that the light catches them in the trees around you.
- You might stop and pick up a rock. Be still with it. See what it has to show you, what it has to tell you.
- You might lean against a tree, or even sit under one for a time. Ask the tree how it can help you to root yourself more deeply within the wild powers of nature which lie at the core of your own authentic power.
- Look at the sky. Feel the breeze, if there is a breeze around you.
- Be aware of the light or the darkness. What are their qualities? What do they have to share with you? Do they echo anything within you?

Civilized man has marched across the face of the Earth and left a desert in his footprints.

Anonymous

◆ See what friends you can make in nature on your walk. See what they have
to teach you. If you need help, ask them for it.

◆ You may come upon a tree or a plant which seems particularly filled with
life, and another which seems terribly sad.

◆ If you feel your new friends calling to you for help, direct your intention
towards bringing them whatever it is that they need.

◆ Here in the atmosphere of a walk on the wild side is the perfect place to
sense the bond of friendship between all things. It is the perfect place to
come to know the spirits of the trees, of the rocks, of the soil, of the air, as
well as the devas that look after the growing things of the earth and the
spirits of nature who live and play in the wildness. They all need our friendship as much as we need theirs.

◆ See what spirit friends you can make during this hour then return to where
you started from.

Bridge Building

*You might like to use colour to draw something that can represent the essence of the spirits you have
seen. You may find that these spirits appear to you – say the spirit of a tree or the spirit of a mountain – in very different form than the tree or mountain appears in ordinary, everyday reality.
Draw or write about its spirit nature. Sing or dance it if you prefer. Make a list of the new friends
that you have made in the spirit world. You may like in the future to come back to visit them.*

STEP INTO THE SACRED

Our perfect companions never
have fewer than four feet.
Colette

This morning I walked my dogs. We followed the same path through the woods, into
fields down to the sea, that I have walked for 20 years. But this morning we climbed
over a fence to come upon 18 perfectly shaped spiders' webs. Eighteen – I know, I
counted them. Suspended between yellow dock plants, now past their prime, every web
glistened with dew. I marvelled at the precision with which they had been made and
wondered how we ever doubt the existence of a divine order in the universe.

This path is sacred to me – not only because it is radiant with life but because it is full of friends I now know so well – the rocks and the oaks, the elders and the willows, the brook and the grasses. We have laughed together and cried together as season gives way to season and year follows year. There is another reason for its sacredness too. The route I take each day is an ancient road. It leads round a twelfth-century castle. Then, if you let it wind all the way to the beach and upwards onto the cliffs, it will take you even further back in history to a megalithic burial ground above the sea. This place in nature is not only made special by its beauty but also by that fact that, for at least 5,000 years, people have walked here, worshipped here, loved here and died here. So it has become a doubly sacred place – both wild with nature and infused with the love of man.

To us they are part of nature, part of ourselves – the earth, the sun, the wind and the rain, stones, trees, animals, even little insects like ants and grasshoppers. We try to understand them not with the head but with the heart.
John Lame Deer and
Richard Erdoes

PATH OF FRIENDSHIP

My path winds down from a country road through a narrow, rock-strewn gully all covered with blackthorn and hawthorn and sycamores. They have grown over it creating a natural arbour, which opens out at the bottom into a glen of ancient trees with a small stream running through it. Sometimes when it has rained hard, the little gully that takes you down from the road is transformed into a torrent of water. For the next few days it is more of a slip and slide to go down the hill than a walk. And when the mud has finally dried I find the water has carved new shapes into the soil.

In the spring wild garlic grows here – powerful little plants with lovely white flowers. They smell like an Italian delicatessen except more raw and wild. You can pick them to put in salads and soups. They have the spirit of the survivor about them. Indeed they can help us survive by destroying the *helicobacter pylori* in the gut which causes ulcers. This is something which doctors are only now discovering, but wise women who have worked with wild garlic for hundreds upon hundreds of years have known it all along. The little plant can also help lower blood pressure that is too high, and readjust cholesterol levels. But eat too much of the stuff and it will make you sick. I know. I have done it. Making friends with plants is just like making friends with people. It takes time and you have to test them out before you come to know them. Aligning ourselves with the spirits of nature helps us to remember our wild origins – origins which we share with them. That was part of my developing a friendship with the wild garlic and with the place in which it grows.

No man is an Island, entire of itself; every man is a piece of the Continent, a part of the main; if a Clod be washed away by the Sea, Europe is less, as well as if a Promontory were, as well as if a Manor of thy friends or of thine own were; any man's death diminishes me, because I am involved in Mankind; And therefore never send to know for whom the bell tolls; it tolls for thee.
John Donne

Communing with a plant spirit to find out about its particular properties is a common practice among shamans. This technique is explained in *Plant Spirit Medicine*, a wonderful book by Eliot Cowan on working shamanically with plants.

Quantum Break 28

COMMUNION WITH A PLANT

Your intention:

TO MAKE A FRIEND OF A PLANT AND DISCOVER ITS ESSENCE

✦ Use your rattle to call in your spirits and shift consciousness.
✦ Go for a walk outdoors, anywhere where there are wild plants growing (if you have no possibility of using the outdoors for this exercise then I would suggest purchasing a plant which you know to be edible and use that in your house).
✦ Stroll with no particular destination in mind.
✦ When you come upon a plant that attracts you particularly stop, speak to it either aloud or silently in your mind. Introduce yourself, telling the plant your name, and explain to it that you have come to learn about the nature of its genus and species.
✦ Ask the plant to reveal its essential self to you. You may also ask for some comfort or healing if you like.
✦ Ask the plant if it has any medicinal uses.
✦ See what other information the plant has to give you. It is important to ask questions here. My experience with plants is that when you accidentally find out something about them and then ask them why they didn't tell you that before, they tend to say that no-one has bothered to ask. Be sure to ask as many questions of your plant friend as you would like.
✦ If the plant will allow you to, pick a leaf or a flower.

- Now rattle softly for yourself again. Call in your power animal or helping spirits while you do a short journey.
- Ask the spirits to show you the essential nature of the plant's genus and species.
- If it is a medicinal plant you might also ask how to prepare and use it.
- Now thank the plant spirit for its time and return to ordinary consciousness.

Bridge Building

Record and compare the information that you have received from the plant, both in its ordinary reality state and from the energy of the whole species in the non-ordinary reality of sacred space. If you have been working with a medicinal plant, after recording the information that it gives you, go to the library and find a good book on herbs. Look up what it has told you. How much of what you have learned is part of the information available through traditional plant medicine resources?

> By studying DNA, molecular biologist have verified that all living organisms are genetically related.
> *David Suzuki*

MORPHIC RESONANCE

All cultures throughout history have had ways of thinking about the quality of a place. They have known that each place has a particular quality or character. The Romans called it the *genius loci* – spirit of the place. Each site has a different personality and atmosphere. Before fifth entity physics came along, nothing in mechanistic science enabled us to explain this in rational terms. Now, using, say, Sheldrake's morphic resonance hypothesis, it is possible to think of places as having holographically-functioning field energies which carry an inherent memory through self-resonance.

It is interesting that the world 'field' was first introduced to science by Faraday who borrowed it from nature where it means simply a piece of land. The most general definition of field is a region of influence or a region of activity. Thinking of the fields of places makes it easier to grasp the revolutionary developments of mysterious interconnecting subtle energy which emerging paradigm scientists like Sheldrake are attempting

> ... civilized man has consistently tried to make the land fit his pattern of farming, when he should make the farming fit the pattern of the land.
> *Vernon Gill Carter and Tom Dale*

Where do 'lifetime memories'
and memories from apparent
previous lifetimes come from?
Can a 10-centimeter-diameter
brain hold 2.8×10^{20} 'bits'
(or more) of information?

Ervin Laszlo

to describe. It also makes it easier for us to talk on a rational level about the power of sacred places on the earth like Stonehenge and Lourdes or megalithic burial grounds. Sheldrake would say they all carry powerful energetic memories. When I walk on the land of the megalithic burial ground near my home I find I can tune into its collective memory. Long before I heard of Sheldrake's work, I did this. We all do this – intuitively. I connected with the wildness of the place and with its history. I climb to the very centre of the megalithic mound surrounded by standing stones whenever I need an answer to a question, or when I feel lost or confused. There I find I can tap into the wisdom of 5,000 years for help. I don't do this often anymore, but every time I do I get the help I am asking for. And it comforts me to know it is there. Sheldrake suggests that there are two senses in which a place can have memory – through the human collective experience of that place and through the memory of the place itself. All over the world we have holy places and places where great men and women have been born or become enlightened or where many people have prayed, like in the temples of Europe and Asia. They all carry great spiritual power – strong morphic resonance. Sacred places such as these are places of pilgrimage. The Australian Aboriginals with their songlines, the Native Americans with their power places, the medieval Europeans with their great networks of cathedrals built on energy lines, all knew about them and how to draw on the spirit of the place to enrich their own lives. It is a basic human need to visit places of power and to connect with the fields of memory and the spirits who live there.

THE SACRED IS EVERYWHERE

Skin-covered drum,
Fulfil my wishes,
Like flitting clouds, carry me
Through the lands of dusk
And below the leaden sky,
Sweep along like wind
Over the mountain peaks!

The Soyot of Siberia

Christ in me, Christ beneath
me, Christ above me,
Christ on my right, Christ
on my left,
Christ when I lie down,
Christ when I sit down,
Christ when I arise,
Christ in the heart of every
one who thinks of me,
Christ in the mouth of every
one who speaks of me,

My own path through the woods sings to me as I walk it – that is whenever I am willing to listen, and provided I am willing to lay aside for half an hour my obsession with doing things and allow myself to be present. There was a time when I would have hesitated to describe this little route as *my* path. 'My' can be such a possessive word. I know full well that it belongs as much to all who have come before and all that will come after me as it does to me, myself. Yet somehow I think of it as mine. For I have always believed that the only way to make something yours is to love it. And love this place I do – in the way I love my home, my lover, my closest friend.

From a shamanic perspective, this sacred place where we walk – my dogs and I – is riddled with nature spirits. You can sense them – especially at dawn and dusk when, according to the Celts, the veil between ordinary reality and the Otherworld is at its thinnest. Sometimes they are mischievous. Other times they seem lost in spaces into which my own mind has never entered.

Each year big men with loud voices come to cut back the overhanging trees exposing the lovely, wild path to direct sunlight. The spirits of the place, the devas who look after the plants, the spirits of the trees and the rocks don't like this. It sends them into hiding. It really is quite ugly what the men with their saws and hatchets do. They hack away at the branches leaving trees and shrubs looking as though they have been raped instead of trimmed. In the beginning this yearly cut-back troubled me a lot. Now it only makes me a little sad. For I have learned from my friend the path that the power of the wild is far greater than the force of their saws and hatchets. Within weeks of being cut, the lovely arbour regrows. Soon I find my spirit friends whose home it is happily playing hide and seek again.

Shamans have always had a timeless awareness of the earth as a living being. They listen to her rhythms and sense her magnetism as they sanctify the four directions (you will be doing this next week). They know the earth's sacred places the way a woman knows her lover's body. They have never heard of fifth entity physics or morphogenetic fields but they feel at one with the subtle energies of a waterfall because energies which echo with their own are within them. Shamans hear the purr of healthy forests. They breathe in the exhilaration of a headland above the sea. They know how to work together with the earth's own wildness for healing and divination, they track her lay lines, and infuse her sacred places with yet more power from their own consciousness. They know where water is to be found. They listen to the rock people and the tree people who are their friends. Sometimes they even bury themselves in the earth in sacred ceremonies of death and rebirth so they will experience in their flesh and bone the cycling energy of the mother that gives birth to us and all of life. And because they know these things, shamans are never alone the way we 'civilized' people so often are.

Christ in every eye that
  sees me,
Christ in every ear that
  hears me.
Christopher Banford and
William Parker Marsh

When humans abuse nature, it is because shamans have not remembered themselves, it is because spirit has not been listened to or seen.
Rowena Pattee

The forest is one big thing – it has people, animals and plants. There is no point in saving the animals if the forest is burned down. There is no point in saving the forest if the animals and people are driven away. Those trying to save the animals cannot win if the people trying to save the forest lose.
Bepkororoti

SANCTUARY OF SOLITUDE
Week Seven Project

We live in an age of
unprecedented uncertainty.
Life on earth is perilously
poised at the precipice of
extinction. Never before has
man possessed the destructive
resources to commit
global suicide.
*Bernard Lown and
Evjueni Chazov*

We humans are a vast system
of systems and subsystems; to
make conscious use of the
complex wisdom of the body
is to achieve a sublime
orchestral experience of the
self and its many ecologies.
Jean Houston

We are the hero of
our own story.
Mary McCarthy

Silence. Solitude. These words strike fear into the post-modern heart. We seem to have forgotten the power of escaping for a time into sanctuary, of listening to the breath or to the heartbeat of the earth. There are too many phone calls to be made, meetings to attend, children's noses to wipe, newspapers to read. Yet solitude has much to teach us. It takes courage to become a learner again. It asks that we trust enough in life to drop for a time all we know (or *think* we know) and to retreat for a day, a week, even only half an hour just to be – quietly receptive to whatever arises within or around us: the intense blue of a tiny flower which sears your senses, burning away every concern for daily life; a wild thought – and where did that come from? The fragrance of cinnamon sprinkled on a bowl of home made yoghurt. Such things go unnoticed unless we spend enough time alone to experience them.

The word 'alone' was once treated as two words: *all one*. To be all one meant to be wholly oneself – all of one piece. This is the great gift of sanctuary. Practised daily, silence and solitude helps heal confusion and mend the frazzled nerves which riddle modern life. Getting away from it all to sit on a rock or at a window and gaze at the sky, or look into the dance of our own mind, helps you come home to yourself. It allows the wildness of your intrinsic being to converse with your more rational side.

Your project this week is to lay aside ten minutes of every day in which you enter the sanctuary of your own being to sit or walk in silence. Allow yourself to become aware of how silence acts upon you. Is it something you are comfortable with or something that you try to avoid? Do you have the sense that there is a richness there that you are not yet tapping into? Be sure to record your experience of the sanctuary of solitude in your Travelogue.

Quantum Break 29

WILD TRACKING

Your intention:

TO DISCOVER THE WILDNESS WITHIN BY ENTERING THE
SACRED SILENCE

Energy follows intention. Until now you have been using the drum or the rattle
to awaken the consciousness matrix and allow it to bring access to quantum
realms. Now, you are ready to experiment with making that shift through silence
alone. There are many benefits to being able to do this. For instance, you may
not always be in a position to use a drum or a rattle comfortably when you want
to enter quantum consciousness for healing, for creativity, for information.
Also, it is important to come to the point where you realize that the drum and
the rattle are nothing more than tools for you to use to practise the craft of shifting consciousness. Once you have learned that craft you may, if you so choose,
gradually wean yourself away from the tools themselves.

I often journey without the sound of a drum or a rattle. I like being able simply
to focus my intention, enter the sacred silence, and then fulfil the purpose of my
journey, without having to rely on anything external. I think it is important that
eventually you develop this skill, otherwise you can end up like Dumbo when
his friend the mouse gave him a feather to hold in his trunk as a talisman to
make him believe that he could fly. The little floppy-eared elephant was under
the mistaken belief that it was the feather which held the power to fly when truly
it lay within himself. The feather was only a reminder of this. But it was only
when he accidentally dropped it that he discovered the truth. This is what you
too will be discovering with this journey, entering the sacred silence.

The devas say that they are
our source of inspiration in
many fields, including science.
Dorothy Maclean

With the exception of its
herbal knowledge, shamanism
generally has been ignored or
scorned by the medical and
academic world. Nevertheless,
shamans were the world's first
healers, first magicians, first
performing artists, and first
storytellers. Shamans can be
defined as native practitioners
who deliberately alter their
consciousness in order to
obtain knowledge and power
from the 'spirit world' which
can then be used to help and
to heal members of their tribe.
Stanley Krippner

- Call in your power animal. Entering the sacred silence is a method for activating your consciousness matrix without the use of any external tool.
- Sit or lie comfortably watching your breath go in and out of your body. Become aware of the way the breath moves. Is it cooler as you feel it come in through your nose? Warmer when it is exhaled?
- Now be aware of your body. Allow any muscle tension simply to sink into the floor beneath you so that you feel deeply connected with the earth.
- Whenever you are ready, it is time to state your intention. Do so silently within your own mind. Then gently do it again and again until you experience a consciousness shift.
- It will take you to a place of absolute stillness within.
- Now let yourself go deep, deep, deeper within. Let yourself move back in time, back to the time of the universe's beginnings.
- Allow yourself to follow all the way back through time.
- Let yourself experience your connectedness with the wild evolutionary power that burst forth at the birth of the universe and which continues to be expressed through all beings.
- See if you can trace the branches of its unfolding back to the original tree from which you come.
- When you do, follow that tree deep down into the roots of your own inexplicable wild order. What do you find there? What do these roots have to tell you about the deepest part of your own being and your connections with the natural world around you?
- When you are ready, give thanks to the spirits who have guided you and prepare to come back through the sacred silence to the room.

A river rose in Eden to water the garden.
Genesis 2:10

One way or another, we were made from the sacred elements that together compose the Earth. We are made from the Earth, we breathe it in with every breath we take, we drink it and eat it, and we share the same spark that animates the whole planet. Our stories tell us this, and so does our science.
David Suzuki with Amanda McConnell

Bridge Building

When recording the journey to the sacred silence, allow yourself to put pen to paper and simply write about it for at least 15 minutes (more if you like) without stopping and without ever picking up the pen from the paper. This practice creates a flow that allows you not to edit what is coming from the deepest layers of your being accessed through the sacred silence.

CALL OF THE WILD

Take a dozen steps into the solemn silence of a rainforest. As you enter this mysterious twilight you are immersed in past and future. You become part of a primeval world where all life feeds upon itself in a perfect balance of dark accord. You can watch as the whole history of creation is being played out before you, around you, beneath you, and you feel part of it. Here, the profusion of plants, insects, fungi, and the bacteria they contain, is wild power in its most concentrated form. Our rainforests are the main repository of the earth's gene pool. They are a source of almost infinitely rich morphic fields which have evolved over billions of years. They are also the most important natural resource we have. Wild virgin land carries a spiritual power which makes not only the human soul but the soul of plants and animals, rocks and mountains sing. Rainforests offer the living organisms of our planet a high degree of primordial life energy necessary for the perpetuation of their life.

Living organisms – from the smallest bacteria to the human body itself – are living contradictions. They challenge all the laws of Newtonian physics. The First Law of Thermodynamics states that the quantity of energy in the world remains constant. The Second is best formulated in terms of *entropy* – a measure of disorder at molecular and atomic levels. It states that energy tends to be constantly degraded from a higher to a lower order. In any system all motion eventually comes to a standstill, differences in electric or chemical potential are equalized, and temperature becomes uniform until finally a permanent state is reached – the whole system fades until it becomes an inert lump of matter. You throw a nail out in the garden. Soon it starts to rust. Then the rust eats away at it so much that in time nothing remains of the nail but powder. This state of thermodynamic equilibrium is what the physicist calls *maximum entropy*. It is what happens when meat rots.

> At the same time, various transpersonal experiences tend to undermine the belief in the mandatory nature of linear time and three-dimensional space by offering many experimental alternatives. Matter tends to disintegrate not only into playful energy patterns ultimately, interchangeable concepts. After the individual has been confronted with a considerable sample of transpersonal experiences, the Newtonian–Cartesian world view becomes untenable as a serious philosophical concept and is seen as a pragmatically useful, but simplistic, superficial, and arbitrary system of organizing one's every day experience.
> *Stanislav Grof*

SUCKING ORDER

Living systems are different. So long as your body is alive, it resists decaying into this inert state of equilibrium. It does this through metabolism – that is by assimilating energy from outside via the foods you eat, the air you breathe, the water you drink, and even the people and places you come in contact with. To stay alive every living organism, ourselves included, must continue to draw on the order of the universe's inherent

> Since after extinction no one will be present to take responsibility, we have to take full responsibility now.
> *Jonathan Schell*

Traditional cultures live in an animated world. Mountains, forests, rivers, lakes, winds and the sun may all have their presiding deities, while each tree, stone and animal may have, or be, a spirit. The spirits of the dead, or of the unborn, may also be eternally present, acting powerfully in the living world, part of the endless circle of time. Such world views may see all death, including that of humans, as simply one stage in the continuum of birth, life, death and rebirth that we see in nature. Human beings are included in this totality of creation participating in various ways in the creative mind of the living Earth. Instead of being separated from the world because of their unique consciousness, they belong to a conscious world in which everything interacts with everything else in a process of continual creation.
David Suzuki with
Amanda McConnell

wildness – an order far beyond our capacity to understand or to define. Nobel laureate Erwin Schrodinger described it in this way: Living systems *suck order* from their environment. Convenience foods, which the Western world now consumes to the exclusion of fresh, organically grown vegetables and fruits, poultry and meat, are not only largely devoid of essential elements such as magnesium and zinc, essential fatty acids and trace elements. They are also largely empty of the wild, life-sustaining energy of Shrodinger's order. Trying to survive on them can have you living in the twilight zone of health and creativity. Just how alive an organism is, just how well it resists decay, disease and degeneration, depends upon the quality of wild, primordial energy on which it draws – on the ordered complexity and richness of its morphic resonance, you could say, or the quality of spirit available to nourish it. This applies equally to the subtle fifth entity field energy scientists are studying as it does to the quality of food it gets.

The magnificence and the wonder of the rainforest lies not only in its beauty but in the ordered splendour of its wildness. It is a wildness which you can palpably feel as you walk beneath its dark canopy of life. Making my way amidst the tangled vines which drip with moisture in this living sea of a thousand shades of green always fills me with wonder, makes me realize just how far we have moved away from experiencing our own wildness in our urbanized, self-centred, mechanistic late-twentieth-century world. It makes me conscious of how desperately we need to reconnect with that wildness in ourselves, come to trust it and work with it in our lives as well as how deeply we need to acknowledge our dependence on life's magnificent, complex, organic order for its perpetuation.

Quantum Break 30

MIDDLEWORLD SPIRIT OF THE PLACE JOURNEY

Your intention:

TO EXPLORE A PLACE IN NATURE BY JOURNEYING TO IT IN THE NON-ORDINARY DOMAIN OF THE MIDDLEWORLD

For this exercise you will need to choose a sacred place. It can be a place that you have seen or a place that you would like to see but have only seen photographs of, such as Avebury, the Taj Mahal, the Pyramids, Bodhi Gaya, the Ganges, Wat Phai Lom. You will be journeying in non-ordinary reality to the sound of a drum. It will be just like any other journey to the upperworld or lowerworld, except that this time you and your power animal will be journeying in the non-ordinary aspects of the middleworld. (On every middleworld journey you do it is essential that you have your power animal with you). You may leave to do a middleworld journey either from where you are right now in physical reality, or from one of the places that you use to journey to the upperworld or lowerworld.

♦ Call your power animal. Explain to him the purpose of your journey, that you will be exploring a sacred site in its non-ordinary aspects. Go through the same preparations that you would go through for an upperworld or lowerworld journey: lie down, cover your eyes.

♦ When the drumming begins ask your power animal to take you to the place you have chosen. See what you can find out about the spirits of the place, the history of the place.

♦ Gather any information that this place may have especially to give to you.

♦ Return with the drum call-back as usual, thanking your power animal and any other helping spirits.

(Then) we, who always think we are small, will feel still smaller. And we will fear to use words. But it will happen that the words that we need will come of themselves. When the words we want to use shoot up of themselves – we get a new song.

Holger Kalweit

It is the story of all life that is holy and is good to tell, and of us two-leggeds sharing in it with the four-leggeds and the wings of the air and all green things; for these are children of one mother and their father is one Spirit.

Black Elk

Bridge Building

Record the experience of your journey. What have you learned from the non-ordinary aspect of the middleworld that you would not have found out by visiting the same place in ordinary reality. How does the information you have received tally with what has been written about this place in books?

Nature has many faces – the wild majesty of waves crashing against rocks, the silent pushing of baby fern heads through leaf mould towards the light, the cool clarity of a white horse grazing in moonlight. So do we as human beings. Moving into communion with nature also helps us remember this and to accept ourselves more fully in all our contradictions. When we consciously make a place for it in our lives, wildness becomes our secret friend and the driving force behind living our authentic power and celebrating our freedom.

Quantum Break 31

CONNECTING WITH THE WEATHER

Your intention:
TO GO OUTSIDE AND FORM A RELATIONSHIP WITH WHATEVER ASPECT OF WEATHER IS PRESENT

✦ Use the same techniques you used for entering the sacred silence. Make sure that you are completely relaxed and well in touch with the powers of gravity before you begin this exercise.

✦ Now go outdoors and allow yourself simply to be with whatever weather is present. Put your head back and let the power of the sun, or the rain, the wind, the snow, or the fog, penetrate your being. See if you can discover the nature of the spirit of whichever element you encounter and begin to develop a friendship with it.

- ✦ Allow into your consciousness an awareness of the particular qualities that each force of nature carries. Many people resist the rain, for instance, and in resisting render themselves closed off from the power that the rain brings to cleanse, refresh, renew and regenerate life. This power also exists within your own consciousness.
- ✦ See if you can let go of any resistance now and just allow yourself to be with the element.
- ✦ You may even discover that the experience of doing this has an ecstatic quality about it.
- ✦ The word ecstasy means to be raised to a high state of feeling, to become enraptured. There is really no other word which more accurately describes the experience of merging with the forces of nature.
- ✦ After ten or 15 minutes, thank the force that you have been working with and return to ordinary reality.

Though we appear to be solid, we are in fact, liquid bodies, similar in a way to gelatin, which also seems to be solid but is in fact largely water 'gelled' by the presence of an organic material.
Daniel Hillel

Bridge Building

Record this experience in any way you like. You may find that a poem works well. You may find that you have been given a power song while making these connections. If so, write it down.

To us the ashes of our ancestors are sacred and their resting place is hallowed ground.
Chief Seattle

FREE BREAKS

During your Free Breaks this week you might like to journey either to the upperworld or lowerworld to find out how you can honour the changing of the seasons, the new moon, the full moon, or the rising and the setting of the sun.

Or, you can try pebble rolling:

Before talking of holy things,
we prepare ourselves by
offerings ... one will fill his
pipe and hand it to the other
who will light it and offer it to
the sky and earth ... they will
smoke together ... Then will
they be ready to talk.

Mato-Kuwapi,
or Chased-By-Bears,
a Santee-Yanktonai Sioux

Sometime this week when you are out on a walk find two pebbles that appeal to you. Ask their permission to bring them home and put them in your sanctuary.

✦ Pick up both pebbles and put them between your two hands.
✦ Enter the sacred silence as you did in Quantum Break 29, and, slowly begin to rub the two pebbles round and round together between your palms.
✦ Listen to whatever messages the rocks are giving you. (This is an exercise that you should allow at least 20 minutes to half an hour to carry out as rocks are slow-speaking people.)
✦ When you have finished, thank the pebbles and either replace them where you got them or, with their permission, incorporate them into your own sanctuary.

CHECKLIST

Day One

✦ Read through the chapter as far as Quantum Break 27.
✦ Do Quantum Break 27 Walk on the Wild Side *to take an hour's walk and connect with the spirits of the place.*
✦ Bridge build.
✦ Read the instructions for Week Seven Project Sanctuary of Solitude on page 210 and begin to work with it.

Day Two

✦ Do Quantum Break 28 Communion with a Plant *to make a friend of a plant and discover its essence.*
✦ Bridge build.
✦ Spend ten minutes in silence as part of your project.

Stories are medicine ...They
have such power; they do not
require that we do, be, act anything – we need only listen.
The remedies for repair or
reclamation of any lost
psychic drive are
contained in stories.
Clarissa Pinkola Estes

Day Three

✦ Do Quantum Break 29 Wild Tracking *to discover the wildness within by entering the sacred silence.*
✦ Bridge build.
✦ Spend ten minutes in silence as part of your project.

Day Four

✦ Do Quantum Break 30 Middleworld Spirit of the Place Journey *to explore a sacred place by journeying to it in the non-ordinary domain of the middleworld.*
✦ Bridge build.
✦ Spend ten minutes in silence.

Day Five

✦ Do Quantum Break 31 Connecting with the Weather *to go outside and form a relationship with whatever aspect of weather is present.*
✦ Bridge build.
✦ Spend ten minutes in silence.

Day Six

✦ Do a Free Break exercise of your choice.
✦ Bridge build.
✦ Spend ten minutes in silence.

Day Seven

✦ Do another Free Break exercise – perhaps trying out pebble rolling.
✦ Bridge build.
✦ Spend ten minutes in silence.
✦ Spend 20 minutes doing your Travelogue.

Life itself is the proper binge.
Julia Child

I would like to learn, or remember, how to live.
Annie Dillard

The future's so bright
I gotta wear shades.
Timbuck Three

Travelogue

✦ How many days this week did you do your Quantum Breaks?

✦ Have you noticed any difference in your attitudes to the living world around you since you have been working with the powers of nature?

✦ Have you felt any connection with the wild order within the universe? Within nature? Within yourself?

✦ Did you allow yourself your ten minutes sanctuary time each day? If not, why not?

✦ Did you experience any blessings of Cocoon Spinning in the connections that you made this week with nature? Did you experience any greater sense of security having connected up with the world around you and the elements?

✦ Were there any other issues this week that you consider significant to expanding the facilities of your consciousness matrix? If so, note them down.

quantum leap 8

Return to the Centre

I stand at the axis of the world. I am the portal through which the quantum vacuum pours forth its abundance. I balance the six directions, I give access to the universe. Come to me and you will know your centre. Enter my field and you can become a conscious creator of your life and the life of the planet. Penetrate my darkness and you shall know rest.

I am the Master of the Centre

Stand at the sacred centre of the universe, the old mythology tells us, and you will be able to know all things. This week you will be experiencing the power of the axis mundi – the world navel. It is the same place Gamow describes out of which the primeval first atom expanded to create the universe. You will be working this locus of expansive power at the hidden centre of the cosmos.

Find your centre. Come to know where you stand in relation to the rest of the universe, and you simultaneously experience both safety and freedom. Try to live without a centre and you will be plagued by chronic feelings of emptiness and fear. The Danish existentialist philosopher Kierkegaard described this experience as 'fear and trembling … the sickness unto death.' It is the chronic emptiness that turns into nihilism and makes it seem that you are living in a wasteland. As human beings we have a constant need to fill ourselves up with spirit. In our society where connections with spirit are not easily made, this can mean filling up instead with an addiction, whether it be to alcohol, sex, drugs, work, fundamentalist religion or shopping. Living in a human body, with all the challenges this brings, is seldom an easy task. Life is too filled with uncertainty, at times with momentous change. To expand your consciousness and experience the freedom of being a multi-dimensional being in the midst of all this, you need to have a sense of where you stand in relation to the rest of the universe and you need to feel safe.

LIFE AT THE CENTRE

Conservation is a state of harmony between men and land. By land is meant all the things on, over, or in the Earth. Harmony with land is like harmony with a friend; you cannot cherish his right hand and chop off his left. That is to say, you cannot love game and hate predators; you cannot conserve the waters and waste the ranges; you cannot build the forest and mine the farm. The land is one organism.
Aldo Leopold

Familial and tribal bonds once created our sense of safety. Now we have to find it in other ways – by connecting deeply with our own centre and from there boldly exploring the ever-expanding universe around us. Throughout most of human history, whether he belonged to a tribal culture or one of the early civilizations in India, Greece, Mesopotamia or Egypt, man knew pretty much where he stood. Thanks to a cosmology and mythology which he shared with his society, he knew his sacred places on the land. He felt pretty sure of what was so and what was not so. He knew that the earth was the centre of the universe and his home was the centre of the earth. From our perspective now, it must have been very comforting to feel that where you stand is at the centre of everything.

Then, late in the sixteenth century a Polish guy called Copernicus came along and pointed out that the earth – far from being the centre of the universe – actually revolves around the sun. Man's safe world fell apart. His discovery was momentous. It challenged the accepted view of reality so profoundly that Copernicus actually waited until he was on his deathbed to reveal his findings. The reverberations of his discovery continue to send ripples of insecurity through us even now. The Copernican revolution inaugurated the 'age of science' which wiped out our sense of the sacred and hurled us into a fragmented, materialistic universe.

In virtually all of the world's mythological and religious traditions, you find the notion of a sacred centre – a place where the confines of the temporal world and all its rules and regulations dissolve away to give us access to the numinous. Stand at the centre and align yourself with the four directions – north, east, west and south. You not only rediscover the security of the centre within your own body, you can access vast spiritual power from both ordinary reality and the quantum realms – in short, from the whole universe.

THE WEEK AHEAD

This week there is lots of experiential stuff to do that will prepare you for working with the body, expanding creativity, and diving deeper into your own soul in the next four weeks. It is like a preparation for what's to come. You will be experiencing the power of the centre. You will be orientating yourself in space in ordinary reality and making a medicine wheel – a mirror in which your universe can be reflected. You will be connecting with the six directions and exploring the axis mundi, which reaches from the depths of the lowerworld through the middleworld all the way to the highest levels of the upperworld and then coming to experience it in your own body. Finally, you will be journeying to your core for rest and restoration, for creativity and to explore the way the universe itself comes into being. Begin by orientating yourself in time and space.

Could not scientists hope to graduate to an entirely complete, truly total vision of the observed and observable world? Unfortunately not: that would be overstepping the scope of science. A more modest (yet already incredibly ambitious) stance is fully warranted. First, because a truly total vision of the known world would include spiritual and metaphysical elements, and these – intuitions of the divine, of soul, and of other transcendent realities – are not accessible to scientific scrutiny, either now or in the foreseeable future. Second, because the items of experience that are accessible to science form an open set. New items could always be added to it, much as quarks, black holes and superconductors were added in the recent past. At any given time even the seemingly most complete scientific vision is only quasi-complete in regard to the vision that could emerge at a later time.
Ervin Laszlo

Quantum Break 32

SPIRITS OF THE FOUR DIRECTIONS

Myths help us to reconcile conflicts and contradictions and describe a coherent reality. They make a meaning that holds the group together and express a set of beliefs; even in our sceptical society, we live by myths that lie so deep we believe them to be reality.

David Suzuki
with Amanda McConnell

Your intention:
TO EXPLORE YOUR SENSE OF CENTRE IN SACRED SPACE

During this exercise you will not be journeying. You will be using your rattle to orientate yourself in time and space according to the four directions: north, south, east and west. This is an excellent way to begin a healing session or to centre yourself whenever you need the support of your cocoon.

You will need to know in ordinary reality in which direction north lies. You will also need your rattle.

+ Darken the room if possible.
+ Sit facing east.
+ Begin to rattle, calling in your spirits.
+ You might like to begin by shaking your rattle in four bursts of say seven shakes each with a pause in between. This can be a useful way to start and end any session of rattling that you do in the future.
+ Call in your power animals and helping spirits.
+ Rattle until you feel power–filled and sense that you are becoming a hollow bone.
+ Now, focusing your intention and rattling in the direction of the east, call in the spirits of the east.
+ Let yourself sense their nature. Do you see any images of colour or animals, qualities or sounds that seem to be connected with the east? What is the nature of the east?

- Now turn your body towards the south and rattle in the spirits of the south. Do you sense any images of colour or animals, qualities or sounds that seem to be connected with the south? What is the nature of the south?
- Now turn your body towards the west and rattle in the spirits of the west. Do you sense any images of colour or animals, qualities or sounds that seem to be connected with the west? What is the nature of the west ?
- Now turn your body towards the north and rattle in the spirits of the north. Do you sense any images of colour or animals, qualities or sounds that seem to be connected with the north? What is the nature of the north?
- Continuing to rattle, let yourself experience what it is like to be seated at the centre of the world – your world – with the spirits of the four directions supporting you.
- After a few minutes you can stop rattling and simply rest in the presence of the compassionate energies which surround you.
- When you are ready, shake your rattle again in four bursts as you turn once again in the four directions to thank the spirits for their presence and let them know that they are free to go now.

Bridge Building

Record what you have perceived about the nature of the four directions. Be sure to write down any images or symbols associated with each of them for you will be using these later in your week's project. You are beginning to create your own medicine wheel. It will become richer and richer as you work with the directions and experience the sense of being at your core.

AXIS MUNDI

The next step is to anchor yourself within the world axis at the centre of your being and connect above and below. You can read about the axis mundi in the Old Testament story of Jacob's Ladder. 'And he dreamed and behold a ladder set up on the earth, and the top of it reached to heaven: and behold the angels of God ascending and descending on it.

For perhaps the first time the landscape of meaning is supplanted by the landscape of fact. Before the Renaissance human beings, like other creatures, occupied a qualitatively heterogeneous world, riddled with significant places. Only the offspring of the Renaissance have ever imagined it to be all the same, neutral matter for transformation and exploitation. This they accomplished by scraping all traces of value from the environment and vesting it solely within the boundaries of the ego. The result is an aggrandizement of the individual human being and the creation of a bare and bleached environment.
Neil Evernden

And, behold, the Lord stood above it, and said, "I am the Lord God of Abraham thy father, and the God of Isaac: the land whereon thou liest, to thee will I give it, and to thy seed; and thy seed shall be as the dust of the earth, and thou shalt spread abroad to the west, and to the east, and to the north and to the south: and in thee and in thy seed shall all the families of the earth be blessed …" and Jacob awakened out of this sleep, and he said, "Surely the Lord is in this place!"' (Genesis 28:10-14, 18-19)

You also find it in the Greek notion of omphalos – the navel or hub of the world which is considered the divine body out of which creation emerges. To the Buddhists it is Mount Meru, centre of the created universe. You see it recreated again and again in visual form in the magnificent sand paintings of Tibetan Lamas. The Hebrews called it the *beth-el* which means the dwelling place of the divine. On the earth this was consid-ered to be Jerusalem. For Christians Jerusalem was also the axis mundi: at one and the same time the place where Jesus died on the cross and where the tree of life grows at the centre of the world. The omphalos is always found at the centre of a circle into which spiritual power from all directions can be drawn and out of which created form emerges. You will even find it in the Chinese symbol for yin and yang and in the magic circle drawn by children on the playground. Even kids know instinctually that once you go inside this circle you gather power. (You are also protected from attack by the oppos-ing team in a game of hide and seek.)

MEDICINE WHEEL

Native Americans have a wonderful way of working with the world axis. It is called the medicine wheel. The medicine wheel is a circle created in time and space, aligned with the four directions and often constructed from small stones. It connects you with all people, all places, and all life. It is like a mirror in which everything in the universe is reflected. It links you up with the powers of the north, south, east and west. Wisdom, it is said, comes from the north. The colour of the north is white. It is the realm of White Buffalo. Illumination is the gift of the east. Its colour is yellow and its power that of Eagle. At the south the colour is green. It is the direction of innocence and purity of heart. Its animal is Mouse. In the west you find Bear and the colour black. He brings the power of prayer and introspection. Each tribe has its own variation on the medicine wheel theme. You will already have begun finding your own in Quantum Break 32 Spir-its of the Four Directions. What is important is that you place yourself at the centre of the four directions in alignment with the spiritual energies of the universe and discover your own centre on the medicine wheel. This starting place, your centre, gives you your own vantage point for looking at the universe – that which is most easy and natural for you to use throughout your life. From this place you will be able to make the experience of the axis mundi one of great power. In time you will also come to know your own world centre and rest in safety and wisdom within it.

BUILD A MEDICINE WHEEL

Week Eight Project

This week you will begin making a medicine wheel in ordinary reality to reflect in visual and tactile terms the experiences you have had in carrying out your Quantum Breaks. You can construct it with pebbles if you like, either indoors at the site of your sanctuary or outdoors – whichever you prefer. There are advantages to both. If you have the luxury of a garden it can be an enormously satisfying experience to make a big medicine wheel which, if you get really ambitious, you might like to plant eventually as a herb garden. Or you can simply create a circle of stones aligned to the four directions that you can sit in the centre of and carry out your quantum work. If you prefer, make a small medicine wheel indoors on which you can place particular objects, colours or pictures at each direction which relate to your experience of the qualities of the energy of each.

Begin by laying out a circle of twelve stones of equal size. Then make a smaller circle using eight smaller stones in the centre. Now connect the larger and the smaller circle up with three stones between the inner and outer ring spanning out towards each of the four directions. Finally you can place in the appropriate places on the circle whatever you choose to represent the powers of each direction for you. Use your medicine wheel for centring, as a place of prayer and healing. Let it remind you of your own personal medicine and the gifts of the spirits through which you have come to know it. And let it gather objects to represent the spirit qualities of each of the four directions as you come to know them better. Your medicine wheel will grow and become richer as your experience of the centre deepens in your own being.

The new meaning of soul is creativity and mysticism. These will become the foundation of the new psychological type and with him or her will come the new civilization.
Otto Rank

It is through ritual that we separate our ordinary selves from our extraordinary possibilities and create the sacred time necessary to address important questions with the attention they deserve.
Carl A. Hammerschlag

THE CENTRE IS EVERYWHERE

The most moving description of the sacred centre that I have ever come across is that of Black Elk who was a Keeper of the Sacred Pipe for the Oglala Sioux. He told his experience to John G. Neihardt who recorded it in *Black Elk Speaks*:

'Then I was standing on the highest mountain of them all, and round about beneath me was the whole hoop of the world. And while I stood there I saw more than I can tell and I understood more than I say; for I was seeing in a sacred manner the shapes of all things in the spirit, and the shape of all shapes as they must live together like one being. And I saw that the sacred hoop of my people was one of many hoops that made one circle, wide as daylight and as starlight, and in the centre grew one mighty flowering tree to shelter all the children of one mother and one father. And I say that it was holy.'

The mountain Black Elk stood upon when he had this experience was Harney Peak in the Black Hills. Later Black Elk told Neihardt the most important thing of all. 'But *anywhere* is the centre of the world.'

When we rest in stillness at the axis mundi, or world navel, we are able to unlock the energies of life, freeing them to stream forth into our consciousness and out into the world around us, carrying their blessings for all. It is the place in shamanism from which we journey into numinous realms – upwards to the upperworld, downwards to the lowerworld, and outwards into the non-ordinary aspects of the middleworld which is the world we live in. And it is enormously important to come to experience your own axis mundi. It has to be a *personal* world centre these days as we have lost connections with our local mythological inheritance. A good connection with the axis mundi provides you with a powerful grounding in ordinary reality for activating the consciousness matrix and journeying into the realms of healing and creativity. That is what we will be doing during the next two weeks in your journey to freedom.

Quantum Break 33

THE CENTRE OF THE WORLD

Your intention:

TO CALL IN THE SPIRITS OF THE SIX DIRECTIONS AND DISCOVER
THE AXIS MUNDI WITHIN

+ This is another exercise which you will do in ordinary reality with your rattle.
+ You will be calling in the spirits of the four directions with your rattle.
+ Follow the guidelines in Quantum Break 32.
+ Once the spirits of the four directions are present, call upwards with your rattle to the spirits of the upperworld, including your Wise One, asking them to join you.
+ Now call in those of the lowerworld, including your power animals. You will also be calling in the spirits of the place.
+ Once all these spirits are present and you are filling up with power, let yourself experience what it is like to be connected with all six directions through the spirit energies that have come from each.
+ Sense the compassionate nature of the energy that enters into your body from all four directions and from above and below.
+ Let yourself enjoy being at the centre of this great three-dimensional cross formed when upper joins lower, east joins west and north joins south.
+ Find out just where in your body these energies meet.
+ What is it like to feel perfectly poised at the centre of this multi-dimensional universe?
+ When you are ready, shake your rattle again in four bursts as you turn once again in the six directions to thank the spirits for their presence and let them know that they are free to go now.

Perhaps a greater demand has never been laid upon mankind: for by this admission (that the earth is not the centre of the universe), how much else did not collapse in dust and smoke: a second paradise, a world of innocence, poetry, and piety, the witness of the senses, the convictions of a poetic and religious faith; no wonder that men had no stomach for all this, that they ranged themselves in every way against such a doctrine.

Goethe

At the centre of the Earth
Stand looking around you.
Recognizing the tribe
Stand looking around you.
Third Sacred Day of the
Lakota Sun Dance

Bridge Building

Record your experience. How was it different to be connected up with all six dimensions rather than only with four? What did you sense about the nature of the spirits of the place? Is the feeling of being poised at the centre of your universe one which was new to you or are you familiar with it? Might it be useful to you to repeat this exercise in the future?

Physical concepts are free creations of the human mind, and
are not, however it may seem,
uniquely determined by the
external world. In our endeavour to understand reality we
are somewhat like a man trying to understand the mechanism of a closed watch. He
sees the face and the moving
hands, even hears its ticking,
but he has no way of opening
the case. If he is ingenious he
may form some picture of a
mechanism which could be
responsible for all the things
he observes, but he may never
be quite sure his picture is the
only one which could explain
his observations. He will never
be able to compare his picture
with the real mechanism and
he cannot even imagine the
possibility of the meaning of
such a comparison.
Albert Einstein and
Infeld Leopold

SCIENCE AND THE SACRED CENTRE

When Copernicus destroyed man's mythological connections to the centre of the world with his revelation that the earth was not the centre of anything, an interesting split took place between religion and science. Before then the world itself and every-thing in it was considered sacred. Now suddenly man, displaced from his centre, became separated from the world and he began to lose his awareness of its sacredness. The world turned into a mechanical thing out there which he could study, describe and manipulate any way he chose. As a result, religion became very anthropocentric in orientation. For man, now alone and thrown out of his place of power, became con-cerned only about his personal connection to an abstract god. He was no longer able to see god in the trees around him, in the changes of the seasons, in the breath of morning. As a result, instead of husbanding the earth as he had when he was aware of its sacredness, he gradually began to exploit it. That is pretty much how things have gone on for 400 years.

Science and sacred mythology – once expressed in the world's great religions – went their separate ways. Newtonian physics and Cartesian philosophy ensured that never the twain would meet. That is how we came to lose our connections with the centre. And the mythologies on which our experience of place depended became to us the curious contrivances of what we considered – in our intellectually superior way – 'primitive minds'.

Since then we have tried to fill the spiritual holes with anything we could – from fast cars to Ph.D.s. The sacred centre of the universe was gone. With it went our own individual experience of the axis mundi and our ability to call on the powers of the six directions to help us live our lives. Our worldview derived from mechanistic science and philosophy destroyed it, presumably for ever, and the last thing anybody ever expected to happen was for science to be putting it back together again. Yet that is exactly what is happening – right now.

There is a whole new world mythology being born right now and it comes – of all things – out of emerging paradigm science. It is developing out of discoveries in astronomy, astrophysics and the exploration of holographically-functioning fields. For the first time in human history as the twenty-first century dawns, science is pointing us towards not a local tribal mythology but a truly global one. Scientists, philosophers and cosmologists are developing explanations of reality that not only restore man's place at the centre of the universe (despite the earth revolving around the sun), they confirm that, as Black Elk taught, each man and woman stands at 'the centre of the world'. And out of this centre the sacred power of the universe flows through each one of us. Let's look at how such a radical change in perspective came about.

MEET THE EXPANDING UNIVERSE

In 1917 Einstein came up with a model of the universe that grew out of his new theory of general relativity. Looking at time as a fourth dimension, he showed that the force of gravity was equivalent to a curvature of this four-dimensional space. Out of this, Einstein revealed that the universe, far from being a static entity – a machine put in motion, adhering to permanent laws as assumed since Copernicus and Newton – must be either *expanding* or *contracting*. Yet this revelation was overwhelming to him. It so went against scientific belief that it frightened even Einstein, forcing him to alter his mathematical equations. So he introduced a 'cosmological constant' to his mathematics so that, in keeping with the paradigms of Newtonian physics, the universe still appeared to be static. By doing this he missed the opportunity to scientifically predict the expansion of the universe. Einstein later referred to this doctoring of his equation as the 'biggest mistake of my life.'

It was not long, however, before somebody corrected him. The Russian mathematician Alexander Friedman wrote to Einstein in the early 1920s to say how much he admired his genius but that, by his own calculation, the one thing missing from Einstein's equations is the fact that the universe is not a static entity; it is expanding. In 1924 the American astronomer Edwin Hubble actually *saw* the universe expanding through his telescope. Before long he called Einstein and invited him to take a look. Meanwhile, the Dutch astronomer Wilem de Sitter had also developed an expanding

Newtonian physics and quantum mechanics are partners in a double irony. Newtonian physics is based upon the idea of laws which govern phenomena and the power inherent in understanding them, but it leads to impotence in the face of a Great Machine which is the universe. Quantum mechanics is based upon the idea of minimal knowledge of future phenomena (we are limited to knowing probabilities) but it leads to the possibility that our reality is what we choose to make it.

There is another fundamental difference between the old physics and the new physics. The old physics assumes that there is an external world which exists apart from us. It further assumes that we can observe, measure, and speculate about the external world without changing it. According to the old physics, the external world is indifferent to us and our needs.

Gary Zukav

model of the universe. Then in 1927 the Belgian abbé Georges Lemaitre worked out his own solution to Einstein's missing link. He suggested that galaxies are fragments which have been thrown out by the explosion of the first atom that brought the universe into being – the *primeval atom*. This, he said, resulted in the expansion of the universe.

Their work set the stage for the big bang theory which came from Russian–American physicist George Gamow in 1948. This was later confirmed by Arno Penzias and Robert Wilson in the 1960s, and – give or take a few bits and pieces – this remains the currently accepted model of our universe. It goes something like this. The universe is not static as Newtonian physics has led us to believe. Neither is it ruled by immutable laws, nor is it eternal. It came into being in a gigantic explosion – a great flaring forth – within which the various elements we have in the world were produced as a result of the extraordinarily high density within the primeval atom and the rapid expansion which this brought about. As the primeval atom expanded, hydrogen and helium cooled and condensed into stars and galaxies. Gamow's work explained the expansion of the universe and what is known as Hubble's law (more about this in a moment).

THE UNIVERSE EXPLODES

From a scientific perspective Newton's notion of a fixed universe – like a box within which all the stars and matter exists – had been laid to rest forever. Later other scientists such as Arno Penzias and Robert Wilson were able to detect and measure the cosmic background of radiation that burst forth from this cataclysmic event and calculate that it apparently occurred some 15 to 20 billion light years away. Scientists not only confirmed that the big bang took place, but also that the galaxies created by it are *rushing* away from each other with an ever-increasing velocity. The farther apart they are the faster they are flying away from the single ineffable point where the birth of the universe happened.

These discoveries are nothing less than mind-blowing. They affect the lives of every one of us. For suddenly the centre of the universe is no longer tribal or cultural. It is not Jerusalem or Mount Meru but right here. The universe, created 15 billion years ago, continues to be created right now with us. For each of us in a very real sense *is* at the centre of this expanding universe. So amazing is this fact, say scientists, that to come to an understanding of how such a thing is possible we need to completely change the way we view reality. And just as the visionaries and mystics have always told us, coming to an

The psychological rule says that when an inner situation is not made conscious, it happens outside, as fate. That is to say, when the individual remains undivided and does not become conscious of his inner contradictions, the world must perforce act out the conflict and be torn into opposite halves.

Carl Jung

awareness of this and 'sitting in the centre of the universe' gives our consciousness access to the same vast spiritual power which brought the universe into being. Bear with me and we'll see if we can follow the route science has taken so we can come to an understanding of how.

HUBBLE'S LAW

While Hubble was calculating the distances of various galaxies from the earth, he discovered that all the galaxies are moving away from us and that the further away a galaxy is from us the faster is the rate of its movement. Galaxies in all directions are moving away from our home in the Milky Way. Because of this, and because of the limiting mechanistic worldview which we inherited, you would naturally assume that the Milky Way is at the centre of the universe. Not so, say the mathematicians and astrophysicists. And to understand how, we need to think in totally different ways. Imagine a balloon with evenly spaced dots painted on its surface. If you were an observer standing on any one of these dots – which would from your point of view be at the centre – you would see all the other dots expanding away from you just the way scientists now see all the galaxies receding from our Milky Way. And no matter which spot you stood on, that would be the centre of the universe coming forth from it as it continues to expand.

Not only has the discovery of Hubble and others shaken science and its belief in a permanent, unchanging, fixed universe, to its very foundations (we are still feeling the shock waves from it and probably will for a long time to come), all this also sounds to the ears of the average person like a contradiction in terms. How can we find ourselves at the very centre of the universe, and at the same time know that the birth of this universe, which took place 15 billion light years away from us, is at the same time happening here and now?

FINDING THE CENTRE

To find the answer we have to go back to the Newtonian–Cartesian-based worldview which, although it has served us well in many ways, is nowhere near large enough to encompass the discovery of what we now know to be true. According to Newton the universe is a huge fixed space – like a big box inside of which particles move about and interact with each other. It is this worldview that all of us have been brought up to

We milk the cow of the
world, and as we do
We whisper in her ear,
'You are not true.'
Richard Wilbur

I rightly conclude that my essence consists in this alone, that I am a thinking thing … And although perhaps … I have a body with which I am closely conjoined, I have, on the one hand, a clear and distinct idea of myself as a thinking, non-extended thing, and, on the other hand, a distinct idea of my body as an extended, non-thinking thing; it is therefore certain that I am truly distinct from my body, and can exist without it.
Descartes

accept – a sense of the universe as a mechanical system devoid of consciousness. Yet the birth of the universe which twentieth-century scientists have discovered is in no way some kind of mechanical birth that took place within Newton's big black box. It was a birth of everything – all the light, all the elementary particles, even *time* and *space* itself. All this, they tell us, literally erupted out of nothing, blazing in an instant out of the mysterium tremendum at the axis mundi – that very point, the centre of the universe which shamans and mythologists, mystics and visionaries have told us throughout history gives us access to sacred power that can change the world. It is found at the centre of the circle and that centre of the circle, with all the power it encompasses, lies within each one of us.

One man, mathematical cosmologist Brian Swimme, has done more than any other to articulate the beauty and monumental significance of these discoveries on our lives. In *The Hidden Heart of the Cosmos* he writes:

> 'The universe began as a titanic bestowal, a stupendous quantum of free energy given forth from the bottomless vaults of generosity … Every place in the universe is at the centre of this exploding reality. From our place on Earth today in the midst of the Virgo Supercluster, all of the universe explodes away from us, just as it does from the perspective of anyone in the Perseus Supercluster. We are at the unmoving centre of this cosmic expansion, and we have been here at the centre from the beginning of time.'

UNIVERSAL CENTRE

The local centre of the universe, the axis mundi, which once formed the core of safety and creativity and gave access to spiritual power in tribal cultures has become a universal centre. We are living in a new universe, one which is continually evolving, reshaping itself, adjusting, creating and destroying as it unfolds. Finally, and here lies the greatest revelation of all, because the cosmic vacuum – Bohm's implicate order – out of which it has come appears in some not as yet understood form of consciousness, it gives our personal consciousness access to the powers of creation and evolution on a highly personal level. By working with the same power that brought about the first flaring forth of the universe, our conscious self-awareness married to our intention may play a direct role, not only in this process, but in the evolution of the world. As Swimme says:

We are the bees of the invisible. We madly gather the honey of the visible to store in the great golden hive of the invisible.
Rainer Maria Rilke

'That which blossomed forth as cosmic egg 15 billion years ago now blossoms forth as yourself, as one's family, as one's community of living beings, as our blue planet, as our ocean of galaxy clusters. The same fecund source – then and now; the same numinous energy – then and now ... to enter the centre of the cosmos is not "mathematical science", nor is it "inside" science, nor is it "owned" by science. *The centre of the cosmos is each event in the cosmos. Each person lives in the centre of the cosmos ... the actual origin of the universe is where you live your life.'* (Emphasis Swimme's.)

So how do you begin to work with such revelations in a practical way? You journey on it.

AT THE CORE

Within the human body are to be found many centres of energy – the seven chakras for instance – these vortices of energy, each of which is related to a different level of consciousness as well as different organs and systems and the Hara – the centre of power within the belly which plays such an important role in the martial arts. There is also a centre known as the *core* at the level of your navel. Dancers know it well as do those who practice t'ai chi, chi kung and yoga. It is something like a gyroscope – a swirling horizontal disk revolving around a vertical axis which is held stable through a dynamic tension of the upward pulling spiritual energies and the force of gravity which anchors you on the earth in space and time. This core is a place of profound peace and dynamism connected both with the axis mundi and with the beautiful medicine wheel at the centre of Native American spirituality. It also appears to be connected with the cosmic centre – that centre out of which the birth of creation happened 15 billion years ago and continues to happen right now.

I knew little about this centre in the body until I came upon it within myself in the midst of a shamanic journey. I was shown a place at the centre of my body below the solar plexus yet above the energy centre of the Hara. It looks like a slowly revolving whirlpool of energy. My shamanic exploration of this place within the body began as I came upon this core again and again while journeying. I was told is the core from which creation and destruction come. Since then I have met a number of shamans who are familiar with it within the human body. New Zealand shaman and healer Rosemareyn van der Sluis is one of them. She describes it in this way, 'This wheel of energy is like

Seldom are surprises allowed to emerge in Western ritual today. Even the Spirit is locked into a box.
Matthew Fox

You are not my enemies, you are my brothers and sisters. You did not do anything to me or my people. All that happened a long time ago in the lives of our ancestors. And, at that time I might actually have been on the other side. We are all children of the Great Spirit, we all belong to Mother Earth. Our planet is in great trouble and if we keep carrying old grudges and do not work together, we will all die.
Chief Seattle

the flat surface of an apple cut in half. It is not the whole apple, but this is an eminently workable blueprint. It is the same blueprint that in the Native American model of spirituality is called the medicine wheel. The lowest part is our earth connection. The top part stands for the spirit, that which we reach toward, and in the middle, the fly-wheel, is the creative centre.'

From my point of view this core looks like a slowly revolving galaxy of stars or light. It revolves in a horizontal plane between the top and bottom of us and it looks very much like what astronomers call a black hole. I and others who have worked with the core have learned that here, at the very centre of this revolving energy in your body is to be found a sacred place of deep quiet, healing, vision, as well as the centre of creative power which parallels that which scientists have been studying in the cosmos. Let's journey into it.

> We can return to a life of morality through telling and listening to stories, through experiencing genuine awe, through participating in rituals and ceremonies. Each allows us to give expression to personal experience while connecting with our communities. We must reinvest our ceremonies and symbols with life-giving, healthful meaning. That is how we can make sense of our lives.
> *Carl A. Hammerschlag*

Quantum Break 34

JOURNEY TO YOUR CORE

Your intention:
TO GO TO YOUR CORE WITHIN YOUR BODY AND DISCOVER ITS PURPOSE

✦ Call in the spirits of the six directions as well as your power animals and any helping spirits you would like to have with you.
✦ Using a rattle or drumming tape let yourself enter deep into the centre of your body to this place that sits in perfect balance between heaven and earth within you.
✦ Remember that for this journey you will be entering into the energetic realm of your body which lies beneath or beyond the physiological level of blood vessels and muscles, organs and systems.

- Look for a slowly revolving disk of energy that sits on a horizontal plane at the level of your navel, or just above. It may look like the movement of stars around the centre of a galaxy. It may appear in some other way to you.
- Notice which direction it is revolving in. Sit on the disk as it revolves. What does it feel like? What is the nature of the light energy you experience from it?
- Let yourself enjoy the beauty of this place and of the circular movement of which you are a part.
- Now move to the centre of this vortex. Let yourself look into the deep velvet darkness of the space you find there.
- Notice what has happened to any worries or mental chatter you may have had with you when you moved to this centre and entered into your core.
- Find out what the nature of this centre – this black hole – is for you and how you can make use of it to enhance your experience of freedom and help you live your own authentic power.
- Remain in this place of quiet for a few minutes. Let yourself enjoy its stillness.
- Gently return to ordinary reality coming back to the room you are in.

Bridge Building

What did you find at the core of your being? What have you learned about how to work with it in your life? Does what you found within you bear any resemblance to Swimme's description of the centre of the cosmos?

SEARCH FOR ECHOES

My shamanic discovery of this place within the body and my fascination with it has led me to explore this phenomenon of the core further. Again and again I came upon this place within the body which I was told is the core within us from which creation and destruction come within us. When something like this comes up again and again in my

It's a funny thing about life; if you refuse to accept anything but the best, you very often get it.
Somerset Maugham

shamanic work it sends me in search of some kind of reassurance that what I have come upon coincides with something also experienced by others. At that time I knew nothing about Hubble, Gamow, Swimme, or the new cosmology. I searched through book after book on human spiritual development and the energy body from which I hoped to find some echo of what I had seen in my journey. All to no avail. I could find lots of material about chakras and about energy centres in the martial arts but nothing to support what I had seen. It was at this point, just about believing that I had experienced something which had little relevance to anyone but me, I came upon a book on astronomy. Within I discovered an amazing outer manifestation of what I had seen within – both a description of the dark centre out of which swirly light emerges and the description of how the universe is now believed to have come into being.

Your conscious mind may be saying – as mine did when I first came across this dark space like a black hole at the core of me – how on earth can a black hole feel safe and comforting? It should be scary and daunting. Maybe in ordinary reality but not in the luminous realms of being we enter on a journey.

To love oneself is the beginning of a life-long romance.
Oscar Wilde

Quantum Breaks 35 & 36

BLACK IS BEAUTIFUL

Your intention:
TO ENTER THE CORE WITHIN YOU AND EXPLORE IT FURTHER

For Quantum Breaks 35 and 36 you will be exploring further the nature of this core within you. You can choose from the suggestions listed below which exploration you want to make. Then for your Free Breaks either journey on another one or, if you prefer, go back and make use of any of the exercises you have worked with in the past eight weeks putting them to use in any way you wish.

Grace strikes us when we are in great pain and restlessness … Sometimes at that moment a wave of light breaks into our darkness, and it is as though a voice were saying: 'You are accepted'.
Paul Johannes Tillich

There are a number of ways of working with your core.

1. The velvet darkness of the centre of your core is a place of great peace where within a few minutes you can experience a sense of rest and restoration. Ten minutes in this place can be worth two or three hours of sleep. Try it.

2. You can use your core to cleanse your body and your psyche of anxiety, confusion and fear when they arise simply by journeying to its velvet stillness at the centre. For just as a black hole in the cosmos literally draws into it every molecule of matter that has outlived its usefulness, so does this sacred core seem to swallow negativity, transmuting it into new life. The power of this can be truly remarkable.

3. Paradoxically, when you feel most empty, going to the emptiness at your core, can fill you up with a rich sense of being. I know no other way to describe it. It is the same experience that you get as you step into any sacred place or when your heart is full of love.

4. Journeying daily to the core in this way for ten to 15 minutes can slowly but inexorably help dissolve away addictive patterns in your life.

5. You can also use a core journey to plant the seed of something that you want to create in your life. You place within the centre your vision and ask it to incubate there until it is ready to burst forth in a new form. All creation comes out of two things: intention and compassion.

> Just trust yourself, then you will know how to live.
> *Goethe*

> True artists and true physicists know that nonsense is only that which, viewed from our present point of view, is unintelligible. Nonsense is nonsense only when we have not yet found that point of view from which it makes sense.
> *Gary Zukav*

Bridge Building

Don't forget to Bridge build. You will be surprised at how, even when journeys or practices you carry out which at the time seem not very important or relevant to you, can turn out a few days or even weeks or months later to offer valuable information, inspiration or guidance just when you are most in need of it.

FREE BREAKS

I would suggest that you use your Free Breaks this week to explore the restorative properties of journeying to your core. Or go back and repeat any of the work you have been doing for any purpose you wish.

CHECKLIST

Day One

+ Read through the chapter at least as far as Quantum Break 32.
+ Do Quantum Break 32 Spirits of the Four Directions *to explore your sense of centre in sacred space.*
+ Bridge build.

Day Two

+ Read the rest of the chapter if you have not already done so.
+ Do Quantum Break 33 The Centre of the World *to call in the spirits of the six directions and discover the axis mundi within.*
+ Bridge build.
+ Take a look at Week Eight Project, Build a Medicine Wheel on page 227.

Day Three

+ Do Quantum Break 34 Journey to Your Core *to go to your core within your body and discover its purpose.*
+ Bridge build.
+ Continue working on your medicine wheel project.

Day Four

+ Do Quantum Break 35 or 36 Core Exercises.
+ Bridge build.

Day Five

+ Do Quantum Break 35 or 36 Core Exercises.
+ Bridge build.

Day Six

+ Do a Free Break exercise of your choice.
+ Bridge build.
+ Complete your work on your medicine wheel project.

Day Seven

+ Do a Free Break exercise of your choice.
+ Bridge build.
+ Spend 20 minutes on your Travelogue.

This is the great realization of the Upanishads as early as the tenth or ninth century B.C. – 'You are it.' The mystery that you're looking for and you think is somewhere external to yourself is not out there at all. It's what you are. You don't have to go anywhere to find the Promised Land. It's here, inside every human being. It's where you are. It's what you are.

Joseph Campbell

Travelogue

+ How many days this week did you take your Quantum Break? Have you been tempted to let them go? What was the experience of going to the core like for you?
+ How did you feel about experiencing your own axis mundi? Was it reassuring? Or something that you already regularly experience?
+ Did you make your medicine wheel? This is something you can continue to develop as you become more and more familiar with your own brand of medicine.
+ Were there any other issues that arose for you this week which you consider important in your own journey to freedom? Describe them.

Climbing the Tree

Your being is not mortal, it is transitory and transformational. Moving through space and time it changes from form to form. Its power and its influence, its sensitivity and awareness go far beyond the limits of your skin. In a very real sense your body is the universe, the world tree at the axis mundi rooted deep within the earth. It grows as you grow towards the heavens. Honour the energies of that tree within. Thanks to its presence, your body is born and dies but it is never lost. A sanctuary, a fortress, a bird in flight towards heaven, the powers of your body are the powers of the universe. Celebrate them.

I am the Spirit of the Body

Remember the joy of tree climbing as a kid? Welcome back. Rooted in darkness and crowned with light, the world tree forms the ladder by which you can travel the universe. Sit in its trunk and know safety. Enter its roots to find the answer to the question, 'what was your original face before you where born?' Slither up its branches and revel in the leaves and petals of becoming.

How often do you rejoice in your body? How often do you feel absolutely at ease in your skin, at peace in yourself and in harmony with your world? For many of us the answer is seldom. Instead we tend to put up with the body rather like some slightly cumbersome baggage we carry with us as we go about. Yet all thought, all feeling, every response to beauty and to horror is mediated through the body. Your body is the medium for experiencing everything in your life. As any healthy two-year-old knows, when it is fully alive you are fully alive. This aliveness is something we often have to rediscover.

THE BODY AS OBJECT

Television, films and advertising are replete with photographs of long-legged pencil-thin females who are meant to be paragons of womanhood against whom we measure ourselves. Magazines and newspapers spend a large part of their time giving us advice about diets, clothes and exercise, which will supposedly help the bodies of their readers approach more closely whatever shape, size and texture the general consensus at any moment considers ideal. Meanwhile millions of women have not a hope in hell of ever looking like that ideal simply because of the way they are built. And they suffer.

This suffering goes deep – far beyond the simple yet painful feelings of inadequacy which come with having been blessed with broad shoulders, big feet or a flat chest when the world you live in tells you you are *supposed* to be different. For implicit in the whole way the body is presented in almost everything we do and think are two far more crippling assumptions. That the *body is separate from the spirit* or person and that it is ultimately *inferior*. These assumptions are anchored deep into Greco–Roman and Christian belief systems which our society has developed. They have led us to view the body either as something not to be trusted – like a wild animal that needs taming lest it gets out of hand – or like a physical object *outside* ourselves to be watched, controlled and manipulated. To work with the body, to live in a body, to feel comfortable with your body, and to be able to make use of its energies as a vehicle for your own freedom, you need to feel OK about being in it. There is no better way to do this than to work with the power of the world tree.

THE WORLD TREE

Like a tree, our bodies are rooted in darkness – the darkness of the womb, the darkness of our ancestral inheritance, the darkness of our deepest longings and our deepest fears. Also like a tree we are crowned with the light of awareness, and as our seedpower grows upwards towards its full enfolding, that light becomes greater and greater. We are continually reaching upwards as a tree does. We are forever growing and renewing ourselves like a tree, letting go of what becomes decayed and no longer serves us. Our roots lie in our past – not within this life but in our primordial past out of which we and all of life has evolved.

We grow in physical stature. We unfold both physically and spiritually around the individual axis – in resonance with the world axis as long as we grow true to our soul's purpose.

This axis allows us shamanically to visit the upperworld and lowerworld and to return to the centre from which we started with absolute safety and control. It allows us to explore the radiant universe and bring back its gifts while remaining grounded in our body and in ordinary reality. In shamanic mythology the world tree, or cosmic tree, is at the centre of the universe. The shaman aligns himself with its place and its purpose. The world axis becomes his axis, the macrocosm becomes the microcosm. Go to your centre and you can experience your central axis or inner tree – the unifying structure from which all individual growth unfolds. Soon you will start to experience an ease of being and a whole new more positive relationship to your body. It can enhance your health and expand your freedom.

> Most of us scale down our dreams to the size of our fears until our vision becomes so tunnelled we see darkness everywhere.
> *Carl A. Hammerschlag*

THE WEEK AHEAD

This week you will be working with one of the most beautiful mythological symbols in the world – the tree of life. Experiencing it within your body grounds the creative power of the axis mundi making it more available for healing, for envisioning and for bringing visions into form. You will be exploring the tree of life as the axis mundi within your body and your being. You will be journeying to discover its importance to your life both from a classical shamanic perspective – tying together the lower, middle, and upper realms of non–ordinary reality – and also as a means of discovering your roots, your genetic and morphic inheritance, and your challenges. Once your connection with

> Here am I
> behold me
> I am the sun
> Behold me
> *North American Lakota*
> *greeting the sun upon its rising*

your own world tree is well established you will learn a technique for healing which takes you deep within the physicality of your being, yet can at times yield fruits far beyond anything you might expect.

Quantum Break 37

CLIMBING THE WORLD TREE

Your intention:

TO DISCOVER YOUR CONNECTIONS WITH AND PATHWAYS TO ALL THREE LEVELS OF THE QUANTUM REALMS

This journey will not only enhance your connections with your own centre it will also give you an alternative way of travelling in the upper, lower and middleworlds. I love travelling this way – first because the tree itself is so full of wonder, and second because it takes me deep within and connects me with the centre of the world. On this journey you will call in the spirits of the six directions to help you climb the world tree that grows through the axis mundi of your own body, which you were working with during your last quantum leap. If you usually journey lying down, you might like to do this one sitting up – especially as you will be working with the tree. This can be a helpful posture to experience your connections with the lower and upperworld as you journey.

◆ Prepare for your journey as always.
◆ Call in the spirits of the six directions including your power animal and any other helping spirits you want to work with.
◆ Centre yourself within the three-dimensional cross where these spirit energies meet within your body.
◆ When you are ready ask the spirits of the six directions to help you explore the world tree which grows up around the axis mundi connecting lower, middle, and upper realms.

One evening a white owl appeared close behind him, along with a man who told him, 'Make yourself a drum and all the equipment a shaman needs. Sing shaman-songs. You will never succeed in being an ordinary individual. If you accept the calling of the shaman, you will become one.'

A Gilyak shaman, reported by Shternberg

- ✦ Let the experience of this tree be felt within your own body. What is its trunk like? Where do its roots begin? Its branches – in relation to your own body?
- ✦ Direct your attention into the earth on which you are sitting.
- ✦ Now travel with your power animal downwards on the roots of the tree into the quantum realms of the lowerworld.
- ✦ What does it feel like to travel in this way instead of taking your usual route to the lowerworld?
- ✦ When you are ready, ask your power animal to bring you back up the world tree into the middleworld.
- ✦ As you travel up the trunk notice its texture and colour. Is it smooth or twisted with vines? Is there anything else you notice on your way up?
- ✦ Now ask your power animal to take you all the way up to the upperworld. How do you move? Do you climb? Fly? How?
- ✦ What do you see as you move upwards? What do you sense? How do the different levels of the upperworld appear to you when you access it in this way?
- ✦ Where in relation to your world tree does your Wise One live?
- ✦ How many different levels do you go through?
- ✦ Ask your power animal if there are any interconnecting passages between the upper, lower, and middleworld.
- ✦ When you are ready, return to the centre of your three-dimensional cross within your body by coming back down the tree with your power animal.
- ✦ Thank your power animal, helping spirits, spirits of the place and of the six directions for their help and return to ordinary reality by opening your eyes and coming back into the room.

In short, both in the need to cast off ordinary thought processes (and ultimately to go 'beyond thought' altogether), and in the perception of reality as one unity, the phenomenon of enlightenment and the science of physics have much in common.
Gary Zukav

Another real thing! I am not dead yet! I can still call forth a piece of soul and set it down in colour, fixed forever.
Keri Hulme

There is only one journey. Going inside yourself.
Rainer Maria Rilke

The woods were made for the
hunters of dreams
The brooks for the fisher
of song
To the hunters who hunt for
the gunless game
The streams and the
woods belong.
Sam Walter Foss

Bridge Building

Compare the experience of travelling on the world tree with the pathways you usually take to go to the upper and lowerworlds. Record your experiences of travelling this way. What did you see, smell, feel, touch, sense, hear? The world tree can be an object of great beauty. Its beauty is also your beauty. You might like to use colour to make a drawing of yours to place in your sanctuary. How does the experience of the world tree at the axis mundi within your body and your being affect the way you experience yourself physically? Psychologically? Spiritually?

You must have a room or a
certain hour of the day or so
where you do not know what
was in the morning paper … a
place where you can simply
experience and bring forth
what you are, and what you
might be … At first you may
find nothing's happening …
But if you have a sacred place
and use it, take advantage of
it, something will happen.
Joseph Campbell

CREATE YOUR WORLD TREE
Week Nine Project

The project this week is an important one. It sounds simple, and in a way it is, but the reverberations from carrying it out can echo for weeks, months, even years in your life. It is to draw or make from papier mache, cardboard or anything that inspires you a representation of your world tree. To do this, you will first need to journey to explore its nature in greater depth than you have already in Quantum Break 37. Once you have brought into some kind of physical form your own experience of the world tree you can take the sacred project further. In fact this is something you might like to continue to work with long after your journey to freedom process has finished. For now, move on to Quantum Break 38 and begin the process.

Quantum Break 38

FINDING YOUR OWN WORLD TREE

Your intention:
TO DISCOVER THE WORLD TREE WITHIN

Each world tree is unique. And the world tree you encounter when you journey to it today is not necessarily the same world tree that you will find when you make a similar journey next week, next month or next year. For it is in the nature of a tree to grow. Trees let go of a branch or a root or bark which has become damaged or rotten or which no longer serves the growth of the tree as a whole. Your own world tree will grow and evolve as you work with it. Just as every journey begins with the first step, creating a physical manifestation of your world tree begins with doing a journey today to find out what it is like. That is your goal now. You will be journeying for any information you can get about what your world tree looks like, feels like, smells like, is like.

◆ Prepare for your journey as always.
◆ Call in the spirits of the six directions including your power animal and any other helping spirits you want to work with.
◆ Centre yourself within the three-dimensional cross where their spirit energies meet within your body.
◆ When you are ready ask the spirits of the six directions to help you explore the world tree which grows up around the axis mundi connecting lower, middle and upper realms.
◆ Begin by examining the roots. What do they look like and feel like? Do they go deep into the earth or do they spread out the way a banyan tree does? Are they big or small? What colour are they? Are they all healthy or are there some of them which are rotting away to feed the earth with new compost?

I pray you … your
  play needs no excuse.
Never excuse.
William Shakespeare

If you want to find the answers to the Big Questions about your soul, you'd best begin with the Little Answers about your body.
George Sheehan

✦ Ask the roots how they would like you to represent them when you are making a physical representation of your tree in ordinary reality.

✦ When you have examined the roots, move up to the trunk. Feel it in your body and then take a look at what it is like. What is its colour? Its texture? Is it tall and thin like a redwood or stocky like a cowry? Are there any markings on the trunk? Are there any animals there? How do you feel about the trunk? Ask the trunk how it would like you to represent it when you come to making your own image of it.

✦ Now move up towards the branches. How many are there? Are they thick or thin? Do they spread mostly outwards or upwards or both? What is their colour and texture like?

✦ Is there foliage? If so what is it like? Needles? Big leaves? Small leaves?

✦ Are there fruits or flowers on your tree? If so what kind? Do they have a fragrance?

✦ Ask the branches and the leaves, the fruits and the flowers (if they are part of your tree), how they would like you to represent them in the model of your world tree that you are going to make.

✦ Ask your tree if it has a name.

✦ Ask the spirit of your tree to help you create a representation of it after you have returned from your journey.

✦ Thank your tree and return to ordinary reality.

Bridge Building

Begin by making a preliminary sketch of your tree just to remind you of what you have learned on your journey about it and also to remind you of what you want to include in your representation. Make a few notes too so you don't forget what you have learned from your tree. Then gather together whatever you need – scissors, coloured paper, glue, sticks, paints, papier mache – to begin your week's project and get started. You can continue with your tree-making doing a little each day or, if you are like me – impatient by nature – you can sit down right now and do the work.

LET YOUR TREE EVOLVE

Part of your week's project is allowing the physical manifestation of your tree to evolve in any direction it wishes to. Trees do that. They shed dead branches and grow new roots. They come into leaf and lose their leaves. They blossom and fruit (at least some do) then they surrender these creations to the earth to become part of some new life form. As you work throughout the week with various parts of your tree see if there are changes or additions that you want to make in your tree model.

THE PRESENCE OF THE PAST

Like a tree, each one of us grows from a spiritual seed planted deep in the past – not just our personal past but the past of the earth and the universe as a whole. So deep can be the roots that feed our seedpower in this life that exploring them can sometimes take you all the way back to the primordial beginnings of the planet. In the journey that follows you will be able to access any level of your inherited power that you like. You can also use this journey at a later time to discover the morphic resonance you have brought with you into this life, to find out what imprints or traces, what joys and sorrows – what in Sanskrit is known as *samskaras* – you have been carrying in your psyche.

Quantum Break 39

AT THE ROOTS OF POWER

Your intention:
TO CONNECT WITH THE CREATIVE POWER OF YOUR BLOODLINE

This journey is an exploration into your origins to connect with your ancestral bloodline, your evolutionary forebears, and earlier experiences of earthly life either in human form or any other form. During this journey you can connect with the deepest sources of your inherited power. You have the opportunity to

> Order is the shape upon
> which beauty depends.
> *Pearl Buck*

discover the nature of your bloodline's unique character. You may even meet an ally or allies which are part of your bloodline who have wisdom or healing or gifts to bring to you while you are on this life's journey. Connect with the positive creative power of your bloodline. Then you can continue to draw on deep wells of spiritual power and guidance for your life.

- ✦ Prepare for your journey as always.
- ✦ Call the spirits of the six directions as well as your power animal and any other helping spirits you want to work with.
- ✦ Centre yourself within the three-dimensional cross where their spirit energies meet within your body.
- ✦ When you are ready, ask the spirits of the six directions to help you explore the roots of your world tree in relation to your ancestral bloodline.
- ✦ Travel up and down the branching roots of your tree – right down to the deepest source of your ancestral power.
- ✦ What does the power of your bloodline feel like? What is its intrinsic nature? How is it unique? What is its highest aim?
- ✦ As you are exploring your ancestral roots, do you encounter any allies there? – ancestral spirits who are caring and friendly and who take a personal interest in helping your seedpower unfold in this life.
- ✦ If so, greet them and find out how they would like to help you in an on-going way.
- ✦ Ask what they can teach you, what gifts they would like to give you or what advice.
- ✦ Ask how best you can support the creative power of the bloodline in the way you live your life.
- ✦ Give thanks to the roots of your inheritance and to any ancestral allies you meet for their creative power, wisdom and gifts.
- ✦ Thank the spirits of the six directions, your power animal and other helping spirits and let them know that they are free to go now.
- ✦ Return.

Bridge Building

You may have a lot to record from this journey. It might be wise to do it in words so you can go back to it whenever you like. It is a great gift to make friends with the creative power of your bloodline. How can you best make a record of the essence of your inherited power? With words? Song? A drawing? Dance? You may want to go back to any spirit allies you have encountered on your journey. Almost every culture in the world, except our own Western culture, honours ancestral spirits and calls on bloodline allies for help and healing when it is needed.

GO FOR JOY

All joy is seated in the body. Your body is more than the vehicle of your consciousness. It is consciousness itself – pure energy in crystallized form. The more blessed, the more loved, the more free your body is – with all its conflicting impulses and contradictions – to explore its place in the vast sea of energy that is life, the greater is your creativity, your power and your capacity for joy. Without your body, without your ears and tongue, you cannot hear the voice of another, neither can you form words to express yourself. Without a nose the delight of tuberose or vanilla will never be known. Without a brain you cannot explore thought or dream dreams.

As a culture we do not feel comfortable with our bodies. We make them into things that are separate from the real us. As a result they appear as dangerous shadows – films filled with inexplicable violence, brutal sex, and a lust for freedom at any cost to ourselves or others. Too often the experience of freedom, the joy of living in the body, the experience of the body as a radiant source of creativity and joy continues to elude us.

Before talking of holy things, we prepare ourselves by offerings … one will fill his pipe and hand it to the other who will light it and offer it to the sky and earth … they will smoke together … Then will they be ready to talk.
Mato-Kuwapi,
or Chased-by-Bears,
a Santee-Yanktonai Sioux

Quantum Break 40

JOURNEY TO JOY

Your intention:
TO FIND THE SEAT OF JOY IN YOUR BODY AND EXPAND IT

You will be taking a middleworld journey deep into the energy of your body and, with the help of your power animal or other helping spirit, seeking out the place of greatest joy. You will ask your body how best you can open out its pathways for joy and freedom. We usually experience ourselves as a Newtonian object. 'I am only the body and something which is one-inch away from my skin has nothing to do with me.' This is what Alan Watts used to call being 'a skin encapsulated ego'. What you find in many ancient cultures and tribal communities is the awareness that this limited way of perceiving the body is only one aspect of it. There are many ways of moving beyond this limited sense of the body to discover its deeper identity. The most delightful of all is to connect with your body's centre of joy and experience its expansion outwards. This journey is best used as an ongoing practice. Carry it out once every two or three weeks and you will soon open up lines of communication between your conscious mind and your body that may have been closed since birth. Some of the benefits of this practice can include a release from the symptoms of long-term stress, readjustment of normal weight, enhanced overall energy and a truly expanded sense of joy. The more you honour your body's capacity for joy, the greater the sense of freedom you feel and the more delight in just being alive. Journey to the sound of a drum, a rattle or through the sacred silence.

Elementary particles in identical quantum states remain instantly interconnected even when separated by finite distances; photons emitted one by one interfere with one another as simultaneous waves; electrons in superconductors flow in a highly coherent manner taking on identical wave-functions; these particles are instantly and nondynamically correlated in different atoms even if they were not previously associated with one another, and they are specifically correlated in the energy shells that surround the atomic nuclei.

Ervin Laszlo

✦ Prepare for your journey as always.
✦ Call in the spirits of the six directions as well as your power animal and any other helping spirits you want to work with.
✦ Centre yourself within the three-dimensional cross where their spirit energies meet at the axis mundi.

- Now, ask your power animal to show you the seat of joy within your body. It may be in your heart, or in your head, in your genitals or your belly or maybe it is all over.
- Once you locate it, enter that place and sit in silence there allowing yourself to feel the joy. Is there a colour you associate with it? A sound? A word? A place? A memory?
- Now ask your power animal to expand the joy you have discovered, letting it flood first the surrounding area of the body where you have located it and then further and further.
- Don't rush anything. Give yourself plenty of time just to savour the joy that is part of living within a physical body.
- Now see if you can let it expand even further – beyond the surface of your skin outwards into the room.
- Can you expand it still further? And further still?
- The limits of the body are not determined by the surface of your skin.
- Can you allow the joy from within to grow from what was a tiny place until it encompasses the universe? This is truly possible thanks to the interconnectedness of all things.
- When you are ready return to the locus of joy within your body.
- Ask if your body has any wisdom it wants to share with you or anything it needs help with.
- Ask your body how best to make this experience of physical joy part of your day-to-day existence.
- Give thanks to the joy, your body through which it has come into being and the compassionate spirits who have helped you find it and expand it.
- Return to the room.

Cold and austere, proposing no explanation but imposing an ascetic renunciation of all other spiritual fare, this idea (that objective knowledge is the source of truth) was not of a kind to allay anxiety, but aggravated it instead. By a single stroke it claimed to sweep away the tradition of a hundred thousand years, which had become one with human nature itself. It wrote an end to the ancient animist covenant between man and nature, leaving nothing in the place of that precious bond but an anxious quest in a frozen universe of solitude.
Jacques Monod

Bridge Building

Record the experience of your journey to joy in any way you like. Then you might like to take a look at the representation of your world tree and see if, after doing this exercise, there are any changes you want to make in it or things you want to add to it. The deeper the connection with your body the more rich the physical representation of your world tree is likely to get. World trees are always developing as we develop and changing as we change. They can also change with the seasons. Be aware of any changes that are appropriate to yours and make them as you can.

I know others who have had really serious sorrows come into their lives. If they can take this positive attitude and absorb it, the bliss experience comes out, and they then realize that what they're affirming is the whole structure of their life. It's an opportunity. It's the incarnation that they've taken to experience – the miracle of this consciousness and the world that they're in. It's very different from saying, 'Ow! This hurts. I'm going over there.' Very, very different. It's the joyous affirmation for the sorrows of the world.

First, you must experience those sorrows as your own sorrows, and then, when you have affirmed those sorrows, you come into bliss. Anyone can try it. It's to find where your pain is and by saying 'yes' to it, the whole new consciousness will suddenly be experienced. You'll be 'saved' as they say.

Joseph Campbell

A CALL TO TRANSCENDENCE

The energies of instinct, of sexuality, of the will to power, of self-assertion, of destruction that come from within us and which we so often fear are the energies that, together with those of compassion and creativity, laughter and healing, inform the whole of life. These energies very often manifest themselves in the forms of gods and goddesses, angels and archetypes. As Karlfried Graf Durkheim said, all these energies are, when you look closely at them, transparent to transcendence. These gods and goddesses of creation and destruction, angels and archetypes are manifestations of the divine power which underlies all manifestations in both the world of form and the formless world. According to mythologist Joseph Campbell, they are necessary parts of our being manifesting through the body's impulse system. They are felt, he said, through the different organs of our body and represent different aspects of living. After all, if we did not have a god or goddess of creation and destruction, spring could not be destroyed to make way for summer or summer destroyed to make way for autumn. Within the body if we did not have the osteoclasts – tiny cells whose job it is to break down or resorb old bone – there would not be the possibility of their opposite – the osteoblasts – to build new bone and we could all end up with brittle, breaking bones.

The body is a holographic manifestation of the universe, a microcosm of the macrocosm. So, like outer life which we see around us, it also becomes a field in which conflict arises as a result of different functions and life energies being in conflict with each other. This is especially true when we have been trained through our education and religions to live from our head and when our heads have been filled with ideas of what we should and should not be, should and should not do. Then we lose our awareness of why these god and goddess energies are expressing themselves from within and we lose touch with our physicality. They are basically divine and marvellous and miraculous energies asking that we listen to them and find ways of putting ourselves in accord with them. Instead we concretize them and demonize them. We forget that they are meant to be transparent to transcendence. As Joseph Campbell says, 'Now a deity that is not recognized and revered and allowed to play into our conscious life becomes an idol. It closes itself and is no longer transparent to transcendence. The energy gets blocked and becomes what we call a devil.' Such 'devils' often manifest in the form of illness.

LISTENING TO SOUL CRIES

This is how we come to experience these life energies within us as something dangerous, separate from ourselves, and we treat them as objects of fear. At this point real conflict arises. Our ego or outer personality does its best to suppress or to silence impulses from within carried in our organs and tissues. We may succeed in suppressing them for a time, in which case our body's capacity for aliveness, joy and communication with the rest of life takes a nose dive. This is when addiction can set in. We use addictions to mask life energies – particularly creative power – that we fear, and we also use addictions to fill up the spiritual emptiness within. In the process we suppress even further these natural forces. If our ability to suppress them goes on long enough we are likely to become ill.

Illness and pain are almost invariably a cry from the soul to pay attention to something that you are ignoring. Otherwise, in some people who have not been able to arm themselves well enough to suppress these life energies, they can push through to erupt as powerful destructive forces: violence, destructive ways. At its most basic level, that of the human body, this means we need to learn to listen to the impulses that arise from within – these often uncomfortable bodily energies – and learn to treat them as whispers from the soul.

I learned this the way I tend to learn everything – the hard way. As a child I was always ill. In my early twenties I suffered from depression with no apparent cause – the kind of thing where you go to the doctor and he tells you he can either refer you for psychiatric treatment or give you a drug. (Then it was tranquilizers like Librium and Valium – now it tends to be Prozac.) However, my instincts told me that the illnesses had something to do with my biochemistry so I chose not to go down either route. Eventually, by accident – except that I no longer believe in accidents – I met a handful of what

Whoever has parted from
  his source
Longs to return to that
  state of union
Rumi

The immaculate conception is not a problem for gynecologists and the promised land is not a piece of real estate.
Joseph Campbell

were probably the most knowledgeable doctors about natural medicine in the English-speaking world. They were all conventionally trained medical doctors yet they had each in his or her own way forsaken symptomatic treatments for using fasting and raw foods, breathing and detoxification to encourage the body to heal itself. What they taught me changed my life. I ended up with more energy than I had ever had before and for a while everything was great.

ASK ANY RAT

Then, after a year or two, I noticed that despite my good diet and all the exercise and meditation I did, I would periodically become quite ill with one thing or another and end up flat on my back in bed for a couple of days. This went on for a few years before I stopped one day to ask myself why. The answer that came made me laugh. 'You are like a rat on a treadmill. Getting sick is the only way to stop you running around.' This little message from within at first shocked me. I thought to myself, what does this illness do for me? Again the answer came loud and clear, 'It puts you to bed and makes you listen to the whispers of your soul.' Right, I thought. What if, whenever I feel like withdrawing from the external frenzy of my life, I go to bed? What would happen then? I found out the answer by doing it: I stopped getting sick. Not only that, but I learned that I get some of the richest inspiration I have ever been given during the odd day or two in bed with a book or some wonderful music. The soul has great wisdom and the body is so often the vehicle for its expression. Eventually learning this led me to discover an even more remarkable secret about pain and illness! When you allow yourself to enter into it within the body, there is no telling how rich a treasure you may find there.

Quantum Break 41
TREASURE HUNT FOR THE SOUL

Your intention:
TO ENTER YOUR PAIN OR ILLNESS AND UNEARTH ITS HIDDEN
TREASURE

Pain and illness, no matter how horrible, are always gateways to a new way of being and always offer the possibility of change. The whole point of pain is to make you focus and concentrate on something. Something is calling to you in very much the same way a child takes hold of its mother's skirts when she is preparing dinner and just keeps tugging at them until she stops and looks to see what the child is doing. It is the numinous realms that are calling you, trying to teach you, trying to help you open to the vastness of your being or make changes in your life through which your seedpower can more fully unfold. The secret is to journey deep enough into the pain or illness to be able to hear what they are whispering to you.

This journey can be done using drumming, rattling, or by entering the sacred silence.

- ✦ Prepare for your journey as always.
- ✦ Call in the spirits of the six directions as well as your power animal and any other helping spirits you want to work with.
- ✦ Centre yourself within the three-dimensional axis mundi where their spirit energies meet within your body.
- ✦ When you are ready, explore the world tree which grows up around the axis mundi connecting lower, middle and upper realms.
- ✦ Let the experience of your world tree be present with you and feel its connections with the rest of the universe while you rest in the centre.

> Symptoms are a way for your body to say 'Listen to me talk for a change'.
> *Carl A. Hammerschlag*

- ✦ Now direct your attention to wherever in your body you feel pain or are conscious of illness.
- ✦ Let your consciousness enter deep into this area. Deeper, deeper.
- ✦ Who or what do you find there?
- ✦ Ask what the illness or pain is there to teach you.
- ✦ See what happens.
- ✦ You can carry on a dialogue with whatever or whomever you find there.
- ✦ When you are ready thank your power animal and compassionate spirits and return.

Bridge Building

You might record your experience in the form of a dialogue if that is appropriate. You may have returned with an image that you can draw in colour and hang on your wall. Often relating to an image – even one you don't understand – in ordinary reality invites the powers of transformation to continue to work their healing and magic in your life in an on-going way.

FREE BREAKS

Use your Free Breaks to further explore working with the body if you want to. You might go into your Inner Reaches of Sacred Space and ask one of the following questions then see what answers you get:

- ✦ How can I make sacred my relationship to my body?
- ✦ What are the limits in space of the energy that is my body? Or are there any?
- ✦ You can also journey to the Spirit of the Body itself and find out which foods are appropriate for you to eat and which are not.

SECRETS THAT PAIN CAN TELL

Throughout the whole of *Journey to Freedom* I have consciously avoided writing much about my own journeys or other people's journeys. This is because it is terribly important that you find out things for yourself. Here I am going to make an exception. For I have discovered that when my students do Quantum Break 41 Treasure Hunt for the Soul, they frequently find their soul or a very wise mentor who is a link between their soul and their outer personality. So amazing is this to me that I still can't figure out why. I mean, why when you go into a place of pain in your body or into an illness should it lead to such richness? Why should you find a being of great radiance sitting in the middle of a crushed knee? This has remained one of the great mysteries of working with the body for me. I don't know how it comes about, I only know that this happens consistently and it tends to blow people's minds. For frequently they come upon so much beauty and they themselves feel so inadequate that they don't know quite how to cope with it or integrate it into their lives.

THE LACEMAKER

I once did a journey into an excruciatingly painful tooth which I had been ignoring for months. It would get better and then worse and then better but it never seemed to clear up completely. Finally I figured out that something from within was calling to me. So I settled myself down one June morning and decided to journey into the tooth itself to see what I could find out. I was not prepared for what I came upon – a being of such beauty that I felt humbled to be in her presence. Like most people, I tend to be highly critical of myself. I know what I consider the bad things about me yet often cannot see the good ones. The being I met is called Lacemaker. She lives in the darkness of a deep cave where she weaves tapestries. Since that first journey at which she appeared – during which I wept just to be in her presence – I have journeyed again and again to her to work with her and open myself to her grace. Should you meet such a being on this journey I would suggest you do the same. The rewards of coming to know Lacemaker have been the greatest I have ever experienced on a personal level. Many of my students have had similar experiences on their own journeys and learned much about how to go forward in their lives.

Shamans often retrieve lost souls, communicate with spirits, emphasize the interconnectedness of their patients with the community and the earth, facilitate spiritual purification for those who have violated social taboos, explain dreams and visions, and stress the importance of spiritual growth, one's life purpose, and being of service to humanity and to nature. These functions rarely attain importance or even respectability in the world views of Western allopathic physicians and other health care specialists.
Stanley Krippner

Here is a record of my second journey to her. It is a dialoguing journey, a technique that I find to be one of the most useful of all. I recorded it word for word as I journeyed:

I journey in search of Lacemaker – weaver of tapestries, creator of beauty. I need to know who she is and what she wants of me. I go to the cave of the Lacemaker – taken there by my power animal. I feel humble and unclean in the presence of the energy there. The holiness of this woman is so beautiful to me. I weep to be in her presence. I feel so unclean. She gives me water to drink. She soothes my fiery skin. She takes my gnarled and ugly hands in hers and holds them, looking into my eyes. She smiles.

LACEMAKER   Do you not know who I am?

LESLIE   No, except that you are someone who is more beautiful than any I have ever seen before.

LACEMAKER   I am the weaver of webs. I am the maker of dreams. I am she who lives in a cave beneath the earth and does her work in silence. I am she who is complete, who loves all things and needs nothing. I am your *essence*, Leslie. I *am* you. It is time that you came to know it.

LESLIE   But how *can* you be me? You are so different from me. My skin is scarred with childbirth, and covered with wrinkles. I have had to learn to survive in the world, no matter what the cost. I am a seller of snake-bite serum – a magician who just keeps moving so that her magic dazzles. I am the fat woman who longs to be leaner but has never been able to be that. I am the teller of tales who wears a thousand masks in the telling. I am she who loves and weeps in her heart for those I see suffering and I am she who could take a gun and kill whosoever steps onto my own territory. I am the rapist and the raped. I am the destroyer and the destroyed.

LACEMAKER   Leslie, do you not realize that you are all of these things because you have to live on the earth and learn the ways of being human? If you had not done this there was no way that I would have been free to weave my webs. Do you not know that you have been willing to be the rough beast that drags its heavy body across the earth that I may stay in the cave and weave my webs? Do you not know that it is your craftiness that has made possible my survival until the time could come when you and I together can weave magic? Do you not know that the things which you so hate in yourself are merely 'skins' that you have been willing to take on in order to move within the world of the living?

Do you not know that it is you who has made the sacrifice, you who has shown the heroism, you who has dared to tread where you fear to create the bonds with the earth that could allow my webs to be woven in the ordinary world? It is you who has the courage, Leslie, not me. I have no need of courage for yours sequesters me here that I may weave.

Do you not know that I am *you*, Leslie? Do you not know that every mask you have ever worn you have worn for my sake that my beauty has the chance to be brought into the world. Do you not know that the sorrow and the grief you have lived when giving birth to your desire to create beauty that carries with it the fragrance of the divine is the sacrifice you made to make that possible? Do you not know that webs cannot be woven without an understanding of the world into which you will bring them? Do you not know? Do you not know that the negativity you so hate in yourself, what you see as fraudulence and cowardice and jealousy and hatred and territorial instinct, have all been necessary to come to this moment?

It is the time to awaken, Leslie. It is time to come to know who I am and to give thanks to the masks and the games and the street-wise survival you have learned. Do you not know, Leslie, that when you chose to be born on this earth you knew what it would cost you and you did it anyway?

You are such a funny creature, Leslie. So stupid. You admire Prometheus. You admire Van Gogh. You admire the heroism that it takes, no matter what the cost, to do what you have come here to do. Yet you are too stupid to know that you have lived and are living this courage every day of your life.

It is not easy for a being of light to become a dense body. It is not easy to choose to become blind and deaf that you may know the blindness and deafness of what it is to be human. It is not easy. Yet you have chosen to do this and you have not forsaken your task.

There is a new birth coming, Leslie. It is a birth that you have earned and one in which you will need to be fully conscious now. For the first web to be woven, the first tapestry to be made is that which brings together all the strands of all of the parts of your human form. It will be sewn with the gossamer threads that flow from my hands. You will find that what you make is sturdy with your human strength yet sings with the fragrance of the divine. This is the time. It has come. Wake up.

True wisdom is only to be found far away from people, out in the great solitude, and it is not found in play but only through suffering. Solitude and suffering open the human mind, and therefore a shaman must seek his wisdom there.
Joan Halifax

The mind of the beginner is empty, free of the habits of the expert, ready to accept, to doubt, and open to all the possibilities …
Shunryu Suzuki

The key is the individual, not the social group anymore. All social groups are bounding groups now, and all social movements are in-group movements, walled-city movements. It's only the individual who can move from one group to another and find the human spirit within himself for whom we have any hope.
Joseph Campbell

LESLIE	What do you want of me?
LACEMAKER	I want stillness and forgiveness towards yourself. I want you to accept me as your true essence instead of continuing to torture yourself with your false ideas of what is good and what is bad. I want you to listen to me and let me guide your hand and your word. You need not pay homage to me. To do so would be to deny the absolute fusion that has to take place now. I am not a separate spirit to whom you turn for help. I *am* you. I am the essence of your being. I am she who chose to come into incarnation in a human body. I am your soul – a being of light, a fountain. I am the white and you, Leslie in human form, are the blood red that completes our incarnation on this earth. I had to cry out in your body causing you great pain that you would hear me for you are very stupid and deaf. Yet it was necessary and it has been done. I want you to allow the expression of my essence in everything you do and wear and say without judgement. I am no more precious than you with all your masks. All of this is divine.
LESLIE	Why are you so silent?
LACEMAKER	I am not wordless as you think. I am what poets call their muse. Except they lie. Their muse is in truth their own soul but most are not willing to take on the responsibility of seeing its beauty and so they distance themselves from this truth. You are not here to distance yourself any more. Your challenge now is to learn to live this truth and let your creations flow out of the fusion between what you see as base metal and truth. The truth is that both are gold although you do not yet see it.
LESLIE	Are you connected with the spirit of the book?
LACEMAKER	She is a manifestation of me.
LESLIE	How do I need to work with you on the book?
LACEMAKER	You need not only to work with me but to live with me every moment of the day. That is why you have sought solitude so much in recent weeks. This will take time. But it will happen. Stay close to me, Leslie, and I will be guided by you and together we will create the beauty you have waited so long for the freedom to create.
LESLIE	Thank you.
LACEMAKER	And you for hearing my call.
LESLIE	I see a Unicorn with you. What is his nature? Is he important to you?

How little do we know
that which we are!
How less what we may be!
George Gordon Lord Byron

LACEMAKER	Yes. He is the animal of liquid gold – the purest manifestation of light – the consciousness of what is known as the Christ. He is my constant companion. We are old friends. He is the bringer of light and transcendence. You can play with him and welcome him into your life if you so choose. He will fill you with light and dispel the self-hatred and criticism. He will do far more as well.
LESLIE	Thank you. Is there anything that you would like me to do to honour you?
LACEMAKER	Nothing whatsoever except open your consciousness to the truth. I AM YOU.
LESLIE	Thank you. Thank you for your wisdom and your love.

Don't identify too strongly with what you now know; that 'truth' is impermanent. Identify with the possibility that at every moment you can emerge from your blind self to see in the dark.

Carl A. Hammerschlag

CHECKLIST

Day One

✦ Read through the chapter up to Week Nine Project, Create your World Tree on page 248.

✦ Do Quantum Break 37 Climbing the World Tree *to discover your connections with and pathways to all three levels of the quantum realms.*

✦ Bridge build.

✦ Begin to prepare your work on your project.

Day Two

✦ Do Quantum Break 38 Finding Your Own World Tree *to discover the world tree within.*

✦ Bridge build.

✦ Begin to work on your project.

Day Three

✦ Read more of the chapter if you have time.

✦ Do Quantum Break 39 At The Roots of Power *to connect with the creative power of your bloodline.*

✦ Bridge build.

The great sea
Has sent me adrift
It moves me
As the weed in a great river
Earth and the great weather
Move me
Have carried me away
And move my inward parts
with joy.
Uvavnuk,
Eskimo woman shaman

Day Four

✦ Do Quantum Break 40 Journey to Joy *to find the seat of joy in your body and expand it.*
✦ Bridge build.
✦ Work on your project if you feel you need to alter it in any way after your journeys.

Day Five

✦ Read to the end of the chapter.
✦ Do Quantum Break 41 Treasure Hunt for the Soul *to enter your pain or illness and unearth its hidden treasure.*
✦ Bridge build.

Day Six

✦ Do a Free Break exercise of your choice, or perhaps use the Inner Reaches of Sacred Space to help you in your relationship to your body.
✦ Bridge build.

Day Seven

✦ Do another Free Break exercise.
✦ Bridge build.
✦ Do whatever work you feel is necessary to complete your project.
✦ Spend 20 minutes on your Travelogue.

Travelogue

✦ How many days this week did you take your Quantum Breaks? What was your experience of working with the world tree within your body?
✦ Have you done your weekly project? Has it changed or evolved in any way since you first created it?
✦ Are there any significant challenges that have come up this week? Describe them.

Fire of Creation

I am the fire. Enter me with your dreams and make them real. I am the power that burns away the dross. I am the heat Hephaestus used to forge his lightning bolts and fashion jewellery for the gods. Creation is no simple task. It asks that you let die that which is false and learn to dance in my heat until beauty emerges from the waste. It demands a descent to the truth, no matter the cost, and a love of the world great enough for you to make the climb back up and offer it the treasure you have found. It is the most exciting journey in the world. Take it and you taste the exhilaration of freedom.

I am the Spirit of Creation

This week finds us face to face with the greatest power in the universe … the energy of creation. Out of the vast potentiality of consciousness comes a flaring forth. How do you wrestle with this dynamic, evolving, self-manifesting power so you can bring your own soul visions into material form? That is the challenge you tackle this week. It can be the most exciting of them all.

Creativity seems to have become one of those new-age clichés. Everybody talks about it, writes about it and gives you ten point plans for how to go about it. When I read some of this stuff I am often struck by a sense that too many people want to reduce the process of creativity to what might more accurately be called 'decorativity'. They seem to be more concerned with helping us control the process of creativity – keeping all of its deepest demands at bay and rationalising its processes – than helping us enter into what has to be the most exciting and challenging experience that each of us ever face: that of bringing into form a vision of our soul.

The important thing is to create. Nothing else matters; creation is all.
Pablo Picasso

PRIMORDIAL LOVE AFFAIR

Scientists tell us that the universe itself was created in an unfurling of monumental potentiality from the quantum vacuum. It burst forth in a dynamic, evolving, ever-changing, self-organizing manner. And it continues to do so. Each moment of its life, each moment of our life, another flaring forth of primal creativity is occurring. The universe's creativity is our creativity and the quantum vacuum out of which it pours is at the very core of our being. As cosmologist Brian Swimme says, 'Our very physical structure is primarily vacuum, we share the very all nourishing abyss that pervades the cosmos. The hydrogen atoms in our body arose after the great condensation following the explosive Primordial Flaring forth. We arise out of this milieu …'

Man can learn nothing except by going from the known to the unknown.
Claude Bernard

So much are the forces of creativity a part of our being that they pervade the whole of our life every moment. You do not have to search for creative power to make what your soul wants to bring into being in your life. But you do need to learn to work with it.

If only human beings could … be more reverent toward their own fruitfulness …
Rainer Maria Rilke

✦ You need to be courageous enough to enter the depths of your soul to access your own transcendent visions – visions which inspire you enough to honour them and enter the fire of creation.
✦ You need to ask for clarity as to how to bring them into being.
✦ You have to fall in love with the wonder of your visions and their beauty.
✦ You have to love them enough and love the world enough to be willing to do what needs to be done to bring them into being as a gift.

Joseph Campbell knew a lot about creativity. His path-breaking book *Hero With a Thousand Faces* has inspired two generations of storytellers and film makers in the act of creation, including George Lucas of Star Wars fame. The book examines the mythological nature of the pathway which each of us has to take many times in our life to connect with the power of our soul and bring back its gifts to the world. It is a pathway that demands letting go of whatever does not serve us to make room for something greater to come through. This is how we continue to grow instead of becoming a crystallized facsimile of who we truly are. Campbell's book is a masterpiece. It can be a great companion during times when you feel that the whole world is being pulled out from under you or you feel a great need to find out what your soul is asking you to do. But it is more than this too. For the whole experience of entering the creative fire and bringing new visions into being is encoded within world myths of the hero's journey which he writes about. Campbell insists that the hero himself actually becomes the navel of the world by following his or her soul path. In doing this he aligns himself with the umbilicus or axis mundi through which divine energies break free from eternity to flood the world of time and space.

INVISIBLE TORRENT

What he is speaking about is another perspective on the creation process that Swimme writes about. For me, creativity is an experience of the highest order of freedom as each of us moves closer and closer to being an authentic expression in our day-to-day lives of what our soul energy is here to celebrate. Campbell says, 'The torrent pours from an invisible source, the point of entry being the centre of the symbolic circle of the universe, the Immovable Spot of the Buddha legend, around which the world may be said to revolve. Beneath this spot is the earth-supporting head of the cosmic serpent, the dragon, symbolical of the waters of the abyss, which are the divine life-creative energy and substance of the demiurge, the world-generative aspect of immortal being. The tree of life, i.e. the universe itself, grows from this point. It is rooted in the supporting darkness; the golden sun bird perches on its peak; a spring, the inexhaustible well, bubbles at its foot. Or the figure may be that of the cosmic man or woman … seated or standing on this spot, or even fixed to the tree … for the hero as the incarnation of God is himself the navel of the world, the umbilical point through which the energies of eternity break into time.' Real creativity means connecting with your soul's visions, moving into the fire of creation and working with them to focus and clarify them, then bringing back the numinous power to wrestle with it until you can shape it into some kind of

Decisions are not made by races, cultures, or nations, unless they are first made by individuals. The most destructive decision that an individual can make is to give away his or her decision-making authority.
Ken Carey

Where there is dismemberment in the beginning there is remembrance at the end.
Alan Watts

Where there is hero, there is shadow.
James Hillman

form. The keys to making it happen are that old familiar duo – intention and compassion: compassion for yourself, for your project, and for the world and the intention to carry out this commitment to manifest your own truth. You have to love your vision enough to bring it into being.

THE WEEK AHEAD

This week is all about working with the fire of creation. You will be journeying to the creative power of your soul to ask what it wants to bring into being. This need not be a big thing – big or small, it makes no difference. For what you are working with here are only the techniques which you can use again and again for creating. It is rather like driving a car. The more you practise doing it the more it becomes second nature. It is the practice that matters, not the size of the vision you are bringing into form. You will explore the primordial energy of creation for yourself and find out what it looks like, feels like and how it moves. You will call in the help of the Great Creator – a spirit on whom you can always call when there is something you want to make. You will also learn to work with the specific spirit of whatever you are going to make. (You might be surprised to find that there is a region of the soul in which the energetic architecture of what you will make lives, waiting for you to call on it.) Despite the nineteenth-century cliché we have all grown up with of the lonely, isolated artist, the truth is, in the process of creating you are never alone. No place in shamanic work are the energies of the spirits more accessible to you than when you are creating. You have only to call for them.

BRINGING YOUR VISION INTO FORM
Week Ten Project

Your project this week is to begin to bring into form a vision you have chosen. If it is a simple vision you may be able to complete it within the next seven days, or even sooner. If it is more complex it will take far longer and you will probably want to come back again and again to the journey work you will be doing this week along the way.

Quantum Break 42

JOURNEY FOR A PROJECT

Your intention:
TO DISCOVER A CREATIVE SEED – SOMETHING YOU WANT TO
BRING INTO BEING

This journey is the first step in working with the fires of creation – that of identifying something you want to create. You will be journeying as you did in Blueprints into Form (Quantum Break 22). This time you will be asking for a project that you would like to carry out. It could be to write a poem. It could be to restructure the management of the people you work with. It could be to create a special place in your home where you can do creative work in the future. For that matter it could be to write a novel or paint a picture, write a song or sculpt a statue. You may find that there is more than one thing you want to create. I would suggest that you choose the simplest one to begin with – it makes no difference what it is as long as the longing to create it comes from your soul. The more you work with this process the simpler it is to take on more demanding projects without feeling overwhelmed.

✦ Begin your journey by singing your power song to prepare, if you have one, and then rattling in the spirits of the six directions, centring yourself within the axis mundi.

✦ Now call in your power animal or any other helping spirit you want to work with.

✦ You may begin your journey from your usual place in nature, or go to the upperworld or down to the lowerworld on your world tree if you prefer.

✦ Ask your power animal to take you directly to the creative centre of your seedpower.

Now, a deity that is not recognized and revered and allowed to play into our conscious life becomes an idol. It closes itself and is no longer transparent to transcendence. The energy gets blocked and becomes what we call a devil. The deity goes into reverse and becomes a negative power, a threatening power. When we forget the deities, we build a life on a program run by the head. The energies coming from the body are ignored and become threatening to the values, the head values, which we have chosen to live for. It's as easy as that.

Joseph Campbell

- When you get to your centre, see what thoughts, seeds, desires or visions are there asking to be realized in your day-to-day life. Ask it to tell you or show you what it is that it wants you to bring into being. You may receive this information in words, symbols or even as a feeling that needs to be experienced somehow.
- Once you have been given this, hold it to your heart in non-ordinary reality and bring your hand to your heart in ordinary reality. Allow it to be absorbed there so that it will remain deeply connected with you after you have returned to ordinary reality.
- Now thank your seedpower and your helping spirits and return to ordinary reality.

Bridge Building

Right away, record whatever you have brought back, being conscious that you have placed it in your heart where you can go to visit it whenever you choose during the creation process.

Quantum Break 43

JOURNEY TO MEET GREAT CREATOR

Your intention:
TO SEEK HELP FROM GREAT CREATOR IN BRINGING YOUR IDEA
INTO FORM

The more you explore the quantum realms the more you realize that just about any kind of help you need is available from the spirits if only you ask for it. This is something most people discover by accident. In this journey you can find out how easy it is to contact the right spirit whenever you need help for some project, for healing, for wisdom. Simply go and ask. Some people like to go to the upperworld and ask their Wise One to take them to the spirit they need. Others prefer to work with their power animal. By the way, it only works when you really care about what you are looking for help with. The spirits respond to passion, compassion and clear intention. Go into non-ordinary reality without clarity about what you want, and you are likely to get nothing of real value.

- ✦ This will be an upperworld journey.
- ✦ Be clear about your intention: to seek help from Great Creator in bringing your idea into form.
- ✦ Begin your journey by singing your power song, if you have one, and then rattling in the spirits of the six directions.
- ✦ Centre yourself within the axis mundi of your being.
- ✦ Now call in your power animal or any other helping spirit you want to journey with.
- ✦ You may start your journey either from the same place in nature from which you always begin, or travel to the upperworld on your world tree if you prefer.
- ✦ Go to your Wise One in the upperworld.

God is really only another artist. He invented the giraffe, the elephant, and the cat. He has no real style. He just keeps on trying other things.
Pablo Picasso

Truth is that which does not contaminate you, but empowers you.
Gary Zukav

Although both the shaman and religious mystics may have been possessed during their 'call' their empowerment lies in the fact that they have overcome the involuntary, helpless, victimized stare of spirit-possession and are cured.
Rowena Pattee

◆ Ask Wise One to take you to meet Great Creator.

◆ When you meet Great Creator make him or her an offering of some kind. It can be whatever you like – a symbol of what you want to create perhaps, a rose, a beam of sunlight – whatever has meaning for you. This is a way of showing your respect for the love and generosity of the compassionate spirits and a practice which you should always carry out when meeting a new helper – especially one of the stature of Great Creator.

◆ Now ask him or her for help and advice in bringing your desire or vision into material form.

◆ Ask also that his power and his guidance remain at your disposal whenever you call on him during the creative process.

◆ You can ask for specific advice if you like – step-by-step stuff – but don't be surprised if he only gives you the next step or two ahead. The creative process is like that. It is as though you can only 'smell the fragrance' of what it is you are bringing into being until you follow one step after another and watch it unfold.

◆ Before you leave Great Creator, ask him or her if it is appropriate for you to be journeying tomorrow to explore the fire of creation in your next Quantum Break. If it is, fine. If it is not then ask if there is some other journey he can suggest which would be more useful for you to do as your next Quantum Break.

◆ Thank Great Creator for his or her help and wisdom, thank your Wise One and your power animal and return.

Bridge Building

Record your journey in whatever way you like. This record can become the beginnings of the blueprint for what you will make. You will probably find yourself adding to it as you go. If your project is a complex or long-term one you may want to return again to Great Creator for help in finding the next step forward from time to time.

ENTERING THE FIRE

Every creative project needs a time of incubation during which, once the tiny seed of its vision is planted in your heart, it can open and prepare to come through the ground as a new plant. Today is the day for it.

Lay aside for a moment your creative project, it is time to investigate the fire itself so you know the kind of power you are able to call on in any creative process you carry out. You are going to be journeying to the creative core within your own being as you did in Quantum Break 34. This time, however, once you get there you are going to ask that it connect you to what Brian Swimme calls the energy of the Primordial Flaring Forth – the initial point at the centre of the universe from which all galaxies were brought into being. The image of the birthplace of all creation runs through every mythological tradition in the world. Sometimes it is the cosmic egg which cracks open to pour forth the world, others it is the great rainbow serpent which creates the world, or God who separates the firmaments and calls out 'Let there be light'. You may, if you prefer, work with any of these images, asking your power animal or Wise One that you be taken to these events. I think you may find it more useful, however, to go straight to your core and connect with this magnificent flaring forth experience.

So shalt thou feed on death,
  that feeds on men,
And death once dead, there's
  no more dying then.
William Shakespeare

Quantum Break 44

JOURNEY TO THE PRIMORDIAL FLARING FORTH

Your intention:
TO EXPLORE THE NATURE OF THE CREATIVE FIRE

You will be journeying to your core with your power animal as you did in Quantum Break 34 then aligning your own core with the creative energy out of which the universe was born some 15 billion light years away. You will be exploring the nature of the energy of creation, and the process by which it produces manifest form out of the cosmic vacuum. (Alternatively you will be journeying at the sug-gestion of Great Creator or exploring one of the other mythological images that carry the story of the creation of the universe.)

✦ Begin your journey by singing your power song to prepare, if you have one, and then rattling in the spirits of the six directions. Centre yourself within the axis mundi of your being.

✦ Now call in your power animal or any other helping spirit you want to journey with.

✦ Start your journey from within the axis mundi and connect with your world tree.

✦ Remember that at the beginning of this journey you will be entering into the energetic realm of your body which lies beneath or beyond the physiological level of blood vessels and muscles, organs and systems.

✦ Ask your power animal to take you to your core.

✦ Look for a slowly revolving disk of energy that sits on a horizontal plane at the level of your navel. It may look like the movement of stars around the centre of a galaxy or it may appear to you in some other form.

✦ In the centre of this disk you enter the space out of which the cosmic vacuum creates form. How does form pour forth from it?

✦ Ask your power animal to align your own creative centre with the creative core out of which the Primordial Flaring Forth brought forth the universe.

✦ What do you feel? What is the nature of this creative energy? Let yourself savour its essence by entering into it knowing that you are perfectly safe to be here under the care and guided by the wisdom of your power animal.

✦ How does creation take place?

✦ What does it feel to be part of it?

✦ Give yourself time to savour the extraordinary nature of being at the centre of this great creative force that has brought you and the whole universe into being.

✦ When you are ready, thank the creative fire for the privilege of being in its presence.

✦ Thank your power animal and other helping spirits for being with you and let them know that they are free to go now.

✦ Return.

Bridge Building

Record what you have experienced in whatever form you choose. There may be ways in which your journey is specifically relevant to the creative project you have undertaken. It may be that the usefulness of the journey lies more in familiarizing yourself with the energy that fuels the process of bringing into material form the visions and longings of your soul. It is a step-by-step process:

✦ *Connect with the numinous energies of creation within your own being.*

✦ *Ask for an idea, a vision or a creative seed.*

✦ *Formulate your intention to bring it into form as clearly as you can by writing it all down or drawing a picture of it.*

✦ *During the entire creative process continually remind yourself that you are choosing to bring your creative seed into being as a gift to the rest of life.*

✦ *During the entire process repeat your intention again and again whenever you get confused or lost in other concerns.*

✦ *Let your creative seed incubate.*

✦ *Work with the energies of Great Creator, either deliberately or by becoming so aligned with his essence that eventually you are able to access his gifts simply by asking for them whenever you are working on a project.*

✦ *Lay aside your personality issues – all the rubbish we grow up with such as 'I can't do this' 'Will anyone like it?' 'I was never any good at anything.' Don't worry, you can always claim them back if you really want to once your project is finished.*

✦ *Love your vision so much that you are willing to do whatever it takes to bring it into being.*

✦ *Love life enough to need to make an offering to it of your creation.*

✦ *Trust the creative power.*

✦ *Let it flare forth without allowing your critical judgement or analytical mind to interfere with the process.*

✦ *Move away for a time from what you have made to give you distance.*

✦ *Come back to what you have made to look at it with an eye of benevolent criticism.*

✦ *Make any adjustments you need to. This is always done with compassion towards your creation as well as towards yourself.*

It is important to remember that whatever we create, it is never anywhere near as rich and beautiful as our original visions. This is in the nature of living in a material body.

And now let us welcome the
  New year
Full of things that have
  never been.
Rainer Maria Rilke

A world that is raw material, resources, dead matter to be made into things, has nothing sacred in it. So we cut down the sacred grove, lay waste and declare that it does not matter, because it is only matter. Just so the slavers of an earlier century declared their merchandise to be incapable of 'proper human feeling'. Just so generations of experimental animals have been sacrificed in the name of research. Pesticides poisoning the lakes and rivers, fish disappearing from the oceans, rain forests going up in smoke – this is the world we have spoken so powerfully into existence, and we will continue to live in it unless we change our tune, tell a different story.
David Suzuki with Amanda McConnell

The beauty of quantum realms far surpasses any representation which even the greatest artist that ever lived could make of it in physical form as a painting or a book, a film or anything else. Yet, if you are true to your vision, and if you keep working with it, what you will create is something absolutely honest and authentic. And, no matter how simple, it will carry with it the fragrance of the divine. That is what art is all about. Your creations carry your authentic power. They are the greatest gifts you can bring to life. All else is mere decorative plagiarism.

MEETING THE ENERGETIC FORM

Your diamonds are not in far distant mountains or in yonder seas; they are in your own backyard, if you but dig for them.
Russell H. Conwell

Every vision from your creative core, every longing for something to be brought into being like your soul itself also has an energetic architecture of its own in the quantum realms. It will either be presented to you in words or symbols, in feelings, atmospheres, or sensed qualities. You can always return to the vision if ever you feel as though you have become side tracked or have lost your way along the path of creating it. There is also a spirit of every project you undertake whose purpose and passion it is to help you during the process of making whatever you are making.

I discovered this in 1994 while I was writing a book for women called *Passage To Power ... Natural Menopause Revolution*. I was really struggling with the thing and I cared passionately about it. For I had discovered just how badly petrochemically-derived herbicides and pesticides (which act as oestrogen-mimics) were damaging the reproductive lives of men and women – indeed all animals. They make women's bodies *oestrogen dominant* – that is filled with too much oestrogen and too little progesterone. This predisposes women to all the female ailments from PMS and osteoporosis to fibroids, endometriosis and cancer of the womb. Yet doctors, unaware of the effect that these chemicals in the environment are having on women, keep prescribing oestrogen when women come to them for help.

IN THE CAVE OF THE CRONE

In writing the book I was trying to weave together the mythological and spiritual passages a woman makes at menopause with her biological ones. Instinctually I knew they fit together but I just couldn't see how. In real distress after working with this thing for some 18 months, I finally journeyed to my Wise One in the upperworld and asked if she could introduce me to the spirit of the book (this was a real long shot, as I did not know that any such spirit existed, but I was desperate). 'Sure,' she said to my amazement, then whisked me off to a cave in the upperworld at the side of a great cliff. I entered this tiny cave to find an old woman – old enough to make Mother Teresa seem like Demi Moore. She was seated behind the most meagre, dismal-looking fire I had ever seen. 'Are you the Spirit of *Passage to Power*?' I asked. 'I am,' she replied. 'How can I help you?'

I proceeded to tell her about all the problems I was having with the book. Among them was the way that my own fear and anxiety and my anger and frustration were not helping get the job done. She answered a few of my specific questions and then she said to me, 'I want you to light a candle on your desk while you are working. Whenever you feel fear or anger, frustration or anxiety arising, pour them into the flame of the candle. It will help keep me warm for the winter.' Moved by her generosity I thanked her for her help. She told me to return whenever I needed any more help and I left.

SACRIFICIAL FIRE

I did as she said. I burnt that candle on my desk and every time all my negative emotions arose I poured them into the candle. Pretty soon the book was going much better. And so, after a while, I forgot to do this and found myself instead falling into the same old patterns of accusing myself of being incompetent and drinking endless cups of tea whenever I didn't feel up to confronting the creative fire and giving over to the process of writing it.

During the time I was working on the book, I must have journeyed to the Crone six or seven times. I went to her with various questions and things I needed help with. Her advice was invaluable. The fourth or fifth time I visited her something important happened. I had asked her for help on one or two problems and she had told me what I needed to know. I was just about to thank her and leave when I looked at her and noticed that she didn't look right somehow. 'What is wrong with you?' I asked. 'It makes me sad that you make so little use of the gifts we give you,' she said.

It was then that I realized that I had been forgetting to pour my destructive negative feelings into the fire of the candle and gone back to struggling with the same old ego junk I had struggled with for years.

It was also then that I came to understand the real nature of our relationship with the compassionate spirits in quantum realms. It is not that they are wonderful, benevolent

It is because we have no sense of reverence, no true belief in the holiness of all Life, that Life is destroyed and tortured, brutalized, starved and maimed while we journey from unempowerment to empowerment.
Gary Zukav

Knowledge of what you love
somehow comes to you; you
don't have to read nor analyse
nor study. If you love a thing
enough, knowledge of it
seeps into you, with
particulars more real than
any chart can furnish.

Jessamyn West

beings so great and all-powerful who bestow upon us poor mortals their gifts. (This was pretty much the idea I had grown up with in a Christian society where we are taught that if we are good little girls and boys the angels in heaven will reward us.) The relationship between us and the compassionate spirits is one of *equal partnership*. They have great power for healing, for vision, for creativity, for joy, which they want to share with all who live on the physical plane. But for them to be able to do so, we have to build the bridges between ordinary and non-ordinary reality that make it possible. This we do by accessing the consciousness matrix and directing our intention and compassion to accomplishing the life-nurturing, life-celebrating, healing and creative tasks we want to carry out.

This was a real revelation to me. In some way which I, with my limited understanding, will probably never comprehend, my pouring my negativity into that candle flame each day *did* help keep the Crone warm through her winter. A partnership is a two-way deal, she taught me. I have burned a candle on my desk ever since when I am writing. Many times I stop to give thanks to the wonderful Crone who taught me all this.

Quantum Break 45 & 46

JOURNEY TO THE SPIRIT OF THE PROJECT

Your intention:
TO MEET THE SPIRIT OF YOUR PROJECT AND ASK FOR HELP

Your vision – your project – is connected with a particular spirit or spirits in non-ordinary reality that can help you bring it into being. He, she or they can help you see how to go about it, help alleviate any blockages you are experiencing and continually infuse you with the sense of spirit as you go along.

This is a journey you will want to repeat again and again as you create, including whenever you get stuck or need help of any kind. Remember that working with the spirit of your project is going to be a partnership inspired by friendship. Honour him or her, and he or she will equally honour you. It is a wonderful gift to work together. You will be doing this journey twice this week for both Quantum Break 45 and 46. See how the information and help that you are receiving from the spirit of the project is different the second time from the first time that you meet.

♦ This will be an upperworld journey.
♦ Begin your journey by singing your power song to prepare, if you have one, and then rattling in the spirits of the six directions.
♦ Centre yourself within the axis mundi of your being.
♦ Now call in your power animal or any other helping spirit you want to journey with.
♦ You may start your journey either from the same place in nature from which you always begin or from within the axis mundi and travel up to the upperworld on your world tree if you prefer.
♦ Go to the upperworld and ask your Wise One to introduce you to the spirit of your project.
♦ When you meet him or her, introduce yourself, offer a gift, whatever you feel is appropriate (remember you can manifest anything you like in non-ordinary reality).
♦ Talk to your new friend about the project. Ask for any advice or help you need on it. Don't try to be a good girl or a good boy, be honest. The spirits respect honesty. It cuts through a lot of nonsense and gets you right to the point of the visit. Remember, they are as keen to help you bring this project into being as you are to have their help.
♦ Gather whatever wisdom or power or advice they offer you.
♦ Thank your new friend and say goodbye for now.
♦ Thank your power animal and other helping spirits.
♦ Return to ordinary reality.

Perhaps loving something is the only starting place there is for making your life your own.
Alice Koller

Learn to get in touch with the silence within yourself And know that everything in this life has a purpose.
Elisabeth Kübler-Ross

Bridge Building

While it is always important to record your journeys as quickly as possible after completing them it is particularly important in this kind of a journey where you may return with quite specific guidance and instructions. You can always refer back to your notes in the process of creating your project.

TROUBLESHOOTING

Seek not outside yourself, heaven is within.
Mary Lou Cook

Everyone makes such a palaver out of the creative process. I think this is because we still want somehow to control it – to be able to stick our big toe into the fire but make sure we don't get burnt. Forget it. If you commit to creation you will most certainly feel the fire throughout the whole of your being for the duration of the process. That is the nature of aligning yourself with the creative power. It is also a great personal gift to your expanding freedom and coming into authentic power. The secret that few people know until they have committed themselves to making the hero's journey that creation demands of us is this: what gets burnt in the process is only that which is old and dead, which you are carrying as 'dead weight' and which you are far better off without. The rewards are not only being able to produce something, no matter how simple, which is authentically yours: dancing in the fire of creation burns away only that which is interfering with the full expression of your authentic power and the experience of living free which all of us long for. For me that is well worth a few smudged fingertips.

FREE BREAKS

If one is a greyhound, why try to look like a Pekingese?
Dame Edith Sitwell

This week during your Free Breaks make use of any of the techniques you have been working with over the past ten weeks which you think might be useful in bringing your vision into form. Remember that the compassion and support of the spirits for any project that honours life and brings that which is true and beautiful into form is virtually endless. You have only to ask. If you never ask, it may never happen.

CHECKLIST

Day One

+ Read the chapter as far as your Week Ten Project Bringing Your Vision Into Form on page 270.
+ Read and do Quantum Break 42 Journey for a Project *to discover a creative seed – something you want to bring into being.*
+ Bridge build.

Day Two

+ Read more of the chapter if you can.
+ Do Quantum Break 43 Journey to meet Great Creator *to seek help from Great Creator in bringing your idea into form.*
+ Bridge build.
+ Begin work on your project if you have not already done so.

Day Three

+ Do Quantum Break 44 Journey to the Primordial Flaring Forth *to explore the nature of the creative fire.*
+ Bridge build.

Day Four

+ Do Quantum Break 45 and 46 Journey to the Spirit of the Project *to meet the spirit of your project and ask for help.*
+ Bridge build.
+ Work some more on your project.

Day Five

+ Do Quantum Break 45 and 46 Journey to the Spirit of the Project *to meet the spirit of your project and ask for help.*
+ Bridge build.
+ Work on your project.

If anything is sacred, the human body is sacred.
Walt Whitman

The body is a sacred garment. It's your first and last garment; it is what you enter life in and what you depart life with, and it should be treated with honor.
Martha Graham

DANCING IN THE FIRE

Ah yes, there is one thing more that it takes. This is where journeying to your core can be particularly helpful to connect up with the fire of creation so you come to trust it and feel comfortable with it. That is as comfortable as anyone can feel knowing that when you dance with this fire it will, with the greatest compassion, burn away from you all that is old and dead, false and confused. Be willing to move into the fire of creation and let it sear away whatever is irrelevant to the process, including any issues of pride or inadequacy which you may carry about yourself. It is a question of just trusting the fire and letting it burn. In the beginning of working consciously with the powers of creativity this is not always easy. It certainly has not been for me.

LUDWIG LESSONS

It is never too late to be
what you might have been.
George Eliot

Although I have written over 30 non-fiction books, made films for television and created God knows how many other things so far in my life – from renovating houses to making salads – I only began to really learn about the creative process when I was faced with writing my first novel: *Ludwig ... A Spiritual Thriller.* It is a complex book that spans two centuries and explores the creation process itself through its two main characters Ludwig van Beethoven and a modern ex-Special Forces officer named Michael, much decorated for his bravery by the American government. Michael, revolted by the corruption he sees around him, is running from himself. While in Vienna, he is handed a manuscript by an old woman. It was written by the doctor who cared for Beethoven in the last four months of his life. It carries with it the energies of creation that Ludwig wrestled with all his life. Michael wants nothing to do with this manuscript and from the moment it comes into his hands his life is turned upside down. The novel is the story of how Michael, a hero in form, is sucked into Ludwig's own experience of the fire of creation to eventually become – to some degree against his will – a hero in truth.

I'd like to share with you how it came into being in order to give you some idea of what entering the creative fire can be like when (like me then) you know nothing about what you are undertaking. I have many times since wished that I had known that I could journey to Great Creator, go to my core to align myself with the universal creative fire and call on the help of the book's spirit in non-ordinary reality. But then I knew nothing at all about these gifts.

One day the fierce wolf that walks by my side will spring on you and rip your abominable guts out. One day, one day …
Jean Rhys

DREAMING THE SEED

The first inkling I had that I would become obsessed with *Ludwig* had come twenty years before with a dream. I dreamed I was standing in the midst of a magnificent garden. Like a garden in one of those fabulous Persian miniatures, it was filled with a myriad of flowers and trees covered with blossoms – all in luminous colours. There was a great pond in the midst of the garden and Beethoven's music was playing. It was nothing of his I had heard before and yet I knew that it was Beethoven. I stood in the garden enraptured by the colours and the sounds. As the music reached a crescendo, the trees and flowers, fruits and sky became transfigured with light. The hand of God – as in the God of Michelangelo's Sistine Chapel – came down from heaven, his index finger touching the centre of the pond and sending ever-increasing circles outwards. It was more than I could bear. I closed my eyes and put my hands over my ears. When, moments later as the music began to descend from its climax, I removed them and opened my eyes the garden was returning to its previous colours and state. A voice within told me, 'It is all right – the next time this comes you will be able to bear the beauty.'

That was all. The dream had occurred in my mid-twenties. I had no idea what it 'meant'. All I knew was that it was some kind of a blessing, for it felt as though something fundamental had shifted in my life – at least in my inner life. From that dream too

I'm alive, eating ravioli and drinking wine. I've escaped. A door has opened and let me out into the sun. Good Morning.
Jean Rhys

I learned something pretty fundamental about myself – something rather strange: I learned that the thing which frightened me most was not the horror of pain, deprivation, or loneliness but rather the intensity of a profound experience of beauty. Real beauty has a devastating quality of truth about it. It brings you in touch with the kind of sacred power that dissolves every boundary of your being. That is – I learned later during the four and a half years I was writing *Ludwig* – what I have always feared most.

CREATIVE ARROGANCE

I had no idea how naïve I was about working with the creative fire nor how arrogant in my assumption that I knew how to make this book from the level of my practical personality. I began the writing the way I have begun every other project – with a lot of organization and the intention to produce 2,000 words a day until it was finished. Frequently I found the writing very difficult and would have to stop for weeks at a time. At one point I discovered that I could not work in the light. I would have to pull all of the blinds in my studio. For weeks I got up and ran for an hour along the cliffs where I live and swam in the sea. Then I returned to the darkened room to write.

In the middle of the way of our lives, I found myself in a dark, dangerous wood.
Dante, Divine Comedy

Before long I was brought to my knees. Everything I had learned about writing simply did not seem to apply. I could not, as I had foolishly assumed, write this book from the same practical, intellectual framework that had worked for all the others. This book demanded something different – it demanded *everything* of me. It had to be written from the soul (a soul which at the time I was not even sure existed). It demanded that I dance in the creative fire. One morning as I ran into the sea at dawn I found myself so filled with despair and frustration at what I perceived to be the impossibility of the task that I wanted to swim out into the sea and not return. What was happening to me? I suddenly knew I had a choice to make: do I live or do I die? There in the white foam as the sun rose over the sea I cried out to whoever in the unseen world would listen: 'OK, if you want to destroy me that is your business but I am not going to help you!'

I could not figure out what was happening to me. I wondered if I was ill. I went to have my endocrine system checked out only to find that most of it – the pituitary, the adrenals, the thyroid – was badly out of kilter. Instead of worrying me, the news delighted me. Now at least I knew what to do. Thanks to my background in natural health I was on territory with which I was familiar. I could find my feet. I went on a seven-week juice fast. The practitioner who examined me was amazed. He had never seen anyone recover so rapidly. This is one of the amazing effects of the wild order of life energy carried in living plants. But the book had to be laid aside for almost six months. For every time I went near it I would find my body filled with energies of such intensity that I felt I could not bear them. It was as though I had fallen into a great numinous sea – a sea in which all things were possible and anything could be brought into being, yet which so completely dissolved the boundaries of my being that I could quite literally not function.

PATIENCE AND HUMILITY

During the years that followed I was to learn a lot about patience and humility. I learned that I was nothing – am nothing – and can do nothing of myself. Yet out of such emptiness, by forcing my intention, new things, I learned, could be born. During the next four years so many internal events occurred that it would be impossible to speak of them all – I suppose much of them went into the novel itself. I made a descent into the underworld of my own psyche which until then I had only read about in books with a distant curiosity.

I was to learn that the experience of such a descent is very different indeed from the sometimes facile description of it in books on psychology. I also discovered that the inner world and the outer one are only reflections of one another – as within, so without, and vice versa. I made passages – not passages of my own choosing, yet passages which from some deep inner part of my soul had been chosen for me. A little like the disciple who follows unquestioningly the will of the guru no matter how irrational or difficult it seems and no matter what his or her personal will may be, I followed the imperative from my soul to stick with the writing and finish the novel – never knowing from one day to the next if I would or even if I could. During the last three months I would get up at three in the morning to begin work, my body stiff with pain for, although most days I ran for an hour along the cliffs, I was so completely immersed in the psychic world out of which the novel came that for weeks I found myself badly neglecting the needs of my body. I would say to it, 'Just support me for a few weeks more then I will help you.'

CATERPILLARS AND BUTTERFLIES

Then one day the novel was finished. Six hours later I left for New Zealand to do a series of lectures and workshops as part of International Green Month. I felt like someone who had come back from the dead – the caterpillar who had bound itself into its cocoon and watched while its body had dissolved into a white gel. Hopefully now it would be reformed again into a butterfly. My passage was over. The world was different. I had to learn a brand new language to live in it.

But what did I learn most from all of this? First that there is nothing to fear from the fire of creation so long as you do not mind having burnt away what you really do not need for your soul energy to be expressed in authentic form in the world. I also learned that there is the most incredible order which regulates our lives even when we perceive ourselves to be in total chaos and that within such order lies a love or a compassion that goes far beyond kindness. It knows exactly what is right and necessary for us from one moment to the next. I suppose I learned a little more about how to trust the order of the universe.

Travelogue

◆ How many of your Quantum Breaks did you do this week?

◆ How has the experience of working with your project felt? Have you been able to lay aside all those negative thought patterns and realize that all it takes for the creative process to manifest your vision into form is clear intention, compassion and loving it more than you love your image of yourself.

◆ Did you have any unique experiences that you had not anticipated which were helpful to your project or did anything happen in ordinary reality that was helpful to its fulfilment? Describe them.

quantum leap II

Entering the Dark

*I move in velvet silence within forgotten spaces of your being. Fear me not.
For when you fear me, you fear your beauty and your power. In the light all
is separate. Within my darkness all is One. When your soul calls, I am
there to wrap my silent wings of transformation around you. Enter me in
friendship. I will introduce you to the magic of angels and archetypes,
deities and destroyers. Look carefully at each, no matter how fearsome
its face. You will find each and every one is a window to the divine.*

I am the Spirit of the Dark

This week is a leap into
the dark – that place
which most fascinates
and terrifies. Goethe
said, 'So long as you do
not have this dying and
becoming you're only
a gloomy guest on this
darkening earth.' We
will be entering the
process of death and
rebirth and digging up
its enigmatic riches.

The dark realms are those transcendent domains about which our culture remains naïve and fearful. But, come to know them as you have in the past ten weeks and you will learn to travel through them with power and confidence. Learn to align yourself in friendship with the transformative power of the dark. It will empower your path.

The dark is the place of seed planting, the realm of incubation, the womb of new life. In its sacred stillness the old and dead are composted to feed the tiny seeds of new life. When they open, their husks fall away, and new plants can grow. There are a thousand thousand seeds within you just waiting to break open when the season is right. When you remain deaf to their call the darkness can rise to swallow you. It is demanding that you husband your soil.

CYCLES OF BECOMING

I am using the term shaman for one who is inspired rather than possessed. The willingly induced state of the inspired I take to be more the state of both the shaman and religious mystic whom Eliade calls prophets.
Rowena Pattee

The issue around which all of this fear revolves is our fear of death. Yet death is an absolutely necessary part of transformation that takes us forward again and again into new life. The old, decayed leaves of the forest must die to fertilize the saplings. In our own psyche whatever we carry that no longer serves the free expression of authentic power must die that we may be spiritually reborn. Death is an initiation that happens to us again and again throughout the whole of our lives. It happens as the moon dies and is renewed every month. You can see it in the way a snake sheds a skin when it needs to grow. As Meister Eckert says, the Kingdom of God – that is a state of transformed and expanded consciousness – is 'for none but those who are thoroughly dead.'

Joseph Campbell's *Hero With a Thousand Faces* talks a lot about coming to terms with the experience of death and the inevitable rebirth which follows. It is central to the growth and spiritual development of human beings in every culture of the world. The death-rebirth cycle lies at the centre of the universal myth of the hero in the process of his or her transformation. Throughout history tribal societies have created rites of passage to celebrate this cycle at times of important biological change such as puberty. Initiates are put through rituals involving non-ordinary states of consciousness in which they connect with the energies of the quantum realms in order to experience the power and the meaning of the death–rebirth process. These rituals celebrate their dying to the old role they have been playing in their society – that of a dependent child – and being born into a new one as a powerful and independent human being. A boy dies. A man is born. From that moment onward nobody in the tribe treats him as a child anymore.

A man might die a thousand deaths in one day and find a joyful life corresponding to each of them.
Johannes Tauler

FEAR OF TRANSFORMATION

Yet our culture has lost touch with death–rebirth transformations and so we fear it. We approach death with anxiety, embarrassment and denial. Thankfully this is changing. The work of Elizabeth Kübler-Ross, Stephen Levine and Ram Dass – all of whom have written wisely about death and worked with the dying – is gradually altering our attitude. So is the in-depth research into near-death experiences where people consistently report the survival of consciousness as well as spontaneous experiences of illumination as the soul separates from the body.

For most of us, the death we fear is not the death of the body (although we often *think* it is). It is the death of the ego – the letting go of the control our personality exerts in our life, for a time, in order to allow an influx of our deeper soul energies to enter. It is this experience that Campbell describes so well in the mythological hero's journey. There death and rebirth represent a kind of membrane or interface in the psyche between the domain of the personal and the vast spiritual realms of the universal. Death is a frontier if you like between psychology and mysticism – a frontier which is only breached by activating the consciousness matrix. With the kind of consistent training which you have had in recent weeks – working with your own matrix and connecting with compassionate spirits in non-ordinary realms – the whole process of death and rebirth can gradually become a friend instead of a source of fear. In truth it is a sacred experience with rewards so great it is impossible to put them into words. One of the most exhilarating rewards is a renewed experience of authentic freedom.

> To become human, one must make room in oneself for the wonders of the universe.
> *South American Indian saying*

> Very great rivers flow underground.
> *Leonardo da Vinci*

THE WEEK AHEAD

This week we will be investigating gifts from darkness. You will do a journey which is one of my favourites: to explore the processes of death and rebirth within nature. You will enter your Inner Reaches of Sacred Space and connect with life and death through a plant, asking it what it can teach you about the process. You will also learn to record your journeys as you go as a prelude for a process of shamanic dialoguing – a technique which can be enormously helpful when so-called crisis occurs in your life – when the dark, transformative energies of the numinous suddenly surface, demanding that you take yet another quantum leap forward. The more you come to understand this death–rebirth process both in nature and in your own psyche, the more easily you will be able to access the radiant energies of new life as well as fearlessly honour the processes that bring them forth.

Quantum Break 47

DEATH AND REBIRTH JOURNEY

Your intention:
TO EXPLORE THE NATURE OF THE DEATH AND REBIRTH PROCESS

The Persian poet Rumi wrote wise words about the energy of death and rebirth:

I died a mineral, and became a plant.
I died a plant, and rose an animal.
I died an animal and I was a man.
Why should I fear? When was I less by dying?
Yet once more I shall die as a man.

Using Rumi's poem as inspiration, journey with your power animal to gather information about the cycles of death and rebirth in nature. How you go and where you go to do this is up to you. You may choose to investigate these cycles in the plant world, in the animal world, or even in realms of story in the form of the hero's journey. My way of working with questions such as this is to go to my power animal and say, 'I need to learn about the energies of the cycles of life and death and I need to make a friend of them. Please take me to the most appropriate place in the universe and help me do this.' Then I just let her get on with things. You have come to the point now in your journey work where you can choose how you want to direct your own journeys. So use my way of working or your own. It is the spirits that are our real great teachers. Go to them with clear intention and compassion for all beings – including yourself – and they will bring you what you ask.

- Decide where you are going to go in non-ordinary reality to learn of the cycles of death and rebirth, where you are leaving from, and how you are going to work.
- Are you going from your place in nature or are you going to work with the world tree?
- Using your power song, rattle in the spirits of the six directions and ask for their help in fulfilling your intention. Call in your power animal and any other helping spirits you want to work with.
- Centre yourself within the axis mundi and then begin your journey.
- Gather as much information as you can about the cycles of death and rebirth.
- You might like to ask how these cycles work within your own life, and how you can best work with them.
- You might like to ask about how to deal with any fear of death which you might still have.
- Find out as much information as you can about the death–rebirth circle of energy.
- Then, bringing back the wisdom and compassion you have been given, thank the spirits that have taught you and helped you journey and return home.

Bridge Building

What did you find? Was it different to what you expected? Record your experience. It is important to get as much of it down as you can because at some point you may have to deal with a hero's journey into the darkness of your own soul and the death of what is no longer useful to you. Being able to refer to this journey will help make the process of death and rebirth, which we all go through many times in our lives, more graceful.

The moon dies and is resurrected. The moon sheds its shadow as the serpent sheds its skin to be born again. So it becomes associated with this problem of the principle of life involved in fields of time – death and rebirth. The sun, on the other hand, does not have a shadow within itself. It's always a crisis when the sun is eclipsed. Something has eclipsed it; the sun hasn't eclipsed itself. The sun is always radiant and so symbolizes the power of life in consciousness disengaged from the vicissitudes of time.
Joseph Campbell

Quantum Break 48

SECRETS OF THE UNFOLDING SEED

The shaman, unafraid, experiences death in order to gain control over the elements and the world of the untamed.

Joan Halifax

Descent to the realm of the dead, home of disease spirits, speaks to the fundamental helplessness of humanity. Encountered in the depths are ravenous spirits that instruct as they destroy. The shaman's receptivity to the world of creatures opens after he or she has surrendered to death.

Joan Halifax

Your intention:
TO DISCOVER WHAT A DYING PLANT EXPERIENCES

Let us, right away, take the whole cycle of death and rebirth a step further and enter into the experience itself by connecting with a plant and asking it to teach you directly what the death–rebirth process is all about. To the average person the idea of being able to connect with a plant is, at best an object of humour, at worst a sign that you need anti-psychotic drugs. But to our tribal ancestors the art of connecting with anything in nature was part of their normal day-to-day life. This is how they learned the secrets of plant healing and how to call on plant power when they needed it to shift levels of consciousness, enabling them to enter quantum realms.

To carry out this exercise you will need a plant with you in ordinary reality. It could be as simple as a sprouted seed or grain that you have bought in the salad section of the supermarket. It could be a herb or potted plant you have in your house. Sit down in front of it and you are ready to begin. This is an exercise you might like to do using your rattle as a means of shifting your awareness into the non-ordinary domain of the middleworld.

- ✦ Call in the spirits of the six directions as well as your power animal and any other helping spirits you want to work with.
- ✦ Centre yourself within the three-dimensional axis mundi where their spirit energies meet within your body.
- ✦ When you are ready, ask the spirits to help you merge with the spirit of the plant in front of you within the middleworld.

- ◆ Ask the plant spirit to introduce you to the experience of giving forth the seed or the bulb from its root as its flower dies to create new life.
- ◆ Go further, if you wish, and allow your own spirit to merge with the spirit of the living plant in front of you.
- ◆ What do you feel as you watch yourself die, giving away your seed or root bulb that new life can live after you?   What do you feel as the seed or bulb begins to grow?
- ◆ When you are ready, thank your power animal and helping spirits and let them know that they are free to go now.
- ◆ Return to ordinary reality.
- ◆ Thank your plant for its wisdom.

The central perception of the multisensory human is that he or she is not alone. The multisensory human does not need to rely solely upon his or her own perceptions and interpretations of events for guidance, because he or she is in conscious communication with other, more advanced intelligences.

Gary Zukav

Bridge Building

Record the experiences you have had in whatever form is appropriate to your experience.

DISMEMBERMENT AND RESURRECTION

At the deepest layer of the mythological hero's journey you will find the ancient shamanic experience of *dismemberment* – an archetypal expression of the death–rebirth energy cycle. Dismemberment is an experience of being torn apart, broken open, swallowed by a whale, exploded into a million pieces. To the ears of those who have inherited the mechanistic worldview and not yet begun to move beyond it, this sounds like the most horrific experience you could ever have. But wait a minute. We are not talking here of an ordinary reality event in which you are drawn and quartered or chopped into little pieces. The healing power that results from such spiritual dismemberment is beautifully expressed in the tales of Osiris, Dionysus and Kali. They tell of a spiritual initiation of the highest order which takes place in non-ordinary reality. It is just such a spiritual experience that the initiation rites in tribal cultures are all about – to get in touch with the regenerative sacred energy that underlines the dismemberment–rebirth experience.

Pursuing their shamanic practices, they have come to realize that what most people describe as 'reality' only barely touches the grandeur, power, and mystery of the universe. The new shamans often cry tears of ecstasy when undergoing and recounting their experiences. They talk with mutual understanding to persons who have had near-death experiences, and see hope where others may see hopelessness.

Michael Harner

The experience of dismemberment always connects you to greater power and vision. Undergoing it can bring some of the greatest experiences of healing and growth possible. You will find this recorded in all shamanic literature. It often takes place during a period of fasting or on a vision quest where the shaman has intensively activated the consciousness matrix to contact the numinous realms more deeply than he has ever done before. As Ralph Metzner says in *The Unfolding Self*, 'Dismemberment is always followed by healing and renewal, intensified fragmentation by wholesome integration.'

Sometimes dismemberment occurs spontaneously when you are journeying for another purpose. You might meet a bear for instance and it eats you alive then digests you and pours the remains out of its body. Or you journey to the upperworld only to find that you are blown into a million pieces, as I was (see quantum leap 2). Should this ever happen to you on a journey give thanks. It is a sign of renewal that can enrich your life and just go on enriching it. Remind yourself that there is nothing to fear in non-ordinary reality in either the upperworld or the lowerworld. Then, in your dismembered condition, let yourself become one with all creation. Such experiences are the spirits' way of cutting away the dead wood from our lives in order to bring us in touch with deeper levels of authentic power and freedom.

Since we cannot change reality, let us change the eyes which see reality.
Nikos Kazantzakis

HONOURING DEATH AND REGENERATION
Week Eleven Project

Your project for the week is to become as aware as you can of the processes of death and regeneration around you. Where do you see signs of them? What do they have to teach you? See if you can collect three or four objects out of what you observe which you can place in your sanctuary to remind you of your own connections with this cycle of renewal that is so important in your own life. Make a place for them in your sanctuary. Sit quietly with them and let their wisdom about the death–rebirth experience further penetrate your consciousness.

MATRIX DIALOGUING

One of the most useful things you can learn to do when you are journeying is to learn to record your journey as you go. There are a couple of ways of doing this. You can use one of the little dictating tape recorders and simply speak your journey into it. Then later you can transcribe your experiences on paper or computer. This technique is wonderful if, like me, you have a lot of impressions when journeying or bring back so much information that you have trouble remembering it all. The only trouble is you have to take the time then to transcribe the journey after you have returned to non-ordinary reality. I find it is easier and more useful to simply type the journey I am doing on my computer while it is happening. (I always use a drumming or rattling tape to do this to help me focus my intention. You need extra support when writing down what you experience whilst journeying.) Typing or writing a journey is something that is simply not possible in the beginning of learning to journey. It would be like trying to focus your intention just by entering into the sacred silence rather than having to rely on a drumbeat or rattle when you are first learning. But after you have been journeying for a number of weeks, with a little practice you will find that both activating your consciousness matrix through the sacred silence and recording your journey in writing as you do it are not at all beyond your capabilities.

If you use a computer and can touch-type – so much the better. You can journey and type as you go and it works beautifully. You can even open your eyes to connect with what you are doing without interfering with the journey once you have got the hang of the technique. It is also a good practice for learning to live and work with a foot in both worlds when you want to or need to. But it does take a little practice. Let's try it.

There is nothing so secular that it cannot be sacred, and that is one of the deepest messages of the Incarnation.
Madeleine L'Engle

If you bring forth what is
    inside you,
what you bring forth will
    save you.
If you do not bring forth what
    is inside you,
what you do not bring forth
    will destroy you.
The Gospel of Thomas

Quantum Break 49

JOURNEY OF THE SCRIBE

When the ten thousand
things become one, then
we return to the centre,
where we have always been.

Plato

Your intention:

TO JOURNEY TO THE NATURE OF THE DARK TO LEARN OF THEIR GIFTS AND RECORD YOUR JOURNEY AS YOU GO

This journey is best done using a drumming tape on a walkman.

◆ Prepare for your journey as always.
◆ Rattle in the spirits of the six directions as well as your power animal and any other helping spirits you want to work with.
◆ Sit down with the lights dimmed and, either with pen and paper or at the keyboard of a computer, write down the intention of your journey. In this case it will be to learn all you can about the regenerative power of the dark.
◆ Now ask your power animal to take you wherever in the universe is most helpful for you to learn about the regenerative powers of darkness.
◆ As you travel, record everything that you experience while it is happening.
◆ While in the presence of the dark learn everything you can about it.
◆ Ask that it give you a gift – something of value which you can bring back to remind you of its nature.
◆ If a gift is given to you, acknowledge it with thanks and write down a description of it and what you think it may have to teach you.
◆ When the journey has finished, thank your power animal and helping spirits and return.

The images of the unconscious
place a great responsibility
upon a man. Failure to understand them, or a shrinking of
ethical responsibility, deprives
him of his wholeness
and imposes a painful
fragmentariness on his life.

Jung

Bridge Building

There will be no Bridge building here since you have been doing this during your journey. But if you are anything like me you will want to read back over the journey you have just recorded a couple of times afterwards. I have the tendency when I am journeying to think that nothing very much is happening and that the information or guidance I am being given is of no particular consequence. When I go back and look again, I am almost always surprised at how rich the gifts the spirits have given me are.

THE INNER REACHES OF DEATH AND BIRTH

In the realm of depth psychiatry, there is no one who has a better handle on the significance of the experiences of death and rebirth, dismemberment and resurrection than Stanislav Grof. Having worked with literally thousands of people with whom he has researched the holotropic realms of non-ordinary reality, Grof has found that virtually all the deep fears which inhibit us revolve around two major issues in a human life – death and birth. Birth events produce vast problems for people. When he talks of birth he is speaking quite literally about the exact experience you have had of birth when you came into this life. The story of how he came to discover this is a fascinating one which goes back to the beginnings of modern psychiatry and the father of consciousness himself – Sigmund Freud.

Freud was first to detect the pathology that came from our separating ourselves from the transcendent. Steeped in his Copernican lineage, he elaborated the gulf between individual perceptions and the objectified world in terms of the human psyche. He identified the unconscious – that part of the human mind which is beyond normal awareness most of the time. He named and described the *ego*, the *id*, the *superego*, and he identified what he called the *Eros*, *Thanatos* and *Oedipus* complexes. However, to Freud, human unconscious consisted of little more than a collection of repressed impulses, memories and dark and dangerous forces, which develop out of life traumas and conflicts between the ego and the id. And, although he described these in an archetypal way, he tended to treat them very much as Newton had his atoms – like lifeless building blocks of the mind.

So he climbed, and he climbed, and he climbed. It was easy work, for the big beanstalk with the leaves growing out of each side was like a ladder ... he saw in front of him a wide, shining white road ...

Jack and the Beanstalk

LABYRINTH OF CONSCIOUSNESS

Then Jung came along and blew the human psyche wide open. He described it as a vast labyrinth of consciousness revealing at every turn archetypal patterns which – far from being nuts and bolts thrown into the Newtonian bin of the unconscious as Freud insisted – make up the very fabric of the psyche. During the first half of his working life, Jung tended to treat these archetypes as purely psychological (he was being true to the Newtonian–Cartesian worldview on which both he and Freud cut their teeth). He spoke of them as interesting subjective phenomena which offered no real information about or knowledge of the universe. In his later years all this changed. Jung began to see the archetypes of gods and goddesses, animals and spirits as mysterious autonomous loci of energy which carry power that adheres to both psyche and matter. Even he himself began to experience them as having external reality – like shamanic spirits. Jung wrote extensively about his own Wise One, Philemon, with whom he had one of the most inspiring human–spirit friendships you could ever read about.

Since Jung, transpersonal psychologists have delved deeper into the archetypal realms that he first explored. By far the greatest of these is Stanislav Grof.

PIONEERS OF CONSCIOUSNESS

Grof was originally trained as a Freudian analyst. But a deep conflict began to develop in him about his work. It was between the theory of psychoanalysis and its practice. He had always been fascinated by symbols from dreams, from art, from revolutions in psychoanalysis as well as by the light they can shed on the psyche. He found himself frustrated by the limitations of what you could do to help people through conventional psychoanalysis and by the incredible length of time it takes to bring people even the most rudimentary help. 'I could not comprehend how you could have a complete "understanding" of a patient's condition and yet do so little to help him,' he says.

The theoretical writings of psychoanalysis seemed so logical to Grof and yet in their practical applications they were neither efficient nor very effective. One day, when Grof was still in Prague, the pharmaceutical company Sandoz sent him a sample of LSD 25 as a tool for exploring psychosis. A small quantity of the stuff, it was believed, could put researchers into a state that psychiatrists were used to seeing and having to cope with in their patients. LSD was originally treated as a tool for psychiatrists to use themselves as a means of entering the distorted realms of the psyche of their patients and then coming back with insights that might enable them to treat their mental illness more effectively. Grof took the drug himself, and having done so, began to wonder if a tool like this was not what psychoanalysis was missing.

DEEP DIVING

Grof joined a group of researchers doing systematic work with psychedelics. These drugs seemed to make the contents of the unconscious surface so that they became available for therapeutic work. Grof tended to treat LSD as a catalyst. He hoped the drug might do for psychiatry what a microscope had done for biology or a telescope for astronomy. And he was quite sure that the drug itself was not therapeutic, it was only a tool. These gadgets don't produce the macroworld – a telescope does not produce galaxies – yet one cannot study them without a tool to make them visible to us.

For three decades since then Grof has studied altered states of consciousness and recorded his discoveries in books which read like a page-turning history of consciousness itself. At first he worked with mind-altering chemicals as a means of activating the consciousness matrix and shifting awareness into holotropic states. Then he turned to working with the breath. With his wife Christina he developed the process of holotropic breathing, a technique of the breath which also gives access to deep levels of consciousness. Unlike psychedelic drugs, it gives the person practising it the ability to work consciously with what he finds in transpersonal realms.

MAPPING THE PSYCHE

Grof concluded that the models that are used in most kinds of psychology and psychotherapy are grossly inadequate for the task. This does not mean that they are false or even useless. They describe the psyche in ways that can be of value provided you are content to work at fairly superficial levels. For the techniques used can only bring about limited results, using tools like free association or face-to-face interviews. To work deeper and more effectively, a person needs to involve himself with experiences in non-ordinary reality the way that shamans do, the way .Kung bushmen do in their healing ceremonies: the kind of thing that happens in deep hypnosis, or when using certain powerful meditation techniques. There is no way you can account for any of

We have drunk the soma and
  become immortal!
We have attained the light, we
  have found the Gods.
What can the malice of
  mortal man
or his spirit, O immortal,
  do to us now?
Make me shine brightly like
  fire produced by friction.
Illumine us, make us ever
  more prosperous
Enthused by you, Soma,
  I find myself rich!
Enter within us for our
  well-being.
Parabola Magazine 1978

the richness of transformation possible to people's lives within the framework of the belief that everything comes out of the individual unconscious. For Grof the old mechanistic Freudian view was completely inadequate as a way of explaining things.

This revelation led him to develop much larger maps of the psyche and to realize that the biographical level of recollective analytical material is little more than the tip of the iceberg. It does little more than scratch the surface of what the human consciousness is all about. You need to add other major levels, all of which are accessible only through the consciousness matrix. The first is what Grof calls the peri-natal level. It describes what has happened to you at or around the time of birth and it is the nature of these experiences that apparently determines greatly how comfortable you are with the death–rebirth energies in your life.

BIRTH TRAUMA

When this level of the psyche is activated through holotropic breathing, people often experience deep confrontations with their fears of death. They may even feel their life is threatened, or that they *are* dying. These feelings can be accompanied by a sense of being trapped or caught in some kind of confined situation as if they were struggling to be born physically – but also to be reborn in a spiritual sense. People who get into the peri-natal level doing Grof's holotropic breathing can feel as though they are physically reliving aspects of their own birth – a phenomenon known as *abreaction*. The experiences coming from this level of consciousness take the form of ego death–rebirth phenomena which Campbell describes so well and which is paralleled in shamanic dismemberment. In history, in anthropology, in mythology, this theme emerges again and again – the theme of dying and being born again and again. It is central to the experience of human life and growth.

Reliving such experiences, much like the shamanic death–rebirth experience of dismemberment, not only helps clear psychological problems, it gives people access to the mystic or numinous dimensions of the psyche, at the same time it often takes you right through the centre of your fear of death and leads you out the other side to expanded freedom. Grof and others have found that people who confront birth and death without any intellectual or religious ideas automatically get in touch with their own genuine spirituality. This experience of spirituality is something that arises quite naturally from within. It is a sense of absolute being and knowing that has nothing to do with whatever religion or culture they have been raised in.

You should be willing to be eaten also. You are food body.
Joseph Campbell

GATEWAY TO THE DEPTHS

Crisis, trauma and peri-natal abreactions can act as a gateway to what Jung called the collective unconscious. Once that gateway is opened, the numinous contents of the psyche erupt into consciousness. So powerful is this experience for every human being who has it that it makes no difference what your previous intellectual beliefs are. You can be an atheist, somebody who hates all religion, a left-brained scientist, a sceptic or anything else. When this great flaring forth from the numinous realms occurs, the lava of your spirituality pours through the whole of your being. Suddenly your spiritual life becomes real and unavoidable. You realize that spirituality is a universal phenomenon in the human psyche and in the scheme of life itself. You also become aware that 'religions' are something quite separate from the experience of spirituality itself. They are codified descriptions of the experiences of spirituality out of which they have been derived. Such are the gifts of the dark.

Here in this spontaneous experience of death and rebirth you enter realms only accessible via the consciousness matrix – realms experienced by mystics, great artists and visionary scientists – the realms you have been working in quite comfortably for the last eleven weeks. Here, too, you tap into true spirituality which, like the volcano itself, is exciting, fascinating, undeniable and liberating. By comparison, most mainstream religions are fossils – doctrines and dogma. They have been created out of what was once, for a few mystics or prophets who found them, a direct visionary experience of other dimensions of numinous reality. So much for our fear of the dark.

Likewise, a Zuni dancer wearing the mask of one of the Kachina gods is doing more than impersonating the Kachina. Transported into an altered state of consciousness by the dancing, drumming, rattling and whirr of bull roarers he 'becomes for the time being the actual embodiment of the spirit which is believed to reside in the mask'.
Michael Harner

Quantum Break 50

THE DEATH EXERCISE

Great works of art are
works of nature just as
truly as mountains,
streams, and plains.
Goethe

Your intention:
TO ENTER YOUR INNER REACHES OF SACRED SPACE, INVITE
DEATH TO VISIT YOU AND FIND OUT WHAT HIS PRESENCE HAS
TO TEACH YOU ABOUT YOUR LIFE

Death is what we fear most. Yet literature is full of experiences of people who
have come close to death and found the experience the most liberating in their
life. They say that when you have been touched by the awesome hand of death
your awareness of the beauty of life and your commitment to living the authenticity of your own life is strengthened. There is nothing like the sense that death
is resting at your shoulder to help you clear away the dead wood in your life and
live in a way that is more true to your soul's purpose.

Living nature is not a
mechanism but a poem.
Thomas Huxley

- ✦ Enter the Inner Reaches of Sacred Space inviting your power animal to be
  present with you while you are there.
- ✦ Activate your senses.
- ✦ What do you smell?
- ✦ How does the air feel against your skin?
- ✦ Sense the earth beneath your body. What is it like?
- ✦ What do you see?
- ✦ Let yourself sink into the beauty that surrounds you.
- ✦ Now invite the presence of death to join you in this sacred place.
- ✦ Feel it at your shoulder.
- ✦ Ask the presence of death what it has to teach you about your life.
- ✦ Look at your life from this place of stillness in the presence of death and
  ask yourself if there is anything you would like to change about it.
- ✦ Is there anything that you want to do which you keep putting off until
  'someday'?

- Is there anything that you are living with which does not serve the graceful expansion of freedom in your life and help you further experience authentic power?
- There is something quite transformative and clarifying about going to a sacred place and spending a little time in the presence of death to examine the way you are living and ask if there is anything that it would be appropriate to change.
- When you are ready, acknowledge the gifts that being in the presence of death has brought you. Thank your power animal and open your eyes.

Bridge Building

Record the experience you have had and make a note of anything you think needs clearing from your life, anything that needs changing and anything you want to do that you have been putting off. The next step in Bridge building is to actually make some of those changes begin to happen. Are you ready to do that?

FREE BREAKS

This week's Free Breaks are truly free to do or not do as you so choose. It can be good sometimes, especially after spending almost twelve weeks of rigorous work with the consciousness matrix, to have a couple of days off. It is a good way to prepare for what lies ahead next week and beyond.

FAMILIARITY BREEDS GRACE

Particles, as isolated or isolatable entities, no longer exist; there are only quarks and the quantum fields they are embedded in. Quarks can only exist in a collective form within hadrons: protons, neutrons, and mesons.

Ervin Laszlo

Having the numinous suddenly erupt in your life can be frightening unless you are already familiar with quantum realms and come to feel reasonably comfortable with its dark places. When some life crisis triggers an eruption it can be enormously helpful to know that you can journey to your Wise One, your power animal and other compassionate spirits to ask for help.

Crisis does not need to be a negative event. Handled positively it frequently portends profound individual change and the unleashing of powerful creative energies. Instead of taking tranquilizers and battening down the hatches when your life seems to be falling apart, it can be useful to look at a crisis as a *pivot for change*, triggered by the death–rebirth energies – a door to the kind of transformation that the caterpillar undergoes: when deeply woven into the silk threads of his cocoon his body dissolves into white jelly only to be reformed and eventually set free as a different creature.

I agree that environmental sanity is about sane science and sane politics leading to a sane society. But how do we acquire this environmental sanity? I, for one, suggest that scientists and politicians will only discover environmental sanity through a spiritual reconnecting to nature. Go sit on the Earth. Spiritual ecology is the modus operandi for achieving environmental sanity.

Jim Nollman

Quantum Break 51

MATRIX DIALOGUING

Your intention:
TO ESTABLISH A DIALOGUE WITH YOUR SOUL AND EXPLORE WHAT IT IS ASKING OF YOU

This is one of the most useful techniques I know when crisis strikes – whether it be big or small. It is so simple too. And you don't have to wait until a crisis arrives in your life to make use of it either. It is helpful when you are uncertain about some course of action or feel somehow that you have lost your way. This journey is best done with the use of a drumming tape.

♦ Be clear about what you want to dialogue with your soul about and write this down before you begin.

- ✦ Prepare for your journey as always.
- ✦ Rattle in the spirits of the six directions as well as your power animal and any other helping spirits you want to work with.
- ✦ With the lights dimmed if possible and either with a pen and paper or the keyboard of a computer, write down the intention of your journey.
- ✦ Now ask your power animal to take you to your soul.
- ✦ When you are in its presence begin by telling your soul what it is you want to know or asking for its comfort or love.
- ✦ Be absolutely honest in your communications when dialoguing either with your soul or with any spirit in the quantum realms. You do not have to be a 'good girl' or a 'good boy'. If you are angry express your anger. If you are in pain, cry out.
- ✦ Record your own words on paper or computer and listen carefully to any reply, recording what is said to you or shown to you or whatever happens during the journey.
- ✦ You can record everything as you would the dialogue of a play (Look back to my Lacemaker journey on pages 262–5 which was done this way.)
- ✦ When you have finished your dialogue, give thanks to your soul, your helping spirits and return.

Bridge Building

When doing a dialoguing journey you will be carrying out the Bridge building process as you journey.

Crisis comes to each of us. It can be triggered by a death, the ending of a love affair, the recognition that one is addicted to alcohol, drugs or work, a dawning awareness that what you have always worked for and what you have achieved no longer holds any meaning for you, the loss of a job or reputation, even the unexpected release of intense emotion and the spontaneous entrance into altered states of consciousness which challenges every notion about what is real and what is unreal.

The dragon is symbolic of one's own unconscious, and killing the dragon and tasting his blood means you've eaten and tasted the life energy which is in your own unconscious and was formerly unknown to you. After Siegfried killed the dragon and tasted the blood, the world of nature spoke to him. He understood the language of the birds and the flowers. So you can go on an underground journey in two ways: one, like Jonah, where the unconscious seizes you and carries you down, the other, like Siegfried, by choosing to take an intentional voyage down.
Joseph Campbell

The confrontation with birth and death is in truth a threshold to the experience of spirituality. It can happen in a literal sense to a woman in the act of giving birth or a man sitting at the bedside of his wife who is dying of cancer. It can also happen in your life when you are having to face the abandonment that happens at the end of a marriage or the disruption in your ordinary life that accompanies the loss of a job. For many it comes in a life-threatening situation, for instance in a car crash when you find yourself standing outside your body looking down on what until then you assumed to be the only reality there was. It can even occur in some kind of spontaneous eruption – often labelled a psychotic break – through which the volatile world of expanded consciousness emerges full blown to shake the very foundations of your life. Such events lead people into the transpersonal realms most know little about. With the techniques you have already learned, should they happen to you, you already have some of the tools most useful in turning a confrontation with the dark death–rebirth energies into what eventually can become a true passage to authentic power.

When the deepest part of you becomes engaged in what you are doing, when your activities and actions become gratifying and purposeful, when what you do serves both yourself and others, when you do not tire within but seek the sweet satisfaction of your life and your work, you are doing what you were meant to be doing.

The personality that is engaged in the work of its soul is buoyant. It is not burdened with negativity. It does not fear. It experiences purposefulness and meaning. It delights in its work and in others. It is fulfilled and fulfilling.

Gary Zukav

CHECKLIST

Day One

✦ Read the chapter up to Quantum Break 47.
✦ Do Quantum Break 47 Death and Rebirth Journey *to explore the nature of the death and rebirth process.*
✦ Bridge build.

Day Two

✦ Do Quantum Break 48 Secret of the Unfolding Seed *to discover what a dying plant experiences.*
✦ Bridge build.
✦ If your creativity project from last week demands your time, honour it.

Day Three

✦ Read the rest of the chapter, and the instructions on page 296 for Week Eleven project.
✦ Do Quantum Break 49 Journey of the Scribe *to journey to the nature of the dark to learn of their gifts and record your journey as you go.*

Day Four

✦ Read the chapter to Quantum Break 50 if you have not already done so.
✦ Do Quantum Break 50 The Death Exercise *to enter your inner reaches of sacred space, invite death to visit you and find out what his presence has to teach you about your life.*
✦ Bridge build.

Day Five

✦ Do Quantum Break 51 Matrix Dialoguing *to establish a dialogue with your soul and explore what it is asking of you.*
✦ Bridge build.
✦ Are you remembering your project for this week?

Day Six

✦ Do a Free Break if you choose, otherwise, take a day off!
✦ Remember to Bridge build if you do a Free Break.

Day Seven

✦ Do a Free Break if you choose, and remember to Bridge build if you do.
✦ Spend 20 minutes on your Travelogue.

I slept and dreamt that life was joy
I awoke and saw that life was service
I acted and behold, service was joy
Rabindranath Tagore

Travelogue

Now, with respect to mythology, the same old motifs are going to be there. They're going to have to be there. They're the motifs of human life. But they're going to have to be related to a new social consciousness – not one of the tribe, not even of the planet. And until that happens, what might be called the new and appropriate mythology for a global consciousness will not have taken place.

Joseph Campbell

✦ How was your experience of death and rebirth?

✦ Has your experience released any fear you may have had of death or crisis?

✦ If you experienced dismemberment, did this bring any changes?

✦ Did you find learning to journey and record your experience at the same time useful? Is it something you want to practise more of?

✦ What did death have to teach you?

quantum leap 12

Lightworks

I am no-thing. Yet from my boundless emptiness do all things arise. Out of me the light is born, the galaxies, the elements, the birds that fly, the rocks, the sea, the bacteria who live within the soil. I am that which can never be described. I can only be experienced. When you have moved beyond your fear of darkness and any fascination with light – there will you find me. There you may enter the silence behind all spirit and beyond all form.

I am That I Am

Remember that old saying – save the best for last? As your journey nears its end we come to the realms of light and boundless freedom. You can enter the space between the atoms. You can explore the quantum nature of gods and goddesses, angels and archetypes. Enter one drop of the universe and the rest pours forth to flood your vision and touch your heart.

In 1965, Arno Penzias and Robert Wilson detected cosmic background radiation and captured the dim glow of particles of light – photons – that were left over from the beginning of time. This confirmed that the universe was born in an instant out of a primeval fireball. Almost 20 years before, Gamow had predicted these elusive particles of light would be discovered. He insisted, as the world's creation myths have told, that the universe erupted into being in a single moment – the very moment at which time and space began. When the radiation from the axis mundi was measured by Wilson and Penzias, it had been travelling a long time. Light moves at 186,000 miles per second – or thereabouts. At that speed, it had taken 15 billion years for those first protons to reach the scientists who captured them out of a universe set in motion so long ago.

AT THE CENTRE

Somewhere in the centre of silence lies a realm even more mysterious and enriching than that of the mythological domains peopled with spirits, gods and goddesses. Consciousness researchers studied and recorded the experiences of people who have touched this place having travelled to the frontiers of spiritual experience in search of answers to the question: 'What do people find to be the supreme principle or creative power?' Perhaps the ultimate area for investigations into human consciousness and non-ordinary reality, this is what we will be exploring next.

THE KING IS DEAD – LONG LIVE THE KING

Einstein's general theory of relativity rang the death knell for mechanistic science. But it dealt with large-scale events like the movement of galaxies and the architecture of the universe. It was quantum theory that put the final nail in the coffin. Quantum theory deals with small things. It developed out of an awareness that atoms both emit and absorb light in quanta – the 'packets' of energy which give light its particulate character. The 'particles' of light themselves are known as photons. Then in 1924 one of the founders of quantum mechanics, Louis de Broglie, who had voiced his ambition 'to succeed in penetrating further into the realm of natural harmonies to come to have a glimpse of a reflection of the order which rules in the universe,' suggested that it was not only light waves that had particulate properties: particles of matter also demonstrate wavelike properties. From then on the image of an atom as a collection of billiard balls gave way to an awareness that all matter has both a wavelike and a particulate nature. And out of that awareness developed the idea of quantum matter fields in which there is no real separation between field and particle in the sense that the field is considered external to the particle. These fields are states of space, or of the *vacuum*.

A few more decades passed. Work with quantum fields led to theories about holographic fields, and to the assertion that we are actually living in a holographic universe. It triggered the suggestion of Harlow Shapley, the hard-nosed Harvard physicist, that there may be 'an additional entity, a fifth one' in the universe in addition to gravitational, electromagnetic, strong and weak nuclear fields. Sheldrake's theory of morphic resonance, which offers a valuable perspective on the power of ritual to influence material reality, and helps make sense of the life-transforming effects of working with compassionate spirits in non-ordinary realms, also sprouted forth from the soil of quantum mechanics. So did the notions of vacuum-based holofields and of the quantum vacuum out of which the whole of our universe appears to have come into being.

VACUUM OF A NEW ORDER

The quantum vacuum is like no other vacuum in the universe. Like David Bohm's implicate order, it is not *empty* but full of energy. Like the axis mundi described by shamans and mystics, in undergoing quantum fluctuations it has the capacity to create new quanta out of 'nothing'. And the parallels between scientific theories about how the quantum vacuum operates and reports from mystics and shamans about the nature of reality are immense.

'We reach into a droplet of the universe,' says Brian Swimme, 'and we find there photons with wondrous stories from the farthest regions of the universe.' The same photons which flared forth from the big bang created hydrogen and helium. They formed our sun. They spilled over into the plants that feed us, and from the plants came the radiant energy of our own bodies – of our own being. But what is the nature of this light?

Holy Mother Earth, the trees and all nature are witnesses of your thoughts and deeds.
A Winnebago wise saying

Almost always it is the fear of being ourselves that brings us to the mirror.
Antonio Porchia

God is in the details.
Ludwig Mies van der Rohe

Only the heart knows how to find what is precious.
Fyodor Dostoyevsky

THE WEEK AHEAD

There is a time for everything,
And a season for every
activity under heaven.
Ecclesiastes 3:1

This is a major part of what we will be investigating this week. You will be moving to the frontiers of quantum realms – really pushing the boundaries of what is known. You will be entering the photon fields of your own body. You will be journeying to the upper-world to investigate what the spirits themselves are made of and glean information about their own deeper nature. You will even be journeying to explore what lies beyond the light in the 'spaces between the atoms'. Finally, you will be seeking answers to the question that man has asked forever. What is the very purpose of creation itself?

We all have angels guiding us
… They look after us. They
heal us, touch us, comfort us
with invisible warm hands …
What will bring their help?
Asking. Giving thanks.
Sophy Burnham

WEAVING THE THREADS
Week Twelve Project

Your project this week revolves around weaving together and recording in your journal the relationships between your own experiences and the things you have learned from the experiences of others, including both the scientists working within the Newtonian–Cartesian paradigm and those working with emergent paradigms. How have the experiences you have had in the past three months in the quantum realms and the things you have learned about worldviews and the expanding universe altered your own view of reality? Record it. Get it all down. You will probably need to spend ten or 15 minutes of each day on this week's project. Certainly you will want to go back over the material in earlier chapters of the book and also look at your own Travelogue reports. What is your view of yourself now? How has it changed? Has your journey work increased the sense of freedom and possibility in your life? If so how? Has working in non-ordinary realms, entering the light and exploring the cosmic vacuum expanded your sense of respect for the nature of the beauty that informs (literally brings into form) your own soul? Your Free Breaks this week are included in the work you will be doing on your project – perhaps the most important you have undertaken on the whole of your journey to freedom.

Whoever you are –
I have always depended on
the kindness of strangers.
*Blanche Dubois in Tennessee
Williams:* A Streetcar
Named Desire

Quantum Break 52

LIGHT OF THE BODY

Your intention:
TO ENTER THE PHOTON FIELDS OF YOUR OWN BODY AND
EXPERIENCE THEIR NATURE

This is an exercise you will do from the Inner Reaches of Sacred Space. It is an exploration into the molecular levels of your body and even beyond into the fields of light. These quantum fields not only *are* you, they can resonate with all others by making discontinuous jumps to any other photon fields in the cosmos.

✦ Prepare for a sacred exercise as you normally would.
✦ Call in the spirits of the six directions as well as your power animal and any other helping spirits you would like to have with you in your inner reaches.
✦ Centre yourself in the three-dimensional cross where these spirit energies meet within your body.
✦ Move into your sacred space.
✦ Give yourself time to really connect in your senses with your special inner place in nature – through smell and taste, hearing and seeing and touch.
✦ Be aware of the earth on which you are sitting.
✦ When you are ready, move down into your own body, deeper and even deeper, beyond its physical nature into the realms of light which constitute its make-up.
✦ Let yourself experience the light within. This is the light that constitutes your own being – the light that is all being.
✦ Now ask specifically to be shown the nature of the quantum proton fields.
✦ What are they like?
✦ Do they interact with other quantum fields – those of your power animal for instance? If so how?

How can one person spontaneously and directly affect the body and mind of another person – perhaps even 'see into' the other across considerable distance and tell what is wrong with him or her?
Ervin Laszlo

Nobody can conceive or imagine all the wonders there are unseen and unseeable in the world.
Francis P. Church

✦ See if you can feel your connections with the fields of the plants around you, of the sun, of the water, the rocks or the earth beneath you.

✦ Give yourself time to explore the nature of the light which is the basis of all life.

✦ When you are ready, thank your helping spirits and the spirits of the inner reaches and return to the room.

Bridge Building

Record what you have found in any way you feel is appropriate.

TROUBLESHOOTING

The only thing you should ever have to worry about in journeying at the outer reaches of non-ordinary reality as you will be doing this week is this: should you have any remarkable and magnificent experiences, don't fall into the messianic trap of thinking you are some super-special expert who needs to go out and teach others what is so and what is not so. Each person has to uncover reality by himself and experience it in his own way. The powerful thing about shamanic work is that it gives each person the chance to do this without ever imposing on them somebody else's rules and regulations. The only guru that there is, is found within.

Don't go the other way either and, if you happen to have little experience of the light or the void, assume that there is something *wrong* with you. Our spirit friends have great wisdom about what is appropriate for us to know at any particular moment in time. Other issues may be far more important in your life right now than an exploration of the nature of cosmic reality. So trust what you get, knowing its teachings are right for you.

Most people identify with the limits of their physical body and think of themselves as Newtonian objects. They believe that anything which is even an inch away from the surface of their skin has nothing to do with them. It is the experience that Alan Watts used to call being a 'skin-encapsulated ego' – a very post-Copernican view of reality. Yet ancient cultures as well as tribal cultures have always been aware that this limited way of viewing who you are – although perfectly valid – is a half truth. There are many ways of moving beyond the skin-encapsulated ego to discover your deeper identity.

Stanislav Grof reports that when people who have activated their consciousness matrix do this there are three major kinds of transpersonal experience that they have:

◆ Those which transcend space. Where we are capable of merging with plants, for instance, as you have been practising in quantum leap 11, or with the energy of an element of the weather as you did in quantum leap 7, or even with the atmosphere of a sacred place to gain information about its nature.

◆ Those which transcend linear time. You have done this too in the exercises you did to connect with your soul's essence carried out at the moment in time when it came into incarnation, and when you followed the roots of your world tree down into connections that can nourish the unfolding of your seedpower.

◆ Those in which you enter the domains of mythology, of gods and goddesses, of Wise Ones, and power animals. This too you have been doing throughout the past weeks. In quantum realms you can also connect with archetypes from the world's religions. You may well have experienced this already too. Many Wise Ones come from this group of spirits. You can be taken to the forge of Hephaestus – husband to Aphrodite and blacksmith to the gods of Olympus, or to visit the realms of the pretas – the hungry ghosts of Mahayana Buddhist cosmology. You can meet a unicorn or Pegasus, the winged horse, or hold the hand of the great goddess Isis.

Yet like many you may have a sense that, just as there is a profound reality that lies behind our own life in the physical realms, so may there be a similar deeper truth behind the spirits who people non-ordinary reality. But if so, then what is it?

'Even if it were a question of my head being cut off and the brain removed, or my belly being ripped open and my heart cut out, or any kind of transference or transformation, I would take on the job at once,' said Monkey. 'But if it comes to sitting still and meditating, I am bound to come off badly. It's quite against my nature to sit still.'
Monkey,
Chinese folktale

Quantum Break 53

JOURNEY TO THE SPIRITS

The Buddhas do not tell
the way; it is for you to
swelter at the task.

Dharmapada

Your intention:

TO JOURNEY TO DISCOVER THE DEEPER REALITY OF THEIR BEING

During this journey you will be exploring the depth of the spirits' energy much
as in Quantum Break 52 where you investigated the nature of the quantum fields
of your own body.

✦ Prepare for your journey as always, by singing your power song and rattling
  in the spirits of the six directions.
✦ Centre yourself within the axis mundi.
✦ Call your power animal or any other helping spirits you want to journey
  with.
✦ Begin your journey by connecting with your world tree.
✦ Now, in whatever way you choose to do it, go to the spirits – your Wise
  One, your power animal, or other helping spirits, and let them know that
  you want to find out the nature of the energy that underlies their own
  existence and the existence of all the other beings who inhabit
  non-ordinary reality.
✦ Pay close attention to where they take you, to any gestures they make or
  symbols they show you, to any words they share with you.
✦ Explore as fully as you can the nature of the reality that lies behind your
  spirit friends and the domains in which they live.
✦ When you are ready, thank them for their wisdom and their generosity
  and return.

Afoot and light-hearted I take
to the open road,
Healthy, free the world
before me,
The long brown path before
me leading wherever I choose.

Walt Whitman

Bridge Building

Record your impressions, perceptions and experiences. Are there any correspondences with what you discovered about them and what you have found about the substrata of your own being?

It is essential for the development of your own authentic power and your experience of authentic freedom that you come to trust and respect your perceptions, not only from what you have experienced during this journey but in all your explorations of non-ordinary realms. What you will find is that the spirits give you exactly what you need to know at any particular moment in time and that these experiences will deepen and broaden as you continue to journey and to develop your relationships with them and the quantum realms. But it can be interesting to know what others have experienced too. For this kind of information there is no better source to return to than the work of Grof.

CLOSE TO THE DIVINE

After carrying out literally thousands of sessions of holotropic breathing to help people activate the conscious matrix and explore the transpersonal realms, Grof found people who had experiences of helping spirits, gods and goddesses and archetypes in non-ordinary realms consistently reported that: although the quality of the experiences they have with spirits is often life-changing, none of these people tend to associate them – even when they appear in the form of deities – with what one might call 'God'. Instead the spirits appear to be, rather like ourselves, forms through which the divine essence can be tasted, touched and savoured.

Joseph Campbell reinforces Grof's findings when he says that much religion is based on a misunderstanding of mythology. He insists that people who don't understand how to read the god and goddess energies which Jung referred to as archetypes, tend to *concretize* them. They turn them into idols to be worshipped, in front of which they abase themselves. 'The problem with Jehovah,' Campbell always said, 'is that he thinks he is God.' In other words he is treated in people's minds as the Ultimate Reality.

Campbell loved Durkheim's view that a deity must always be *transparent to transcendence*. It should always act like a window to the divine beauty and truth and power which underlies all existence including our own. It needs to be looked on as a symbol, if you like, through which you reach for the numinous. 'Any deity which gets stuck in its archetype creates a situation where a worship of idols is taking place. Rather than allowing people to adore the experience of transcendence, it tends to block them in a misunderstanding that in concretization of the deity is the divine itself and therefore to block their being able to experience the ultimate nature of the numinous,' says Campbell.

STEP INTO THE VOID

Somewhere at the centre of silence lies a realm even more mysterious and enriching than that of the mythological realms peopled with spirits, gods and goddesses. People who have travelled to the frontiers of spiritual experience in search of answers to the question: 'What is the supreme principle or creative power?' come back with fascinating reports. It correlates exactly with the teachings of many of the world's great religions. In Grof's words: 'Time after time, people compared the Absolute to a radiant source of light of unimaginable intensity, though they emphasized that it also differed in some significant aspects from any forms of light that we know in the material world. Yet to describe the Absolute as light entirely misses some of its essential characteristics, particularly the fact that it also is an immense and unfathomable field of consciousness endowed with infinite intelligence and creative power.'

OK. Then the issue becomes, when and how do people who are familiar with the realms of non-ordinary reality come to feel that they have really *arrived* – that they are in touch with the supreme nature of the universe – that they now sit at the cradle of everything? When do they have the sense that they understand what it is all about – or at least when do they have the experience of being in a state when even asking such a question seems beside the point?

Those who make channels for water control the waters; makers of arrows make the arrows straight; carpenters control their timber; and the holy control their soul.
Dharmapada

LIGHT REPORTS

There are two different experiences which people who explore the transcendent realms in great depth consistently report. One is an experience of the void – an emptiness that is super-ordinated to everything else and appears to underlie everything. The other is an encounter with boundless light – a light that embraces all and encompasses within itself every polar opposite. Not surprisingly, perhaps, you often find an experience of all-pervading light in reports of mystical encounters in every major religious tradition in the world, as well as in the descriptions of poets, prophets, alchemists and shamans. The physician Paracelsus spoke of the 'light of nature'. He insisted that our clairvoyant dreams and visions as well as the instinctual abilities of animals were made possible by this light in nature. 'Nothing can be in man,' he said, 'unless it has been given him by the light of nature.' And presumably in the sixteenth century when he lived he had no knowledge of quantum proton fields.

Arctic explorer Knud Rasmussen, who has written extensively of the experience of shamans in his *Intellectual Culture of the Iglulik Eskimos*, reports that an experience of all-pervading light is often experienced by shamans. 'Every real shaman has to feel *quamaneq*,' one of the Eskimo shamans told him, 'a light within the body, inside this head or brain, something that gleams like fire, that enables him to see in the dark, and with closed eyes see into things which are hidden, and also into the future.'

Mystics from Teresa of Avila and St John of the Cross, to the Sri Aurobindo and the Tibetan saint Milarepa all tell of the experience of illumination in mind, body and spirit which comes after you have gone through a period of darkness. It comes in a flash. Even St Augustin writes of it in his *Confessions*:

> 'I entered into the secret closet of my soul, led by Thee ... and beheld the mysterious eye of my soul the Light that never changes ... It was not the common light that all flesh can see, but different ... It was higher because it made me, and I was lower because made by it. He who knoweth the truth, knoweth the Light: and who knoweth it, knoweth eternity.'

An experience of light was also at the core of Jesus' transfiguration on the mountain. At that point his personal life ended and the *passion* began which quickly led him to Jerusalem and to the crucifixion. When it happened, James, John and Peter looked at him: 'His face shone like the sun, and his clothes became white as light.' Gnostic and Neoplatonists call the soul *augoeides* – lucid, radiant, luminescent, splendidly shining.

American naturalist Henry David Thoreau also speaks of the nature of this transcendent light when he writes:

> 'I hear beyond the range of sound,
> I see beyond the range of sight,
> New earths, and skies and seas around,
> And in my day the sun doth pale his light.'

There cannot be self-restraint in the absence of desire; when there is no adversary, what avails thy courage? Hark, do not castrate thyself, do not become a monk: chastity depends on the existence of lust.
Rumi

It is the soul's duty to be loyal to its own desires. It must abandon itself to its master passion.
Rebecca West

All you need is deep within you waiting to unfold and reveal itself. All you have to do is be still and take time to seek for what is within, and you will surely find it.
Eileen Caddy

And poet Walt Whitman in his *Leaves of Grass* describes his own experience of illumination:

'As in a swoon, one instant,
Another sun, ineffable full-dazzles me,
And all the orbs I knew, and brighter, unknown orbs;
One instant of the future land, Heaven's land.'

Quantum Break 54

JOURNEY TO THE LIGHT

At the time of the change of
the Moon his pain is great.
Wolfram von Eschenbach
Parzival

Your intention:
TO EXPLORE THE NATURE OF LIGHT

In this journey you will be going to the upperworld either using a drumming or rattling tape or by travelling in the sacred silence. Begin to connect with the self-luminating domains of quantum reality in which, as Meister Eckhart writes: 'The light of the soul's core overflows into the body which becomes radiant with it.' This journey can also help you establish a connection – however tenuous at first – with the light of healing and grace which you can then journey to whenever you like. I only learned about the light realm from shaman friends who journey to it regularly, often daily, to renew their energy and bring greater clarity to how they live their lives day to day.

It is important to lay aside your tendency to think of journeying to the light as a 'big thing' and just do it. We have so often become overawed by such things and led to believe that we are not 'worthy' even to consider that an experience of light could be 'allowed' in our lives. Try not to make a big deal of it – just begin to make your connections with the light realms and see what there may be in them for you. If such an exploration is not relevant for you at this time, your spirit friends will let you know this, in which case simply lay this journey aside for a while. You can always come back to it later.

+ Prepare for your journey as always, by singing your power song and rattling in the spirits of the six directions.
+ Centre yourself within the axis mundi.
+ Call your power animal or any other helping spirits you want to journey with.
+ In whatever way you choose to travel – either up the world tree or to the upperworld from your usual leaving place – begin your journey.
+ Ask your power animal and Wise One to take you through a hole in the fabric of reality into the realm of pure light.
+ What is this realm like?
+ Let yourself bask in its beauty.
+ Is the light so great that it wipes out everything?
+ How do the cells of your body feel in this place?
+ What can the light teach you?
+ When you are ready, thank your helping spirits and return.

Bridge Building

How can you best record your experience? In words, in colours? In sound? Dance? How?

The Buddhas have a saying: 'joyful participation in the sorrows of the world.' Only then are you really in the field of life. Life isn't meant to be happy. That's not what it's all about. Ah, the damage that is caused by that attitude. All life is sorrowful. Sorrow is the essence of life. But can you handle it? Are you affirmative enough with your relationship to life to say 'yea' no matter what? The extent of your power to say 'yea' is the extent of your power to love and when you begin to have hates, and when you begin to knock people down, and say, 'No! No! This one, this Hitler, or Stalin, they're monsters!', then you have lost your bliss. They are manifestations of life too. Your limitation and understanding and experience is measured by the boundary of your love.
Joseph Campbell

RESISTANCE TO THE LIGHT

An unempowered personality cannot complete the task of its soul. It languishes in an inner sense of emptiness. It seeks to fill itself with external power, but that will not satisfy it. This sense of emptiness, or something missing, or of something wrong, cannot be healed by satisfying the wants of the personality. Gratifying needs that are based upon fear will not bring you to the touchstone of purpose. No matter how successful the personality becomes in accomplishing its goals, those goals will not be enough. Eventually it will hunger for the energy of its soul. Only when the personality begins to walk the path that its soul has chosen will it satisfy its hunger.

Gary Zukav

There is so much palaver surrounding our experience with light. The first time I came in touch with transcendent light was in my twenties. It happened to me in the dream I spoke about in quantum leap 10 – the dream of transfiguration which years later led to my writing my first novel. I was terrified by the beauty of such all-encompassing light. It was too much for me to handle. And so I closed my eyes and put my hands over my ears. 'The next time such beauty comes,' I was told, 'you will be able to bear it.'

The first time I did the journey which you have just done I was still resistant to it. But, at the insistence of a friend, I did it anyway. I found the whole experience fascinating. The most important thing I learned from it is that entering the light realm is not an experience allowed only to 'good' people. Light is so fundamental to our being in every sense that we can never move fully into our own freedom or live out our authentic power without acknowledging it.

And, if such illumination comes spontaneously in our lives, we should not in any way consider ourselves 'special', 'extra holy', 'enlightened'. The light, like the void, and our friendships with spirits, power animals, gods and goddesses is not reserved for a specially-elected holy group of people. It is one of the gifts of being human. And just because you experience illumination this does not make you a saint or a guru. However, the more familiar we allow ourselves to become with the totality of human possibilities, including the experience of light, the richer our lives become, the greater our experience of freedom, and the more gracefully do we move into authentic power. Light belongs to everyone regardless of religion, race or cultural origins.

THE DYNAMIC VOID

The other state which consciousness researchers find people tend to experience when they feel themselves to be in touch with the supreme nature of the universe is that of the Void, which in some sense underlies everything – perhaps even the light itself. The Void is a non-ordinary state of consciousness in which you touch this emptiness. There is simply nothing there. And yet this nothingness is in some way conscious of itself. Such things will never be understood by the intellect. Their experience closely resembles the descriptions scientists are now coming up with of what they call the dynamic void or cosmic vacuum out of which the first flaring forth that created the universe emerged. In the words of Ervin Laszlo:

'There is now a growing body of evidence that the interconnecting holofield is a specific manifestation of the cosmic quantum vacuum. But just what is the quantum vacuum? The term seems mysterious, yet it refers to one of the most important, and as yet least understood, aspects of the physical universe. A deeper look is eminently worth our while … Matter, as we have seen, is best viewed as a product of space – more exactly, of the vacuum's universal zero-point field that fills space. The seemingly solid objects that populate our world, and the flesh and bones that make up our body, are not constructed out of irreducible building blocks we could properly call "matter". The things we know as matter – and that scientists know as mass, with its associated properties of inertia and gravitation – are the results of subtle interactions in the depth of this space-pervading field. In the new vision there is no "absolute matter", only an absolute matter-generating energy field.'

Quantum Break 55

INTO THE VOID

Your intention:
TO JOURNEY TO EXPLORE THE EXPERIENCE OF THE VOID

You can do this journey in either of two ways. You can go to the upperworld – as is set out below – or you can journey to what I call the 'spaces between the molecules' – the quantum vacuum itself within your own body.

+ Prepare for your journey as always, singing your power song and rattling in the spirits of the six directions.
+ Centre yourself within the axis mundi.
+ Call your power animal or any other helping spirits you want to journey with.

The mathematically formulated laws of quantum theory show clearly that our ordinary intuitive concepts cannot be unambiguously applied to the smallest particles. All the words or concepts we use to describe ordinary physical objects, such as position, velocity, colour, size, and so on, become indefinite and problematic if we try to use them of elementary particles.
Werner Heisenberg

In the history of the collective as in the history of the individual, everything depends on the development of consciousness.
Carl Jung

Action on behalf of life transforms.
Joanna Macy

- ✦ In whatever way you choose to travel – either up the world tree or to the upperworld from your usual leaving place – begin your journey.
- ✦ Ask your power animal and Wise One to introduce you, through a hole in the fabric of reality, to the experience of the Cosmic Void or the quantum vacuum.
- ✦ What is this realm like?
- ✦ Is it peaceful, dynamic or both?
- ✦ How do the cells of your body feel when you touch this place?
- ✦ What can you learn here about the nature of reality?
- ✦ How does being here affect your view of your own life?
- ✦ Allow yourself to remain for a time in this space.
- ✦ When you are ready, thank your helping spirits and return.

Bridge Building

Record what you have experienced by whatever means you feel most appropriate.

OUT OF NO-THING

The experience of cosmic emptiness which people who have had it refer to as the Void should more properly be called the 'pregnant Void'. It has nothing to do with a sense of emptiness within that we associate with a sense of meaninglessness in life. It is a state which goes beyond time and space, is unchangeable, and transcends all opposites – from good and evil to light and dark, stasis and motion, agony and ecstasy – the lot. Grof has found that people in holotropic states who experience both the clear light of absolute consciousness and the cosmic emptiness report that these two experiences are interchangeable and identical. Yet from the point of view of our logical mind they certainly seem very different.

THE FINAL QUESTION

The question which often arises out of all this is an unanswerable one yet a lot of fun to explore too. It is WHY? Why did absolute consciousness, the Cosmic Void, the quantum vacuum, choose to bring forth the world of form anyway? Let's journey on it:

Quantum Break 56

THE PURPOSE OF CREATION

Your intention:
TO GO EITHER TO THE QUANTUM VACUUM OR THE LIGHT AND ASK THE PURPOSE OF CREATION

✦ Prepare for your journey as always, singing your power song and rattling in the spirits of the six directions.
✦ Centre yourself within the axis mundi.
✦ Call your power animal or any other helping spirits you want to journey with.
✦ Travel in whatever way you choose – either up the world tree or to the upperworld from your usual leaving place or into the 'quantum field spaces between the molecules' of your body – to connect with the light or the void.
✦ When you have connected ask the question 'Why was the universe with all its myriad forms created?'
✦ See what you get.
✦ When you are ready, thank your helping spirits and return.

The universe is a living, creative, experimental experience of discovering what's possible at all levels of scale, from microbe to cosmos.
Margaret J. Wheatley and Myron Kellner-Rogers

We bear the universe in our being as the universe bears us in its being. The two have a total presence to each other and to that deeper mystery out of which both the universe and ourselves have emerged.
Thomas Berry

Bridge Building

Record whatever your experience has been. It can be interesting to compare your own information on this with that of others. I never do this until after I have had the opportunity to explore issues such as this on my own through my own eyes. Afterwards I go digging in books on science, mythology and transpersonal psychology to see if the answers to certain questions or the experiences that I have had find echoes in the experiences of others. Stan Grof's most recent book – and in may ways his most fascinating – is The Cosmic Game. *It is a wonderful source for this kind of information both from the point of view of depth psychology and also in respect to the earlier recorded experiences of mystics and visionaries from the world's great religious traditions on these issues. I find him one of the world's most brilliant and at the same time most simple human beings. His work has inspired me for a very long time.*

Far from there being an 'end' of science, our period will see the birth of a new vision, a new science whose cornerstone encloses the arrow of time; a science that makes us and our creativity the expression of a fundamental trend in the universe.

Ilya Prigogine

Exploring the nature of what you might call the Absolute or Supreme Cosmic Principle, in whichever way you perceive it, people find they generally experience it one of two ways: either someone feels himself to have lost all boundaries and merged with the source of creation – the experience which the great Vedanta mystic Ramakrishna described as *being* the sugar – or one still maintains the vestiges of personal identity in which case one *tastes* the sugar by becoming witness to the *mysterium tremendum* of existence and remains in highly personal relationship to it. Sometimes it is the relationship of the beloved which you find in the Sufi tradition, or in the case of Christianity, Jesus experienced it as that of the child to God the Father.

CHECKLIST

Day One

+ Read as much of the chapter as you can.
+ Take a look at the instructions for Week Twelve Project Weaving the Threads on page 314, and begin work on it.
+ Do Quantum Break 52 Light of the Body *to enter the photon fields of your own body and experience their nature.*
+ Bridge build.

Day Two

- ✦ Do Quantum Break 53 Journey to the Spirits *to discover the deeper reality of their being.*
- ✦ Bridge build.
- ✦ Continue to work on your project.

Day Three

- ✦ Read the chapter to Quantum Break 54 if you have not already done so.
- ✦ Do Quantum Break 54 Journey to the Light *to explore the nature of light.*
- ✦ Bridge build.
- ✦ Continue to work on your project.

Day Four

- ✦ Read the rest of the chapter if you have not already done so.
- ✦ Do Quantum Break 55 Into the Void *to journey to explore the experience of the void.*
- ✦ Bridge build.
- ✦ Work on your project.

Day Five

- ✦ Do Quantum Break 56 The Purpose of Creation *to go either to the quantum vacuum or the light and ask the purpose of creation.*
- ✦ Bridge build.
- ✦ Work on your project.

Day Six

- ✦ Work on your project for your Free Break this week.

Day Seven

- ✦ Work on your project for your Free Break this week.
- ✦ Spend 20 minutes on your Travelogue bringing it all together.

Remind yourself that you are supported, that you are not going it alone upon this Earth. Dwell in the company of your nonphysical Teachers and guides. Do not discriminate in terms of what you can and should ask and speak about. Just assume and live in the beauty of the bond. Do not fear dependency. What is wrong with being dependent upon the Universe, whether that is your Teachers or Divine Intelligence? You do what you do for yourself and the Universe and your nonphysical Teachers and guides are there in assistance. They will never do it for you. It is not possible for them to do it for you. Delight in the dependency. Give your guides and Teachers permission to come closer.

Gary Zukav

Just trust yourself, then you
will know how to live.
Johann Wolfgang von Goethe

What I so love about shamanic work is that when you are accessing the consciousness matrix it gives you the possibility of finding out what is true for you. That is the only truth that is of any value – not my truth, nor Grof's truths, nor the truth of mystics and saints or shamans, nor the church's truth, or anybody else's. All of the tools and techniques you have been working with for the last twelve weeks belong to the most useful collection of practices I know for expanding your experience of truth. I suppose they are rather like the exercises a dancer does at the bar to develop her muscles and poise, her physical stamina and to practise her ways of moving. It is the dance that you do with them afterwards that matters. It is *your* dance. Trust it.

Travelogue

+ How did you find this week's journey?
+ Were the things you discovered directly related to the way you live your life? If so how. If not, why not?
+ How was your week's project? Did it give you some perspective on just how much your awareness has expanded as a result of the process you have been through?

quantum leap 13

Freedom

I am the vehicle on which you can travel to the ends of the universe. I let you celebrate the sheer exuberance of living from one moment to the next. I am the winged victory rising upwards. She sings the song of your soul. I remind you that you are an instrument in the creative evolution of the universe. Welcome my presence with all your being. I am an arrow shot forward into your future. Choose your target, focus your intention and let go.

I am the Spirit of Freedom

We've arrived at the all-important thirteenth leap. The programme has done the job of getting you to the rooftop so you can see. Take a look at the possibilities from here. Freedom encompasses the whole of your being and enables you to do what you want. Authentic power fuels its movement. Where will you go from here? The possibilities are endless.

Because of the
interconnectedness of all
minds, affirming a positive
vision may be about the most
sophisticated action any
one of us can take.
Willis Harman

The process is finished. The circle of twelve is complete. By now you have walked through the halls of science, gathered the tools of the shaman, gazed through the eyes of the mystic, and been seared by the fire of creation. You may even have broken the boundaries of time and space in touching the quantum vacuum out of which the universe was created. It is the same power that flares forth right now from your own axis mundi and goes right on flaring forth. So now it's time for that all-important thirteenth leap: the leap to freedom.

FEAR OF FREEDOM

When I was a kid I had an uncle – a big man with hands like hams and a voice that was soft as silk and smooth as butter. He was the warden of a prison in California. His house was on the prison grounds. When you went to visit him, you had to drive through three sets of gates to get to it, and once inside it always felt to me like I was one of the prisoners. There was no way out. My uncle was a gentle, powerful man. So great was the respect the Governor of the state had for him, he would always call my uncle out to deal with riots in any other top security prisons. I guess he knew a lot about human nature.

Without a global revolution
in the sphere of human
consciousness, nothing will
change for the better … and
the catastrophe towards which
this world is headed – the
ecological, social,
demographic, or general
breakdown of civilization –
will be unavoidable.
*Vaclav Havel, president of
Czechoslovakia*

One day my uncle told me something I never forgot: 'Leslie,' he said, 'It is a funny thing about prison. I have seen men take red pencils and mark their calendars for twenty years. They hate each moment spent in this place. They count the weeks and months and years until parole. Then one morning, sure enough, the day arrives. Dressed in a suit, with an extra pair of shoes wrapped in a newspaper stuffed under an arm, a prisoner walks through that gate to become a free man. You'd think that would make them happy wouldn't you? Well, I will tell you this: there aren't many who don't want back in. All that freedom stuff is scary. Men want to know where the next meal is coming from and where they are going to sleep at night, and what's gonna happen at 8 o'clock next morning. We're all a lot like that. I think we get used to following other people's rules. We would rather complain about the freedom we don't have than use the freedom we do.'

WHAT FOR?

I guess that is part of living free. Each of us has to decide whether or not we want to use the freedom we have been given and, if we do, then we need to figure out what for. In the past eleven weeks you have been exploring non-ordinary domains. You have met gods and goddesses, Wise Ones and compassionate helpers in the quantum realms. You have spoken with them, listened to them, worked with them, been given advice by them and created friendships with them. If you so choose after the thirteen quantum leap programme is finished, you can broaden your experience of transpersonal realms to deepen your connections with the spirits there, and draw on their wisdom and share their gifts with the world in which you live. For me the exploration of non-ordinary reality continues to be a source of endless fascination, creativity, strength and joy. I love the friendships I have made there. I am constantly surprised by the wisdom of my spirit friends and partners. They are as real to me as the desk in front of me, as my dog Moonbeam who lies beneath my feet as I write. I love and honour them as I love and honour my parents and my sons and my daughter. I am inspired by their wisdom and their compassion. I am moved to tears by their willingness to come to me and provide help when I need it most at times when it feels as though my energy is giving out and I cannot find another word to write.

In recent weeks your hard work and the focus of your intention to carry out the exercises that form the structure of *Journey to Freedom*, you have connected up with your own authentic power which is ultimately the universe's power. So, now what are you going to do with it?

TO BE AND TO WATCH

As humans our position in the cosmos is unique. We have the capacity for self-reflection. Where animals sense something, we sense that we sense. We can not only be *in* the world, we can stand back and *watch* it. We can look back to the past and forward into the future. And we find ourselves at a unique moment in history: we are no longer imprisoned in the mechanical universe in which we once thought we lived.

Our universe is an expanding one – an evolving one. Native Americans talk of honouring 'all our relations'. They mean our rock friends, our tree friends, the sun in the heavens and the soil between our toes. Astrophysicists tell us that the creation process

Mindfulness must be engaged. Once there is seeing, there must be acting. Otherwise what is the use of seeing?
Thich Nhat Hanh

In the history of the collective as in the history of the individual, everything depends on the development of consciousness.
Carl Jung

The responsible rapprochement of human consciousness with the powers of the collective psyche, that is the task of the future.
Erich Neumann

did not just happen once 15 billion years ago. It continues to happen right here and now – in us and all around us. It is actually part of us and we of it. Where once the whole shebang was seen as lifeless matter in empty space, we now view it as a living sea of energy in which we swim. Such knowing has shifted us from a view of separation and isolation towards perceiving wholeness and interconnections.

SHAPING MATTER

Emerging paradigm scientists speak of timeless, spaceless interacting fields and holographic minds. They tell us we are – each one of us – deeply embedded in the web of life which we ourselves help weave. They tell us that consciousness shapes matter. They say that, like the cream-stealing bluetits, when enough of us are aligned in our thinking and clear about our goals we can – if we so choose – redirect the future of the planet. What part do you want to play in this process?

You have already taken giant steps towards finding the answer to this question. You have had the courage to go back in time and merge with your seedpower – that absolutely unique essence which is you. You have wanted to find out about your own unique brand of seedpower. In the past three months you have gathered tools and techniques which enable you to travel anywhere in the universe and to call for whatever help you need to bring forth that essence in what you do. This is what living in authentic power means.

Each of us has our place within the evolving universe – a place which is so unique and so invaluable that for us not to know about it or honour it creates distortions in the weaving of life's web. This week is a good time to begin finding out what yours is.

While the weekly exercises, projects and processes of *Journey to Freedom* are officially over, the skills you have learned and the insights their use may have brought you go on and on. You can keep on using them if you so choose to spin cocoons that make your life-transitions more graceful to gain help and healing when you need it, or bring both of these things to others who ask you for them. Now you know how to connect with creative power and you have begun to play with bringing your visions into form. You have begun to explore the vast wonders of the universe and revel in its beauty and its wonder. You may want to continue, as I do, to journey daily for clarity and guidance about what lies before me, to connect up with my friends in the quantum realms, to work out how to handle something which is challenging me.

EASY AS RIDING A BIKE

The process you have been through by moving from one quantum leap to the next, like the leap of protons themselves, is discontinuous. It transcends time and space. This process is a process of the soul. The things you have learned you will never lose. It is like riding a bike. You think you have forgotten how, when it has sat in the cycle shed for a few years, only to find that five minutes of wobbly pedalling has you back on track. They open up possibilities, access new power and create new visions and they will simply go on doing so. Once the consciousness matrix is activated it never goes to sleep again. If you do choose to continue to work consciously with it the benefits are even greater: you will go on and on making quantum leaps in your life. You will experience more and more synchronicities in your life. You will become more aware when great swells from your soul arise out of the sea of consciousness. And, respecting their authenticity even though you may not 'understand' them, you will ride them with trust and excitement to the next shore.

During this last week, there are some important journeys you can do. I have not set them out in the same way as I have done before because you already know how to journey. You know how to call in the spirits of the six directions, how to align yourself with the axis mundi and in doing so with the creative power of the cosmos. You know that the only real limitations to what can be done working in non-ordinary reality through the consciousness matrix come from limitations to your imagination. For instance, I would never have dreamed that I could journey to the spirit of a book I was writing or a film I was making until, desperate and struggling with my own inadequacies and trying to do it all from the tiny spaces of my left brain, I went in desperation one morning to the upperworld for help from my Wise One, asking, hope against hope, if I could meet the spirit of the book. In meeting the Crone I not only found help finishing the book I was writing, but my whole way of looking at my relation to gods and goddesses, angels and archetypes, changed. I learned about *partnership*.

Ask and you shall receive, they tell us. But the implication, at least in our Judeo-Christian culture is that to receive we have to be good little girls and boys. Then, if we are lucky, the great angels or god himself might take pity on us. That is simply not the way it works. Self-abasement only leads to a feeling of powerless on the one hand and spiritual arrogance on the other.

We don't need to make another person believe like we do to feel comfortable with them. What is important is the willingness to let stand another person's experience of their experience – to live in comfort in their experience and our own – knowing that we inhabit a common reality. When I see the ground we share as spiritual experience, it lessens the anxiety I feel about enormous differences between us.
Mwalimu Imara

But are we being dreamed by a single divine intelligence, by God, or are we being dreamed by the collective consciousness of all things? … We cannot ask if the part is creating the whole, or the whole is creating the part because the part is the whole. So whether we call the collective consciousness of all things 'God,' or simply 'the consciousness of all things,' it doesn't change the situation.
Michael Talbot

CARROT WORSHIPPERS

So think as if your every
thought were to be
etched in fire upon the sky
for all and
everything to see. For so,
in truth, it is.
So speak as if the world
entire were but a
single ear intent on hearing
what you say.
And so, in truth, it is.
Mikhail Nimay

Years ago my daughter Susannah and I wrote a book about the health enhancing properties of raw foods called *Raw Energy*. From the point of view of physics, raw foods carry wonderfully complex energy fields which when we eat them resonate with our own, raising the aliveness of our cells and expanding our capacity for health and healing, joy and vitality. It is all perfectly true. Eat 50% to 75% of your foods raw and it rejuvenates your body and transforms your looks and well being. Some people, however, mistake the 'map' for the 'territory'. They read the book and figure that they will find God in a carrot. Then they want to know how many carrots they need to eat to get close to him. So they go overboard, consume nothing but raw foods, and feel enormously self-righteous about the whole thing.

Occasionally I get a letter from somebody like this. They thank me for writing the book, let me know how raw foods have changed their life and tell me how wonderful it is that *we* (presumably they mean Susannah, me and them) know the 'truth' – and isn't it a pity the rest of the world suffers in ignorance.

Now, I am quite sure that God is in a carrot. But God is in everything else too – from the sweet peas in the vase on my desk to the greedy arms dealer who exploits human life, destroying himself in the process. You see, these 'carrot-lovers' think the Raw Energy approach to eating is a pat formula for perfection. In truth it is only a useful tool for empowering your health and clarity. Don't make the mistake they do. Never think of the *Journey to Freedom* programme as an end in itself, or that it holds the power of your freedom and authentic power. It is nothing more than a useful and beneficial process to help you get in touch with both. The real power comes from your own soul and nowhere else.

By the way, I usually deal with the carrot worshippers by writing back to thank them for their letter and letting them know that I am most certainly not one of the 'elect' since I drink three bottles of cheap red wine a day and dance on tables. (Of course it is a total lie since I hate cheap wine and am saving two things to learn only after I turn 80: dancing on tables and playing golf.) But it does the trick.

ONE WORLD

The convergence taking place between emerging paradigm science and the experience of mystics and shamans is rapidly expanding our sense of what constitutes reality. Data from quantum physics, the work of Sheldrake and Bohm and Laszlo are moving us towards a realization of the interrelatedness of all things – seen and unseen. So long as we were living with limited worldviews, what we experienced around us only confirmed our sense of limitation. We went on perceiving ourselves as nothing more than a material body. Everything continued to seem solid and separate. Time continued to be only linear in nature – flowing from yesterday to today and on to tomorrow. And all events appeared to be connected in simple, single-cause-single-effect chains.

Once you activate the consciousness matrix and allow yourself to experience the nature of quantum realms, you see how limited such a view has been and you begin to move towards a sense of wholeness with the rest of the universe. You start to see and smell, taste and touch the interrelatedness of all things. They become *real* for you. You begin to look at the world around you more as a flow than as a collection of nuts and bolts. The solid structures on which the Newtonian–Cartesian world had been built give way to a sense of process in which everything is related to everything else in highly complex ways – far too complex for the intellectual mind alone to comprehend. One of the great ironies of where we find ourselves at the beginning of the millennium is that we are beginning to perceive ourselves more the way emerging paradigm science is telling us that the universe is put together. Who would have thought it?

Since the universe and everything in it is intimately interconnected, our relationship to it becomes central to experiencing our freedom and living our authentic power. The challenge now is to bring into balance the key relationships in our lives – the inner and the outer world, the intuitive and the rational, the expansiveness and the containment of structures. And then to align our visions with the gods of the rest of the universe. For when we are aligned in this way, the power that we can call on to fulfil our own lives and to make a significant contribution to the world is virtually unlimited.

To find out how this alignment works best in your own life, you might like to do some more journey work this week, recording in your journal what you discover as you have been doing all along. (In fact you might like to do some of these journeys more than once, or repeat them whenever you feel you need to in the future. The depth of

I lay on the bowsprit, facing astern, with the water foaming into spume under me, the masts with every sail white in the moonlight, towering high above me. I became drunk with the beauty and singing rhythm of it, and for a moment I lost myself – actually lost my life. I was set free! I dissolved into the sea, became white sails and flying spray, became beauty and rhythm, became moonlight and the ship and the high dim-starred sky! I belonged without past or future, within peace and unity and wild joy, within something greater than my own life, or the life of Man, to Life itself.
Eugene O'Neill

The universe is a communion and a community. We ourselves are that communion become conscious of itself.
Thomas Berry

We have great freedom and that's a blessing. What must happen is that some mythological instruction should be added to our freedom so that the individual can find his own myth, his individual meaning in that freedom.
Joseph Campbell

I will tell you what I learned myself. For me a long, five – or six mile walk helps. And one must go alone and every day.
Brenda Ueland

Today a new sun rises for me; everything lives, everything is animated, everything seems to speak to me of my passion, everything invites me to cherish it.
Anne De Lenclos

Before I built a wall I'd ask to know
What I was walling in or walling out.
Robert Frost

understanding and clarity and the spiritual power available to you seems only to expand the deeper you explore the questions.)

Here are my suggestions. You may come up with even better ones on your own.

✦ Journey to explore the nature of your role on earth.
✦ Journey to connect with your vision (or visions) for the planet's future.
✦ Journey to find out where you are in relation to your visions.
✦ Journey to discover how the thrust of your soul's purpose best aligns itself with the purpose of the planet.
✦ Journey to seek the help you need from your friends in quantum realms to bring your visions into being.

The mere exploration of these questions opens us up to discovering our alignment with the universe. It is all part of that old magic duo – intention and compassion.

LET IT ALL UNFOLD

Having been brought up in the American ethos of 'the harder you work the faster you get where you are going', the spirits have had a lot to teach me. For instance, they taught me it just ain't so. They also taught me something that may really surprise you. It certainly has me. Yet it is probably the most important thing I have ever learned: That we as human beings are not designed to do anything except to direct our intention towards what we want to accomplish. Then, provided we continue to do this with compassion both for ourselves and the rest of life around us, sooner or later we bring into manifestation what our soul is seeking.

The key is that what you want has to be what you *really* want from the level of your soul – not somebody else's idea of what you should want, or some notion that you have happened on with your conscious mind. The rest takes place by itself. Sounds amazing? That's what I thought. But it is absolutely true. It works. If you want to pick up a book from a table across the room, you do not have to think about every little movement that is going to make it happen. You simply focus your attention and let your body do it for you. Just hold the intention, trust the focus of the energy which your consciousness is pouring out of you and let it happen. It works equally well big or small. After all you don't put a seed in the ground and then pull it up to see how it is growing. But if you are a gardener or a farmer, you might well think about your crop every day.

THE POWER OF INTENTION

This is the great power of human consciousness. The conscious mind uses its ability to focus intention to accomplish something then the energy of the universe aligns itself to bring it into being. But what you want has to come from deep enough. That is why it is useful to journey again and again to the essence of your soul and learn to listen to its whispers. It is the passion and the wonder of the soul's longing that fuels the help of the spirits and calls in the power of the universe to fulfil that longing. It quite literally works miracles. But don't take my word for it. Experiment and see what happens.

Even more powerful than focusing your intention for personal ends is the power we have when, with the help of the spirits, we focus our intention together with the intention of others in a shared vision. Thanks to the way in which the universe is one, the spirits are our partners, and quantum fields communicate with quantum fields, our *shared* visions can reshape the future of the planet.

In the world we live in, where ecological disaster seems to follow ecological disaster, this is our greatest challenge. I suspect it will also be our greatest joy. The future of the planet may well rest in the hands of visions we share with others. We humans have screwed things up because our worldview was just not big enough. But that is changing rapidly. We broke it and I figure we can fix it. Emerging paradigm scientists tell us that the power we have to influence the course of evolution is immense. It all comes through the power of consciousness focussed into shared visions for the future.

My prayer is that we connect with the deepest levels of our own soul, envision that future in which each of us has a unique role to play, merge our compassion, focus our intention for the earth, and see what kind of future we can make for all of us. Who knows, like the bluetits, we may not only have the pleasure of drinking the cream each morning but the satisfaction of knowing that we have helped to bring that cream into being.

To work magic is to weave the unseen forces into form; to soar beyond sight; to explore the uncharted dream realm of the hidden reality.
Starhawk, The Spiral Dance

Beauty is an ecstasy; it is as simple as hunger.
W. Somerset Maugham

'Forty-two!' yelled Loonquawl. 'Is that all you've got to show for seven and a half million years' work?'

'I checked it very thoroughly,' said the computer, 'and that quite definitely is the answer. I think the problem, to be quite honest with you, is that you've never actually known what the question is.'
Douglas Adams

FURTHER READING

What follows are three lists of books which in one way or another have deepened my understanding of some of the subjects covered in *Journey to Freedom*. I have starred those that I believe to be particularly valuable or truly path-breaking.

PSYCHOLOGY AND CONSCIOUSNESS

Assagioli, Roberto, *Psychosynthesis*, New York, Basic Books, 1980.

Bowie, Fiona, and Davies, Oliver, (ed), *Hildegard of Bingen: an Anthology*, SPCK, Holy Trinity Church, Marylebone Road, London, 1990.

Cameron, Julia, *The Artist's Way*, Pan Books, Macmillan Publishers Ltd, 25 Eccleston Place, London, 1995.

*Campbell, Joseph, (ed) *The Portable Jung*, Penguin Books Ltd., Harmondsworth, UK, 1976.

Drury, Nevill, *The Visionary Human*, Prism Press, The Thatched Cottage, Partway Lane, Haxelbury Bryan, Sturminster Newton, Dorset, 1998.

Eckhart, Meister, *Meister Eckhart*, translated by Raymond B. Blakney, New York, Harper & Row, 1941.

Frankl, Victor, *Man's Search for Meaning*, New York, Washington Square Press, 1963.

Franz, Marie-Louise von, *Psyche and Matter*, Shambhala Publications, Boston and London, 1992.

Goleman, D., *Emotional Intelligence: Why It Can Matter More Than IQ*, Bantam Books, New York, 1995.

*Grof, Christina, and Grof, Stanislav, *The Stormy Search for the Self*, Jeremy P. Tarcher Inc, Los Angeles, 1990.

*Grof, Christina, *The Thirst for Wholeness – Attachment, Addiction, and the Spiritual Path*, HarperCollins*Publishers*, New York, 1993.

*Grof, S., and Bennet, Z., *The Holotropic Mind: The Three Levels of Human Consciousness and How They Shape Our Lives*, Harper Publications, San Francisco, 1992.

*Grof, S., and Grof, C., *Beyond Death: The Gates of Consciousness*, Thames & Hudson, London, 1980.

*Grof, S., *Beyond the Brain: Birth, Death, and Transcendence In Psychotherapy*, State University of New York Press, Albany, 1985.

Grof, S., *LSD Psychotherapy*, Hunter House, Pomona, CA, 1980.

Grof, S., *Realms of the Human Unconscious: Observations from LSD Research*, Viking Press, New York, 1975.

Grof, Stanislav MD., and Grof, Christina, *Spiritual Emergency*, Jeremy P. Tarcher Inc., Los Angeles, CA, 1989.

*Grof, Stanislav, *Beyond the Brain: Birth, Death and Transcendence in Psychotherapy*, State University of New York Press, Albany, 1985.

*Grof, Stanislav, *The Adventure of Self-Discovery: Dimensions of Consciousness and New Perspectives in Psychotherapy and Inner Exploration*, State University of New York Press, Albany, 1988.

*Grof, Stanislav, *The Cosmic Game: Explorations in the Frontiers of Human Consciousness*, Newleaf, Gill & Macmillan, Dublin 8, 1998.

*Grof, Stanislav, with Bennett, Hal Zina, *The Holotropic Mind*, HarperSanFrancisco, San Francisco, 1993.
*Hammerschlag, Carl, MD., *The Theft of the Spirit*, Fireside, Rockefeller Centre, 1230 Avenue of the Americas, New York, NY 10020, 1994.
*Huxley, Aldous, *The Perennial Philosophy*, Harper & Row, New York, 1970.
*Jung, C.G., *Symbols of Transformation, Collected Works*, vol. 5, Bollingen Series XX, Princeton University Press, Princeton, NJ, 1956.
Jung, C.G., *The Archetypes and the Collective Unconscious, Collected Works*, vol. 9, 1. Bollingen Series XX, Princeton University Press, Princeton, NJ, 1959.
Keen, Sam, *Fire in the Belly*, Bantam, New York, 1991.
Keleman, Stanley, *Living Your Dying*, New York, Random House, 1976.
Koestler, A., *Janus*, Random House, New York, 1978.
Leonard, George and Murphy, Michael, *The Life We Are Given*, A Jeremy P. Tarcher/Putnam Book, 1995.
LeShan, Lawrence, Ph.D., *The Medium, The Mystic and The Physicist*, Arkana, Penguin Books USA Inc., 375 Hudson Street, New York, 1995.
Levi-Strauss, Claude, *The Savage Mind*, University of Chicago Press, Chicago, 1966.
Maslow, A., *Religions, Values, and Peak Experiences*, Ohio State University Press, Columbus, OH, 1964.
Metzner, Ralph, *The Unfolding Self*, Orbis Press, 1122 Grant Avenue, Suite C, Novato, CA 94945, 1998.
Monroe, R., *The Ultimate Journey*, Doubleday, Garden City, NY, 1994.
Murphy, Michael, *The Future of The Body*, Jeremy P. Tarcher, New York, 1992.
Netherton, Morris, and Shiffrin, Nancy, *Past Lives Therapy*, William Morrow, New York, 1978.
Neumann, Erich, *The Origins and History of Consciousness*, Bollingen Series XLII, Princeton University Press, Princeton, NJ, 1973.
*Odent, Michael, *Primal Health*, Century Hutchinson Ltd., London, 1987.
Rank, Otto, *Beyond Psychology*, Dover Publications, New York, 1958.
Rilke, Rainer Maria, *Sonnets to Orpheus*, translated by M. D. Herter Norton, New York, Norton, 1942.
Rumi, *Rumi: Poet and Mystic*, translated by Reynold A. Nicholson, Unwin Paperbacks, London, 1978.
Stevenson, I., *Children Who Remember Previous Lives*, University of Virginia Press, Charlottesville, VA, 1987.
Stevenson, I., *Reincarnation and Biology: A Contribution to the Etiology of Birthmarks and Birth Defects*, Praeger, Westport, CT, 1997.
Targ, Russell, and Katra, Jane, *Miracles of Mind*, New World Library, Novato, California, 1998.
Tart, Charles (ed)., *Transpersonal Psychologies*, Harper & Row, New York, 1975.
Tart, Charles T. (ed), *Body, Mind, Spirit*, Hampton Roads Publishing Company Inc., Charlottesville, VA, 1997.
Tulku, Tarthang, *Dynamics of Time and Space: Transcending Limits on Knowledge*, Dharma Publishing, Oakland, CA, 1994.
Wambach, H., *Life before Life*, Bantam, New York, 1979.
Watts, Alan, *The Spirit of Zen*, Grove Press Inc., New York, 1958.
Wilber, Ken, *The Atman Project: A Transpersonal View of Human Development*, Theosophical Publishing House, Wheaton, Illinois, 1980.
Wilber, Ken, *Up From Eden*, Anchor Press/Doubleday, New York, 1981.
Wilber, Ken, *The Eye of the Spirit*, Shambhala Publications, Boston, 1997.
Wilber, Ken, *Sex, Ecology and Spirituality*, Shambhala Publications, Boston, 1995.
Woolger, Roger, *Other Lives, Other Selves*, Doubleday, New York, 1987.
Zukav, Gary, *Thoughts from the Seat of the Soul, Meditations for Souls in Process*, Fireside, Simon & Schuster, New York, 1989.
Zweig, Connie, and Abrams, Jeremiah, *Meeting the Shadow*, Jeremy P. Tarcher/Putnam Book, G.P. Putnam's Sons, New York, 1991.

SCIENCE AND PHILOSOPHY

Barrow, John D., and Tipler, Frank J., *The Anthropic Cosmological Principle*, Oxford University Press, London and New York, 1986.

Barrow, John, *Theories of Everything*, Clarendon Press, Oxford, 1991.

Bateston, Gregory, *Mind and Nature*, E.P. Dutton, New York, 1979.

Bateston, Gregory, *Steps Toward an Ecology of Mind*, E.P. Dutton, New York, 1979.

Bentov, Itzhak, *Stalking the Wild Pendulum*, Bantam Books, New York, 1979.

Berry, Thomas, *The Dream of the Earth*, Sierra Club Books, San Francisco, 1988.

Bohm, David, and Hiley, B.J., *The Undivided Universe*, Routledge, London, 1993.

*Bohm, David, *Wholeness and the Implicate Order*, Routledge & Kegan Paul, London, 1980.

Breathnach, Sarah Ban, *Simple Abundance*, Bantam Books, London, 1997.

Capra, Fritjof, *The Web of Life*, Anchor Books, Doubleday, New York, 1997.

*Carey, Ken, *The Third Millennium*, HarperSanFrancisco, HarperCollins*Publishers*, 10 East 53rd Street, New York, NY 10022, 1991.

Crick, F., *Life Itself, Its Origin, and Nature*, Simon & Schuster, New York, 1981.

Crick, F., *The Astonishing Hypothesis: The Scientific Search for the Soul*, Scribner, New York, 1994.

Davies, P.C.W., and Brown, J.R. (eds), *The Ghost in the Atom*, Cambridge University Press, Cambridge, 1986.

Davies, Paul, and Gribbin, John, *The Matter Myth*, Simon & Schuster, New York, 1992.

Davies, Paul, *God and the New Physics*, Simon & Schuster, New York, 1983.

Davies, Paul, *The Mind of God*, Simon & Schuster, New York, 1992.

Dickinson, Terence, *Exploring the Night Sky*, Firefly Books, Buffalo, New York, 1997.

Eccles, John, and Robinson, Daniel N., *The Wonder of Being Human*, Shambhala Publications, Boston and London, 1985.

Edelman, Gerald M., *Bright Air, Brilliant Fire: On the Matter of Mind*, Basic Books, New York, 1992.

*Elgin, Duane, *Awakening Earth*, William Morrow and Company Inc., New York, 1993.

Elgin, Duane, *Voluntary Simplicity*, Morrow, New York, 1981, revised 1993.

Elgin, Duane, and LeDrew, Coleen, *Global Consciousness Change: Indicators of an Emerging Paradigm*, San Anselmo, CA, 1997.

Elgin, Duane, *Collective Consciousness and Cultural Healing*, Alonzo Environmental Printing, 1997.

Gimbutas, Marija, *The Civilization of the Goddess*, HarperSanFrancisco, HarperCollins*Publishers*, New York, 1991.

Gleick, James, *Chaos*, Viking, New York, 1987.

Gore, Al, *Earth in the Balance*, Boston, MA, Houghton Mifflin Co, 1992.

*Goswami, Amit, *The Self-Aware Universe*, Putnam, New York, 1993.

Heisenberg, Werner, *Physics and Philosophy*, Harper & Row, New York, 1985.

Hines, B., *God's Whisper, Creation's Thunder: Echoes of Ultimate Reality in the New Physics*, Threshold Books, Brattleboro, VT, 1996.

Hoyle, F., *The Intelligent Universe*, Michael Joseph, London, 1983.

*Huxley, A., *Perennial Philosophy*, Harper and Brothers, New York and London, 1945.

*Huxley, A., *The Doors of Perception* and *Heaven and Hell*, Penguin Books, Harmondsworth, UK, 1959.

Kafatos, M. (ed), *Bell's Theorem, Quantum Theory and Conceptions of the Universe*, Kluwer, Dordrecht, 1989.

Kauffman, Stuart, *The Origins of Order: Self-Organization and Selection in Evolution*, Oxford University Press, Oxford, 1993.

Kuhn, Thomas, *The Structure of Scientific Revolutions*, 2nd ed, University of Chicago Press, Chicago, 1970.

Laszlo, Ervin, *Introduction to Systems Philosophy*, Gordon and Breach, New York, 1972.

*Laszlo, Ervin, *The Creative Cosmos*, Floris Books, 15 Harrison Gardens, Edinburgh, 1993.

*Laszlo, Ervin, *The Interconnected Universe*, World Scientific, London and Singapore, 1995.

Laszlo, Ervin, *Evolution, The General Theory*, Hampton Press, Cresskill, NJ, 1996.

*Laszlo, Ervin, *The Whispering Pond*, Element Books Inc, PO Box 830, Rockport, MA 01966, 1996.

Lindley, David, *The End of Physics*, Basic Books, New York, 1993.

Mander, Jerry, *In the Absence of the Sacred*, Sierra Club Books, San Francisco, CA, 1992.

Margulis, Lynn, and Sagan, Dorion, *Slanted Truths*, Copernicus, Springer Verlag New York Inc., 175 Fifth Avenue, New York, NY 10010, 1997.

*Narby, Jeremy, *The Cosmic Serpent: DNA and the Origins of Knowledge*, Jeremy P. Tarcher/Putnam, 200 Madison Avenue, New York, NY 10016, 1998.

Pagels, Heinz, *The Cosmic Code*, Bantam Books, New York, 1990.

Peat, F. David, *Einstein's Moon*, Contemporary Books, Chicago, 1990.

Penrose, Roger, *The Emperor's New Mind*, Oxford University Press, New York, 1989.

Pribram, Karl, *Brain and Perception: Holonomy and Structure in Figural Processing*, The MacEachran Lectures, Lawrence Erlbaum, Hillsdale, NJ, 1991.

*Prigogine, Ilya, and Stengers, Isabelle, *Order Out of Chaos: Man's New Dialogue with Nature*, Bantam Books, New York, 1984.

Roszak, Theodore, *The Voice of the Earth*, Simon & Schuster, New York, 1992.

Russell, Peter, *The White Hole in Time*, HarperSanFrancisco, San Francisco, 1992.

Schroeder, Gerald L., *Genesis and the Big Bang*, Bantam Books, New York, 1990.

*Sheldrake, Rupert, *A New Science of Life*, Paladin Books, Granada Publishing, 8 Grafton Street, London, 1984.

Sheldrake, Rupert, and Fox, Mathew, *The Physics of Angels*, HarperSanFrancisco, HarperCollins*Publishers*, New York, 1996.

Sheldrake, Rupert, and Fox, Matthew, *Natural Grace*, Bloomsbury Publishing plc, 38 Soho Square, London, 1997.

*Sheldrake, Rupert, *The Presence of the Past*, Times Books, New York, 1988.

Sheldrake, Rupert, *The Rebirth of Nature: The Greening of Science and God*, Bantam Books, New York, 1991.

Smoot, G., and Davidson, K., *Wrinkles in Time*, W. Morrow, New York, 1993.

Stapp, Henry P., *Matter, Mind, and Quantum Mechanics*, Springer Verlag, New York, 1993.

*Suzuki, David, with McConnell, Amanda, *The Sacred Balance*, Greystone Books, Douglas & McIntyre Ltd, 1615 Venables Street, Vancouver, 1997.

*Swimme, Brian, *The Hidden Heart of the Cosmos*, Orbis Books, Maryknoll, New York, 1996.

*Swimme, Brian, *The Universe is a Green Dragon*, Bear & Company Inc., PO Drawer 2860, Santa Fe, NM 87504, 1984.

*Tarnas, Richard, *The Passion of the Western Mind*, Random House, 20 Vauxhall Bridge Road, Pimlico, London, 1991.

Teilhard de Chardin, Pierre, *The Phenomenon of Man*, Harper & Row, San Francisco, 1965.

Teilhard de Chardin, Pierre, *The Future of Man*, Harper & Row, San Francisco, 1964.

Thorne, K., *Black Holes and Time Warps: Einstein's Outrageous Legacy*, W. W. Norton, New York, 1994.

Tompkins, Peter, *The Secret Life of Nature*, Thorsons, HarperCollins*Publishers*, London, 1997.

Watts, A., *The Book about the Taboo against Knowing Who You Are*, Vintage Books, New York, 1966.

Weinberg, Steven, *The First Three Minutes*, Basic Books, New York, 1988.

White, John, *The Meeting of Science and Spirit*, Paragon House, New York, 1990.

Whitehead, A. N., *Process and Reality*, Macmillan, New York, 1929.

Wilber, K., *A Sociable God: Brief Introduction to a Transcendental Sociology*, McGraw-Hill, New York, 1983.

Wilber, K., *Sex, Ecology, and Spirituality: The Spirit of Evolution*, Shambhala Publications, Boston, 1995.

Wilber, K., *The Eye of Spirit: An Integral Vision for a World Gone Slightly Mad*, Shambhala Publications, Boston, 1997.

Wilber, Ken, *A Brief History of Everything*, Gill & Macmillan Ltd, Goldenbridge, Dublin 8, 1996.

Wilber, Ken, *The Eye of the Spirit*, Shambhala Publications, Horticultural Hall, 300 Massachusetts Avenue, Boston, Massachusetts 02115, 1997.

Wilber, Ken, *The Marriage of Sense and Soul*, Newleaf, Gill & Macmillan Ltd, Goldenbridge, Dublin 8, 1998.

Yockey, H., *Information Theory and Molecular Biology*, Cambridge University Press, Cambridge, 1992.

Zohar, Danah, *The Quantum Self*, William Morrow, New York, 1990.

Zukav, Gary, *The Dancing Wu Li Masters*, Bantam Books, New York, 1989.

MYTHOLOGY AND SHAMANISM

Achterberg, Jean, *Imagery in Healing*, Shambhala Publications, Horticultural Hall, 300 Massachusetts Avenue, Boston, Massachusetts 02115, 1985.

Alexander, Jane, *Spirit of the Home*, HarperCollins*Publishers*, London, 1998.

Berggren, Karen, *Circle of Shaman*, Destiny Books, One Park Street, Rochester, Vermont 05767, 1998.

Bleakley, Alan, *The Fruits of the Moon Tree*, Gateway Books, Bath, 1991.

Brown, Joseph Epes (ed), *The Sacred Pipe: Black Elk's Account of the Seven Rites of the Oglala Sioux*, New York, Viking Press, 1953.

Brown Jr, Tom, *Awakening Spirits*, The Berkley Publishing Group, 200 Madison Avenue, New York, NY 10016, 1994.

Campbell, Joseph (ed), *Man and Transformation*, Papers from the *Eranos Yearbooks*, Bollingen, Series XXX, vol.5, Princeton University Press, Princeton, 1980.

Campbell, Joseph (ed), *Myths, Dreams and Religion*, Spring Publications Inc., Dallas, Texas, 1988.

Campbell, Joseph, *Creative Mythology, The Masks Of God*, Arkana, Penguin Books USA Inc., 375 Hudson Street, New York, 1991.

Campbell, Joseph, *Myths To Live By*, Bantam Books, New York, 1973.

Campbell, Joseph, *Occidental Mythology*, Arkana, Penguin Books USA Inc., 375 Hudson Street, New York, NY 10014, 1991.

Campbell, Joseph, *Primitive Mythology, The Masks Of God*, Arkana, Penguin Books USA Inc., 375 Hudson Street, New York, 1991.

*Campbell, Joseph, *The Hero with a Thousand Faces*, Bollingen Foundation Inc, New York, Princeton University Press, Princeton, New Jersey, 1968.

*Campbell, Joseph, *The Hero's Journey*, Harper & Row Publishers, San Francisco, 1990.

*Campbell, Joseph, *The Inner Reaches of Outer Space*, Perennial Library, Harper & Row Publishers Inc., New York, 1988.

Campbell, Joseph, *The Mythic Image*, Bollingen Series C, Princeton University Press, Princeton, NJ, 1990.

*Campbell, Joseph, *This Business of the Gods*, Windrose Films Ltd, PO Box 2000, Caledon East, Ontario, 1989.

Campbell, Joseph, *Transformations of Myth Through Time*, Harper & Row Publishers Inc., New York, 1990.

Cloutier, David, *Spirit Spirit Shaman Songs*, Copper Beech Press, Brown University, Rhode Island, 1980.

Cook, Roger, *The Tree of Life: Image for the Cosmos*, Avon Books, New York, 1974.

Cowan, Eliot, *Plant Spirit Medicine*, Swan Raven & Co, PO Box 726, Newberg, OR 97132, 1995.

Cowan, Tom, *Fire in the Head: Shamanism and the Celtic Spirit*, HarperSanFrancisco, HarperCollins*Publishers*, 10 East 53rd Street, New York, 1993.

Cowan, Tom, *Pocket Guide to Shamanism*, The Crossing Press Inc., Freedom, CA, 1997.

*Cowan, Tom, *Shamanism as a spiritual practice for daily life*, The Crossing Press Inc, PO Box 1048, Freedom, CA 95019, 1996.

Cumes, David, MD., *Inner Passages Outer Journeys*, Llewellyn Worldwide, St Paul, Minnesota, MN 55164-0383, 1998.

Doore, Gary, (compiled by) *Shaman's Path*, Shambhala Publications, Horticultural Hall, 300 Massachusetts Avenue, Boston, Massachusetts 02115, 1988.

Drury, Nevill, *The Elements of Shamanism*, Element Books Ltd, Dorset, 1997.

Drury, Nevill, *The Shaman and the Magician*, Arkana, Penguin Books Ltd, 27 Wrights Lane, London, 1987.

Drury, Nevill, *Vision Quest: A Personal Journey Through Magic and Shamanism*, Avery Publishing Group Inc., New York, 1989.

*Eliade, Mircea, *The Sacred and the Profane*, Harcourt, Brace & World Inc., 1959.

Eliade, Mircea, *The Forge and the Crucible*, Harper & Row, New York, 1962.

Eliade, Mircea, *The Two and the One*, Harper & Row, New York, 1965.

Eliade, Mircea, *Images and Symbols*, Sheed & Ward, New York, 1969.

*Eliade, Mircea, *Shamanism: Archaic Techniques of Ecstasy*, Princeton University Press, Princeton, NJ, 1972.

Eliade, Mircea, *A History of Religious Ideas*, 3 vols, University of Chicago Press, Chicago, 1979.

Eliade, Mircea, *Ordeal by Labyrinth*, University of Chicago Press, Chicago, 1982.

Foster, Steven, with Little, Meredith, *Vision Quest*, Fireside, Simon & Schuster, New York, 1992.

Gregg, Dr Susan, *Finding the Sacred Self*, Llewellyn Publications, St Paul, Minnesota, MN 55164-0383, 1997.

Halifax, Joan, Ph.D., *Shamanic Voices: A Survey of Visionary Narratives*, Arkana, Penguin Books, New York, last printing 1991.

Halifax, Joan, Ph.D., *The Fruitful Darkness: Reconnecting with the Body of the Earth*, HarperCollins*Publishers*, New York, 1993.

Halifax, Joan, *Shaman: The Wounded Healer*, Thames and Hudson Ltd, London, 1988.

Hall, Nor, *The Moon and the Virgin*, Harper & Row Publishers, New York, 1980.

Harner, Michael (ed), *Hallucinogens and Shamanism*, Oxford University Press Inc., New York, 1973.

*Harner, Michael, *The Way of the Shaman*, HarperCollins*Publishers*, 10 East 53rd Street, New York 10022, 1990.

Henderson, Joseph L., and Maud Oakes, *The Wisdom of the Serpent: The Myths of Death, Rebirth and Resurrection*, New York, Collier Books, 1963.

*Ingerman, Sandra, *Soul Retrieval*, HarperSanFrancisco, HarperCollins*Publishers*, New York, 1991.

Ingerman, Sandra, *Welcome Home*, HarperSanFrancisco, HarperCollins*Publishers*, New York, 1993.

Kalweit, Holger, *Dreamtime and Inner Space, The World of the Shaman*, translated by Werner Weunsche, Shambhala Publications, Boston, 1988.

Kalweit, Holger, *Shamans, Healers, and Medicine Men*, Shambhala Publications, Boston, 1992.

*Kharitidi, Olga MD., *Entering The Circle*, HarperSanFrancisco, HarperCollins*Publishers*, New York, 1996.

King, Serge Kahili, *Kahuna Healing*, Quest Books, The Theosophical Publishing House, 306 West Geneva Road, Wheaton, Illinois 60187, 1983.

King, Serge Kahili, *Mastering Your Hidden Self*, Quest Books, The Theosophical Publishing House, 306 West Geneva Road, Wheaton, Illinois 60187, 1996.

Kryder, Rowena Pattee, *Sacred Ground to Sacred Space*, Bear & Company, Santa Fe, NM, 1994.

Larsen, Stephen, *The Shaman's Doorway – Opening Imagination to Power and Myth*, Station Hill Press, Barrytown, NY, 1976, 1988.

McGaa, Ed, Eagle Man, *Mother Earth Spirituality*, HarperSanFrancisco, HarperCollins*Publishers*, New York, 1990.

McGaa, Ed, Eagle Man, *Rainbow Tribe*, HarperSanFrancisco, 10 East 53rd Street, New York, 1992.

McLuhan, T.C. (compiled by), *Touch The Earth*, Touchstone, Simon & Schuster, New York, 1971.

Mehl-Madrona, Lewis, *Coyote Medicine*, Rider, Ebury Press, Random House, 20 Vauxhall Bridge Road, London, 1997.

Mindell, Arnold, *The Shaman's Body*, HarperSanFrancisco, HarperCollins*Publishers*, 10 East 53rd Street, New York, NY 10022, 1993.

*Neihardt, John G. (as told through), *Black Elk Speaks*, Bison Books, University of Nebraska Press, London, 1988.

Nicholson, Shirley (compiled by), *Shamanism*, The Theosophical Publishing House, Wheaton, Ill, 1987.

*Osbon, Diane K, (selected and edited by) *Reflections on the Art of Living: A Joseph Campbell Companion*, HarperCollins*Publishers*, New York, 1991.

Otto, Rudolf, *The Idea of the Holy*, Oxford University Press, London, 1910.

*Pere, Dr Rangimarie Turuki, *Te Wheke: A Celebration of Infinite Wisdom*, Ao Ako Global Learning New Zealand Ltd, New Zealand, 1997.

Rainbow Spirit Elders, *Rainbow Spirit Theology: Towards an Australian Aboriginal Theology*, HarperCollinsReligious, HarperCollins*Publishers* (Australia) Pty Ltd., Blackburn, Victoria, 1997.

Roth, Gabrielle, and Loudon, John, *Maps to Ecstasy – Teachings of an Urban Shaman*, Nataraj Publishing, Novato, CA, 1989.

Sanchez, Victor, *The Teaching of Don Carlos*, Bear & Company Publishing, Santa Fe, NM 87504-2860, 1995.

Sansonese, J. Nigro, *The Body of Myth*, Inner Traditions International, Rochester, Vermont, 1994.

Savinelli, Alfred, *Plants of Power*, Taos, NM, 1993.

Stevens, Jose, Ph.D., and Stevens, Lena S., *Secrets of Shamanism – Tapping the Spirit Power Within You*, Avon Books, New York, 1988.

*Storm, Hyemeyohsts, *Seven Arrows*, Ballantine Books, New York, 1973.

Tyson, Donald, *Scrying for Beginners*, Llewellyn Publications, St. Paul, Minnesota, 1997.

Walsh, Roger N., MD., Ph.D., *The Spirit of Shamanism*, Tarcher/Perigee Books, New York, 1990.

RESOURCES

LESLIE KENTON

Leslie's website gives full information on all of her books, workshops, videos and audio tapes. http://www.qed-productions.com/lesliekenton.htm

Alternatively please write to her at HarperCollins*Publishers*, 77–85 Fulham Palace Road, Hammersmith, London, W6 8JB.

SHAMANISM

Organizations

The Sacred Trust (Great Britain)

The Sacred Trust is a non-profit educational organization which offers an ongoing curriculum of training and workshops with some of the most important and influential teachers of shamanism from around the world. For a copy of the current programme of events (including many of Leslie Kenton's shamanic workshops) and their book and audio mail order catalogue contact: The Sacred Trust, PO Box 603, Bath, BA1 2ZU. Telephone 01225 852615. Fax 01225 858961.

The Foundation for Shamanic Studies (United States)

The Foundation for Shamanic Studies, founded and led by Michael Harner, actively helps to preserve shamanism where it is threatened and to revive it when invited. The Foundation also studies the effectiveness of shamanic healing methods in contemporary life, and offers an extensive teaching programme. For further information contact The Foundation for Shamanic Studies, PO Box 1939, Mill Valley, CA 94942, USA. Telephone (415) 380 8282. Fax (415) 380 8416. Website address www.shamanism.org

Academy of Shamanic Studies (New Zealand)

The Academy of Shamanic Studies promotes the awareness and realization of the interconnectedness of spirit in all creation as a practical way of life. It aims to teach shamanism in a way that honours the cultural heritage of each person, and the spirit and vibrations of the land. For further information contact Jan Natusch, Academy of Shamanic Studies, PO Box 5417, Wellesley Street, Auckland, New Zealand. Telephone/Fax (64) 952 15 366. Email jan.natusch@clear.net.NZ

Drumming and Rattling Tapes

A selection of high-quality recordings, including *Michael Harner's Shamanic Journey Series, Rattle, Double Drumming and Multiple Drumming* is available from The Sacred Trust, PO Box 603, Bath, BA1 2ZU.

A new series of journeying tapes and CDs created by Leslie Kenton is currently in preparation. Contact The Sacred Trust for details.

Publications about Shamanism

Sacred Hoop

UK-based magazine which focuses on the shamanic paths as they express themselves in this country. Good interviews with visiting teachers, useful sections on everything from drum to rattle making; book and tape reviews; what's on guide etc. Quarterly. Telephone 01834 860320.

Shaman's Drum

American quarterly journal which explores shamanism in its rich variety of forms. Often contains very good photography and always offers the latest important news regarding the plight of indigenous peoples. For more information contact The Sacred Trust.

SPIRITUALITY

Organizations

Centre for Creation Spirituality

Begun by Matthew Fox, the Centre for Creation Spirituality offers lectures, workshops, tapes and the Techno-cosmic Mass. For further information contact Centre for Creation Spirituality, 2141 Broadway, Oakland, CA 94612, USA. Telephone (510) 836 4392.

Centre for Creation Spirituality (UK)

For information on talks and workshops held in the UK contact Ingrid Hankins, Centre for Creation Spirituality (UK), St James's Church, 197 Piccadilly, London W1V 0LL. Telephone 0171 287 2741. Fax 0171 734 7449.

SCIENCE AND CONSCIOUSNESS

Organizations

Grof Personal Training

For further information on Stanislav Grof's Holotropic Breathwork contact Cary Sparks, Grof Personal Training, 20 Sunnyside Avenue, A 314, Mill Valley, California 94941, USA. Telephone (415) 383 8779. Fax (415) 383 0965.

California Institute of Integral Studies

A unique college offering Masters' degrees in East-West Psychology, Philosophy and Religion, Organizational Development and Transformation, Integral Health Education and other emerging paradigm subjects. For further information contact California Institute of Integral Studies, 9 Peter Yorke Way, San Francisco, CA 94109, USA. Telephone (415) 674 5500.

INDEX

Lectures and Workshops
with Leslie Kenton

Leslie Kenton regularly presents events based on her published work.

These include public lectures, one-day and weekend workshops as well as residential events at sacred sites throughout the world.

Leslie's subjects include:

➤ **HEALTH AND WELL-BEING**

➤ **AWAKENING SPIRITUALITY**

➤ **JOURNEY TO FREEDOM**

If you would like information about these events, please contact:

Bright Idea Productions Limited
Tel: +44 (0)7000 782494
Fax: +44 (0)7000 782949
E-mail: info@bright-idea.co.uk

AUDIO TAPE SETS ARE ALSO AVAILABLE

Bright Idea
PRODUCTIONS LTD